Shivaji

India's Great Warrior King

Vaibhav Purandare

JUGGERNAUT BOOKS
C-I-128, First Floor, Sangam Vihar, Near Holi Chowk,
New Delhi 110080, India

First published in hardback by Juggernaut Books 2022
Published in paperback by Juggernaut Books 2023

Copyright © Vaibhav Purandare 2022

10 9 8 7 6 5 4 3 2 1

P-ISBN: 9788195996919
E-ISBN: 9789391165963

The international boundaries on the maps of India are neither purported to be correct nor authentic by Survey of India directives.

The views and opinions expressed in this book are the author's own. The facts contained herein were reported to be true as on the date of publication by the author to the publishers of the book, and the publishers are not in any way liable for their accuracy or veracity.

All rights reserved. No part of this publication may be reproduced, transmitted, or stored in a retrieval system in any form or by any means without the written permission of the publisher.

Typeset in Adobe Caslon Pro by
R. Ajith Kumar, Noida

Printed at Gopsons Papers Pvt. Ltd. Noida

For Vikrant

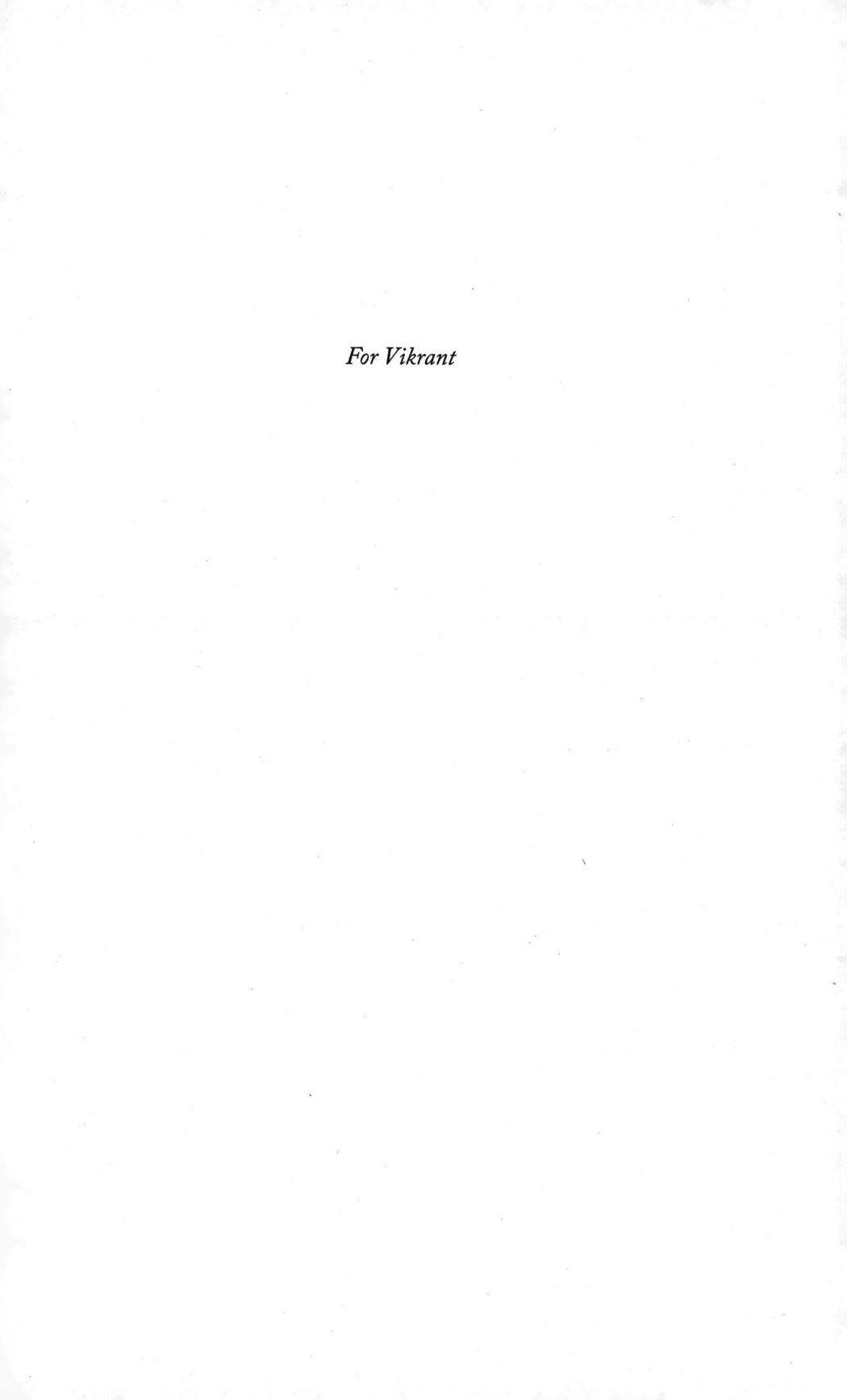

Contents

Introduction	1
1. A Child of the Deccan	17
2. Notice to the Adil Shah	34
3. Notice to the Mughals	54
4. Daggers Drawn	70
5. Narrow Escapes and British Prisoners	86
6. The Nocturnal Strike	105
7. The Sack of Surat	123
8. A Naval Enterprise	137
9. Setback and Retreat	153
10. Showdown and Escape	179
11. A Push for Reforms	198
12. Shivaji Strikes Back	217
13. The Crown	230
14. The Final Phase	251
Notes	262
Select Bibliography	293
Acknowledgements	297
Index	298
A Note on the Author	309

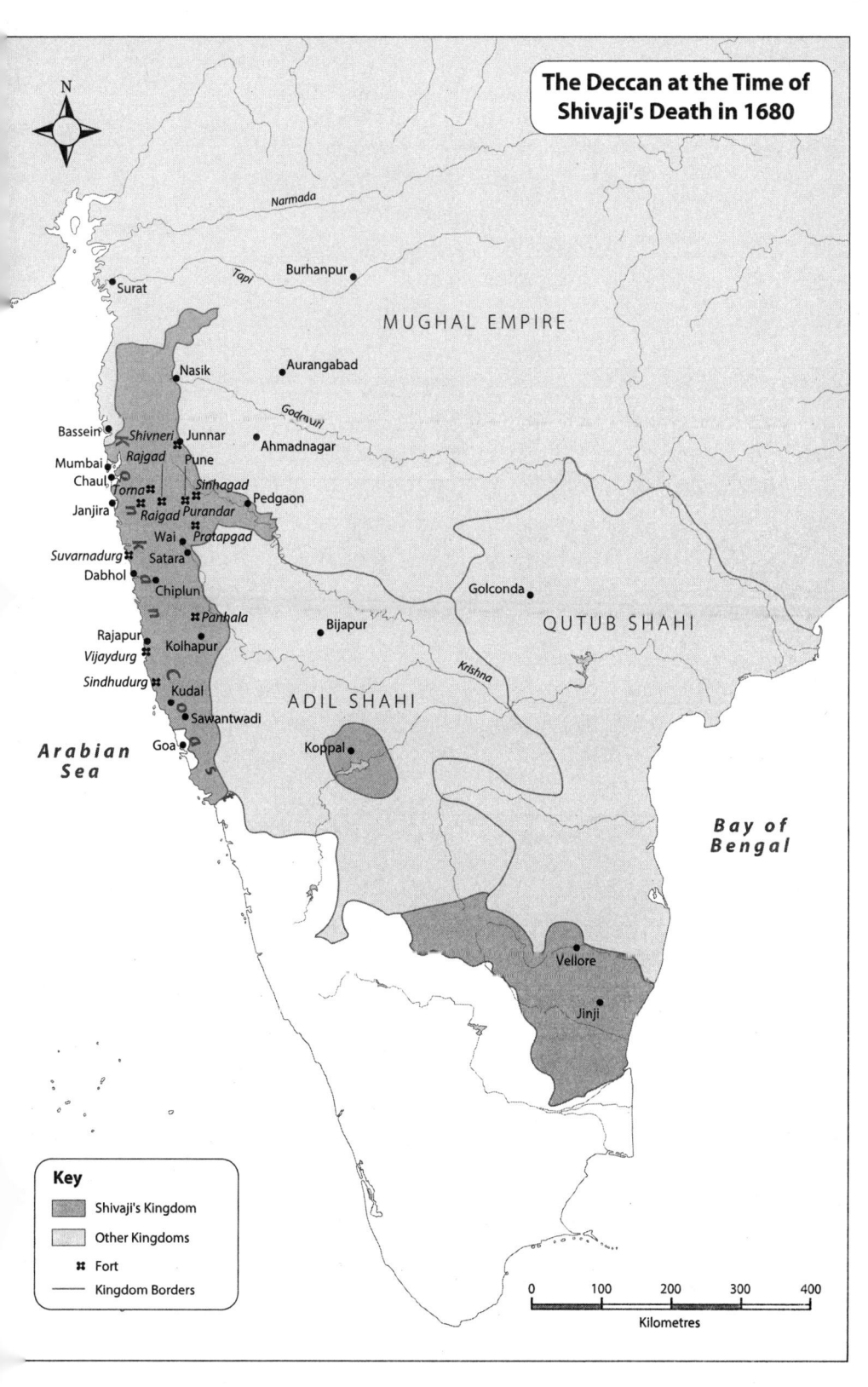

Introduction

Imagine an individual ranged against an empire. If that sounds like a grossly unequal situation, imagine that the empire is among the world's biggest and most powerful of its time. You would think the imbalance of power would be too great for even a semblance of a serious contest.

However, the Maratha Shivaji Raje Bhosle, son of Jijabai and Shahaji Raje Bhosle, did not merely put up a fierce fight against the mighty Mughal empire when it was at the height of its glory under its sixth emperor, Aurangzeb, in the seventeenth century. He actually sparked a movement that coursed through the Deccan and sowed the seeds of the empire's fall and destruction. In the process, Shivaji set up his own independent state, anointing himself Chhatrapati – bearer of the *chhatra* or royal umbrella. He fashioned his own template of governance and of political and revenue administration, framed policies of responsible and responsive conduct for the new state's officials, both civilian and military, and gave robust expression – by way of words and actions – to values of religious plurality at a time when Aurangzeb was actively and aggressively distorting those values.

Chhatrapati Shivaji is a singular figure in the early modern history of India because he shaped a political revolution in his native Deccan which had implications for the entire map of the Mughal empire, which included in its sweep Afghanistan in the north-west and Bengal in the east. When he was born in 1630, the western part of the Deccan he came from had three Islamic sultanates: the Nizam Shahi of Ahmadnagar, the Adil Shahi of Bijapur, and the Qutub Shahi of Golconda. While all three were constantly warring, the Mughals, ever increasing in strength, were pressing in from the north in a bid to conquer the southern parts and wipe out the sultanates. The constant warfare of these four kingdoms caused huge turbulence in the Deccan, unsettling populations and fitfully shifting the contours of its politics. The Marathas of the western Deccan had emerged as highly competent military personnel in the sixteenth century, but they were engaged entirely in serving one or the other of these four powers, either as generals who took and implemented orders or as foot soldiers.

Shivaji's father, Shahaji Raje Bhosle, was a military general of note. He played a stellar role in propping up the Nizam Shahi Sultanate in its last years in the 1630s; he had, besides, important stints with the Adil Shahi rulers of Bijapur and also a short one with the Mughals. Astoundingly, Shivaji launched his rebellion in his teenage years by capturing four hill forts belonging to Bijapur. He later had to backtrack to save his father but continued to swim against the main political current of his times, which was, for the Marathas, to join one or the other well-established kingdoms. He persisted with his rebellious actions, forming a solid, cohesive bond with the ordinary, nameless people and peasants of the hills, and winning friends and comrades who would help him raise the political structure he was seeking to create. His opponents realized that though he was an outlier, the Maratha rebel was a clear and present threat because of his natural charisma – which always disarmed people – his smart strategizing, his military skills and his leadership.

Aurangzeb was on top of the world at the time Shivaji attacked his territories but as a sharp and alert military commander himself, he was not dismissive of Shivaji. Just like Bijapur had done before him, he publicly called Shivaji all sorts of names, describing him as 'a mountain rat',[1] yet immediately directed the full might of the empire against the emerging rebel. Aurangzeb was acutely conscious that Shivaji's greatest strength lay in his hill forts and treacherous terrain and that he was deploying the Maratha guerrilla playbook devastatingly against his opponents. It was a captivating contest between two superbly pitted rivals, Shivaji's insurrection growing in size even as Aurangzeb repeatedly applied an incredible amount of pressure and the Mughals vastly outnumbered the Marathas.

Broadly, Shivaji's career had three stages. The first was from his childhood until 1656, the first twenty-six years of his life. It was marked by his early deeds as a rebel. The second phase covered the dramatic decade from 1656 to 1666. The battle of wits and the action during these ten thrilling years, as Shivaji took on both Bijapur and Aurangzeb, were extraordinary. From time to time, Shivaji suffered setbacks as the confrontation raged, and there were points when he found himself staring at an abyss and things looked hopeless for him. The manner in which he picked himself up and hit back at both the Adil Shahi and the Mughals makes this decade one of the most fascinating in the history of early modern India. The third phase – from 1666, when Shivaji was thirty-six, until his death at the age of fifty in 1680 – combined consolidation and expansion even as the conflict between Shivaji and Aurangzeb played out relentlessly, capturing attention across the length and breadth of India.

Shivaji was shrewd enough not to engage in pitched battles with his enemies. This allowed him to calibrate his stand and take the measure of his opponents before he made his responses. He also offered concessions to his opponents and made retreats in order to give himself time to re-equip himself and his forces and to make further gains on the ground. One of his outstanding qualities as a military leader and statesman was that he was as brilliantly adept at holding himself back as he was at launching the most boldly daring and seemingly impossible of attacks.

Among the things that left Shivaji's opponents flummoxed was the steadfast loyalty of his lieutenants and followers, mostly people drawn from ordinary families in the Deccan. One of his closest aides, Baji Prabhu Deshpande, held off a major Bijapuri onslaught in 1660 in a narrow pass in the mountains with a group of just 300 men to enable Shivaji to reach a place of safety; in the process Baji Prabhu laid down his life, becoming a legend in his own right.

In 1674, Shivaji took the momentous decision to crown himself sovereign, a declaration of the establishment of his own independent state, and in heraldic terms, the start of a new era. By giving his rule legal, official status, he robbed Aurangzeb, Bijapur, Golconda – or anybody else for that matter – of the opportunity of accusing him of overstepping the line. From now on, he was going to deal with them all as an equal. He had pulled off something that hardly anyone could match up to.

At the time of his death in 1680, when he was only fifty years old, Shivaji had left for his successors such a wealth of inspiration that despite Aurangzeb's hurried march to the Deccan to recapture lost ground, they succeeded in ensuring that the Mughal emperor stayed in the south and could never go back to the north for a quarter of a century, up until his death in 1707. In the first half of the eighteenth century, the rule of the Marathas reached its apogee as they conquered the major part of the subcontinent, their territory stretching from Attock in the north (in present-day Pakistan) to Bengal in the east before the British came and took over.

One of Shivaji's most remarkable achievements was the building of his own naval fleet. He was alone among his contemporaries in recognizing the importance of the seas and demonstrated a political and strategic vision in this regard that all the other rulers sorely lacked. The foreign powers – the Portuguese, the Dutch, the British and the French – were reluctant to share sea power with him. In fact, they often showed open hostility, and Shivaji had to nuance his positions with them, alternating between demonstrating his strength and opening negotiations. Shrewd general-statesman that he was, he was as deeply wary of and sceptical about the *firangs* as he was about all of his other adversaries. He remained constantly alert to their shenanigans, took forceful, uncompromising and retaliatory actions where necessary, and reminded them constantly that they would have to accept things on his terms – a quality that stands out given the rapaciousness, especially of the British East India Company, that revealed itself later on and proved costly to the people of the subcontinent.

If Shivaji improvised in war, he innovated in peace or whenever he got some respite from warfare. Before he had turned twenty, he had started resettling populations in and around Pune and in the Maval valleys of the Sahyadri mountain ranges. He offered incentives for increase in cultivation and for bringing wastelands under the plough. In the second half of the 1660s and the first half of the 1670s, he carefully reorganized the entire civilian administration in his territories, which had by then grown considerably in size. He took away a great deal of the powers of officials who had hereditary grants to collect revenue and were in the habit of extorting from the local population. This assault on the deeply entrenched vested interests was extraordinary in its boldness because it placed the political reorientation he was effecting at risk of disruption and sabotage at all levels, but it endeared him to the people and showed him to be a fearless pioneer.

Shivaji cared for his people. He strictly forbade his army from taking anything from the lands and fields of ordinary peasants and farmers. Those of his soldiers who flouted these rules and troubled the peasants and local villagers were punished. Among his more notable written directives was that not a blade of grass should be touched and no grain of food taken by force. If the soldiers did that, he stated, the villagers would think of them as worse than the Mughals, underlining the nature of the subjugation of the people under Mughal rule.

Shivaji was a liberator. He came in as a breath of fresh air for people in the Maratha country, who were not used to being treated with such respect by their rulers. Having said that, it should also be underlined that he was a man of his times. The revolution he achieved was brought about through armed resistance and all the fiercely aggressive warfare methods that were de rigueur in the seventeenth century: violent and debilitating attacks on enemies; capture of embattlements, arms, ammunition and personnel; despoilment of the adversary's critical geographical areas; and infiltration of enemy territory and plunder. The armed political revolution was in sync with the martial combat techniques of the times.

As British rule in India spawned a new national consciousness in the nineteenth century, leaders of the freedom movement began looking up to Shivaji as a source of inspiration. His determination, his steely resolve, his persistence, his overcoming of deadly difficulties, and his statesmanlike qualities that enabled him to realize his goals were seen as traits to emulate. The movement holding up Shivaji as a national icon for the unity of the Indian people in their fight for political emancipation gained momentum because he appealed both to the educated and the unlettered, the new elite who had imbibed Western ideas of enlightenment and the masses who were deeply traditionalist in thought and action. His rule was seen as reflecting justice, equity and tolerance. Thus it was that among the earliest to hail Shivaji as an exemplar was the Maharashtrian social reformer Gopal Hari Deshmukh, a stern critic of orthodoxy and ritualism. In an article in 1848, Deshmukh hailed Shivaji as a living legend.[2] Deshmukh's contemporary, Jotirao Phule, who eventually got the title 'Mahatma', wrote a *powada* (ballad) in Shivaji's honour in 1869. Phule attacked Brahmins and considered British rule a blessing because he believed it had ended Brahminical orthodoxy. In his *powada*, which he said he was writing for the so-called lower castes such as the Kunbis, Malis, Mahars, Matangs, Phule said Shivaji was a great king because the *rayats* (peasants) were happy with his rule, and he had framed new laws for them and taken care of the ordinary people.[3]

Deshmukh's writings resonated with the educated sections in western India and Phule's with ordinary farmers. Soon there emerged a brilliant national leader who successfully enlisted the support of both the masses and the elite in the name of Shivaji. That leader was Bal Gangadhar Tilak, popularly known as Lokmanya. He launched in 1896 the annual Shivaji festival on the Maratha hero's birth anniversary, and it resonated through the length and breadth of India. Tilak used Shivaji's story to make his fiery statement: 'Swarajya is my birthright.' In western India, people of different intellectual persuasions were now citing Shivaji's life and work: the scholar, jurist and moderate M.G. Ranade, the radical young revolutionary V.D. Savarkar, and the famous Marathi playwright Ram Ganesh Gadkari.

In Bengal, the Marathas had for long been seen as unwelcome invaders. But Shivaji's image, wedded to the national movement, brought about a drastic revision of perception. This change was sparked off by the writer Bhudev Mukhopadhyay as early as 1857, the year of the great revolt, followed by the depiction of Shivaji by the nationalist R.C. Dutt as a national hero.[4] When Tilak launched a movement to repair Shivaji's memorial at Raigad in 1895, among those present on the dais to address the gathering was Surendranath Banerjea, president of the Indian National Congress and then the most popular leader of Bengal.[5] In 1902, the celebration of the Shivaji festival began in Bengal; two years later, Rabindranath Tagore wrote a poem describing Shivaji as 'the King of Kings'; and the fire generated by the 1905 partition of Bengal saw to it that the next year, the Shivaji festival was observed there in a way 'hardly surpassed in Maharashtra itself'.[6] The nationalist leaders Bipin Chandra Pal and Aurobindo Ghose, and the revolutionary journal *Jugantar*, among others, interpreted Shivaji's life and ideals for their fellow Bengalis; Aurobindo in particular wrote a ballad for Shivaji's warrior Baji Prabhu Deshpande who had sacrificed his life to protect the Maratha leader, and a poem, 'Bhavani Mandir', where, referring to Shivaji's mother goddess Bhavani (Durga), he wrote, 'Chosen of Shivaji, Bhavani's swords / For you the Gods prepare.'[7] The revolutionary Anushilan Samiti adopted Shivaji's war cry of '*Har Har Mahadev*'. Comparing Shivaji with his contemporaries, Tagore wrote that Shivaji's movement was of greater significance than that of the Sikhs because while the Sikhs, like the Marathas, were full of valour, Shivaji had a well-conceived plan of building up a nation.[8]

The first biography of Shivaji in Urdu was written by a leader from the northern parts, the patriot Lala Lajpat Rai: he wrote his book in 1896, the very year in which Tilak started the Shivaji movement in

Maharashtra.⁹ Just as in Bengal, in the first two decades of the twentieth century, a series of writings on Shivaji in Hindi in the United Provinces and in the Assamese language in the north-east made fervent appeals to people to take up the cause of political freedom. At the same time, Shivaji began to figure prominently in more and more specimens of confiscated and proscribed Indian literature, especially in Marathi and Bengali, with the result that he increased in stature in the national imagination until Mahatma Gandhi's idea of non-violence came to dominate public consciousness.

However, such was Shivaji's story and legend that even Gandhi recognized his greatness. In many ways Shivaji was a product of his early modern times, as we have noted, and his work had involved armed hostilities throughout, as well as pillage and sackings. Most apostles of non-violence in the independence movement acknowledged that in the medieval to early modern era there was no other way to fight against unjust rulers than armed resistance. And in post-Independence India, parties of almost every kind of ideological leaning have tried to appropriate Shivaji. They cite his ideas of political, civic and administrative reforms as models worthy of adopting – not literally, because times have changed and monarchies have been replaced by a democracy – but in terms of the foundational concepts of justice and fairness underlining his vision and his actions.

So what kind of state was Shivaji trying to establish? Was it a secular state, as some have asserted, or was it Hindu, as some others have declared? Or was it simply a Maratha empire? The answer I have arrived at is that Shivaji was not out to establish a secular or non-religious kingdom, nor was he bent on founding a Hindu theocratic state. He was establishing a Hindu polity – one that was broadly inclusive, tolerant and all-encompassing and at the same time drank deep of the fountain of Hindu culture and civilization. His deep sense of his own religion and its spirituality made him regard Hindus and Muslims as equal, and he saw religious discrimination as abhorrent, immoral and unacceptable. Shivaji recruited Muslims in his army, just as he recruited Marathas and other Hindus, and two of his navy admirals, Darya Sarang Ventjee and Daulat Khan, were Muhammadans. One of his bitterest critics, the official Mughal chronicler Khafi Khan, who called him a 'hell-dog', put it in writing that Shivaji had strictly instructed his soldiers to treat with the greatest respect the Muslim holy book, the Quran, if they came across it.

The element of Hindu identity, though, is inescapable in Shivaji's life and courses through his career right from the beginning. Evidently the Islamic conquest of India, and of the Deccan in particular in the late thirteenth century, had ramifications for the lives of the vast majority of the region's population. Shivaji noticed that despite the rise of the Marathas as accomplished soldiers of rank, the highest military ranks were still denied to them. The Adil Shahi, the dominant power in the western Deccan, had been tolerant, even pluralistic, in the sixteenth century, but things had changed in the seventeenth century. And once Aurangzeb sat on the Mughal throne when Shivaji was in his twenties, the empire turned increasingly hostile towards Hindus. From the 1660s onwards, Aurangzeb began a reign of social and economic repression, making Hindus pay customs duties which Muslims were exempted from paying, and ultimately imposing the discriminatory *jaziya* tax on 'unbelievers', in response to which Shivaji wrote his famous letter to the emperor. Renaming of places in the Deccan by the Islamic powers was also rampant during this period; all seals of the state and its officials were issued in Persian in contrast to the earlier tradition of Hindu rajas, including those from the Deccan, to use either Sanskrit or the local languages.[10]

Shivaji's actions show he was responding to what he was seeing all around him. His father's and mother's own seals were in Persian. But Shivaji, at the age of sixteen itself, chose Sanskrit as the language of his seal, making an unequivocal statement in the Persianate Age. Many Deccani kings who were Hindu – among them Pratapa Rudra and Kapaya Nayaka – had taken, from the time of the Delhi Sultanate's invasions from the north, the title of Sultan for themselves. Shivaji took the title Chhatrapati after the word '*chhatra*' of Hindu rajas of the past.

Tagore was thus accurate in saying in an article in the *Modern Review* in 1911 that Shivaji had 'in his mind the ideal of setting up a Hindu Empire',[11] as did Tilak and B.C. Pal. Jawaharlal Nehru too accepted in his *Discovery of India* that Shivaji 'was the symbol of a resurgent Hindu nationalism'.[12] But Shivaji's Hindu state was for Hindus and non-Hindus alike and did not conceive of any difference in treatment between the two.

There are, thus, two kinds of people who would not be able to term his state as one after their own heart. One group would be those who believe in discrimination and domination in the name of faith, and would like to overstate Shivaji's role as a protector of the faith. Shivaji did once issue an order to his soldiers saying 'cows and Brahmins' should not be harmed, but it is utterly reductive and misleading, and a case of reading history backwards for the benefit of modern-day religious conservatives, to label him 'protector of cows and Brahmins' for this reason.[13] In his era, the ritualistic and caste-based order was strong, and with cows and Brahmins symbolizing such an order, he was sending out a reassuring message to the larger, tradition-bound society. There's nothing to suggest he attached any special importance to these two categories. All the evidence is that he stood by so-called Brahmins and non-Brahmins alike, as much for the Ramoshis and other tribals who were among the guardians of his forts as for the Marathas, Kayasthas, Kolis, Bhandaris and Muslims like his navy admiral Daulat Khan who fought shoulder to shoulder with him.

The second set of people who cannot claim his state as their own are those who see the affirmation of Indian civilization in the denial of the terms 'Hindu' and 'Hinduism'; this group attempts to stall any discussion and dialogue on the likely trauma that Islamic conquest over a period of several centuries caused to Hindu cultural identity, despite the element of syncretism that may have existed parallelly, and also seeks to excuse the undeniable religious dimension of the attacks on Hindu temples by framing them as mere assaults on seats of power.[14]

The term 'Hindawi' was current during Shivaji's times in the Deccan, and it indicated the vast majority of the land's Hindu population, its diverse tribal population, and indeed, all the indigenous peoples.[15] It included, interestingly and increasingly over time, the majority of Deccani Muslims who, having entered over the seas through the western coast centuries ago, had been absorbed as one with the land and had made the land their own – as against those coming in more recently from the northern parts who were seen as being imbued with a different set of values.

What of the 'Maharashtra dharma' then, which has been named in some of the poetic verses of the seventeenth century, particularly those of the Lord Ram-worshipping saint Ramdas, as denoting Shivaji's state? Is it evidence of a Maratha state? Shivaji's state was of course a Maratha state. Deeply and profoundly so. His self-respecting Maratha mother Jijabai gave him spine and spirituality; his father Shahaji and the Bhosle family as a whole, with its military feats, awakened him to his potential; the hardiness and dedication of his fellow Marathas and the resilience of the native Kunbis and other peasants that Phule spoke about were the sinews of his power; and the deeply humanistic philosophy of the Maharashtrian bhakti saint-poets, from Namdeo and Dynaneshwar to Tukaram, lay at the core of his worldview.

The reference to 'Maharashtra dharma' by Ramdas, an unstinting admirer of Shivaji, points to a set of ethical, spiritual and cultural values and principles of the Marathi-speaking regions, which were all part of a broader Hindu identity. The stories of the Ramayana and Mahabharata which Shivaji's mother told him constituted the same cultural heritage, as did the ochre flag he selected for himself and the Maratha war cry of *'Har Har Mahadev'* in the name of Lord Shiva. The fundamentally Maharashtrian and macro Hindu civilizational identity are not unreconciled here; in fact, they are truly culturally united. If that were not the case, Shivaji would not have asked Chhatrasal, a youngster of the Bundela clan in the north, who approached him seeking to join his army in the early 1670s, to head home instead and set up a state of his own against the Mughals and against Aurangzeb.[16]

In the final phase of his life in the second half of the 1670s, Shivaji's campaign of conquest covered large parts of present-day Telangana, Andhra, Karnataka and Tamil Nadu. This is yet another sign that his political dream was not restricted to the Marathi-speaking regions, though Maharashtra would always be the nucleus and the heart. The 'what ifs' of history are tantalizing. Shivaji died in 1680, having marched all the way up to the eastern coast. What more lands would he have conquered and administered is something we can only guess. But his successors among the Marathas did not restrict themselves to Maharashtra either; they ventured deep into the northern and eastern parts of Hindustan.

In writing this biography of Shivaji, I had to sift through a vast collection of papers, documents and books in the Marathi language. The majority of the Marathas' own records were burnt during enemy assaults or destroyed by the Marathas themselves after Shivaji's death as their conflict with the Mughals intensified and as the Mughals under Aurangzeb took Raigad and other important forts, where the top official documents were stored. Whatever family papers still survived in the homes of a few Marathas were hidden by them after the end of the Peshwa era in 1818 for fear of the new British rulers cracking down on them on suspicion of an anti-British conspiracy by those still owing their allegiance to the Maratha rulers. The British brazenly confiscated the records they found, not allowing the public any access to them.

But slowly, as national consciousness grew in the late nineteenth century, an archival movement of sorts developed in western India, with its proponents urging families to hand over documents to historians who could preserve and examine them and simultaneously appealing to the British Raj to open up the archives they had concealed. The efforts bore fruit. The pioneering Maratha historian who led the archival movement was V.K. Rajwade. He painstakingly collected, at the turn of the century, twenty-one volumes of documents, chiefly private papers of Maratha families and official state correspondence in the nature of orders or revenue arrangements. These are indeed priceless for any historian, and so they proved for me in the research, as did the materials put together by generations of scholars of the Bharat Itihas Sanshodhak Mandal of Pune like B.G. Paranjpe, D.B. Parasnis, K.N. Sane, K.V. Purandare, D.V. Apte, D.V. Kale and G.S. Sardesai. Sardesai's eight volumes of *Marathi Riyasat* provide an encyclopaedic view of Maratha history and of the long Maratha–Mughal conflict. During his time – broadly the first half of the twentieth century – not only scholars writing in Marathi such as T.S. Shejwalkar, K.V. Keluskar and V.S. Bendrey but also those writing in English apart from Sardesai himself – such as Jadunath Sarkar, M.G. Ranade, K.T. Telang, Bal Krishna, Surendra Nath Sen, C.V. Vaidya and H.G. Rawlinson – contributed handsomely to exploring Shivaji's life and times. Five modern-day historians stand out as their heirs – G.H. Khare, Setumadhavrao Pagadi, Narhar Kurundkar, A.N. Kulkarni and G.B. Mehendale (who wrote in both English and Marathi) – for their work looked at new discoveries and findings and interpreted them for the present generation. Yet most of their writings remain accessible largely to scholars of history. It is with a deep dept of gratitude that I have referenced them extensively in this book so that they can reach the twenty-first century reader curious to know and learn about Shivaji.

The English works on Shivaji in particular, most of them published in the first half of the twentieth century, suffer from a surfeit of outdated material. Jadunath Sarkar's book *Shivaji and His Times* is a case in point. For decades it was regarded as the standard English work on Shivaji. Sarkar, unfortunately, got several things wrong, most of which Marathi historians subsequently either pointed out or corrected with corroborative evidence. To give an example, Sarkar wrote that Shivaji had renamed the Kondhana fort as Sinhagad after one of his closest lieutenants, Tanaji Malusare, was slain there during a spectacular assault on the Mughal garrison in 1670 and said, '*Gad aala, pan Sinha gela*' (The fort's won, but the lion's dead). The legend made its way into textbooks and in the popular imagination in Maharashtra and has been repeated endlessly, in ballads, cinema and the theatre. The truth, though, is that Kondhana was always called by its other name of Sinhagad, and there are letters extant from before Tanaji's death that mention the name. It was precisely because it was called Sinhagad that Shivaji used the lion metaphor – and not the other way round. This book looks at this myth and several other stories that have acquired popular and legendary status, but it separates fact from fiction and presents the real Shivaji of history, whose life is so filled with drama that it scarcely requires further embellishment in the form of made-up tales.

Sarkar and most other English biographers of Shivaji, including the British official Dennis Kincaid, also almost totally neglected two crucial contemporary works on Shivaji's life. These works are by Shivaji's officials and chroniclers Parmanand, who wrote *Shivabharat*, and Sabhasad, who wrote *Sabhasad Bakhar*. Their writings throw considerable light on Shivaji's life. The exact words that a recent biographer of Thomas Cromwell used about his close contemporaries writing about him can be applied to Parmanand and Sabhasad: 'We need to remember that ... they were *there*,' and 'we need to respect their observations and comprehend their limitations and concerns.'[17] The overlooking of their texts has seriously hindered writings on Shivaji's life in English, and one of my aims in this book is to reinstate their works in his narrative.

I cannot read Persian, but translations of Persian works and official documents and records of the Mughals, of the Nizam Shahi of Ahmadnagar, of Bijapur and of Golconda by Sarkar, G.H. Khare, Pagadi and so many others helped me to record the point of view of Shivaji's adversaries and to understand how they perceived him and changed their perceptions of him and responses to him over time. Sarkar's translation of documents in the Rajasthan archives helped to illumine elements of Shivaji's visit to Agra, his imprisonment and his escape. The officials of the British East India Company wrote copiously about their activities all across peninsular India in the seventeenth century, and they recorded lots of details about Shivaji and his actions, including his two raids on Surat. I have critically examined their records for those details and for their sometimes adversarial and sometimes transactional perspective. Similarly, records of the Portuguese rulers of Goa and their officials, translated from the original by the scholar P.S. Pissurlencar, and the diaries of the French official of Pondicherry Francois Martin at the time of Shivaji's southern campaign of the late 1670s provided rare and rarely quoted accounts of Shivaji.

Interestingly, the first foreign biographer of Shivaji was a Portuguese man based in Marmugao in Goa during his lifetime, Cosme da Guarda. Though his biography was published in 1695, that is, fifteen years after Shivaji's death, da Guarda had spoken to many people in the Deccan before writing it, and it provides interesting insights into how Shivaji was seen by the people of the region during that time and of contemporary discussions around his personality, politics and his momentous clash with Aurangzeb. The Italian traveller Niccolao Manucci was part of the Mughal army and had the opportunity to meet Shivaji and have conversations with him. He recorded much material in his diaries which I have consulted and, where relevant, quoted. Other European travellers and officials such as Francois Bernier, Jean de Thevenot and Jean-Baptiste Tavernier also left accounts, in the classic European style of documenting most of what they were observing around them. Their observations came in handy at times where the account was plausible and the evidence supportive; their flights of fancy, as indeed those of all the others, Sabhasad and Parmanand included, I have roundly rejected.

Shivaji Maharaj as Chhatrapati marked a point of serious departure in the politics and military history of early modern India, a point that needs close examination in order to understand the picture that emerged later in the subcontinent. His life was an expression of popular will and an eloquent demonstration of political will. He gave himself up to the task of fusing his people into a nation, with a sense of mission, and thwarted Aurangzeb's ambition of conquering all of Hindustan. The spirit Shivaji was imbued with endured after his death, and his motivations for state-building still constitute a template for Indians in the twenty-first century. This book places him on the stage of the seventeenth century as the leading actor that he was and charts his journey, at times from truly serious failure to dazzling success, but – to paraphrase what Aurobindo Ghose once wrote about him[18] – always ultimately in the direction of undermining a vast empire and creating a political entity whose values still haven't been extinguished.

1

A Child of the Deccan

It was Friday, and the sun had already set behind the mountains surrounding the steep, craggy hill of Shivneri. These peaks lay at the northern end of the long Sahyadri range, which vertically divided the Marathi-speaking regions of western India into two distinct halves: one stretched up to the Arabian Sea some 40 kilometres away, and the other was a land of chasms and crevasses sloping down to arid plains that somehow fused together into a triangle, one as rough-hewn and ragged as the heights above. Atop the Shivneri hill was an eponymous fort, located a forbidding 3,500 feet above sea level. It was a sanctuary of sorts, towering above Maratha lands riddled with conflicts between four competing kingdoms, and that was why Jijabai, the pregnant wife of Shahaji Raje Bhosle, had sheltered there as she awaited the birth of their child.

The child was born that very evening, on 19 February 1630. He was named Shivaji. Three centuries later, scholars and politicians would still be sparring over the date of his birth, and committees would discuss whether it was 27 April 1627 or 19 February 1630. A credible account, penned by the Marathi poet Parmanand on the orders of the Chhatrapati himself, cites Falgun Vadya Tritiya 1551 according to the Hindu calendar, which corresponds to 19 February 1630. This is confirmed by the Jedhe Shakavali or Jedhe Chronology, a contemporary account of a family aligned to Shivaji, as well as an inscription in Thanjavur and three horoscopes of

Shivaji found in Rajasthan. The sources which mention 27 April 1627 are chiefly those recorded over a hundred years after he had passed on.

Why has this controversy carried on for so long? It has much to do with the turbulent history of the region and Shivaji's emergence as a historical, political and quasi-religious figure. As stated earlier, most Maratha records of his times were destroyed during the Mughal–Maratha conflict in the Deccan – a corruption of the Sanskrit word *dakshin* meaning 'south' – in the wake of his death. Those that remained were mainly family histories and letters related to land grants and other administrative matters. Gradually, in the late nineteenth and early twentieth centuries, historians in India began to gather the documents that were still around, and the first date to emerge was the 1627 one. As Shivaji developed into an icon during the Indian freedom movement, this year came to be established in popular and cultural memory as Shivaji's birth year. Shivaji Jayanti was started and popularized by Bal Gangadhar Tilak. As more accurate documents emerged – the Jedhe Shakavali was brought to light by Tilak himself in 1916 – it became clear 1630 was the right date. But historians and others who had made the claim for 1627 would not give up, which is why confusion still exists.

Going back to that rugged hilltop in Shivneri: how was the new baby welcomed? If you believe the hugely popular, Broadway-meets-Bollywood Marathi theatre production on Chhatrapati Shivaji's life that has been running to packed houses since the early 1990s, Shivaji's birth is announced by a woman who comes running out of Shivneri fort breathless with excitement and exclaims '*Mulga! Mulga! Mulga!*' (It's a boy! It's a boy! It's a boy!). She's followed by an enthusiastic bunch of Marathas sounding their *tutari*, a traditional trumpet-like instrument, hurling *gulal* or celebratory colours in the air, daubing the stuff on each other's cheeks, and waving the ochre Maratha flag while sweets are distributed liberally. Mounted on a lavish scale, this play, written, produced and presented by a famous balladeer,[1] is sometimes performed on a stage so broad and wide that mahout-controlled elephants walk from end to end, imperiously, and horses stride across in beautifully choreographed scenes. Stirring stuff for playgoers, who already know what the boy is going to do when he grows up, but actually quite far-fetched. The fort was chosen by Shahaji, a Maratha nobleman doing his duty on the battlefield at the moment of his son's birth, to keep his wife – who had lost other babies – safe in an atmosphere of precarity and peril. Given that, boisterous revelry would have been out of the question. More likely, the expressions of joy were subdued.

Jijabai and Shahaji had had five children before Shivaji, all sons. Only one, Sambhaji, born circa 1620, had survived. They had arranged his marriage, two years before Shivaji's birth, at the same fort where the sixth child had now arrived. The names of Shivaji's other four siblings were never recorded. They likely died in infancy. Naturally, the parents were anxious that the newborn should survive. To their great relief, he did; Sambhaji, though, died in a battle in Kanakgiri in Karnataka, in his thirties. Three years after Sambhaji's death, Shivaji would give his own firstborn his brother's name.

A common theory around Shivaji's name, mentioned in the latter-day and highly unreliable Chitnis Chronicle,[2] is that it comes from the Hindu goddess Shivai, whose idol stood in a temple on Shivneri fort. But in his record of Shivaji's life, the poet Parmanand states simply that he was named 'Shiv' because he was born at 'Shivgiri' or Shivneri fort.[3] There's little to show that the fort itself was named after the goddess; it's possible the name of the fort came first and the temple deity's name was derived from that. However, it's plausible that 'Shiv', 'Shivneri' and 'Shivaji' all have their origins in the name of one of Hinduism's most powerful deities. The Bhosle family, we know from records, was devoted to Lord Shiva. Besides, Bhimashankar, one of Shiva's *jyotirlingas* – the twelve spots across India where he, according to legend, cast his celestial beam – is not far to the south-west of Shivneri.

Whatever the provenance of Shivaji's name, Shivneri was nevertheless an appropriate setting for his birth given his lineage on both sides. The Bhosles claimed descent from the Sisodia clan of Rajasthan, which was of noble extraction, but the earliest specific location they're traced to, sometime around the middle of the sixteenth century, is Verul or Ellora. Home to some of the most magnificent rock-cut Hindu, Buddhist and Jain caves in the world and now recognized by UNESCO as a global heritage site, Ellora was held by Shivaji's ancestors as one of their hereditary tracts of land. Cut into the Shivneri hill, too, on three sides, are nearly sixty rock caves, nowhere near as extraordinary as those of Ellora and quite devoid of ornamentation, but significant nonetheless for their two *chaityas* or prayer halls, several quadrangular *viharas* or cave homes for itinerant monks, some open cells and chambers, a few small halls with benches running along their side walls, a few roof paintings, nine inscriptions and a number of cisterns. Jijabai's father was Lukhji Jadhavrao from the Jadhav clan, 'Rao' being an honorific. What is Jadhav in Marathi is Yadava in Hindi: the Jadhavs were genealogically linked to the Yadavas, a Hindu dynasty that ruled over considerable parts of the Deccan between the twelfth and fourteenth centuries CE. The town of Junnar (the northernmost town in Pune district) and four hills around it with their individual cave groups – the Shivneri hill on the town's south-west, the Tulja hill to the west, the Ganesh hill to the north, and Manmodi to the south[4] – once belonged to the Jadhavs.

The Bhosles were Marathas, and so were the Jadhavs. For centuries, the term 'Maratha' denoted a resident of the Marathi-speaking parts. A fifth century CE. Sinhalese document described a region as 'Maharattha,' the eleventh-century Islamic chronicler Al Baruni called the place south of the Narmada 'Marhat Des,' and the fourteenth-century Muslim writer Ibn Batuta stated those living around Daulatabad were 'Marathas'.[5] In the fifteenth and sixteenth century, people from the Marathi-speaking regions who entered military service and obtained positions came to be identified as Marathas. In time, the Marathas, because of their military tradition, developed, like the Rajputs, as a distinct social group, differentiating themselves from others. Broadly, the entire Maharashtrian community has been referred to as Maratha across India for generations; in this book, the word will denote the wider community except when referring to the distinctive group called the Marathas.

Their positions were all held in the Islamic kingdoms of the Deccan, best defined, in the context of the Middle Ages, as that part of the Indian land mass south of the Vindhya mountains. Maharashtra was a part of the Deccan region.[6] It chiefly comprised three parts: sections of the Konkan or western coastline where Marathi was the chief language, the Ghats and the Desh.[7] The Ghats were mountains that rose over 40 kilometres inland from the coastline and successfully blocked the monsoon clouds coming in from the south-west, keeping the hills rocky, dry and not very conducive to cultivation. The Desh was the plateau that began where the Ghats ended and got narrower as you went further east. One part of the Desh, which lay in the shadow of the mountains, was similar in nature to the dry and the largely farm-resistant areas along the heights; the other part was productive, helped along considerably by three rivers that ran along its length before moving from the Marathi parts to the east: the Tapi or Purna to the north, the Godavari roughly at the centre, and the Bhima–Krishna to the south. The rivers were life givers and some of the most ancient dwellings came up around them, including the famous pilgrim centre of Pandharpur on the banks of the Bhima.

The local population, who grew 'mainly wheat, cotton and pulses and very little rice',[8] impressed the seventh-century Chinese Buddhist pilgrim Hsuan Tsang, who has provided one of the earliest descriptions of the region:

> Men are fond of learning and studying both heretical and orthodox books. The disposition of the people is honest and simple; they are tall in stature and of a stern ... character. To their benefactors, they are grateful; to their enemies, relentless. If they are insulted, they will risk their lives to avenge themselves. If they are asked to help one in distress, they will forget themselves in their haste to render assistance.[9]

The language of the locals was known as Maharashtri – 'from Maharashtra' – at least from the third century CE. Maharashtri was the Prakrit or vernacular child of Sanskrit. One of the oldest surviving anthologies of poetry from South Asia, the *Gathasaptasati* ('700 verses in *gatha* form'), was compiled in Maharashtri Prakrit around the second century CE by a Satavahana king and has 700 verses, almost all of them about love. According to the scholar Martha Ann Selby, Prakrit grammarians considered Maharashtri 'the Prakrit par excellence',[10] and the Sanskrit poet Kalidasa (fourth to fifth centuries CE) used Maharashtri in his dramas, getting female characters to speak verses in the language.[11]

In time Maharashtri became Marathi, and from the eighth to the thirteenth centuries it grew further. The precocious sixteen-year-old Dynaneshwar wrote his famous commentary on the Bhagavad Gita at the end of the thirteenth century and a Hindu religious ferment in the form of the bhakti or devotional movement overtook the land, rising in opposition to ritualism, orthodoxy and caste oppression. The bhakti movement ran almost parallel to the entry and establishment of Islam in the Deccan, and in part may have been a response to the decline in superiority of the Hindu faith, decaying under the burden of dead ritual.

The Marathas rose in military service in the sixteenth century, by which time the Deccan had been completely overrun by Islamic kingdoms. The first Muslim invasion of the region was led by the Delhi sultan's nephew Ala-ud-din Khilji in 1296. Until then, all Muslim invasions had been limited to the northern parts, and the Deccan had four regional Hindu kingdoms roughly formed along linguistic lines: the Yadavas with their capital at Devagiri in the Marathi-speaking western Deccan, the Kakatiyas in the Telugu-speaking Andhras, the Hoysalas of Karnataka, and the Pandyas of Tamil country.

Khilji's assault on Devagiri, and the riches he took from that capital of the Yadavas, helped to cement his claim on the Delhi throne. The Tughluq dynasty, which succeeded the Khiljis, also took Devagiri in 1327. The assaults of the Ghaznavids on Delhi in the tenth and eleventh centuries and the establishment of the Delhi Sultanate in 1206 had already led to the influx of military and administrative personnel from Central Asia. With Devagiri now taken by Sultan Muhammad bin Tughluq, renamed Daulatabad and given the status of a second capital, one-tenth of Delhi's Muslim population was moved there. The Marathas were until this point not known to be engaged in military activities, preferring instead to be tillers of their lands. Using Daulatabad, situated 13 kilometres north-west of Khadki (latter-day Aurangabad in the Marathwada plains) as a base, the Tughluqs swooped down on Warangal in the eastern Deccan and destroyed the regime of the Kakatiyas there, razing the big Swayambhu

Shiva temple near the fort, renaming the place Sultanpur, and forcing the local raja to climb up the ramparts of his fort and genuflect in the direction of Delhi.[12] Eventually, the four Hindu kingdoms were wiped out, and the rule of the Tughluqs, too, ended soon afterwards as a result of twin rebellions. In its place emerged, by the middle of the fourteenth century, two successor states: the Bahmani Sultanate and the Vijayanagara kingdom.

In the first half of the sixteenth century, three momentous changes occurred on the South Asian landscape: Babur, a descendant of Genghis Khan the Mongol and also of Timur the Turk, founded the Mughal empire in the north; the Portuguese captured Goa on the western coast; and the Bahmani kingdom of the Deccan, after about 150 years, splintered into the five separate states of Ahmadnagar, Bijapur, Bidar, Berar and Golconda. Though opposed to each other, four of these kingdoms got together to crush the already weakened state of Vijayanagara at the battle of Talikota in 1565.

It was under these four kingdoms that the Marathas sought military service, and their rise as competent soldiers was the result of four factors. The first was that tensions were always running high between the Arab-Turkish Muslims or 'Afagis' coming in from the north, the so-called 'Westerners' arriving on ships from the Persian Gulf, and the Deccanis, who by the sixteenth and seventeenth centuries saw themselves as indigenous Muslims. These constant tensions made the Deccan sultanates look to the local Marathi-speaking population for recruits.

One of the sultans was particularly welcoming of the Marathas and their language. Ibrahim Adil Shah I, who came to power in 1535, sacked the majority of his Persian-origin troops, mostly Shias from Iran, and recruited Deccani Muslims in their place. And to check the power of these 'Deccanis' and the 'Afagis', he chose the Marathas for his troops. Adil Shah I also decided to get public accounts of his kingdom recorded in the native Marathi and Kannada instead of Persian, which was the language used before him.[13] The second reason for the rise of the Marathas was their close links with the native populace, which helped the sultanates – most of whom were Shias as distinct from the Sunnis ruling the north – to establish a direct connection with the people of the region, consolidate their rule and get a grip on administration right down to the village level. The third was the drying up of 'Turkish' and other Muslim recruits coming in from the north from the time the Mughal empire began to expand southwards; it was mostly the Mughals that the Muslims entering from Central Asia or the Persian Gulf would increasingly serve. And the fourth was the easy and swift manner in which the Marathas took to cavalry and other soldierly duties.

Among the Maratha families whose members became prominent nobles in the Deccani kingdoms during this period were the Bhosles and the Jadhavs. In addition to the family base of Ellora, the Bhosles, in time, gained Chamargunda near Ahmadnagar and Pune as their *jagirs*. A *jagir* was an area where the *jagirdar* or holder of the *jagir*, while professing loyalty to a particular kingdom, maintained a body of troops under him for military service, held forts for a kingdom, and enjoyed land assessment rights. Allegiances were fluid as battles for territory were almost unceasing, and a *jagirdar* often attached himself to the state that had – either in keeping with or against his will – his *jagir* under its control. These *jagirs* were transferable, so a fief holder often preferred to keep his *jagir* rather than his fealty to a particular state in case his area was seized by a rival kingdom.

Shivaji's grandfather Maloji acquired prominence as a noble with the Nizam Shahi kingdom, which controlled most of the north and northwest parts of the upper Deccan. He served the kingdom particularly well under Malik Ambar, the Ethiopian regent of the Nizam Shahi state who put up a strong defence of the northern Deccan from 1600 until his death in 1626. In pushing back the forces dispatched, first, by Emperor Akbar to conquer the Deccan in 1600 and right through the reign of Jahangir, who continued the assault on the borders of the Nizam Shahi kingdom until his death in 1627, Ambar excelled in his role and was smartly assisted by the Maratha forces under his command. Ambar became known for his deployment of Marathas and his faith in their abilities, and was the first to use *bargir-giri* or guerrilla warfare to deadly effect with the help of the terrain-knowing Marathas.

After Maloji, Shahaji carried forward the martial tradition of the family and became one of the Nizam Shahi's leading chieftains, distinguishing himself in the battle of Bhatvadi of 1624 in which Malik Ambar's men held off the combined forces of the Mughals and the Adil Shah 16 kilometres to the east of Ahmadnagar.[14] It was after the death of Malik Ambar that Shahaji played a truly starring role in the kingdom's affairs. While he too, like the other Maratha *sardars*, had in the past switched sides and worked with the Mughals and the Adil Shah, from 1633 to 1636 he single-handedly held the Nizam Shahi banner aloft and kept the state afloat, anointing – just like Ambar had done before him – a young scion of the Nizam Shah's family. Though the Mughals pressed down undeterred on a kingdom considerably weakened, Shahaji, leading a band of 12,000 troops (5,000 directly under him and the rest of the Nizam Shahi state), at one point succeeded in capturing Nasik and Trimbak in the north, Sangamner and Junnar in the central parts, and sizeable chunks of 'Tal' Konkan or the southern end of the Marathi-speaking Konkan.[15] The Mughals nevertheless crushed the Nizam Shahi Sultanate finally in 1636. Crucially, among the empire's commanders in the Deccan who led the campaign against Shahaji in this last phase of the Nizam Shahi Sultanate was Shaista Khan,[16] who would later become one of the major opponents of Shivaji. After the Nizam Shahi's collapse, Shahaji took up service with the Adil Shahi of Bijapur.

Jijabai's family, the Jadhavs, were *deshmukhs* or headmen of a *pargana* (a group of anything between twenty and hundred villages, akin to a modern district or subdistrict) in Sindkhed, not too far to the east of Ellora, so the two families were known to each other. Jijabai's father, Lukhji Jadhavrao, was a noble of eminence and much sought after by both the Nizam Shahi and the Mughals, evident from the fact that he shifted allegiance from one to the other seven times in a fifteen-year period between 1614 and 1629.[17] In his memoirs, Jahangir wrote of a battle against Malik Ambar's forces in 1616, where, just before hostilities began, 'Jado Ray' (Jadhavrao) was among the 'influential leaders' of the 'Bargis' (Marathas) who defected to the Mughal side along with his body of troops.[18] The 'Bargis', Jahangir noted, were 'a hardy lot' and 'a centre of resistance in that (Deccan) country'.[19] A representative of the British East India Company at Burhanpur, Nicholas Bangham, said in his report to the English factory at Surat, on 18 November 1621, that the latest from the court of Prince Shah Jahan was that 'Jaddoo Raye [Jadhavrao], one of the principall generalls of the Decanns, is revolted and receaved at this court with great honour'.[20] And the Adil Shahi kingdom's chronicler of the period mentioned both Jadhavrao and his son-in-law Shahaji Bhosle – calling them 'Jadav Rao' and 'Shahjiu Bhosle' respectively – as among the Maratha leaders in two campaigns, one in 1614 and the other ten years later.[21]

Their families were well matched in terms of social class in a medieval to early modern age set-up. Shahaji was married to Jijabai when he, as a teenager, 'had just about sprouted a moustache' in the early teens of the seventeenth century. 'Jijau', as the girl was called lovingly by her parents, was five to seven years younger to him. Parmanand described the young Jijabai at the time of her wedding as 'well-born' and 'lotus-eyed', 'with radiant black hair' and 'a visage so soft it looked like a blossomed lotus'. Shahaji, he wrote, was 'generous, humane, spirited, well-skilled in fighting, endowed with all excellent qualities'.[22]

Some years after the marriage, ties between the Bhosles and the Jadhavs were seriously fractured. One day, so the story goes, the Nizam Shah's *sardars*, including Jadhavrao, Shahaji and others had gathered in his durbar. After the sultan withdrew, they were all on their way out when, at the exit to the palace, they heard a commotion. An elephant of a *sardar* named Khandagle had run amok. The elephant injured some members of Lukhji Jadhav's contingent, prompting Lukhji's son and Jijabai's brother, Dattaji, to try and rein the wild animal in. Possibly interpreting Dattaji's move as an attack on the Sultanate, Shahaji and his cousins rushed to the elephant owner's rescue, and there was a major clash in which Dattaji was killed by one of Shahaji's cousins, Sambhaji.[23] In turn the angry Jadhavs killed Sambhaji, and Shahaji himself injured his arm in the melee. Finally the sultan had to step in to end the fight. With one member of each family killed, much bad blood was created.

Jijabai must have been completely torn, mourning the pointless death of a brother, and on the other hand, witnessing her husband's agony at the equally pointless death of his cousin.[24]

Believing that the sultan had favoured the Bhosles in this incident, which took place circa 1623, Lukhji Jadhav made one of his famous defections to the Mughal side. When he was back later with the Nizam Shahi, a much greater shock awaited him. Sometime in June–July 1629, information trickled in that the new Mughal ruler, Shah Jahan, was soon going to launch a campaign in the Deccan. Suspecting that Lukhji Jadhav was among the generals planning to switch over, the Nizam Shah summoned him to his durbar in Daulatabad. The moment he entered the durbar with his sons on 25 July, Lukhji was suddenly set upon and murdered by assailants who had got the sultan's go-ahead. Three of his sons – Raghav, Achloji and Yashwant – were also killed in cold blood.[25] Lukhji's wife and Jijabai's mother, Girjai, had accompanied him to Daulatabad. She, along with her surviving son Bahadur and Lukhji's brother Jagdevrao, immediately left the camp in which she was staying and headed to the family fiefdom of Sindkhed for safety. The Jadhavs soon switched loyalties to the Mughals, and revolted by the murders, Shahaji too went over to the Mughal camp, despite the previous cooling-off with his in-laws' family. Thus it was that at the time of Shivaji's birth, Shahaji was with the Mughals (he would leave in 1632 to try and save the Nizam Shah's state).[26] He held land rights in the Pune and Chakan areas, but the Nizam Shahi didn't hurry to take back those lands; the Adil Shahi did, and he had to fight his fight. While he was doing so, Jijabai was ensconced at Shivneri fort in Junnar district, which was near Pune.

Shivneri was then under a Maratha *sardar* called Shriniwas Vishwasrao. Shahaji and Jijabai had arranged the marriage of their son Sambhaji sometime in 1628–29 to Jayanti, the daughter of this *sardar*. A pregnant Jijabai would be safest with Sambhaji's in-laws, Shahaji felt,[27] and 'with the permission of his relative [Vishwasrao]' left her 'at Shivneri fort itself, together with her attendants'.[28] Far from enjoying noisy celebrations at the time of Shivaji's birth, Jijabai, sheltering in a home that was neither

her own nor that of her parents, would have had to keep a low profile. To make matters worse, the Deccan was hit by a terrible famine from 1629 to 1631. The *Badshah Nama*, the account of the first two decades of Shah Jahan's reign, said of the year 1630:

> A total want in the Dakhin and Gujarat. The inhabitants ... were reduced to the direst extremity. Life was offered for a loaf, but none would buy; rank was to be sold for a cake, but none cared for it ... The numbers of the dying caused obstructions in the roads.[29]

Shivaji spent the first six years of his life with his mother Jijabai at Shivneri. Shahaji was in and out of the place, first fighting for the Mughals in the Deccan and then attempting to shore up the flagging fortunes of the Nizam Shahi. When Shivaji was born, Shahaji was in the midst of a conflict with one Darya Khan at Nevasa near Gujarat. He first set eyes on his son after the twin rituals of the boy's *annaprashan* (the first time a baby is fed food) and *suryadarshan* (the infant's sighting of the sun) had been carried out; this means, going by the usual timing of such ceremonies, that the father beheld the son well over a month after his birth.[30] Soon the little one was moving about on all fours, playfully 'chasing his own shadow in the sun and trying to catch it'. Before long, as he learnt to walk and run, there were many small things that held his interest and excited him. He was quite taken with 'horses and elephants of clay, preferring them to the real ones belonging to his father' and would 'run after a bunch of peacocks to get hold of their flowing tails'. He also picked up pretty quickly the sounds made by peacocks, parrots, nightingales, horses and elephants and would imitate them with absolute ease; and he would often naughtily put the fear of God in the minds of his and his mother's adoring attendants by springing upon them all of a sudden with the roar of a tiger.[31]

As a little boy, Shivaji was extremely active and agile. And he had striking features. His nose was sharp and pointed; his forehead was broad and of an excellent proportion; and he had an endearing smile. An English chaplain who saw him later in life observed that Shivaji had a 'quick and piercing eye' and described him as 'whiter than any of his people'.[32] The boy would be dressed in a tunic, with a *pagdi* on his head and an ornamental tuft called an aigrette, and he had slightly long hair on the sides. In adulthood, as records maintained by English officials tell us, Shivaji grew to be a man of middle height, with an erect bearing, and whenever he spoke, it appeared as if he were smiling.[33] Shivaji's earliest foreign biographer Cosme da Guarda, noted similarly that Shivaji was 'quick in action' and 'lively in carriage', 'with a clear and fair face', and his 'dark big eyes were so lively that they seemed to dart rays of fire'.[34]

When Shivaji was six years old, the Nizam Shahi fell, the Mughals and the Adil Shahi splitting its dominions among themselves. Shahaji joined the Adil Shahi state and was immediately sent by his new masters on a campaign, led by Ranadulla Khan, to conquer Karnataka. From 1636 his base was Bangalore (now Bengaluru), and once the Adil Shahi had won Bangalore, the town was gifted by Ranadulla Khan to Shahaji as his *jagir*. Shahaji chose to stay there for good. With him was the older son, Sambhaji, and his own second wife. Well after his marriage to Jijabai, Shahaji had married Tukabai Mohite,[35] sister of Sambhaji Mohite, a fort commander in the Pune–Supe belt. He had a son by her, Ekoji or Vyankoji, a little after Shivaji's birth.[36] Shivaji would have a fraught relationship all his life with this stepbrother, who would go on to become the founder of the Thanjavur Maratha Raj. Shahaji also had at least two and at the most four sons by other women outside of marriage; in an act of extraordinary loyalty at a critical moment in Shivaji's life, one of these stepbrothers, Hiroji, replaced him in a confinement chamber in Agra when the Maratha leader made his escape from Aurangzeb's custody![37]

It seems likely that in 1637–38, Shivaji and Jijabai went to live with Shahaji in Bangalore. If Shahaji had gained Bangalore, he had also retained some of his earlier *mokasas* or areas where he had revenue collection rights, particularly across his Pune *jagir*. In these areas he appointed Dadoji Konddev, a *kulkarni* or account keeper (of the Brahmin caste), as his agent. According to one account, Dadoji was told to shift Jijabai and Shivaji from Shivneri in Junnar to Pune, and according to another, it was only Dadoji who was in Pune, whereas Jijabai and Shivaji were based in Bangalore with Shahaji until Shivaji turned twelve years old. A third possibility indicated is that while Dadoji alone looked after Shahaji's Pune estate from 1636 to 1642, Shivaji and Jijabai intermittently moved between Pune and Bangalore until Shivaji turned twelve.

Even though it was the eldest son, Sambhaji, and the youngest, Ekoji from the second wife, who were always with him, Shahaji's affection for Shivaji does not seem to have wavered, regardless of how little he saw his younger son between the ages of six and twelve. Shivaji, the records tell us, was 'extremely dear' to his father, and Shahaji sincerely believed it was after Shivaji's birth that his own life had taken a turn for the better, for he 'had seen much prosperity'. *Shivabharat* also states that though Shahaji had more than one wife, it was 'Jadhavrao's daughter, Jijabai' who held 'pride of place in his heart'.[38]

At the age of seven, Shivaji was ready to learn the letters of the Marathi or Devanagari alphabet, his father felt; he appointed a good tutor for his son and the children of some of his close associates. Shivaji was a quick learner when it came to writing and later gained expertise not only in horse riding and elephant riding but in archery, marksmanship, and wielding both the spear and the sword.[39] Once Shivaji had turned twelve, Shahaji summoned him, along with Jijabai and Dadoji, to Bangalore – which suggests they had moved back to Maratha country at least some time before that – and asked him to officially take charge of his Pune *jagir* from then on.[40] Shahaji gave his son 'some elephants, horses and infantry' and equipped him with some 'material resources' as well.[41] Importantly, he sent with him Shamrao Nilkanth as the *peshwa* or prime minister, Balkrishnapant – a cousin of Shahaji's agent in Bangalore Naropant Dikshit – as the *mujumdar* or auditor, Sonopant as the *dabir* or counsellor, and Raghunath Ballal as *sabnis* or head clerk.[42] Shahaji was thus equipping Shivaji with staff and entourage he could rely on in overseeing the *jagir*'s affairs.

Some nineteenth-century Marathi chroniclers write of Shivaji's visit to Bijapur at the age of twelve. According to their version, Shahaji took the boy to the sultan's court, where the self-respecting Shivaji created quite an embarrassment for his father by refusing to pay obeisance to the Adil Shah despite his father's express instructions. The same tale has it that Shivaji was appalled by the sight of cow slaughter in Bijapur, and according to one British official and chronicler of Shivaji's life, Dennis Kincaid, he went to the extent of registering a 'public protest' there against the killing of cows.[43] The reality is that the whole thing is an invention and an interpolation by these chroniclers to show Shivaji as rebellious and claim that he had an early dislike of Islam and of Muslims. But, as discussed earlier in the introduction, he never demonstrated any personal dislike of Muslims or their faith; instead, he continued grants to mosques given before his time and, as we have noted, explicitly told his soldiers to treat holy men of the faith, and especially their holy text, the Quran, with respect. Shivaji went to Bangalore at that time to see his father, and never did the two travel to Bijapur together.

A much more important event than a visit to the Adil Shahi capital did occur in Shivaji's life at the age of twelve, just before he left Bangalore for Pune. His parents got him married. His bride was Saibai, the daughter of Mudhoji Naik Nimbalkar.[44] The Nimbalkars, whose original surname was Pawar, were the same family of Phaltan that Shahaji's mother Umabai hailed from.[45] So ties of kinship already existed, which made the fixing of the matrimonial alliance easier. We know astonishingly little about Saibai, who died quite early, in the year 1659, just two years after she gave birth to Sambhaji, their first offspring. An incident recorded by the Marathas' nineteenth-century British chronicler James Grant Duff is about the only one that mentions her role in her husband's life, and suggests that it was quite political. In 1648, Shahaji Raje Bhosle was placed in a dungeon by the Adil Shah, whom he was then serving, on the suspicion that he was aiding his eighteen-year-old son Shivaji's rebellious activities. Shivaji had then captured a few forts around Pune, and the Adil Shah saw it as an egregious act of disloyalty. The door of the dungeon had only a small opening, and 'he was told that, if within a certain period his son did not submit, the aperture should for ever be closed'. Shivaji saw the danger his father was facing. Saibai offered her husband her firm opinion at this critical moment: she told him that he shouldn't submit, and that 'he had a better chance of effecting Shahjee's liberty by maintaining his present power, than by trusting to the mercy of a government notoriously treacherous'.[46]

Eventually, Shahaji was released after Shivaji played his cards wisely and well. Shivaji married eight times, two of these marriages taking place while Saibai was still alive, in an age in which marriage was an instrument of politics and geopolitics.

Shahaji's affection and fondness for Shivaji, and his authorization for him to run his *jagir* at the age of twelve notwithstanding, the big emotional anchor for Shivaji right through his childhood was his mother – and she would remain so later in his life too. Resolute in her patience and fortitude, Jijabai was a remarkable woman. She had suffered the trauma of a clash between her own family and that of her husband, which had led to a loss of lives. She had seen the greater trauma of the cold-blooded killing of her father and brothers in the Nizam Shah's court. During long periods of her pregnancy and during the first six years of Shivaji's life and the time spent between Bangalore and Pune, her husband was away for extended periods of time, and she faced tremendous uncertainty and anxiety. She remained in the fortress of her elder son's in-laws for years, a setting far from comfortable despite a number of attendants around; there was no saying when forces hostile to her husband or to her son's relatives might storm the fort or the *jagirs* of Bangalore and Pune. The possibility of a kidnap, if not outright slaughter, was a real one in particular when she was at Shivneri; at the very least, there could be an attempted assault that might result in injury, a frightening prospect for a mother raising a small child. Situated in the heart of the western Deccan, Junnar and its surroundings were one of the chief battlegrounds where armies of various states had clashed for supremacy, and the battles either continued during the early years of Shivaji's life – leaving in their wake desolation and ruin – or were replaced by a ceasefire that was more an uneasy lull before a storm than genuine peace.

In spite of the deeply patriarchal society she doubtlessly inhabited – a society in which the exterior or interior lives of women like her were never vividly rendered by contemporary chroniclers, resulting in a serious paucity of authentic information for modern-day biographers – Jijabai was not altogether without agency as a woman. She had been brought up in relative comfort in Sindkhed, the daughter of a distinguished noble; and even in the Bhosle clan, there was evidence that women had certain undeniable rights. For example, the region of Ellora which Shivaji's great-grandfather and Maloji's father (Babaji Bhosle) had inherited was a legacy from his mother's side and not a paternal gift. As we know, Jijabai also had with her – in Junnar and in Pune – numerous attendants and staff members appointed by Shahaji. That was more than many other women of the time could ask for. But there was, without doubt, serious turbulence in the air.

In Jijabai's case, the turbulence was both physical, in her surroundings, and psychological, in the overall uncertainty of her situation. In spite of that she raised Shivaji with tremendous emotional vigour. It may have been her reserves of self-belief, and her sheer hope in the future despite everything she was witnessing, which might have kept her going while dedicating her time and effort to her growing son. Or she might have been inspired by Hindu religious texts such as the Puranas or the twin epics Ramayana and Mahabharata, the staple spiritual and intellectual diet for women of the era as well as their children with their stories of valour, strength and the ultimate triumph of truth. Whatever it might have been, in Jijabai, her son Shivaji evidently saw the kind of steel that would be his inner and intimate armour as he began to carve out his own destiny.

2

Notice to the Adil Shah

Pune was a ghost town in 1630–31. If anything was in abundance there, it was wolves and other beasts. It had been little more than a *kasba* to begin with – a village with a marketplace where people from neighbouring villages converged once a week to buy their essentials. But the depredations of warring armies had laid it waste, and one general (called Murar Jagdev) of the Adil Shahi kingdom in particular had brutally vandalized it when the Nizam Shahi found itself cornered after Malik Ambar's death, apparently going to the extent of getting donkeys to drive a plough around the place and implanting an iron rod in the soil – both signs to indicate the *kasba* was cursed. Whatever little crop, cultivation, vegetation and human habitation still remained was wrecked by the Deccan famine of 1629 to 1631.

So resettling the population and recovering a semblance of normal life was the top priority. Dadoji Konddev, an agent of Shivaji's father, had launched that work when he was asked by Shahaji to look after the family *jagir* in 1636. With Jijabai and Shivaji moving there in 1642 and with Shahaji's younger son officially assuming charge, resettlement and rehabilitation picked up pace. As all the houses in the village had been either destroyed or burnt, Dadoji immediately initiated the construction of a comfortable dwelling for the mother–son duo. It would be a one-storeyed structure, called Lal Mahal; a little enclave to be built around it would be named Shivapur; and around the house, there would be an orchard.

Dadoji declared war on the wolves, promising monetary reward to anyone who would kill them and also the tigers and other wild animals that prowled around. Cultivators were wooed with specific offers. Land was given to them at a nominal rent for the first year; in later years, the rent would increase only marginally, they were promised. Of every ten trees planted, the plot owner could have one to himself and pay taxes for the others; of the total crop, one-third would be taken by the *jagirdar*, and two-thirds would remain with the plot owner. After a long time, lands were measured, ownership or rental status ascertained, and wells and canals built; remuneration was paid for those who worked on them.

Shahaji's *jagir*, though, was much bigger than the *kasba* at its core. There was the broader Pune *pargana* or district comprising more than 250 villages. To the main *kasba*'s south-east were Supe and Shirwal, districts with about sixty and forty villages respectively. And there were the Mavals, the mountainous valleys to the west of Pune. If a diagonal line were drawn from the *jagir*'s western corner of Lonavla to its other, south-eastern corner of Indapur, it would cover 200 kilometres.[1]

Naturally, the effects of the developments in Pune were quickly felt in the wider *jagir*. Several of Pune's erstwhile villagers, displaced and destitute, came back, relieved to get cash for killing beasts and equally relieved to return to cultivation and more normal ways. Many rural folk and hill people had also descended into poverty as a result of the famine and political instability. This was the environment in which Shivaji, just a teenager at the time, gradually began to emerge as an authority figure. As he started taking matters in his own hands, he was astute enough to extend land and revenue arrangements similar to those in Pune all across his father's *jagir*, ensuring that more and more land came under cultivation and irrigation. The response was encouraging. 'New crops were reared in every village; mango, tamarind, pomegranate, lemon came to be planted afresh.'[2] The result was that quite a lot of ordinary people from one end of the *jagir* to another found productive and paying work and a sense of hope.[3]

Of greatest significance were the teenaged Shivaji's forays into the Mavals, which, apart from the Pune *pargana*, were directly under him; for the other areas, as yet, Dadoji was both directly and indirectly responsible. The twelve hills and valleys, each with their individual nomenclatures but collectively known as the Mavals, were among the most neglected parts of the upper and western Deccan. They were not easy to access; their soil was rocky and impoverished; cultivation was sparser than elsewhere and spread chiefly next to the streams flowing along the hill slopes. The people were hardy and resilient. Their identities – Maratha, Kunbi, Bhil, Koli or any other – were distilled into a single term, 'Mavale', which simply meant 'the people of the Mavals'. Indeed, 'Maval' itself was a generic term derived from the word *mavalti*, denoting the areas (valleys) where darkness descended first as the sun went down behind the mountains. Sunset or not, large parts of the valleys were always blanketed in shadow, so the name Maval had stuck.

If the administration everywhere was hamstrung by political and military conflict, in these parts it was often mostly absent, with many officials not even setting foot on what they considered insupportable soil, with risky cliffs, edges and ravines. And the hill people and fief holders such as the *deshmukhs* (district-level revenue collectors) fought interminable succession battles for whatever land and assessment rights there were on offer. These land fights, which might have been endemic because families depended almost entirely on these lands for their sustenance and survival, constituted the principal weakness of the region and its inhabitants.

Remarkably, Shivaji made these very cliffs, edges, ledges and ravines that were studiously avoided by so many his chief stomping grounds; and the young men of the area became his bosom mates. Shivaji was athletic, supple, extremely active and adventurous. He began to spend virtually all day in these inaccessible parts, venturing with his friends into treacherous corners where even horses feared to tread, and examining the heights and the depths, the gaps and the gorges, the slippery slopes and the occasionally smooth but hard-to-detect and barely visible pathways. From an early age he had natural personal charisma and demonstrated a genuine warmth towards those he reached out to and befriended. He was intensely curious, keen to get together a bunch of buddies, and to know the people who lived in his father's *jagir* and around it really well. For the hills and its inhabitants he showed what they perceived to be a natural, spontaneous affinity, and he started making deep connections with the land and its ordinary people. His easy nature and his soft, winning smile in particular – noted by several contemporaries who met him[4] – disarmed even sceptics who initially kept a cautious distance from their new, and very young, administrator. Three members of his band of brothers are particularly notable: Tanaji Malusare, Yesaji Kank and Baji Pasalkar. They would contribute very handsomely to Shivaji's life and work.

One of the most pervasive myths of Maratha history is that around this time, at a very young age, Shivaji, along with a few select mates, took the oath of 'Hindawi Swaraj' in the temple of Raireshwar in 1645.[5] Two letters purportedly reminding a certain Dadaji Naras Prabhu of this oath, claimed to have been written by Shivaji himself, have been cited to suggest that such a thing happened. However, both the letters have been conclusively established by outstanding historians of the Maratha period as latter-day forgeries. The manipulation was apparently done by Dadaji Naras Prabhu's family in an attempt to establish its claim over one of the Mavals, Rohid Khore, in a protracted property dispute.[6] Not surprisingly, though, the romantic oath-taking episode, with Shivaji and his Maval associates drawing blood from their fingers with their swords and sprinkling a few drops on Lord Shiva's *linga* in the temple while taking their vows, has proved to be enduring in public memory. Evocative in its appeal, it has been an intrinsic part of textbooks in Maharashtra, not to count the number of movies and plays in which it has been depicted.

However, there is no doubt that Shivaji's bond with his friends from the Mavals was formidably strong, and they rewarded his attachment to them many times over. Bereft and largely forgotten, the Mavals, on the outer edges even of Deccani consciousness, would be the womb from which Shivaji's independent state would emerge.

Soon after Shivaji turned fourteen, the Adil Shahi kingdom began to express its distrust with the goings-on in Shahaji's *jagir*. Shivaji was not just scanning the territory and establishing contact with the local populace. As the Adil Shahi state well knew, apart from befriending the common folk, he was getting in touch with the hereditary *deshmukhs* and acquainting himself with other officials as well. There were the *patils*, for instance, who were in charge of revenue collection at the village level, and the *kulkarnis*, who kept the village books in order. The *deshmukh* did at the wider district level what the *patil* did in the village, and the *deshpande* or *deshkulkarni* maintained the district's accounts.

All these state functionaries were termed *watandars* or holders of the *watan*, an Arabic word for land, and their rights were hereditary, though they could be withdrawn at any time if *watandars* incurred the ruler's wrath. They were also responsible for bringing lands under the plough and keeping track of sowing and harvesting patterns within their jurisdictions. For the duties they performed, they were paid in cash and kind from collections from their own domains and thus from the villagers themselves; in addition, they were entitled to receive 'voluntary' gifts from villagers and from the twelve *balutedars* or service providers who were part of every village set-up, such as the potter, barber, tailor, ironsmith and carpenter, among others. Those who owned lands were called *mirasdars*, and they in turn were the principal remunerators of the twelve *balutedars* and the big contributors to a *patil*'s and *deshmukh*'s kitty. There were those from outside the hamlet, too, who occasionally came to do odd jobs; they were described as *upri* (outsiders) and couldn't claim any social rights if they clashed with a native dweller. Together, the *watandars*, *mirasdars*, *balutedars* and *upris* formed the four branches of a village unit, and Shivaji was closely familiarizing himself with all of them.

Importantly, a *patil* or *deshmukh* was often called to offer military service or assistance to the state by mobilizing and even leading forces. Equally importantly, there were forts across the region whose commanders were appointed by the durbar and were directly under the state's control. These commanders often cocked a snook at local-level state officials and acted independently. What became evident to Bijapur early on was that Shivaji and Dadoji Konddev had started speaking to some of them as well.

Why did that matter? Had Shivaji rebelled against the Adil Shah? He hadn't, up until that point. While Shivaji's reaching out to local officials had got Bijapur's antenna up, these efforts by themselves would not have resulted in any action. What complicated matters was, typically, a factional fight in the Adil Shah's court. Shahaji Raje Bhosle had done extremely well under the patronage of the Bijapur general Ranadulla Khan. In 1643, however, Khan died, and his intra-state rival, Mustafa Khan, rose in stature. Earlier, Shahaji had been given the endearment *farzand* (son) by the Adil Shah for his feats in the southern campaigns;[7] now, he was vilified as a troublemaker. On 1 August 1644, Sultan Muhammad Adil Shah issued a *farman* or directive to Kanhoji Jedhe, one of the more powerful *deshmukhs* of Maval, stating that 'Shahaji Bhonsla' had 'become a rebel against this august Court', that Shahaji's agent Dadoji Konddev was up to no good in Kondhana district in the neighbourhood, and that Jedhe must immediately join Khandoji Khopde and Baji Ghorpade who'd been dispatched to 'destroy' Konddev.[8] Another *farman* of the same period states that the hands of a representative of Shahaji near Kondhana had been cut off as punishment.[9] Was this representative Dadoji Konddev? There's no evidence to that effect, but decades and even centuries later, an interesting myth came to be circulated about Dadoji Konddev. According to it, Dadoji once plucked an apple from the orchard he had built in Shivapur near Lal Mahal. But it then occurred to him that he hadn't asked his master, Shivaji, if he could take it and so, in order to publicly discipline himself, he chopped off the arm that had pulled out the fruit. Is the myth related to the factional fight? We have no way of knowing.

What we do know, however, is that Shivaji's father's estates in Pune and Supe were taken away from him after the Adil Shah's orders. The Adil Shah's forces attacked these estates in 1644 on the suspicion that Shahaji was revolting, and took over the area for four months. But the rift was clearly not deep because the lands were restored, by the end of the same year, for reasons that were never made clear.[10]

Apart from the vagaries of the Adil Shahi court, the young Shivaji also became aware of the growing strain of bigotry in the court (which may have been a factor that went against Shahaji during the standoff). The days of the state practising pluralism, as in the sixteenth century, were fading, and fanaticism had taken root. By the fourth decade of the seventeenth century, except for Shahaji and Baji Ghorpade, 'the high barons of Bijapur were Muslims'; as many rajas from the south had joined Bijapur after asking Shahaji to mediate on their behalf, his rivals 'poisoned Adil Shah's ears against him' by alleging Shahaji was trying to become independent with the support of the rajas.[11] While Shahaji's patron Ranadulla Khan was around, the poison hadn't seeped in; after his demise, it did.

Shivaji could not but be aware of all of this because the reigning Muhammad Adil Shah had pronounced three openly discriminatory regulations against Hindus, who formed the majority of his state's population. The first stipulated that only Muslims be appointed governors in the provinces, while Hindus could be given clerical and non-executive posts; no executive responsibilities, and no governorships, would go to Brahmins and other Hindus, for they were 'disturbers of the land and the faith'. The second order said all efforts must be made to 'propagate the rules of Islam', with 'no infidel' being allowed to insult, oppress or claim equality with a weak Muslim; Muslims who injured infidels, on the other hand, need only be admonished orally 'but never ... punished in any way for the sake of the infidel'. Third, Muslims were told to refrain from participating in 'infidel celebrations like Holi, Diwali, Dassehra' because these were 'bad', though, as a concession, these celebrations were not banned, so the Muslims couldn't 'object' to them or 'obstruct' them either.[12]

When Shivaji started issuing orders in his own name at the young age of sixteen, though only as administrator of his father's *jagir*, the language he chose for making his official seal was Sanskrit. This was a direct departure from the well-established norm of the Persianate Age: his father Shahaji, mother Jijabai and Shahaji's agent Dadoji all had their seals in Persian, as did the other Hindu chieftains of the various Muslim kingdoms. The Persianization of the courts and of administrative documents was near-complete during this period. Yet Shivaji seemed to have made a conscious choice, and the language of the seal is the first unmistakable evidence of the Hindu element in Shivaji's political philosophy. His Hindu worldview looked at all religions as sacrosanct. But with a clear sense of his own cultural and religious identity, an identity he did not want obliterated or deliberately sidelined, he embraced and endorsed Sanskrit in order to underline that sense of selfhood.

Interestingly, the vernacular Marathi was also used in official correspondence at the time. All the letters and *farmans* were issued in Persian, and wherever necessary, for the comprehension of local officials and the local populace, their translations were readily made and provided by the Islamic states. Even so, the Marathi copies of letters and other correspondence never carried official seals in the vernacular. The official signature had the element of both legality and sanctity, and Shivaji's act of choosing Sanskrit, the sacred language of the Hindus in which the two great epics and important sacred texts like the Vedas, the Upanishads and the Puranas had been composed, even over his native Marathi, was definitely a statement.

Shivaji's official imprint was hexagonal in shape, and on it was inscribed a line: 'Ever increasing in luminosity like the moon at the start of the brighter half of the lunar month and esteemed across the world, this seal of Shivaji, son of Shahaji, shines for the betterment of all.'[13] The earliest letter which carries his Sanskrit imprint is from 28 January 1646, and it is about an extraordinarily decisive verdict that Shivaji gave at the very young age of sixteen. This was on a complaint of sexual assault made by an ordinary village woman against a *patil* in Khede Bare near Pune. The ruling went like this:

> To the officials, *deshmukhs* and *deshkulkarnis* of Khede Bare:
> The *mukadam* [another name for *patil*] of Ranjhe village in Khede Bare, Babaji Bhikaji Gujar, committed an act of sexual misdemeanour while carrying out his responsibilities in the village. The matter was reported to Saheb [Shivaji]. The Saheb ordered that he [the *patil*] be arrested immediately and brought before him. The offence was established after an inquiry. So Babaji was sacked from his post and his hands and legs were cut off. At that time, Sonaji Banaji Gujar of the Purandar fort made a plea that Babaji be handed over to him as he was his relative. The request was granted and Babaji was fined 300 Padshahi *hons* (a unit in currency). As Sonaji is Babaji's kin and Babaji has no offspring, Sonaji

Banaji Gujar has been granted the post of *mokadam* of Ranjhe village now and 200 Padshahi *hons* recovered as fee for the government treasury. No one should obstruct him in the discharge of his duties.[14]

The ruling, delivered in a period when capital punishment was deemed acceptable, was welcomed by the majority of commoners who had seen officials not being held accountable for their actions, or sexual misdemeanours not being taken seriously. By promptly punishing a sexual offender, Shivaji was giving the ordinary villagers what they had long hoped for: a modicum of accountability from officials. This act is among the earliest where Shivaji truly becomes the expression of a popular will. By several such acts and measures in his life, he became a darling of his people, who felt that he represented light at the end of the tunnel. And if this light slowly grew brighter and spread wider, they were bound to appreciate it, initially quietly and increasingly openly as Shivaji started gaining new aides and allies. For the violation of women's bodies and psyche he would continue to demonstrate a zero-tolerance policy, which was extraordinary and radical for the age he lived in. It convinced the ordinary folk in the Deccan hills that he had a gift for empathy and that the most vulnerable of them could expect from him justice, equity and fairness.

There has for long been a debate about whether Shivaji sought to establish his own raj right from the beginning or whether his story should be seen as one of an expanding vision. It is clearly evident from his early decision on his seal and his act of punishing the *patil* of Ranjhe that he was keen to branch out on his own. He believed in a new way of doing things. He started out as a natural rebel, the son of a *jagirdar* militating against the well-established system of doing and arranging things, and then he began moving inexorably in only one direction: of freeing his land from the culture of oppression, suppression, harassment and ignominy heaped by the many sultanates and the mighty empire of the Mughals who had their original home on the steppes of Central Asia. The rest of Shivaji's life – with all its victories, defeats, compromises, adjustments, retreats – has to be seen in the light of this clarity of thinking and intent he demonstrated at the age of sixteen.

Shivaji's initial moves may well have made entrenched stakeholders in the system wary, but he was not a man to be deterred by such considerations, and he continued to take bold steps, even beyond the domain of administrative procedure.

He was careful while Dadoji Konddev was around as the overall custodian of Shahaji's *jagir*. After his death in 1647, Shivaji, not yet eighteen, moved quickly. Within a year and a half, he took four forts, all just to the south of Pune *pargana* and highly useful for a pushback in case the Bijapur force, which had attacked in 1644, attacked again. With control of the forts, Shivaji had the means to block Bijapur's advances from the south into his own estates in and around Pune, and also receive early warnings of any advance.

The most crucial of these was Murumbdeo, which Shivaji renamed Rajgad. Situated more than 4,574 feet above sea level,[15] it had a base that ran across several kilometres, making any siege difficult. Shivaji found it unoccupied, saw its potential and further built on it. The spotting itself was smart work, made possible by the fact that Shivaji wasn't cooped up in his home or principal *kasba* of Pune but was busy exploring the Mavals where this citadel stood. From the top the fort provided a nearly 360-degree view of its surroundings, including the vast sprawl to the west that led to the Konkan coastline. Shivaji's distinctive creative contribution to its natural strength was the construction of three *machis* or flat-lined terraces in three directions. Each of these terraces, at approximately 4,000 feet above sea level, was over a mile wide, had two or three tiers, and was fortified with walls; the result was that they virtually became independent forts in their own right, offering protection to the topmost part, known as the *bale-killa*, where the residential quarters and offices would be built.[16]

The Mughal chronicler of Aurangzeb's reign reluctantly conceded Shivaji's astuteness, stating:

> The infernal Shiva after getting possession [of Rajgad] made terraces on three sides around it on a lower level [*machi*] and there built three strong forts, namely *Suvela* and *Padmavati* situated towards Konkan uplands, and *Sanjivani* on the side of Konkan lowlands; he thus made its capture by any enemy impossible ... The infidel ... had formed a triangular enclosure,

which is called a *sund* [elephant's trunk] in the language of military fortification, by erecting two thick walls from the postern-gate (wicket) of the fort of *Padmavati* to the end of the hillock, and making these two walls meet at a point. Below both of these (walls) the path declines so sharply and is so full of slippery holes that no one can pass there on foot.[17]

Further, the Mughal historian wrote, in an age in which no attacks could take place from the skies, 'Fort Rajgad is a hill second only to the fort of the towered sky. Its circuit is twelve *kos* [one *kos* is around 2 kilometres]. Imagination cannot estimate its height. Its thorny jungles and spectre-haunted chasms can be traversed only by the wind. Nothing can descend on it except rain!'[18]

The other unoccupied fort Shivaji took almost simultaneously was Torna. About 7 kilometres to Rajgad's north-west, in later years it came to be known as the Eagle's Nest and the 'sentinel' of Rajgad, which went on to become Shivaji's capital until 1670. Torna towered above any other fort in the vicinity, even above Rajgad, at 4,600 feet. According to legend, Shivaji found some war materials there and a stack of funds,[19] which he used for the purpose of arming his Maval associates, carrying out construction work on Rajgad, and repairing some dilapidated structures that stood atop Torna itself.

The first fort Shivaji won by way of either assault or subterfuge was Kondhana or Sinhagad, right in the centre of a ring of forts around Pune and thus of strategic significance. Held earlier by the Khiljis and later by the Bahmani kingdom, it had passed eventually into the hands of the Nizam Shahi. Post 1636, it was held by the Adil Shahi and included in Shahaji's *jagir*, where it was unequivocally stated, unlike in the case of most other forts, that it would be under Shahaji's representative. But after the passing of Dadoji Konddev, the Adil Shah took it away from Shahaji's control and appointed Mian Rahim Muhammad as the in-charge.[20] Two reliable chronicles of Shivaji's life have given differing versions of how Kondhana was seized: one, by Sabhasad, says it was by assault, after which 'Shivaji established his own military outpost (*thana*) there',[21] and the other, Jedhe Shakavali, indicates it was by diplomatic manoeuvres initiated with the assistance of Bapuji Mudgal Narhekar, the *deshpande* of Khede Bare, one of the Mavals.[22] Kondhana's other, equally well-known moniker, was Sinhagad; the two names were used interchangeably.

Shivaji next zoomed in on the fort of Purandar which, unlike the other three forts on Pune's south-west, was slightly to its south-east and would help to ring-fence the chief village of the *jagir*. Purandar was under the Adil Shahi, and its commandant, a Brahmin named Nilo Nilkanth Sarnaik or Nilkanth Rao – 'a friend and neighbour of Shahaji and his family'[23] – had died recently, triggering a squabble among his three sons over who would get to keep it. Shivaji offered to mediate, threw all three brothers into prison, and took over the fort. Soon the brothers were released, and each was given *watan* grants beneath the fort; they accepted the grants offered by Shivaji and pledged loyalty to him.[24]

All along, as he went about gaining these first four forts, Shivaji cleverly professed total loyalty to Bijapur and when asked by the Adil Shah, his father Shahaji said he was holding them on the Sultanate's behalf, either because they stood abandoned or needed order and organization.[25] Initially Bijapur didn't have much to complain about, as Rajgad and Torna were without any troops, but Sinhagad, held by a Bijapur-appointed commander, was a different matter. It was a prized possession owing to its location and steep slopes; and it had a reputation that the other three forts hadn't earned. Why had Shivaji taken that one if he only wanted to fortify Bijapur's position, the Adil Shah wondered. And he concluded correctly that what he was seeing in Shivaji was a rebel taking his first few bold steps.

The backlash for Shivaji came in two ways: his father Shahaji was once more in trouble with Adil Shah, who also sent out a force to put down Shivaji's incipient rebellion – and received a response that took him completely by surprise.

But first, Shahaji's story. At the time, he was part of a military campaign under the leadership of Mustafa Khan, laying siege to Jinji deep in Tamil country. As noted earlier, Mustafa Khan deeply disliked Shahaji, who'd been close to his bête noire Ranadulla Khan. He accused Shahaji of non-cooperation during the siege, implying Shahaji was using his influence with the Hindu rajas of the south against Bijapur. This accusation was bolstered by tying Shahaji to Shivaji's activities.[26]

Early on the morning of 25 July 1648, Bijapur nobles 'Baji Ghorpade, Yashwantrao and Asad Khan'[27] entered an unsuspecting Shahaji's chamber in the Jinji camp and placed him in fetters for alleged disobedience. Until December, when the Jinji fort was won by the Adil Shahi forces, he was kept in custody there. And though Mustafa Khan died in November before the siege ended, Shahaji remained out of favour and was sent back to Bijapur in chains along with the loot of eighty-nine elephants under the watch of the general Afzal Khan, who had distinguished himself in the battle. Once in Bijapur, Afzal Khan was felicitated and Shahaji was thrown into prison on the court's orders.[28]

Days after Shahaji's arrest, Adil Shah sent one fighting unit to his Bangalore base, where Shahaji's older son Sambhaji beat it back. A second force was sent against Shivaji. It was to be led by Fatah Khan. This Khan was not an Adil Shahi leading light, unlike the other three – Ranadulla, Mustafa and Afzal – and was chosen because Shivaji was, at this stage, seen as a minor irritant who could easily be shown his place. Shivaji didn't have a large force, and Fatah Khan, with just a couple of thousand people, could effortlessly take care of things – or so Adil Shah believed. Just to make sure, he wrote to the *deshmukhs* around Pune ordering them to join Fatah Khan's men.[29]

The resistance put up by Shivaji's men in this very first violent skirmish with the Adil Shahi turned out to be of the kind of steel and remarkable resolve Bijapur hadn't bargained for. Fatah Khan left for Sinhagad from Bijapur, which was over 280 kilometres away, but along the way he heard that Shivaji had moved to the fort of Purandar, so the Bijapur forces were turned in that direction. Purandar had a string of hills covering about 4 kilometres and rising progressively in height from left to right. From the summit, both east and west were easily visible, an advantage for a defender with a small force – unlike Sinhagad, where a defender could be taken by surprise owing to the vertical climb. Shivaji's own sources of intelligence were very reliable: he got to know that Fatah Khan was moving towards Belsar, 24 kilometres to the east, to set up camp there, but also that he had asked one military unit, under Haibatrao Ballal, to shift out midway and take the route to Shirwal at the back of the fort so an attack could be launched from the rear. One morning, as Ballal's team entered Shirwal, they suddenly discovered four groups of Marathas led by Kavji Kondhalkar, an enthusiastic aide of Shivaji from the Maval region, each a hundred horsemen strong, lying in wait. With Kondhalkar were – and here we get the names of some of Shivaji's earliest associates recorded by his official chronicler Parmanand, with effusive praise – Godaji Jagtap, 'the destroyer of enemies', Bhimaji Wagh, 'brave as the real Bhima', Sambhaji Kate, 'deflator of an adversary's pride and brawn', Shivaji Ingle, 'wielder of a deadly spear', the 'fearless' Bhikaji Chor and his brother Bhairav, 'as fierce in combat as the real Bhairav' (Shiva).[30]

Seeing them, Ballal asked his team to quickly move to a small mud fortress in the vicinity held by a local revenue official; once everyone was inside, the gates were slammed shut. The Marathas chased and, climbing up, started hammering on the fortress's mud walls with clubs, iron rods and stones even as those inside responded with medieval to early modern era guns, arrows, spears, oil, and burning pieces of cloth and coal. In the melee, Kavji broke open the fort's gates, and the fight turned bloody. Ballal, mounted on his horse, charged at Kavji but was struck by his rival in the chest with a spear. Panicking, Ballal's men abandoned the fortress and fled in the direction of Belsar, meant to be the advance base. There was another shock in store for Fatah Khan one evening: a crack squad of about a hundred Maratha horsemen led by the young Bajaji Naik Jedhe – a member of the Jedhe *deshmukh* family loyal to Shivaji – carried out a raid and caused much commotion before returning to Purandar.

The twin surprises meant Fatah Khan had to launch a frontal attack immediately. The Bijapur army had a number of Pathans, and at their head was Musa Khan, with Fatah Khan himself at the rear. Among the others in Khan's army were right-flank leader Mattaraj Ghatge and left-flank head Baji Naik Nimbalkar of Phaltan, both Marathas with links to the Bhosle family; Shahaji's mother was from the Nimbalkar family of Phaltan,[31] and so was Shivaji's wife, Saibai. (In the force sent to attack Shahaji's Bangalore *jagir*, too, there was a Maratha Brahmin, one Vitthal

Gopal.³²) The clash, which began with Shivaji's men opening cannon fire and gunfire on the attackers, ultimately climaxed into a hand-to-hand fight, and according to Parmanand, both sides fought hard.³³ When Bijapur's captain Musa Khan was killed, the attacking army turned around and fled; Shivaji lost Baji Pasalkar, the *deshmukh* of Muse Khore and a close aide.³⁴

Contrary to expectations, the teen rebel Shivaji had retained Purandar. Viewed under a military lens, the Marathas' first encounter with Bijapur had gone according to plan, with plenty of weaponry, gold, horses and elephants seized after the retreating army had disappeared.³⁵ But the victory was bittersweet. Bijapur still had a great hold over Shivaji, with his father in an Adil Shahi prison. Shivaji had tried to gain some leverage of his own before the conflict against Fatah Khan, by opening a line of communication with Prince Murad Bakhsh, then the Mughal *subahdar* or governor of the Deccan. Murad Bakhsh was Mughal emperor Shah Jahan's fourth and youngest son, after Dara Shukoh, Shah Shuja and Aurangzeb. The Mughals were at that point not pressing in on Bijapur's northern boundaries, but their ambitions were intact; only the timing remained to be chosen.

In the event, Shivaji didn't have to rely on the ploy of either offering to help them or serving under them. Bijapur agreed to release Shahaji provided Shivaji gave up Sinhagad and Sambhaji let go of the town of Bangalore; Shivaji would be allowed to keep Purandar. Shivaji acquiesced, and Shahaji was set free on 16 May 1649, after a period of ten months, and promptly sent off on a military campaign by Bijapur.

Giving up Sinhagad was not an easy decision for Shivaji. His political enterprise was new, and the young Mavale soldiers, all charged up, had lined up behind him and defended the Purandar fort to the hilt. He needed to keep their morale high, which would be difficult if he returned Sinhagad, over which the conflict had erupted. Apart from the fact that his father was incarcerated in a dungeon, there was another concern: Bijapur might send a far bigger force to quell Shivaji. Would it make sense for the Marathas, when their leader was barely nineteen years old and still mobilizing men and materials, to get involved in an enlarged scale of warfare? Clearly, the answer in Shivaji's mind was no. The return of Sinhagad carried a timely message for Shivaji that the creation of a new political reality required vigil, relentless hard work and persistence in the face of setbacks and difficulties which would inevitably arise with a gargantuan empire on one side and long-established Deccani kingdoms on the other. Another confrontation with Bijapur loomed, but in good time.

What Shivaji did in the following decade showed that the message did not go unheeded.

First, he determinedly went about securing and strengthening his control over those parts of his father's *jagir* where it was still tenuous. These included Chakan *pargana* to the north of Pune, and Supe, Baramati and Indapur *parganas* to the east.[36] This meant a greater geographical spread – even if the *jagir* was still being held, though mostly in name, for Bijapur – more local officials either cooperating or being made to toe the line, the gaining of more fortresses, and wider scope for recruiting personnel for the troops and for acquiring gunpowder materials, swords, shields and other arsenal.

Quite a few *deshmukhs* had aligned themselves with Shivaji already, and more came into the fold as Shivaji's hold grew, but these officials, as we have seen previously, had much at stake in the existing order. Shivaji knew right from the start that while they would be immensely useful if brought around, with their local knowledge, manpower and the levies they brought, he would be making an egregious mistake if he relied on them for his army. So instead of overdependence on the *deshmukhs*, he focused on building his cavalry and infantry, and later his navy, under his own watch; all his military personnel were paid directly and not from a *deshmukh*'s coffers even if their men would be told to join expeditions and valued.[37]

Some of the *deshmukhs* played truant, some frequently changed sides, and others were openly hostile to Shivaji. Among those in the hostile camp was Sambhaji Mohite, the brother of Shahaji's second wife, Tukabai. He had been given charge of the Supe *pargana* by Shahaji. The young Shivaji's response was to arrange a familial meeting with Mohite and have him arrested; his property was confiscated, and the *pargana* seized.[38] When Shivaji sought to take over the Rohida fort, situated near Torna and Rajgad which were already with him, he faced resistance from the Bandal *deshmukhs* who controlled it. A member of the *deshmukh* family, Krishnaji Bandal, was killed as Shivaji's men launched an assault. The Bandals capitulated, declared allegiance to Shivaji, and handed over the citadel. In gaining Rohida, Shivaji also obtained a new and genuinely trustworthy associate: Baji Prabhu Deshpande, a minister who had worked with the Bandals.[39] Baji Prabhu would, in time, leave his own imprint on Maratha and early modern Indian history by courageously holding off a Bijapur force in serious pursuit of Shivaji at the cost of his own life. Another Shivaji loyalist was Kanhoji Jedhe and his family. The *deshmukh* of Kari near Bhor in Pune district, Jedhe had gone along with Shahaji to the south and had even been imprisoned along with another aide, Dadaji Lohakare, when Adil Shah had imprisoned Shahaji. After the release of all three from prison, Shahaji asked Jedhe to head to Pune and to be in Shivaji's service.[40]

In undertaking these activities and forging such partnerships, Shivaji took full advantage of the disarray created in the Bijapur court after Muhammad Adil Shah suffered a paralytic attack in the second half of the 1640s. Though Adil Shah's wife the Badi Sahiba had taken charge, things continued to be in a state of flux until Adil Shah's death in 1656 and the ascension to the throne of his successor, Ali Adil Shah.[41] In the year of Muhammad Adil Shah's death, Shivaji struck. In January that year, he made the bold move of stepping out of his father's *jagir* and capturing Jaawali, a famously inaccessible corner of Adil Shahi territory.

Jaawali, situated across the southern boundary of Shivaji's possessions, was a place where even the Adil Shah's troops feared to tread. So what if Bijapur was supposed to be in charge? The only writ that ran was of the More family, the local *deshmukhs*. The Mores, whose surname was a variant of Maurya, were only nominally with Bijapur and enjoyed autonomy owing to the dangerous nature of the terrain. Jaawali was a den of deep, dark valleys – eighteen compared to the twelve in the Mavals – and even more remote and thickly forested than the Mavals, with precipitous drops, unexpected chasms and bewildering gaps that could turn into death traps. Strategically, Jaawali, close to the modern-day hill station of Mahabaleshwar, carried its own significance: at its heights, it provided a bird's-eye view of the Sahyadri mountains that ran along its length on the left as well as the southern and south-eastern parts of the Deccan; from its depths, it opened the route on to the Konkan coastline on the west, and in its innards, rather paradoxically, it allowed for seclusion, secrecy and a degree of safe distance from everything that stood around it.

Shivaji had only recently helped the Mores end a family feud over succession. The ruler of Jaawali carried the title of 'Chandrarao', and the various valleys had their own individual chiefs, all from the same More family, who reported to him. In 1648, the then 'Chandrarao' (Daulatrao More) had died without leaving an heir, and a dispute broke out about who would succeed. Daulatrao's wife adopted a child named Yashwant from one of the valley subordinates, the Mores of Shivthar, and Shivaji helped ensure the boy's smooth takeover.

Quickly afterwards, the Mores turned antagonistic towards Shivaji, refused to acknowledge his dominance of the northern parts, and defied him openly. Evidently they were unhappy that the *deshmukhs* and other Maratha officials in the western Deccan, who'd been in awe of them for decades, were submitting to Shivaji; some were even finding common cause with him. Their aura was in danger of being diminished, as was their special status within the Bijapur realm. Worse, the rival was now close to their borders and could challenge their authority.

Shivaji had the Mughals to the north and north-west of his domain and Bijapur to the south and south-east. If he wished to get into the Konkan, a region in which he was keenly interested, Jaawali was key. If he took it, he would also cut Bijapur off from areas in the western lowlands it ruled and could stride across to the seafront. Shivaji had kept quiet from 1649, building his strength silently and gradually without disturbing any of the big powers. He waited, extremely patiently, for his opportunity. And it was after a period of nearly seven years that he was now making his next big move because he saw Jaawali as a strategic area, useful both for the expansion of his writ and for getting a foothold in the coastal corridor.

Shivaji initially proposed negotiations with the locally ruling Mores and some sort of agreement with them. When the Mores wouldn't yield, he held out the threat of an attack. Dismissively, they wrote to him:

> As regards your threat of arms, we heartily welcome your proposal: Come today instead of tomorrow and with whatever number of troops you wish. Why do you talk of having become an independent king? Who calls you a king? You are an upstart of yesterday. You may make any boasts in your own home but no one is going to listen to them. Come to Jaawali and see what kind of a reception you get in this difficult region. We respect the honours that the Sultan of Bijapur has bestowed on us. We respect his commands, come what may.[42]

In January 1656 Shivaji marched into the seemingly impenetrable region. First, Hanumantrao More, who was propping up Yashwant or Yashwantrao, was killed in a fight. Besieged, the incumbent Chandrarao – Yashwantrao – fled to the hill of Rairi, a stronghold of the family on Jaawali's northern edges. Accompanying him were his two sons, Krishnaji and Baji. Shivaji parked himself in the valleys for two full months, consolidating his occupation, and asked Yashwantrao to surrender.[43] The family document or *bakhar* of the Mores states Shivaji wanted to leave a small tract of territory for them, but he soon found out they were 'carrying on secret correspondence with the Ghorpades of Mudhol against Shivaji'.[44] When Yashwantrao descended from Rairi in May 1656, Shivaji had him executed. Yashwantrao's sons were taken captive to Pune, where they were found engaged in communication with Bijapur and 'put to death'.[45] It was a wipe-out of a clan of mandarins long convinced of its own invincibility.

Having made an example of the Mores, Shivaji took, along with their region, the fortress of Rairi. He renamed it Raigad; from the early 1670s onwards, it would be his capital, and he would get himself coronated there in 1674 and make it formally his capital. Plus, Shivaji ordered the construction of a fort alongside the Sahyadri mountains that ran along Jaawali. It was done in a year's time, and it would be called Pratapgad. On

Shivaji's instructions, an idol of the family goddess Bhavani, an incarnation of Durga, was placed inside the fort.

Shivaji was twenty-six years old when he captured Jaawali. He had marked the soft launch of his political enterprise by capturing four forts near Pune in his teenage years; for the big launch he had worked gradually, taking almost eight years, and very carefully.

If Jaawali's capture set alarm bells ringing in Bijapur, Shivaji followed up by making further advances which triggered concerns even in the Mughal establishment. One man who took particular notice of what he was doing was Shah Jahan's third and most ambitious son, Aurangzeb.

3

Notice to the Mughals

The blowback was inevitable. Shivaji knew that Bijapur would want to make him eat humble pie in Jaawali. So, having created a divide between the western and eastern parts of the Adil Shahi state by taking eighteen apparently impenetrable valleys, he quickly captured the crucial port centres of Kalyan and Bhiwandi; and further down the coastline, moved against the Siddi rulers of Danda-Rajpuri, who were of African origin. He conquered all except the town of Danda-Rajpuri itself and the sea fort of Janjira, which was part of the wider Danda-Rajpuri belt and also held by the Siddis. He then proceeded south, going as far as the southern borders of Dharwad district in Karnataka. From there, his forces had to retreat after a pushback from Bijapur's local commanders. But Shivaji's ambitions of branching out on his own were no longer a secret. With his speedily obtained new possessions, he had contravened key conditions of his father's agreement with Bijapur, which forbade him from attempting to capture any of the Adil Shahi's possessions.

He decided to calibrate his moves. His first step towards doing so was to tell Bijapur that new gains near the coast were for Adil Shah and not for himself, and would be a check against the Mughals. Simultaneously, the by now twenty-six-year-old Shivaji began communicating with the Mughals, as he'd done previously following his father's arrest.

The Mughal factor had become more important. Shah Jahan had returned to his capital, Agra, after pulverizing the Nizam Shahi in 1636 and had appointed his third son Aurangzeb as *subahdar* of the Deccan. Born in 1618, Aurangzeb was twelve years older than Shivaji. He consolidated his hold on parts of the Nizam Shahi Sultanate such as the city of Ahmadnagar that had come into the Mughal kitty, settling revenue matters and other related issues. He also took over the town of Khadki near Daulatabad, first established by Malik Ambar, and renamed it Aurangabad after himself. But suddenly, in 1644, he quit his post as governor in a huff, accusing his father of favouring his eldest son, Dara Shukoh. The following year, after the father and son patched up, Aurangzeb was sent as governor to Gujarat. In 1647, he was plucked out from there and sent to Afghanistan to fight off the Bukhara armies of Uzbekistan on the one hand and the Shah of Persia's forces on the other, both of whom were pressing in on the Mughal empire's borders. Through Afghanistan lay the pathway to Hindustan, as the Indian subcontinent was termed by all those who coveted it, and Shah Jahan was keen that intruders be repelled. Though Mughals under Aurangzeb were forced to retreat from Balkh in northern Afghanistan and later from Kandahar, there was no doubting the Mughal prince's skills as a commander, especially after another Mughal force led by his brother Dara Shukoh faced an even bigger defeat in Kandahar soon afterwards. Besides, during his stint in the north-west, Aurangzeb had acted as governor of Sindh and Multan.[1]

In 1652 Aurangzeb was reappointed governor of the Deccan by his father.[2] He was an experienced general by now, having faced attacks from the Uzbeks and Hazaras in northern Afghanistan and the Persians in Kandahar and having had to deal with, and put down, various Afghan and Baluch tribal clans in Sindh and Multan.[3] And he was hungry for success. As the death of the Adil Shah late in 1656 threw the Bijapur durbar into chaos, Aurangzeb began a campaign against both the Adil Shahi and Qutub Shahi states. Shivaji, having strengthened himself by taking Jaawali, and seeing the Mughals on the offensive against Bijapur, thought the moment was ripe to hammer home the advantage.

He got his opportunity when Mulla Ahmad, the local commander of Kalyan in the northern Konkan region, which was part of the Adil Shahi kingdom, was called by the new ruler, Adil Shah II, to the kingdom's capital to deliver accumulated revenue. Shivaji struck swiftly, his men waylaying the Bijapur commander's forces near Purandar, while they were transporting the revenue. Shivaji's men carried all the wealth with them to Rajgad, while another set of men captured Kalyan, Bhiwandi and the Mahuli fort near Kalyan. Shivaji knew that a considerable amount of traffic moved to and from Kalyan into the Deccan, and any control over such a trade route was bound to be beneficial. Other significant parts of northern Konkan were captured equally speedily, whether it was Chaul, another important port near Alibaug, Rajmachi, which provided a vantage view of the coastal belt, or Lohagad.[4] The Marathas must have taken heart from their success against the African Siddis. They seized a few forts belonging to the Siddis, but before they could get hold of the two major fortresses of Danda-Rajpuri and Janjira, the Siddis sued for peace.[5] Later, the powerful Bijapur general Afzal Khan was quoted by Parmanand as saying in a letter that among Shivaji's 'offences' was the conquest of parts controlled by the Siddis, 'which had driven the Africans into a corner and made the Siddi ruler furious'.[6]

There is an apocryphal story, perpetuated in folklore, that Shivaji's general, Abaji Sondev, captured Mulla Ahmad's attractive daughter-in-law in Kalyan, and sent her to his master in Pune. According to this story, Shivaji apologized to her and sent her back, and is also said to have said to her, 'If my mother Jija Bai had possessed your beauty, I too should have looked as handsome.'[7] A far more reliable insight into Shivaji's attitude towards women from the enemy camp is an incident at Panvel's Prabalgad fort, one of more than twenty that the Marathas captured in northern Konkan. In the fight, led by Shivaji himself, the fort commander of Bijapur, Keshri Singh, was slain. When Shivaji went up the fort, he found plenty of hidden treasure – mohurs, *hons* and gold bars – but also Singh's elderly mother and his two children, cowering in fear. Shivaji touched the mother's feet and sent her back to her home town Deulgaon in a palanquin, escorted by his own security detail. The bodies of Keshri Singh and others who had fallen in battle were, on Shivaji's orders, consigned to the flames 'with due rites and honours'.[8]

Shivaji's focus on the western coastline was abundantly transparent right from the hard launch of his political and military career at Jaawali. The land powers – Mughals and the various sultanates – had left almost the whole of the seafront to the *firangs* (the Portuguese, the English, the Dutch and the French) who had gradually established their sway. They controlled the movement of all ships and vessels, even those which took the top officials of northern Hindustan and southern Deccan and their families and friends to Hajj for the holy pilgrimage mandated by Islam. Unlike all his other contemporaries, including Aurangzeb, Shivaji saw fully and quite early the vast potential of the sea, and his aim in getting closer and closer to the seawaters was to control the coastline corridor because it could yield political, economic and negotiating power – which would obviously be useful for a rising political force pitted against far stronger rivals.

So, after northern Konkan, Shivaji swooped down on the southern parts of the coastal belt, seizing the stretch from Chiplun to Sawantwadi, just to the north of Goa. The 'Sawant' or local ruler of Wadi – in Bijapur's employ but finding himself increasingly at odds with its rulers – capitulated and signed a treaty pledging loyalty to Shivaji. This Sawant had in his possession a sword manufactured in Europe that Shivaji found beguilingly glistening; Shivaji bought it from the Sawant for 300 *hons*. He named it Bhavani, after his patron goddess. (Centuries later, the Congress chief minister of Maharashtra, A.R. Antulay, would claim, in a political stunt, that the Bhavani sword was in Britain's Buckingham Palace, having been presented to the Prince of Wales by the Maharaja of Kolhapur in the nineteenth century, and vow to get it back. Historians were sceptical, and eventually, Britain's Queen Elizabeth herself scotched the story, replying to a Maharashtra legislator who had written to her, that no such sword existed in England. However, the *neta*'s stunt ended up becoming a part of the state's political memory.[9])

The Marathas also ventured further south into Karnataka, but were rebuffed. Still, Shivaji had made the kind of considerable gains he had envisaged. He now possessed a big portion of the lands very close to the western coastline, from parts lying north of Bombay right down to the border of Goa. He had even managed to regain the fort of Kondhana, which he had been forced to give up, much against his wishes, to secure his father's release in 1649. How he took it back is not clear from available records, but the symbolism of this recapture was immense for him. He could be satisfied that he had, in a way, redeemed his father's, and his family's, honour.

Shivaji's forces had even had a brief skirmish with the Mughal commander of Junnar, Mohammed Yusuf, during his Kalyan campaign, forcing the latter to retreat to his base.[10] But it ended there because Shivaji had no intention of opening up another front. At least not at that juncture. Shivaji saw a scrap with the Mughals as no doubt inevitable since Aurangzeb had set his sights on annexing every bit of the Nizam Shahi state that had gone to the Adil Shah two decades earlier, and the Maratha leader was targeting precisely that territory, especially in northern Konkan. Yet for the moment, it was in Shivaji's interest to put it off. So, he opened a line of communication with Aurangzeb – the first time he was deliberately and directly engaging with the Mughal empire after a gap of seven years.

Not a single one of the close-to-a-handful letters Shivaji wrote to Aurangzeb in this period have survived. It's likely the originals, or their copies at any rate, were part of the papers burnt by the Mughals after their invasion of Shivaji's territories following his death. What we have to go by are Aurangzeb's replies to his letters, which give us a fair enough indication of what Shivaji was professing.

Aurangzeb first referred to Shivaji's message to him in a letter he sent to Multafat Khan, the governor of Ahmadnagar, in July 1656. He told the Khan, who was supervising the area around Shivaji's territory, that he ought to 'keep the path of correspondence with Shivaji open' and 'write to him in such a way as to encourage him to offer his loyalty to the [Mughal] durbar'. Such correspondence would make Shivaji 'more and more willing' to serve the Mughals, Aurangzeb stated.[11]

Just a few months on, soon after Shivaji had made advances into Bijapur's domains, he wrote to Aurangzeb once again, asking that he be allowed to retain those areas on behalf of the Mughals. Shivaji's idea was that this would help him achieve twin objectives, which were obviously left unstated: deny Bijapur's claims and block immediate Mughal aggression. Aurangzeb welcomed the offer, as his missive to the Mughal *wazir* or prime minister Muazzam Khan suggests, yet he included in it an unmistakable note of warning to Shivaji. The clever, accomplished and experienced military leader that he was, Aurangzeb was among the earliest to have understood Shivaji's ideas and objectives. Shivaji was not as innocuously out to toe the line of the Mughals or the other established powers as he pretended to be, Aurangzeb realized. He informed the Mughal *wazir* that Shivaji's representative had, barely days ago, approached him with his letter stating that if Shivaji were granted *mansab* or land and revenue rights for the regions he'd recently captured, he'd stick to the path of allegiance and service and merge those parts with the Mughal empire.

'I have written to him [Shivaji] spelling out some conditions in relation to loyalty and service that he'd have to meet,' Aurangzeb stated. 'I will let you know when he replies. If he follows our orders, fine. Else, they [Shivaji and his men] would be trampled underfoot by our powerful army and punished for their actions.'[12]

By the time Aurangzeb next wrote about Shivaji, he was himself experiencing quite a high. Towards the end of 1656, Shah Jahan gave Aurangzeb the go-ahead for a march on Bijapur. By March 1657, the Mughal prince had laid siege to the Bidar fort in south-eastern Deccan. From there, he wrote to the Ahmadnagar governor Multafat Khan, referring to Shivaji's 'requests and demands', which apparently had been made one more time, while at the same time informing the Khan that the siege of Bidar was going well for their side. In the following month, Aurangzeb had captured the Bidar fort and was planning to press on to Kalyani, the old capital of the Chalukyas west of Bidar and now under Bijapur's control. Before he moved forward, he wrote directly to Shivaji.

Aurangzeb was at this stage working actively to get into his fold *sardars* belonging to the Deccani kingdoms, and his big recent catch had been Mir Jumla, the *wazir* of the Qutub Shahi of Golconda who had acquired as much of a reputation for his military skills as for looting rich temples of the south, melting their Hindu idols made of copper, and casting them into cannon.[13] Aurangzeb put it in writing that he was willing to formally recognize Shivaji's rights to the Bijapur forts he'd captured and also to the port of Dabhol in southern Konkan, along with Dabhol's dependencies in the neighbourhood. In return, Shivaji had to pass a loyalty test: with Aurangzeb headed for Kalyani, the Maratha had to provide armed assistance to the Mughals on this campaign.[14] Hardly had the ink on the writing reed dried, however, that Aurangzeb discovered that Shivaji had instead quickly cleared a disloyalty test: he had launched raids on the Mughal territories of Ahmadnagar and Junnar in south-western Deccan.

Why did Shivaji choose this moment to strike? Right through 1655 and 1656, Aurangzeb had been making fuzzy assurances to Sri Ranga Rayal, the last nominal ruler of the Vijayanagara dynasty, even offering him protection against any attacks by Bijapur and Golconda. The assurances had ultimately resulted in zero protection for Ranga Rayal and the extraction of a lot of protection money from him by the Mughals.[15] Shivaji firmly believed that Aurangzeb, albeit momentarily in a mood to offer sops to him to gather support, would similarly dump him the moment he was no longer needed. And he had no desire to be in Aurangzeb's camp or company anyway. He, in fact, saw the moment as appropriate for a strike against the Mughals. Daringly, one night, Shivaji climbed the walls of Mughal-controlled Junnar 'with rope-ladders',[16] and after slaying the fort's guardians, walked off with 3,00,000 *hons*, 200 horses, and plenty of clothing and jewellery.[17] From there his men rode to the entrance of Ahmadnagar, the chief base of the Mughals in the Deccan. The troops stationed there beat back a Maratha assault on the *peth* or locality beneath the fort, but the attack rattled the local Mughal governor so much that he ordered all inhabitants of the area to immediately shift all their property inside the fort.[18]

This was Shivaji's first and clearest notice to the Mughals in his very own Deccan, and it confirmed Aurangzeb's conviction that Shivaji was not in the game for the sake of the established powers. Shivaji was fighting for his own free dispensation, for his people in the Deccan, for freeing the Deccan of powers that in his opinion didn't care about the region or its inhabitants but saw it as a colony to be held down by force of the sword, exploited, looted and suppressed. Shivaji deemed it all to be toxic control by outsiders, and he wanted the place to be rid of them. His decision to carry out raids in the Mughal territories of Ahmadnagar and Junnar betrayed the workings of his mind, whatever he might have been writing in his letters to Aurangzeb.

Aurangzeb ascribed the surprise Maratha raids to awful negligence by his local commanders. He scolded the Ahmadnagar fort in-charge Multafat Khan for lack of foresight and dereliction of duty and asked the generals Nasiri Khan, Kartalab Khan and Iraz Khan – who were then with him at Bidar – to leave immediately for Ahmadnagar with a force of 3,000. Two other military officers, Hoshdar and Rao Karna, who were on their way to Bidar to join Aurangzeb's campaign, were told to head to Ahmadnagar instead. And Shaista Khan, the governor of the Malwa province of Rajasthan, was instructed to send an additional force of 1,000 to the areas attacked by Shivaji, with an experienced military man at its head. Thus a Mughal force of almost 5,000 was immediately dispatched to fence off the Mughal kingdom's south-western borders.[19]

But Aurangzeb was obviously enraged, and he desired more than mere protection of his own frontiers. The legendary conflict between the Mughal and the Maratha, which was to see many twists and turns over decades, had finally begun in the real sense. Aurangzeb directed at once that the arena of the combat itself be changed. Enter Shivaji's *jagir*, he told his men. In letter after sharply worded letter in subsequent months, he spoke of exacting urgent and utter revenge on Shivaji, though not without voicing his impatience and incomprehension at what his own officers were doing. After his raids on Junnar and Ahmadnagar in April–June 1657, Shivaji hadn't lain low. On the contrary, he had, right up until December, continued to make swift and sudden incursions into these districts every now and then, giving the Mughal armies no respite at all and preventing them from settling into any kind of military or administrative steadiness.

The two big rivals were sizing each other up and testing each other.

'Invade the enemy's territory, don't spare any effort in ransacking the villages there, and reduce it to ashes. Destroy that territory in every way possible,' Aurangzeb told his generals, expressing his frustration over what he considered their initially slow progress towards Junnar and Ahmadnagar when Shivaji's men were all over the place.[20] Attaching to Shivaji's name – which he spelt as 'Siva' – the Perso-Arabic suffix *makhu*, meaning 'one who has invoked someone's (in this case, the Mughal prince's) wrath', Aurangzeb asked his men in another message to 'promptly descend into the cursed and condemned man's areas' and 'pillage, slaughter and imprison without mercy, so that the scene of devastation will trigger in his mind concerns about the actions he has undertaken and stop him from pursuing his aims'.[21] In another letter, he underlined how 'important' it was that 'the cursed Siva' was 'punished' for 'his impudence and intransigence'. If, in the process of the Mughal badshah's armies razing his territories, Shivaji stepped forward to oppose them, then, Aurangzeb made clear to his men, 'use the sword to remove the swelling in his head'.[22] After one of his *sardars*, Nasiri Khan, sent him a report in June 1657 that Shivaji and his army had retreated from the Mughal fields of Junnar, Aurangzeb was relieved but found it inexplicable nevertheless that the general had not pursued the Marathas as vigorously as he wanted. 'That ill-intentioned man's rebellion has to be wiped out,' Aurangzeb asserted,[23] displaying a sense of urgency seemingly lacking in his commanders. Till that happened, Aurangzeb warned his men to be always 'on the alert' against Shivaji and 'carry out a detailed probe into his activities'.[24] As for those 'people, *deshmukhs* and *patils* living in Mughal territory' who had 'instigated the enemy', Aurangzeb suggested their 'shoulders be freed of the burden of their heads'.[25]

Early in 1658, Aurangzeb left for the north to stake his claim to the throne as reports of Shah Jahan's serious ill health and impending death gathered momentum. Pounded badly by the Deccan *subahdar*, the Adil Shahi kingdom had already signed a treaty with the Mughals, agreeing to hand over several parts that belonged to it. With Aurangzeb away, Bijapur dilly-dallied on fulfilling the terms of the treaty. Shivaji himself had launched his first fusillade of attacks against the Mughals and was looking for time to consolidate what he had got; he was determined to be in the fray for the long haul, and not be just a flash in the pan or manifest a brief flicker of revolt. He knew Bijapur was now going to look for opportunities to pursue him, and he made up his mind, at this moment of strained relations with the Mughals, to conciliate Aurangzeb rather than challenge him further immediately. To reach out to Aurangzeb at that point was tricky, he knew, but he perceived it to be necessary. Just as he had waited seven long years to strike against the Mores of Jaawali in his first move of expansion, he could do with a period of stability to strengthen and deepen his hold over the areas he had gained instead of going all out at once. As noted earlier, he considered this policy of rebellion and aggression alternating with periods of apparent, on-the-surface compliance and restraint to be immensely valuable: it would allow him, if indeed he could pursue it intelligently and successfully, to steadily expand his footprint, and to survive even during periods when he needed to backtrack. Two steps forward, one step back, four steps forward, two steps back. He would still be the gainer in the final analysis, getting more of a foothold than he had had when he started. And the quiet periods would provide him valuable time to securely hold the places he had won, so that any future challenges could be rebuffed.

Shivaji thus wrote twice to Aurangzeb, in quick succession: first in November 1657, around the time news of Shah Jahan's ill health first filtered out and just before Aurangzeb began his journey northwards, and the second time in February 1658, the arc of both his letters moving towards submission.

In response to the first of these two of Shivaji's letters, Aurangzeb wrote to Nasiri Khan, the Mughal general now in charge of Ahmadnagar:

> What you have written in reply to the letter of the defeated and disgraced Shivaji is approved by the Prince. Although it is proper to extirpate that miscreant, and after his manifestations of crime and hostility he cannot

even in his imagination hope for any safety from us, yet, if he acts as you have written to him and sends a trusty agent to you, and if you find his demands worthy of being reported to the Prince, then you should write the nature of his desires in your letters to the Prince. Remain ever on the alert![26]

The second response was sent in April 1658 when Aurangzeb had reached Ujjain, and it was addressed directly to Shivaji:

I have gone through the letter you sent me through your envoy Raghunath Pandit, as well as the letter you have addressed to Krishnaji Bhaskar Pandit [a Mughal representative]. What you are seeking is thus clear to me.

Your offences are too many and don't deserve any pardon. But you have demonstrated your intention of being loyal and in service and have expressed your contrition over your offences. Ours is not a durbar that persecutes, so I have pardoned your offences on the condition that you stay steadfast on the path of service and obedience. True loyalty is the means to obtain rank and fortune. You must strive to demonstrate it.

You have written that if you are given all the *mahals* and forts and areas in the Konkan which were part of your *watan* [ancestral domain] once all the Nizam Shahi territory now with the Adil Khan comes into the possession of the Mughal Badshahi, you will send Sona Pandit [Shivaji's envoy] to us. And if we grant all your requests, you will send a good force – of not less than 500 horses – with a general of yours to us, join all other Badshahi officers in protecting the Badshahi frontiers, and not allow any dust of revolt to be raised anywhere in that territory.

I hereby instruct you: Act according to your promises. Once you have received this letter, send to us with the aforementioned Sonaji your letter with your demands and requests, and I will grant those. See that you stick to the path of loyalty and don't deviate in any way from it.[27]

Aurangzeb got himself crowned Mughal emperor in July 1658 after defeating his elder brother Dara Shukoh in battle and imprisoning his father Shah Jahan and other sibling Murad Bakhsh. As the first coronation was a hurried one, he crowned himself with pomp a second time in June 1659, and this time his accession was more decisive as he had succeeded in capturing Dara Shukoh. Shivaji had, in the meantime, sent Sonaji to the durbar with his letter, and Aurangzeb wrote back to him just days after his second coronation, on 14 July 1659:

> Know that God has adorned my banners with victory and defeated and crushed my rivals who were enemies of the Faith ... On the 24th of Ramzan, the imperial throne was made resplendent by my accession.
>
> The letter that you had sent me by the hand of one of your servants has reached me. Remain firm in your loyalty and service to my throne, which will be the means of realizing your hopes. Amir-ul-umara Shaista Khan has been appointed subahdar of the Deccan. Act according to his orders and never deviate from his instructions. Exert yourself so that the things you have promised may be carried out in the best manner and your prayers may be granted.
>
> I have established peace throughout the empire. Dara Shukoh has been captured with his family and followers on the frontier of Bhakkar [in Sindh]. God willing, Shuja too will soon be annihilated.
>
> Know my favour to be turned towards you. A robe of honour is conferred on you for your exaltation. Written on 4th Zilqada 2nd regnal year.[28]

It is clear, however, that Aurangzeb was not convinced by Shivaji's attempts to placate him. Privately, even after he had replied to some of Shivaji's early letters professing loyalty, he wrote to Mir Jumla warning him about the Maratha's activities. After Nasiri Khan had departed from his district in the Deccan, Aurangzeb told Jumla, 'Attend to it [the district], as *the son of a dog* is waiting for his opportunity.'[29] Similarly, he wrote to the Adil Shah who had signed terms of peace with the Mughals: 'Protect this country. Expel Siva who has sneaked into the possession of some forts of the land. If you wish to entertain his services, give him *jagirs* in the Karnatak, far from the imperial dominions, so that he may not disturb them.'[30]

Shivaji, for his part, had his sights set not on any robes of honour that Aurangzeb might send, but firmly on the sea. In doing so he was breaking new ground. As we have noted earlier, the Mughals and the Deccan sultanates had been quite insular about the sea that surrounded the land on all sides, concentrating on inland territories, despite the fact that the waters were so crucial to trade and to the movement of goods and even weaponry for states that were almost entirely military in nature. It was almost as if the *firangs* – as the Portuguese, the English, the Dutch and the French were called – and to a lesser extent the African Siddis on the west coast, were given bragging rights and a monopoly on the vast seafront, with the interior kingdoms being merely content with arrangements that would enable the unimpeded movement of commodities, horses and other things. These arrangements chiefly meant the grant of a 'passport' by the foreign powers for ships carrying goods for the various kingdoms inland to be allowed into the ports, harbours and creeks in the first place and for the goods then to be carried inland.

Why almost no one linked such a trade corridor to defence and security is bewildering, and what made matters worse for any states which were Hindu in nature and character was the peculiar religious diktat of the orthodoxy that it was 'unholy' to cross the seas. Anyone who allegedly 'polluted' himself thus would have to undergo a ceremony of 'purification', a practice that continued until the early years of the twentieth century. Shivaji, however, was unmindful of such taboos. He was looking at the gigantic, untapped waters and the beckoning coastline as a magnificent opportunity and a critical zone of state defence and security. And he had begun serious work in that respect.

Soon after capturing Kalyan, Bhiwandi and Prabalgad near Panvel in 1657, Shivaji had ordered the construction of twenty small armed ships in the creeks beneath these three towns. For this purpose he had commissioned Portuguese officers, better shipbuilders than the indigenous people of the region, along with some locals to assist them. Around 400 people were involved in the work, according to details recorded by Portuguese officials.[31] At the head of the shipbuilding teams were two Portuguese siblings, Roe Leitao Viegas and Fernao Leitao Viegas. Shivaji had proclaimed that he wanted the ships, each of which would have the ability to carry twenty people, to take on the Siddis of Janjira and Danda-Rajpuri. They could help cut supply lines to the Janjira fort which the Marathas were eyeing and block the Siddis' attacks along the shores.[32]

All three creeks fell under the subdistrict of Bassein or Vasai, where most of the ports were under Portuguese control. The chief Portuguese official at Bassein, Antonio de Melo de Castro, wrote to his bosses in Goa, which was under Portuguese rule, that Shivaji wanted timber transported to the creeks from the sea for building the ships and was also asking for 'an exit to the sea via [our] ports'.[33] The Bassein captain sent his own opinion with the letter: that Shivaji's ships should not be permitted any sort of exit. These were his reasons: there would be born this way 'a pirate at home'; if Shivaji's men seized some ships, their armada would grow; relations with him weren't close enough to rule out apprehension or wariness; if he had motives beyond menacing the Siddis, this could possibly threaten the island of Sashti to the north of Bombay; and finally, he had employed seafarers on regular salaries, and they'd already become so bound to him that the Portuguese were finding it hard to find a 'single sailor' for their own fleet.[34]

The Goa advisory council agreed. The order they issued on 19 July 1659 is recorded in the Goan archives. It said:

> A son of Shahaji, the rebel nobleman of the Adil Shahi court, has captured the territory around Chaul and Bassein and has become quite powerful. He has built some men-at-war (a reference to the small ships) in Bhimdi (Bhiwandi), Kalyan and Panvel, ports in Bassein Taluka. We are forced, therefore, to be cautious. To ensure that these men-of-war do not set sail, we have ordered the Portuguese Captain not to let them come out of these ports.[35]

Shivaji simultaneously made more demands on the Portuguese. He wrote to the Goa governors that when his men had recently approached the Siddis' frontiers, the Africans had received active assistance from the Portuguese captains at Bassein and Chaul. He wanted the Goa authorities to write to the local captains asking them to desist from helping the Siddis against him. The Goa council debated this issue and came to the conclusion that the best course of action for the Portuguese would be to send letters to their Bassein and Chaul captains telling them it was 'necessary to maintain amiable relations with him [Shivaji] because he is powerful, has control over Kalyan, Bhiwandi and the entire Konkan, and can cause immense harm to Portuguese interests'.[36] Another letter would be sent to them at the same time, asking them to 'ostensibly' offer no support to the Siddis but to 'secretly' do so if they wished, ensuring that no one, least of all Shivaji, had any idea.[37] They were obviously feeling the need to check Shivaji.

Shivaji was spreading alarm all around: amongst the Portuguese, the Mughals and, most of all, Bijapur. He had launched his most aggressive offensive against the Adil Shah's lands. By 1648–49, in the early phase of his career, Shivaji had consolidated his hold over his father's *jagir*, but ten years on, he had expanded his footprint substantially. From Thane district to the northern tip of Goa he was all over the Konkan, except for the big ports still held by the Portuguese, the Siddis and, in some cases, by Bijapur. He was moving southwards inland as well and had, from the valleys of Jaawali, entered Satara district. The southern half of his father's *jagir* in Pune district was of course still with him. He'd raided areas north of that district, in the Mughal domain of Junnar, and had pressed on to parts of Karnataka besides, from where his men had been repelled.

Shivaji had captured at least forty forts, his cavalry had a strength of 10,000, with 7,000 using state-owned horses and 3,000 relying on what various cavalrymen themselves brought in. He had appointed a close confidant, Netaji Palkar, as the head of cavalry. His infantry too had swelled to 10,000, with his other trusted aides such as Yesaji Kank and Tanaji Malusare at its helm. The top rung of the civilian administration was being reset. There was a new *peshwa*, Moro Trimbak Pingle, in place of Shyamraj Nilkanth, who had aged (Pingle would, in addition, head the army in the Konkan); and replacing the earlier incumbents, Nilo Sondev was the new accountant-general, Abaji Sondev the chief of correspondence (*surnis*), and Gangaji Mangaji the writer (*waqnis*). Individual areas too were being taken care of: Abaji Mahadev was appointed the chief official in Kalyan, Krishnaji Bhaskar was going to be administrative in-charge in the Mavals, and Anaji Malkare became head of the fort of Purandar.[38]

However, the truth was that the threat he posed to the Adil Shahi, then still the most powerful state in the Deccan, was very much manageable. For all of Shivaji's systematic build-up of forces, Bijapur's military and civilian strength, and its expanse of territory were far wider; it was much better equipped in terms of resources and the number of local officials it could order or summon, because it was a well-established power. Also, Shivaji's forces had so far fought more or less isolated armies and acquired either not-so-well-guarded forts and areas or totally abandoned ones. Was he really equipped to stand up to a regular, sizeable and well-armed, well-provisioned force?

The prevailing sentiment in the Adil Shah's court was that the rebel needed to be put in his place before he became a bigger threat and chipped away further at the kingdom's strength, and before he acquired more men and material. And who better to do so, the Adil Shahi ruler thought, than Afzal Khan, a Bijapur general known as a powerful crusher of enemies.

4

Daggers Drawn

His actual name was Abdulla Bhatari, but he is much better remembered as Afzal Khan. An Afghan noble at the Bijapur court, Afzal Khan was one of the leading commanders of the Adil Shahi army. He was tall, imposing, heavily built, and highly skilled at fighting important battles and seeing military campaigns through. He had had a long stint in Karnataka from the late 1630s, where he'd worked alongside Ranadulla Khan and one of Ranadulla's favourite nobles, Shahaji. He had easily subdued a number of Hindu rajas in the south and appropriated their domains. He had been entrusted the challenging task of fending off Aurangzeb's assault on Bijapur's territories from 1656 onwards, a measure of his exalted status in the Adil Shahi hierarchy, and had done creditably despite the challenges involved. He had been the governor of Wai, the region in which Jaawali stood, and knew the terrain extremely well; and with that came his deep knowledge of the fickle nature of the *deshmukhs* and other local officials. He could get these officials on his side; he had the political will, the military might and the fearsome reputation to do it.

For the dead ruler Muhammad Adil Shah's chief queen, Begum Badi Sahiba, and the new incumbent Ali Adil Shah, Afzal Khan was the go-to man for tasks which needed to be accomplished any which way, with a brazen disregard for means. For Afzal Khan could be blunt and decisive, and he had a ruthless streak. There were many examples of how he would stop at nothing to achieve his and his sultan's aims. He had, in 1639, extended an invitation to Kasturi Ranga, the raja of Sira in the south, to his *shamiana* or pavilion, giving him solemn assurances of safety and promising to sign a peace agreement, but 'put him to death', according to the *Muhammadnamah*, an official account of Muhammad Adil Shah's reign.[1] When internecine feuds broke out in the Bijapur durbar immediately after Muhammad Adil Shah's death, three senior generals were murdered in rapid succession, allegedly at the behest of the Badi Sahiba. Afzal Khan was instrumental in hatching the plot to kill at least one of them, his factional rival Khan Muhammad, if not all three. He denounced Khan Muhammad to the Badi Sahiba as someone who had gone over to Aurangzeb's side. This was at just the time Bijapur had found itself besieged by Aurangzeb's army. The accusation, though false, had its effect: when Khan Muhammad was on his way to see the Badi Sahiba in court, he was stabbed to death in the streets of the capital.[2] Afzal Khan was, in addition, a religious bigot and prided himself on attacking Hindu shrines. The Portuguese captain in Chaul in the northern Konkan wrote in a letter in 1664 that Afzal Khan had ordered the demolition of all Hindu temples in Upper Chaul.[3]

Shivaji was entirely conscious of the fact that for him in particular, there was one more factor to be borne in mind: Afzal Khan seemed to nurse a certain antipathy for the Bhosle family. Initially, he and Shahaji Raje Bhosle had worked together as part of Ranadulla Khan's team, but soon, Afzal Khan had moved on to other factions. And it was he who had placed Shahaji in fetters at Jinji in 1648 and dragged him all the way to Bijapur, to be put into a dungeon, on the suspicion of disloyalty. Shivaji, his mother and his father were also convinced that Afzal Khan had had a role to play in the death of Shivaji's elder brother Sambhaji in Kanakgiri in 1654. As a matter of fact, Sambhaji and Afzal Khan were in the same contingent on this campaign, but Afzal Khan had, it was strongly suspected, deliberately not moved quickly enough to back Sambhaji up when he had badly needed reinforcements.[4]

Interestingly, shortly before Afzal Khan went off to lock horns with Shivaji, the latter's father, still in the service of Bijapur, was told by the Badi

Sahiba to rein in his son immediately. He shrugged off all responsibility. 'He [Shivaji] is no longer under my control. I am a faithful dependant of the Badshah. Though Shivaji is my son, His Majesty may attack him or deal with him in any way he likes. I will not interfere,' he wrote to the durbar from Bangalore.[5]

For Shivaji, Afzal Khan's name evoked bitter memories: of his father's ill treatment, and his elder brother's death. Just two years earlier, Shivaji's wife Saibai had delivered a baby boy, and Shivaji had named him Sambhaji after his brother. The birth of the child was a moment of great celebration for Shivaji, his wife Saibai and his parents, and 'great festivities took place' and 'many deeds of charity were performed'.[6] But on 5 September 1659, when the child was barely two, tragedy struck, with Saibai's death after a protracted illness.[7] Shivaji had no time to grieve, though. Afzal Khan was already threatening his frontiers.

Afzal Khan's boast on the floor of the Bijapur durbar on the day he stepped up to launch his mission against Shivaji has been recorded by a host of sources. 'Who is Shivaji? I will get him here in chains, and I won't even have to get off my horse to do that,' he declared proudly.[8]

Very little is known about Afzal's family background, except that he was born close to Bijapur, most likely, as Aurangzeb has recorded somewhere, to a woman who worked as a cook for a living.[9] Historians have surmised that if we take his age to be around eighteen to twenty years when he is first spoken of as a young man in the Deccan campaigns of the late 1630s, he would be around forty in 1659. Shivaji, on the other hand, was then just twenty-nine.

Shivaji's chronicler Sabhasad says Afzal Khan set out with a military strength of 12,000 horses besides infantry, but the figure of 10,000 cavalry cited in Bijapur's official records seems more likely.[10] A question debated over and over again is whether Afzal Khan set out with the intent to kill Shivaji. Or was he meant to get the rebel to simply submit to Adil Shahi authority, and if he didn't, to capture him and drag him along to Bijapur?

This is one debate on which written records do provide answers.

The official historian of the Bijapur court, Nurullah, spelt out the orders issued by the Adil Shah to Afzal Khan:

Ali Adil Shah, on seeing that the prevalence of the Muhammadan religion was not possible unless the bramble of infidelity was burnt up in the fire of the enemy-consuming sword, appointed Afzal Khan with 10,000 horsemen, to chastise and extirpate that wicked man Shivaji ... At the time of giving the assignment to Afzal Khan, Adil Shah had instructed him that in case Shivaji on being hard pressed by the Bijapuri forces, in his habitual deceptive manner offered to make a peaceful submission, the Khan must not listen to him but follow no other policy than that of flinging the fire of death on the harvest of his life.[11]

Bijapur was clamouring for death to Shivaji, and it said so without mincing any words.

Launching his 'Mission Shivaji' sometime in April 1659, Afzal Khan proceeded towards Wai, the province he had previously governed. As mentioned earlier, Jaawali was part of the Wai region, and the town of Wai itself – a flat land where Afzal Khan had decided to set up camp – was just beyond Jaawali's southern boundary, within earshot of Shivaji's newly conquered hill terrain. By heading straight there, Afzal Khan wanted to tell the Marathas that he was taking them head-on. Over a month after his departure from Bijapur, a *farman* issued by the Adil Shah reached Kanhoji Jedhe, the *deshmukh* of Kari in Pune district. The *farman*, dated 16 June 1659, stated:

I begin in the name of the Merciful and Kind God.
 The whole world belongs to God.
 Imam Ali Adilshah
 Son of
 Mohamed Adilshah
 Since the beginning of the year 1069 (1659), Shivaji out of narrow-mindedness and evil propensities has started troubling the Muhammadans residing in the Nizam Shahi Konkan. He has plundered them. He has also captured several forts in our territory. Therefore, in order to drive him out and conquer him, we have appointed Afzal Khan, possessed of valour and prestige, the most capable and efficient of our noblemen ...

as the Governor of that province and sent him with a most formidable army. You must therefore carry out his commands, obey him and do all the offices of a servant, and defeat and exterminate Shivaji. You must not give quarter to Shivaji's men, wherever they may be or from wheresoever they may come, but must kill them.[12]

Here again, the words 'exterminate' and 'kill' were pronounced. There was to be no doubt about what was to be done.

The Adil Shahi wanted to peel off as many of Shivaji's *deshmukh* partners as possible, and Afzal Khan, on his way to Wai, himself wrote to Kanhoji Jedhe's son Shivaji Jedhe and Vithoji Haibatrao of Gunjan Maval. He told both of them that a Maratha Brahmin, Krishnaji Bhaskar Kulkarni (who would soon be acting as Afzal Khan's envoy to Shivaji in the tense days leading to their face-off), had spoken to him about them 'in appreciative terms' and that they should join him in his endeavour so they could earn the promotion and advancement they desired. With Kanhoji's son he had to adopt a particularly reassuring tone, because the family had linked itself with Shivaji. 'We are aware that your father and brothers have been serving Shivaji Bhosle for some ten or twenty years,' he wrote. 'But you need have no hesitation about that. You should come to our presence. You will not suffer on that account. You are a friend of the Court.'[13]

Similar letters were sent to other *deshmukhs,* and by the time Shivaji reached his newly constructed fort of Pratapgad on the western border of Jaawali in July 1659, in direct response to Afzal Khan parking himself just outside the hill territory's eastern borders, he found that two Maratha chiefs from the Utravali area, Kedarji Khopde and Khandoji Khopde, had indeed already joined his adversary. Shivaji was aware that Kedarji and Khandoji were cousins and had quarrelled bitterly with each other for land rights. Shivaji himself had settled the fight in favour of Khandoji Khopde. But Khandoji, along with his cousin, had still gone over to the other side. So had some other Marathas, like 'Ghorpade, Naikji Pandhare, Naikji Kharade, Kalyanji Yadav, Mambaji Bhosle, Rajaji (Zunzarrao) Ghatge and one Kate'.[14] They had all joined Afzal Khan's army – comprising, among others, generals like Ambar Khan, Yakut Khan, Muse Khan, Hasan Khan Pathan, Ranadulla Khan (Junior) and Ankush Khan – with their armed squads when he was on his way to Wai. Afzal Khan's choice of Wai itself – when he could have easily headed to the Pune region instead, where Shivaji and his family had recently taken to staying in the fort of Rajgad – had to do with a Maratha chief who was accompanying him. This was Prataprao More, one of the More brothers who had fled to the Adil Shahi durbar after Shivaji's conquest of Jaawali. He had a personal vendetta against Shivaji, and he promised to impart his knowledge of the difficult and densely wooded place to Afzal Khan so that the Adil Shahi could win it back. Afzal Khan was at once convinced by More's talk that getting control of Jaawali was tantamount to establishing sway 'over all of Wai, over the Sahyadris and also over the sea with its coastline', for Jaawali's 'secret pathways' could steer him into all kinds of directions.[15] If a single stone could bring down a multitude of birds, why go around picking up more, he thought.

For many *deshmukhs*, the situation was delicate. Bijapur could claim that they owed their authority and legal status to the Sultanate and that it had every right to conscript them in its war on Shivaji. If they sided with Shivaji, they'd be publicly declaring themselves rebels. Kanhoji Jedhe was one of those who wrote to Shivaji telling him about Afzal Khan's letter. Shivaji wrote back:

> I have learnt everything from the letter you wrote ... You and he [Afzal Khan] have been on friendly terms for a long time. So go you must. But if you decide to go in person, or to send any of your sons, first take his word of honour, and then go, else there may be treachery. Have some good man as an intermediary and then go. Perhaps you think of going in person; and you have no suspicion on your mind. Still it would be better to send one of your sons, with some men, after taking a proper promise. Make some excuse or other, and do not go in person. I have written to you about either alternative. You are wise. It is unnecessary to tell you more.[16]

Kanhoji pored over the contents of this note and went straight off to meet Shivaji, his five sons in tow. He told Shivaji, 'Your father has obtained an oath from me and sent me into your service. I will stay true to it. I am at your service with my five sons and all my men, and we will fight to death for you. Let anyone have our *watan* then. But we will stick to our word.'[17] But wouldn't his *watan* be in danger if he did that, Shivaji asked. Kanhoji replied that he'd happily give up his *watan* to be with Shivaji. Could he do so by tipping some water off his right hand, which was the ceremonial Hindu way of renouncing things, Shivaji inquired gently. So Kanhoji did exactly that, and Shivaji's instant response was to tell Kanhoji to move his own family out from Kari in Bhor to Talegaon for some time; there was grave danger to the Jedhe family, he said. Then Shivaji and Kanhoji had milk and rice together, and the Jedhe family document records that with their hands placed on the *bel-roti* (the *roti* and the *bel* leaf), they took oaths; in addition, Shivaji promised that he and his descendants would look after Jedhe and his future generations.[18] Shivaji had tested Kanhoji's loyalty, and once Kanhoji had cleared the test, the leader had offered his own undying attachment to him, a connection that he said wouldn't be severed come what may. Once Shivaji was convinced that someone was totally with him, it was in his nature to dedicate himself to that associate in a similar, avowedly comprehensive fashion; here he was doing precisely that with Kanhoji.

On his way to Wai, Afzal Khan caused much devastation, especially in temple towns such as Pandharpur. Merchants, priests and others were forced to foot his army's bill, which came to an estimated two and a half lakh rupees a month. Afzal Khan threatened the *deshmukh* of Phaltan, Bajaji Naik Nimbalkar, that he'd have him crushed by an elephant if he didn't pay a ransom of two lakh rupees.[19] The Marathi chronicles state that he desecrated the Vitthal idol at Pandharpur and the Bhavani (Durga) idol at Tuljapur.[20] Now, Tuljapur was not along Afzal Khan's route at all, so it's unclear if he sent his cavalry there to cause devastation or had desecrated the shrine on some other, earlier occasion, if at all he did so.[21] At any rate the Adil Shah's court historian wrote that Afzal Khan had ordered his troops to unleash mayhem across the territories Shivaji had seized, including parts to the north of Wai, and had sent some of his men independently to several areas.[22] 'In a short time,' wrote the Adil Shah's chronicler, 'the Khan made the country seized by Shivaji the riding ground of his troops ... The dust raised by the horses' hoofs of our heroes blinded the eyes of the enemy ... Many of the latter were slain and the rest fled into holes.'[23]

Realizing that Afzal Khan's intent was to draw him out into the open, Shivaji was determined not to fall into that trap. From here on, a contest of cunning diplomacy began between the two fierce rivals. Afzal Khan asked Shivaji to come down to the plains of Wai, where his forces would outnumber Shivaji's before they could descend from the Sahyadris and from the next-door valleys of Jaawali; Shivaji, in turn, attempted to get the Khan to meet him in the labyrinthine denseness of the valleys.

In their own ways, they started dissembling, Afzal Khan acting uncharacteristically avuncular after handing out a generous dose of admonition and threats, and Shivaji pretending to be absolutely terrified at the prospect of facing the much-feared Khan. Afzal Khan's first, and rather stern message to Shivaji, sent with his envoy Krishnaji Bhaskar Kulkarni after the rains had receded in October 1659, read:

> The insolence you have lately been showing at every step has greatly upset and hurt the Adil Shah. The territory which, after the fall of the Nizam Shah, the Adil Shah had taken for himself, and which he later gave to the Mughals in order to establish a peace pact with them, that same territory, full of hill forts, you, son of Shahaji, have taken and appropriated. The Raja of Danda-Rajpuri is filled with rage because you, who have been consistently fortunate, have deprived him of his territory. You attacked and seized the expansive lands of the Chandra-raj [Chandrarao More], which were considered absolutely unconquerable. What was more, you took Kalyan and Bhimpuri [Bhiwandi] and demolished the mosques of the Muhammadans there ... Without giving any thought to your own strengths, you imprisoned *kazis* and *mullahs* and posed hurdles in the paths of the Muhammadans. The Adil Shah has sent me on this mission because of the way you have assumed emblems of imperial sovereignty,

have been unjustly sitting on a golden throne, have arrogated to yourself powers to grant favours and punishments, and have haughtily refused to pay obeisance to whom it is due ... The considerable force I have got along with me is beckoning me to begin hostilities against you at once. Brave men like Muse Khan, wishing to start battles with you, and sardars keen on capturing Jaawali have been encouraging me to move forward. So it is best that you follow my orders and sign terms of peace with me, and return all the hill forts and territories you have taken.

The great and strong forts of Sinhagad and Lohgad, the fort of Purandar and the city of Chakan, and the territory between the Nira and Bhima [rivers] – surrender all of these to the incredibly powerful Delhi Badshah. Jaawali, which you snatched forcibly from the Chandra-raj – that, too, the Adil Shah asks you to hand over to him.[24]

The second message, which was conciliatory, also sent with Krishnaji Bhaskar Kulkarni, suggested that Shahaji and Afzal Khan had been very close, which they never were:

Your father has long been a great friend of mine. So you are not a stranger to me. Come and see me. I will get the Badshah [Adil Shah] to confirm your possession of the Tal [southern] Konkan and a *jagir* as well. I will also get confirmed your possession of the forts you have captured. I will get for you further distinctions and military equipment from our government. In doing so I would give you as big a *saranjam* [fiefdom] as you want. If you would like to see the Badshah you could do so, but if you wouldn't, I will get for you an exemption from regular appearance at the court.[25]

Shivaji delivered his response through his own envoy, Niloji Pant Bokil. Every line of it was framed to put Afzal Khan on top of the world:

You vanquished and annihilated all the rajas of Karnataka. That you have shown at least so much compassion for me is a great thing. Your prowess is beyond comparison, and your heroism is fiery. You are truly a jewel on this earth, and you don't have in you the slightest bit of deceitfulness or perfidy.

If you are keen to glimpse the glory of this forest, please come to Jaawali and see it for yourself. I think it would be best for you to come here. It is just the thing, and the only thing, that will remove all my sense of fear and even provide to me a touch of glory.

Without a man as extraordinarily valiant and accomplished as you, I feel, the armies of the arrogant Mughals and the Adil Shah are worthless. Come along, and be careful on your journey. I will surrender to you all the forts I have taken and, of course, Jaawali too. It is hard for me to even look you in the eye, but once you are here, with all my doubts totally removed, I will place the sword that's in my hand in front of you in submission. When your army is in this ancient and colossal forest, it will experience the soothing shadows of the world beneath ours.[26]

A few more messages were exchanged through the two envoys, broadly similar in argument, persuasion and reassurance, and it was Shivaji's clever and fluent diplomacy that won the day. Afzal Khan finally agreed not only to go on to Jaawali but to meet Shivaji on an extended clump of a hill just beneath the Pratapgad fort, where Shivaji had tactically moved ever since Afzal Khan had left for Wai. The words of unstinting, extraordinary praise and the impression of mortal dread of an intimidating opponent conveyed by Shivaji must have boosted Afzal Khan's confidence. But another factor was equally at work. Embedded in the last sentence of Shivaji's letter was an invitation not just to the Khan alone, but to *all* of his army to move to Jaawali. For a veteran campaigner like the Khan, this carried a lot of weight. He would be there with all his forces and not on his own.

Shivaji made it clear to his men that Afzal Khan's army must be given smooth passage into the wooded zone. Some of the Maratha spies had already gotten into the Bijapur camp and were relaying information regularly to Shivaji. Soon, he got to know that Afzal Khan's move to Jaawali was proceeding unhindered, and that the Bijapur general was bringing along most of his troops, but not heavy equipment or elephants which would not be able to contend with the valley's crevasses. The Bijapur force set up camp in the village of Par, which was near the river Koyna, more than 1.5 kilometres to the south of Pratapgad.[27]

A one-on-one interaction was fixed for the afternoon of 10 November 1659. Several terms were mutually agreed in advance. Afzal Khan would come, fully armed, in a palanquin to the pavilion that Shivaji would build on the flattish clump beneath Pratapgad. He could bring two or three guards with him. Shivaji too was permitted to carry arms and to bring the same number of guards. He would descend from the fort and extend a warm welcome to Afzal Khan, with gifts. Shivaji and Afzal Khan could each be accompanied by not more than ten of their courageous and trusted soldiers who would keep vigil at the distance of the shot of an arrow. Once both sides were thus properly primed and secure, the two chieftains would have a private conversation.[28] That was the plan, on paper.

Closer to the day of the meeting, Shivaji summoned his military contingents from the Ghats and the Konkan and asked them to stealthily enter the jungles on either side and stay there in a state of high readiness. He said Afzal Khan's army must have absolutely no inkling of their movements or their presence, a task not too hard for the Mavale who were adept at quietly moving in the mountains and keeping below the radar until they could spring a surprise. If there was a stirring in the forest, the explanation was easy: there were too many beasts of prey lurking there, and it could be a tiger, lion, bear or pig.[29] It was best not to check.

Shivaji made yet another smart move before the meeting. Afzal Khan's best generals – Muse Khan, Ankush Khan, Yaqut Khan, Hasan Khan and even Mambaji Bhosle, who happened to be a cousin of Shahaji's – were with him on the banks of the Koyna. Surely the Khan himself and all of them deserved lavish gifts? Knowing from his spies that Afzal Khan's entourage included plenty of jewellers who had carried their wares to do business en route, Shivaji sent a request to the Khan: could he please send them all up to Pratapgad, so that he could buy their best ornaments to present to the Bijapur eminences? Afzal Khan sent them with alacrity, and Shivaji, to prove his sincerity about buying the gifts, not only bought their best wares but asked the jewellers to stay back as his guests in the fort.

There was great concern in the Maratha camp, and in Jijabai's mind and the minds of Shivaji's council members in particular. They well remembered Afzal Khan's other encounters. Jijabai was with the two-year-old Sambhaji at Rajgad, and her anxiety was greater on account of the distance. Shivaji himself was acutely aware of the jeopardy he was facing. On the eve of 10 November, he held a meeting of his senior council members and told them that if he met with success, all would be well, of course. All the same, he said, he had to give them instructions on how the affairs of state had to be run and managed if he were killed. To his soldiers lurking in the forest's depths, his words were concise: 'If, in spite of himself agreeing to a pact, Afzal Khan doesn't stick to his word, I will order the horns to be blown. If you hear them, destroy his army.'[30] Legend has it that Shivaji that night had a dream in which Goddess Bhavani appeared and assured him of success, that she then entered his Bhavani sword so as to imbue it with her own incredible strength.[31] That legend has morphed into a version in which the goddess herself handed over the Bhavani sword to Shivaji in his dream. As noted earlier, it was bought from the Sawant of Wadi.

From the top of Pratapgad fort, the *shamiana* put up for the meeting looked resplendent on the morning of 10 November 1659. It had a 'richly decorated canopy', its carpets were magnificent, and the cushions and other furnishings matched the importance of the visitor. Shivaji prepared himself carefully after having bowed to the sun god in the morning and prayed to Goddess Bhavani. After a light lunch in the afternoon, he put on a white tunic with a sprinkling of saffron. Inside was a coat of mail. Beneath his embroidered turban was a steel cap, and he carried with him a *bichwa* (scorpion), a sharp, curved dagger so named because it resembled the arachnid. According to some sources, the *bichwa* was hidden up his right sleeve; according to others, he held it in his right hand; and according to still other sources, it was pressed against his belt.[32] In his left hand he clasped the *wagh-nakh* (tiger claws), a set of steel claws small enough to be concealed from view. Apart from the ten armed men who were allowed to be an arrow-shot away, he would be accompanied by two companions: Jiva Mahala, a skilled swordsman, and Sambhaji Kavji, who had previously killed one of the Mores of Jaawali. Each of the two aides had with him a *patta* (a non-curved sword), a *firang* – a sword of foreign make – and a shield.[33]

When Afzal Khan started off for the rendezvous, he was accompanied by a thousand swordsmen and musketeers. Shivaji's envoy Pantaji Pant Bokil, who was with the Khan, understood instantly what was happening. He went up to the Khan immediately and asked him not to take so many military men along when the agreement had stated that neither should bring along a fighting unit. Pantaji argued that if Afzal Khan insisted on having so many armed men, Shivaji, who was anyway worried about meeting such a fear-inducing military general, would 'head back to the fort and the meeting will not take place'.[34] So Afzal Khan kept them all back and took with him ten trusted aides who would stay at the agreed-upon distance and three companions who'd be nearer him. Two of those companions were arms bearers, and the third was his envoy, Krishnaji Bhaskar Kulkarni.

Once he got the news that Afzal Khan had reached the pavilion, Shivaji started his walk down the fort. As the two eventually caught sight of each other, they exchanged smiles. Advancing further, Shivaji entered the *shamiana* and mounted the raised platform where Afzal Khan stood, their aides stationed inside the tent on either side now. Afzal Khan opened his arms for an embrace, and Shivaji accepted it, the difference in height between the two palpable: Shivaji was a head shorter. The embrace suddenly felt uncomfortable to Shivaji, for Afzal Khan had in a split second held him around the neck in a tight grip; then, he had drawn his 'straight-bladed dagger' with his right hand and struck him on the side. Though taken by surprise, Shivaji reacted very swiftly, putting his left arm round the Khan's waist and tearing out his intestines with the *wagh-nakh*. With his right hand he struck the *bichwa* into Afzal Khan's side, and as the Khan staggered and screamed, 'He's struck me, kill him at once!' Shivaji stepped back from the platform.

First Afzal Khan's envoy, Kulkarni, was upon him with a sword, and Shivaji parried the attack from the fellow Maharashtrian. The next moment, all of Afzal Khan's aides, the two companions as well as the armed men at a distance, charged forward. Among them was Sayyid Banda, an expert swordsman. He was killed by Jiva Mahala before he could attack Shivaji. A chaotic confrontation ensued. According to one version, Afzal Khan's head was chopped off by Shivaji with his sword. According to another, the lurching Khan was taken out of the tent by some of his guards and placed in a palanquin, with Shivaji's men giving chase instantly. Shivaji's soldiers first slashed the legs of the palanquin bearers and then cut off Afzal Khan's head. Either way, Afzal Khan's men, highly capable fighters no doubt, were clearly stupefied by what had just happened. The Maratha soldiers quickly killed most of them, one after the other: Afzal's nephew Rahim Khan, Abdul Sayyid, Bada Sayyid, two Maratha Hindus, Pilaji and Shankaraji Mohite, Kulkarni and four other Muslims. The assailants – the members of Shivaji's armed guard – were, apart from Jiva Mahala and Sambhaji Kavji, Kataji Ingle, Kondaji and Yesaji Kank, Krishnaji Gaikwad, Surji Katke, Visaji Murumbak, Sambhaji Karwar and Ibrahim Siddi, the last of them an Abyssinian Muslim.

Soon enough, the horns sounded from the head of the fort, and as Afzal Khan's men, waiting in their camps, wondered what was going on, the Mavale emerged from the jungles from all sides, falling upon them with unconcealed fury. Not surprisingly, there was total panic. While some of the Adil Shahi soldiers attempted to flee, several recovered from the initial shock and put up a brave defence, but they were surrounded and at a disadvantage in hostile terrain. It was a bloody massacre. According to a report that reached the Rajapur factory of the English, 3,000 men were killed. 'All (those) who begged quarters holding grass between their teeth [indicating surrender] were spared, the rest were put to the sword.'[35] Prataprao More managed to escape and guided some others who were escaping on the way out of Jaawali. Among those who went with him were Muse Khan, Hasan Khan, Yaqut Khan and Afzal Khan's older son, Fazl Khan. Shahaji's cousin Mambaji Bhosle was among those slaughtered on the Bijapur side, and several others, such as two of Afzal Khan's younger sons, and Ranadulla Khan (Junior), Ambar Khan and Zunzarrao Ghatge, were taken into custody.

The booty that fell into the lap of Shivaji's men, from Jaawali as well as Wai, was massive: apart from all the arms, artillery, tents and other infrastructure for a moving army, they seized 4,000 horses, 1,200 camels, 65 elephants, 2,000 bundles of clothing and ten lakh rupees in cash and jewellery.

Shivaji carried out a detailed assessment of the damage beneath Pratapgad and ordered all the captured men to be freed and sent back to their homes 'with money, food and other gifts'.[36] He announced pensions for the widows of the Mavale who had died in the battle and monetary rewards of 25 to 200 *hons* for those of his men who had been wounded, depending on the seriousness of their injuries. If any of the Marathas who died had sons who were grown up, they were recruited into the army; and the fighters who had excelled were given handsome rewards.

In the cold aftermath of the Adil Shahi force's defeat, Khandoji Khopde was among the escapees who approached Shivaji. He had betrayed Shivaji, no doubt, but Shivaji's trusted aide, Kanhoji Jedhe, put in a word for the apparently remorseful Khopde, and he was reluctantly accepted back by Shivaji. But not for long. When he began occasionally going up to Shivaji on his own, Shivaji, on seeing him around one day, summoned his aides and ordered Khopde's right hand and left leg to be chopped off. Kanhoji Jedhe was most upset and remonstrated with Shivaji; he asked him what had been the value of his own intercession then. Shivaji told him, 'I spared Khopde's life only because you intervened. I have only cut off the hand that held the sword against me and the leg that carried him to the enemy. I haven't deprived him of his *watan* [land grant]; I will continue it.'[37] Almost 400 years after this incident, the name 'Khandoji Khopde' is still a synonym for betrayal in Maharashtra.

The outcome of the encounter with Afzal Khan was a pivotal moment in the life of Shivaji and the state he was seeking to build. Given Afzal Khan's record and his openly stated motive of going in for the kill, the setting, the situation and the stakes were such that only one of them could have survived.[38] Shivaji out-thought, outplanned and outmanoeuvred the formidable Adil Shahi commander, drawing him intelligently first into the heart of Jaawali and later on to Pratapgad, and Shivaji's military decimated Bijapur's sizeable troops by making the fullest use of its strategic advantage. As a result, Shivaji's name entered the consciousness of all the powers, indigenous and foreign, across the subcontinent, making the Marathas feel that mounting a major challenge to bigger and far more established rulers was possible, if their leadership, strategy and teamwork held. But this dramatic and highly charged moment under their inspiring captain also meant that the challenges to the Marathas were going to swell further, and that increasingly forceful attempts would be made to stamp out Shivaji's emerging power before it could strike deeper roots.

5

Narrow Escapes and British Prisoners

It would not have been surprising if Afzal Khan's death had left both the Adil Shah and the Mughals stupefied by Shivaji's exploits. A world in which the twenty-nine-year-old son of a *jagirdar* from a corner of the Deccan had raided their domains with impunity, and had just pulled out the entrails of a legendary general, must have seemed truly bizarre.

The best course was to fight this 'menace' together and squash him, and that's what they eventually decided. If the Adil Shah and Begum Badi Sahiba, reeling from the shock of the Afzal episode, wanted to retaliate swiftly, Aurangzeb, too, finally secure on the Mughal throne, was itching to get back at Shivaji for daring to raid Mughal-ruled Junnar and parts of Ahmadnagar. Dots they might be on the map, but they belonged to a mighty empire.

Shivaji, in anticipation of this tie-up, and because he wanted to act while Bijapur was still in shock, did not let the grass grow under his feet after Afzal Khan's death. Barely a fortnight later, he went deeper into Bijapuri territory, taking the fort of Panhalgad or Panhala near Kolhapur, the kingdom's western headquarters, and forts around it. One of these, Khelna, was named Vishalgad by Shivaji, a name that would, as we will soon see, come to carry tremendous resonance in Maratha history. Shivaji also sent his cavalry chief Netaji Palkar to Raibag, Gadag and Lakshmeshwar – all in present-day Karnataka – on a raid. He returned with plenty of booty.

Meanwhile, an Abyssinian apparatchik in Bijapur named Siddi Jauhar saw a chance to rise. Though he was the chief of the province of Karnool in modern-day Andhra Pradesh, the court mistrusted Jauhar, regarding him as self-serving and not particularly loyal. Sensing an opportunity to restore some trust in himself, Jauhar sought the sultan's approval to march against the rebel Shivaji, and Adil Shah, eager to damage Shivaji in any way possible, gave him 15,000 troops. Before long, Jauhar and his men had surrounded Panhala, whose loss had infuriated the Adil Shah. Shivaji, who was at Rajgad, near Pune, swiftly made a 200-kilometre dash to Panhala on horseback. If Jauhar was going to target Panhala, then Shivaji wanted to be right there at the spot and lead his men from the front. This he had done all along, whether in capturing his first four forts in the Deccan hills, in attacking Jaawali, in raiding Mughal-dominated Junnar, and in taking on Afzal Khan. Planting his feet into the flanks of his horse and charging at the head of a few hundred men to Panhala was once again a measure of his personal sense of daring.

There, he found himself well and truly under siege. Jauhar turned out to be a first-rate besieger, leaving no window open, no corner unattended. He also enlisted the support of several underlings, among them Afzal Khan's son, Fazl, evidently anxious to crush Shivaji, the Marathas Baji Ghorpade and the Sawant of Wadi, ever shifting sides depending on where their advantage was; there were also the Siddis of Janjira, who recognized Shivaji as a threat.

As Jauhar's men encircled Panhala, Shivaji's principal hope was that the siege would lift automatically with the arrival of the monsoon in June 1660. To the surprise of the Marathas, it did not. As the rain poured, Jauhar's tents and covers, strong enough to withstand its fury, carried the day, along with a supply system the Marathas could not disrupt. It was they, rather, who were facing problems getting provisions into the fort. Netaji Palkar, launching attacks in vain from the outside on the Bijapur troops' in-coming supplies,[1] had to face the embarrassment of being scolded by Jijabai when he headed back to Rajgad.

Jijabai was 'filled with anger', writes Parmanand, but when she spoke to Netaji Palkar and Siddi Hilal, a general accompanying him, her tone was nevertheless 'soft and serious'. Without exploding, she told them in a calm but determined tone that her 'life' – meaning Shivaji – was under siege, and she would now herself head to Panhala and 'bring back Jauhar's head', because both Netaji and Hilal had 'surprisingly given up all shame' and, instead of fighting for their leader, had 'simply found their way back to Rajgad'. Both offered the materfamilias their deepest apologies and returned to the place of the siege, where Wahwah, the 'angry, proud and powerful' son of Siddi Hilal, known for his 'remarkably big and red eyes', fought valiantly but ended up being trapped by Jauhar's men. Felled from his horse, an unconscious Wahwah, 'his bow broken and body riddled with blows', was carried off by Jauhar's men to their camp. The sight destroyed the morale of Hilal's men. Netaji too was beaten back.[2]

Enter the Mughals. They were now moving inwards from the northern end of the Maratha frontiers. Aurangzeb's hand-picked general, his own maternal uncle, Shaista Khan, was leading the troops. Of Persian origin, Shaista Khan was the nephew of Jahangir's queen Nur Jahan and an accomplished military man in his own right. He had served earlier as governor of Malwa and contributed substantively to Aurangzeb's recent onslaught against Golconda. In July 1659, as Shivaji was grappling with the threat posed by Afzal Khan, Aurangzeb had appointed Shaista Khan governor of the Deccan. His base was Ahmadnagar, and from there he set out in February 1660 for Pune. He didn't go in the normal, straight south-west line to that hamlet in which Shivaji had spent his teens. He drew a curve, first going south, capturing fort after fort in Supe, Baramati and other spots, and keeping detachments in all these places so the route of the Marathas would be blocked, before turning to Pune. His forward march went largely unopposed, and in a couple of places where it met resistance, the Marathas were forced to retreat.

When Shaista Khan reached Pune in May 1660, he realized the Marathas had, adopting a scorched earth policy, destroyed grain and fodder in and around the *kasba*, and asked its residents to flee. The many rivers around Pune would be in spate through the monsoon, so getting food and supplies from Mughal lands, which lay across the waters, was going to be hard. Thus, in mid-June, Shaista Khan moved his camp for the rains to Chakan, about 28 kilometres north of Pune. This way, he'd still be in command, and his troops would face few rain-related difficulties, with the troublesome, raging river waters that could disturb the supply chain at some distance.

Trapped inside the fort of Panhala, Shivaji felt his options shrinking. But one day, to his surprise, he saw an unusual sight. Rocky Panhala was neither as imposing nor as broad as Rajgad or Raigad, and from inside the fort, it was possible to see the ground below. So, Shivaji was watching when a new lot of mortars and shells rolled up one morning. This ammunition was carried by white-skinned men in lengthy, full-sleeved red jackets buttoned up almost to their chins, in defiance of the sultry weather. Leading the men – from the East India Company, notorious for its rapacity – was Henry Revington, the head of the British factory at Rajapur. He had spotted a chance to sell the Company's mortars and shells to Siddi Jauhar for the Panhala siege, and the Rajapur factory's officials recorded diligently that he received 'a most courteous and noble reception unto the camp of said generall, Syddy Jore'. 'Jore' had sent a team to 'Collapore' to bring Revington to his camp, rolling out the red carpet as it were with a 'pallanken', a horse and 'around 100 persons with an ellephant'.[3]

While Shivaji was seeing the Company's men for the first time, his forces had already had a brush with them. A few months before, the governors of Dabhol and Rajapur (local chieftains whose names are not known) had taken refuge at the Rajapur factory, while the Marathas were pursuing them to seize three junks – sizeable, flat-bottomed boats with squarish sails – belonging to Afzal Khan, after his death. The Marathas asked the British, who had themselves been trying to recover some dues from the governors, to hand over the junks and the governors to them, and the Company's officials refused.[4] They said they couldn't hand over the governors to the Marathas for reasons of faith. 'Wee denyed,' the Company's Rajapur officials wrote, 'being not consistent with our religion to deliver up any man to his enemy that comes under our protection.'[5] The Dabhol and Rajapur governors then requested the British to take over the junks; they claimed one that weighed 300 tonnes and renamed it the *Rajapore Merchant*, telling the governors that 'wee would (maintain) possession of her till the rest of the mony was paid'.[6]

Shivaji's official at Rajapur at once demanded that the British hand over the *Rajapore Merchant*, which they refused to do until their dues were paid. Shivaji's angry men then detained the British broker in Rajapur, Velji, and a local trader named Vagji.[7] The British sent out a warning to the Marathas that they would 'fire the town [of Rajapur, which was now with Shivaji, though the port and waters weren't] about them, if they delivered us not our broker'. But the Marathas whisked Velji and the local trader up a hill and beyond, forcing the British to send one of their officials, Phillip Gyffard, for talks. The audacious Marathas refused to negotiate with Gyffard; they detained him as well along with the other two.

The matter was serious enough for Revington, the head of the Rajapur factory, to write a letter to the Company's Council at Surat to seek advice on whether the Company should give away the junks in exchange for the freedom of its men. Interestingly, 'Sevagy' (Shivaji) comes off very well in this letter. Revington wrote that the Marathas could keep Gyffard and the two others as prisoners 'so long as wee cann have a letter carried to there master Sevagy, who is so great and noble a person as wee beleive hee will never maintaine this action of detenying any of us upon so unreasonable (an) accompt (account)'.[8] Subsequently, the British officials of Rajapur sent a letter addressed to 'Sevagy, Generall of the Hendoo Forces', urging him to release their officials and naming one of Shivaji's men, 'Dorogy', as the man who had effected the arrests and because of whom they had suffered.[9] Velgi was subsequently released by the Marathas after twenty-five days and Gyffard and the local trader after more than a month, and there the matter ended for the moment.

Shivaji, when news of the episode reached him, was not pleased that the Company's men had not handed over the junk to the Marathas. And here they were suddenly at the foot of Panhala, inexplicably propping up Jauhar. Shivaji found this gratuitous meddling in his fight with Bijapur infuriating. But he could deal with all of that later. The vital thing for him was to find a way out of the encirclement as soon as possible. But how? All exit routes were sealed, and Jauhar had set up checkpoints on every side.

Narrow Escapes and British Prisoners

Shivaji had never had any problem in writing letters of submission while at the same time nursing in his bosom the deep desire and sturdy resolve to be free. On this occasion, too, he decided to write to Siddi Jauhar accepting submission and surrender. He said he would hand over Panhala to Jauhar and not cross swords with Bijapur. This might seem like an echo of his note to Afzal Khan, but the situation was very different. Shivaji had been under siege for four months, and was looking for a way. However, as always, he was also strategizing. He was hoping that Jauhar's patrols would slacken, and they did, a little, on hearing the news. It was only natural that they should, after being on alert for months.

Shivaji made up his mind to try and make his escape. His personal courage, demonstrated earlier on so many occasions, came into play again. Shying away from a life-threatening risk was not his style. He relied tremendously on his own initiative, on charting a path of intrepid, clear-eyed action for his associates and followers. He had been squeezed into one place for too long already, and the supplies were fast drying up. Leaving an escape bid for too late might make the attempt itself altogether futile, he believed; if that happened, the siege would remain, the provisions would wither away, and the morale of his supporters might drop to the point of preventing any possible fightback or rearguard action on their part. There was such a thing as acting *in time*, and the time was now – or it could well be never. Taking on established sultanates was itself a gargantuan risk, and he would be wiped out if he continued to be inside the confines of Panhala much longer. He was convinced that leave he must, and in such a way that he could spring one of his eye-popping surprises and declare his own, and his men's, superb efficacy in turning the tables on the opponents. One of the attributes of his personality and leadership was that all his risk-taking was married to resolute self-belief – a belief in himself, his people and his destiny. With that self-belief, he proceeded to put a daring plan into action.

The next day, 13 July 1660, Shivaji and his men waited for the sun to go down. Once darkness had set in and it had started to drizzle, Shivaji began his stealthy descent from the fort, on foot, with 600 of his Mavale compatriots. Riding on horseback would have given away the game.

Nature favoured him, with the showers getting more intense within minutes: though the ground was squelchy and slippery, and stepping into puddles could result in a dangerously audible plop-plop, it also meant that those patrolling the many checkpoints would be seeking cover and perhaps be a little less agile than otherwise. In an especially tense moment, Shivaji and his Marathas slipped past a corner near a checkpoint on the western end, which his highly reliable spies had already identified as being the most vulnerable. Once past it, they briskly picked up pace. They really had no choice. The fortress of Khelna was a good 43 kilometres away, and it was going to take many, many hours for them to get there on foot.

Shivaji wasn't walking. He was seated in a palanquin, and men took turns carrying him through the slush. The reasoning was that identification of the leader would be easy in the dark if he were in a palanquin and if it came to a skirmish with the rivals. Knowing where the leader was would help the followers draw a ring of security around him if there was any trouble and also not expose him to a one-on-one fight with anyone from the rival camp. It was a tense journey. The Marathas needed to cover enough distance for Bijapur's cavalry to have to struggle to catch up with them when their escape became known. Even if a third of Jauhar's 15,000 men came galloping to them too soon, 600 Marathas, despite being fully armed, would be no match.

As it happened, a couple of Jauhar's scouts did catch sight of the Marathas, and as soon as the information was received back in Jauhar's camp, an impetuous and hot chase was launched, with Jauhar and Afzal Khan's son Fazl at the head of the Bijapur troops astride their horses. The Marathas were intercepted close to the pass of Ghodkhind, and a violent fight began. In the melee, the Marathas took a swift decision: Shivaji would start moving forward in the direction of Khelna, while a decent-sized Maratha squad tried to block the enemy on this very narrow pass. Most of the men who stayed back at the pass were part of the Bandal *deshmukh*'s contingent, and their helmsman was Baji Prabhu Deshpande. He was probably in his early forties, and in some books and in popular imagination he has been pictured as a bald, moustachioed man with a round face and a tuft of hair at the back, as affected by Brahmins, though he in fact belonged to a community called Chandraseniya Kayastha Prabhu, known as the caste of scribes. Another set of images depicts him as lean-faced, wearing a small *pagdi*, and sporting a Hercule Poirot–like moustache, with a gentle, trust-me smile playing on his lips.

For hours, as the Bijapur forces dashed against the Marathas, Baji Prabhu and his band held their ground, taking blows more severe than the rain that now fell in buckets. In the course of his heroic resistance, Baji was attacked, was grievously injured and died. In many tellings of this story, he is said to have lain down on the ground, blood streaming down his forehead, staying alive only until he heard the booming of guns from the fort of Khela, which showed Shivaji had finally and safely reached his destination.[10] In popular accounts, soldiers of the Adil Shahi are shown whirling around Baji Prabhu and fighting him from all sides. He's a man possessed and unfazed. He almost circles around fearlessly, taking them all on, his sword clashing against so enemy swords. The sounds of the clanging swords envelop the entire narrow pass and its surroundings, penetrated occasionally by a massive roar that Baji Prabhu lets out in his display of resistance. Soon the little streams running through the pass and the rocks there, big and small, are drenched in blood – the blood of Adil Shahi soldiers, and also the blood of Baji Prabhu who, for all his superlative effort, is suffering a hundred cuts but still standing tall, like a one-man impenetrable army. The truth is that there is no denying that the Marathas built a veritable wall to beat back wave after wave of the Adil Shahi troops on that slender pass in the mountains and gave their leader safe passage.

From the fort of Khelna, Shivaji soon proceeded to Rajgad to see his anxious mother. Parmanand notes that 'a flood of tears flowed from Jijabai's eyes', and Shivaji spent the entire day with her, giving her a detailed account of what had happened.[11] There was so much to tell about those four months in which he had found himself trapped inside Panhala, his daring escape, his 40-kilometre run to safety, and Baji Prabhu and his team's remarkable resilience in the face of the massive onslaught.

Shivaji's escape under cover of darkness was deeply embarrassing and humiliating for Siddi Jauhar, who was all but certain he had his man. Equally worrying for Shivaji's rivals was the indomitable spirit shown by Baji Prabhu and his team. It was proof that things were changing for the sultanates of the Deccan. Shivaji had, with his personality and keen leadership, changed the mindset of the local people. He had imbued them with a sense of Maratha pride, and was stirring them to acts of extraordinary courage and sacrifice, acts that might have been deemed inconceivable just a couple of decades ago, given their low-key presence in the increasingly Islamicized states. The Marathas had earlier risen in military service in the various sultanates, but always as slaves, and they were always denied the very top posts, no matter how able they were. As noted earlier, Bijapur had even put it in writing that the high posts were not to be given to non-Muslims, and the Mughals had never granted any of the highly prized posts to a Maratha. Shivaji had roused in the Marathas a desire to be their own people controlling their own destinies and challenging a political order that had ensured that they did nothing but the sultan's bidding. The Marathas were no longer accepting of the status quo, no longer reconciled to duties under a sultan or a Badshah.

Further evidence of their evolving mindset under Shivaji's leadership was provided by the challenge to Shaista Khan from within the confines of the minor fortress of Chakan. Having moved, as we have seen earlier, to Chakan for the monsoon season, Shaista Khan thought he'd take the relatively weak fortress quite easily. His men pounded it with big pieces of Mughal artillery, but the Marathas, led by their doughty commander Firangoji Narsala, held on for fifty-four days, forcing the Mughals to carry a mine under one of the towers on the afternoon of 14 August 1660. The mine's blast stunned the defenders, blowing various Maratha soldiers to bits, and created a wide opening, only for the Mughals to discover that behind those lines the Marathas had built a mini-mountain of earth, which they used effectively as a shield to strike at the attackers with 'rockets, musket-shots, bombs and stones'.[12] Thrusting ramrods into the barrels of their muskets, the defenders prepared to fight and fire afresh after every little setback. It took close to twenty hours even after the mine explosion for the Mughals to evict the defending Marathas. Given how absolutely inconsequential the fortress was, the casualties for Shaista Khan's side were far too many: 268 killed and 600 injured.[13]

The Mughals had another disquieting experience. One of the reasons Shaista Khan had moved to Pune and Chakan was his realization that Shivaji's northern dominions were vulnerable while he was occupied near Panhala. Shaista Khan asked one of his generals, Salabat Khan, to occupy the port of Kalyan near Mumbai and instructed the experienced Deccan campaigner Kartalab Khan, who had recently successfully attacked the Qutub Shahi's Parenda, to assume control of the broader northern Konkan, which stood totally exposed.

To go there, Kartalab Khan's men and women had to descend from the Sahyadris, and along the path downward lay Umbarkhind, a narrower pass than Ghodkhind, near Bor Ghat in the vicinity of Lonavla. Shivaji instructed his cavalry not to obstruct the enemy's passage until Kartalab Khan's unit had entered and filled the Umbarkhind pass completely, from its front end to the rear. The path was so horribly constricted that two soldiers could barely walk side by side, and taking elephants and artillery through was particularly onerous. But the Mughal force wasn't unduly worried; there was utter quiet in the woods, and no enemy anywhere in sight. Suddenly, when Kartalab's men had least expected it, there was an eerie rustling in the trees on both sides, and the Marathas appeared as if out of nowhere, showering arrows and firing their muskets. Taken aback, the Mughal side and its leaders fought valiantly, but the Marathas pounded their positions and made flight impossible. Amid the frenzied fighting, the earth turned a flaming red in the blood of the dead and the wounded. Almost as a symbol of the existential threat confronting Kartalab's unit, there appeared Shivaji astride his horse, surveying the chaotic scenes.

Veering close to collapse and with fatalities rapidly ticking up, Kartalab's side concluded it had to save itself from being steamrollered. Among Kartalab's soldiers who had fought quite boldly until that moment was a Maharashtrian woman mounted on her own horse. She was the wife of the deceased ruler of Berar's Mahur province, and she had been given the title of 'Rai Bagan' or 'royal tigress' by Aurangzeb for her battlefield exploits. Rai Bagan's real name was Savitri. Her husband, Udaji Ram, had held the *jagir* of several places in Berar and had been loyal in his service to the Mughals. When he died in the first half of the 1630s, the Mughals continued the *jagir* in his then minor son's name, but the son too died in 1658. Savitri's grandson, Baburao, was too small to carry out the *jagirdar* responsibilities, so she took it upon herself to run its affairs. The Mughals had for long held undisturbed sway in the Berar region, but after Aurangzeb's ascension to power, a local chieftain named Harchand Rai proved to be something of an irritant, and news reached Aurangzeb that he was quite recalcitrant. When Aurangzeb issued orders to the local *jagir* holder to put down the rebellion, Savitri picked up the sword herself and led Mahur's soldiers against Harchand Rai. Her march was successful; defeating the rebel, Savitri restored complete Mughal rule in those parts, prompting Aurangzeb to bestow the title of 'Rai Bagan' on her.[14]

According to Parmanand's account, it was Rai Bagan who spoke for all her fellow soldiers in the midst of the Umbarkhind carnage, advising Kartalab that the Mughal army had better wave the white flag to escape what she described as 'the jaws of death'.[15] By the time this conversation took place amid the crisis, the Mughal soldiers were also struggling with an acute scarcity of water. According to Parmanand, Rai Bagan said to the leader of her unit, Kartalab Khan:

> The army was put into your care, but you behaved wrongly and thoughtlessly in entering this forest, the lair of that lion, Shivaji ... The enemy wants to take you alive and carry you away. You, like a blind man, have been caught in this forest and still want to fight. A man should show his prowess only if there is a possibility of success; otherwise, what he does qualifies as rashness, and it brings on ridicule. So now surrender immediately to that chief [Shivaji], and save yourself and the army.[16]

Hearing this, Kartalab immediately sent off an envoy to Shivaji, who, says Parmanand, was wearing his armour including a helmet, and holding a long spear in his right hand. Against Shivaji's waist was a sword in its scabbard, hanging by a golden belt; against his sash was tied a large shield; and he had, besides, a bow and arrow close at hand.[17] Begging to be let off, Kartalab Khan suddenly invoked his apparent closeness to Shahaji Raje and agreed to hand over everything to Shivaji.[18] Hundreds of swords, spears, shields and other armour were surrendered by his soldiers; the elephants and the horses were given away as well, along with other property. All this for safe passage.

Shivaji had bounced back with a vengeance after tasting the depths of despair at Panhala. He saw a window of opportunity in the southern Konkan and felt the momentum now gathered could help him there. The Marathas easily took the ports and major trading stations Dabhol and Rajapur, which meant they'd get a share of the revenue generated from goods going inland and outward. Kudal and Sangameshwar too were captured, and Goa seemed just a gallop away. Bijapur's governor of the southern Konkan, Rustam-i-Zaman, gave up almost without a fight. This meant Shivaji now had under him almost the full Konkan stretch from Bassein to Goa's borders; going inland, his domain covered the major part of the Sahyadris, which, of course, was under attack at that moment from Shaista Khan.

On capturing Sangameshwar, Shivaji assigned the task of guarding it to Tanaji Malusare, among the most trusted of his lieutenants, and himself proceeded further south. However, Malusare came under serious attack from Surya Rao Surve, the local ruler of Shringarpur which was part of that region. When Shivaji heard of this, he returned immediately. He had a score to settle with Surve of Shringarpur. In the past, this local ruler had played a double game, helping Bijapur when he saw it expedient to do so and at times pretending he was with Shivaji. Notably, Surve had sided with the Mores of Jaawali during Shivaji's crucial battles with them. Reports of Shivaji marching back reached Surve, and he fled his own province in sheer fright, enabling Shivaji to reclaim Sangameshwar without a fresh bout of confrontation. Soon Surve was petitioning Shivaji. He was keen to surrender and to be in Shivaji's service, he said. Shivaji, initially bent on reprisal, accepted him without reserve, to Surve's surprise. Perhaps Shivaji's anger against the man had been satiated by his very first act on entering Surve's residence in his absence. Surve had at the time made a throne-like fancy seating arrangement for himself in his fief, where he was in the habit of receiving visitors. Shivaji had taken one look at it and, ferocity in his eyes, kicked it to the ground in a display of high indignation. Along with the extravagant chair, the anger too had gone.[19]

However, Shivaji had not forgotten the sight of the British East India Company rolling in grenades during the siege of Panhala, or the saga of Afzal Khan's junks. After subduing Surve, he entered Rajapur, where it had all played out, and where the Company's factory was located, and decided both to penalize the Englishmen there and to assert his dominance over the town, which according to *Shivabharat* was 'a wealthy emporium', with 'the merchandise of Arabia, Persia, Egypt, Africa, China, Europe … imported there for sale'.[20]

Shivaji promptly asked the English officials in Rajapur to call on him, and the moment they did so, he ordered that they be placed in fetters. In all, eight British men were arrested, among them Henry Revington, the factory's chief official, Randolph Taylor, another official who was slated to succeed Revington as head of the factory, a medical surgeon named Robert Ward, and Phillip Gyffard, who had previously been detained by the Marathas for over a month during the affair of the junks. The Dutch, who had their base in Vengurla nearby, recorded that the British East India Company's Rajapur factory was 'entirely stripped' by Shivaji's men, 'even the floor being dug up in search of hidden treasure'.[21] Pointing to the reasons behind Shivaji's actions, the Dutch noted that the British had 'received no compensation for the munitions of war which they lent to the King of Bijapur for use against Shivaji, but they have suffered great damage from that rebel on their account'.[22] The Marathas, they added, 'also plundered many foreign merchants, who yearly bring goods to Rajapur from Persia and Muskat'.[23]

The British East India Company was at the time a nascent power and far from being the force it eventually became in the eighteenth century. Though Jahangir had given it permission in 1618 to build a trading station or factory in Surat, it was only eight years later that it established its first fortified hub on the Coromandel coast; that, too, had been wound up by 1632. The Madras settlement came up soon thereafter, becoming a major centre, and so did Rajapur and other trading stations, though Surat remained the heart of its operations along the western coast. When the British prisoners of the Marathas were moved inside the Rairi fort in 1662, Charles II got the island of Bombay as a dowry gift from the Portuguese, but so obscure was this island that for some time the East India Company's officials in London were wondering where exactly it was, some even making the guess that it was 'somewhere near Brazil'.[24] Hardly anyone would have realized in the 1660s that the Portuguese and Dutch powers would lose their might almost completely in the future and the British East India Company would become the predatory global corporation that it turned out to be.

Some of the arrested British officials were confined by the Marathas inside the fort of Songad near Pen in the Konkan and the others at the fort of Wasota, a little further inland. Shivaji directed one of his officials, Raoji Somnath, to take charge of Rajapur's affairs and to watch over the captured Company officials. Soon Raoji Somnath communicated to the arrested men that they would be released if the British agreed to assist Shivaji in his campaign against the Siddis of Janjira.[25] Their immediate answer was that the Company would offer no such assistance, but as time went by and it became increasingly clear that liberty would not be so easily obtained, they began to dangle the carrot of possible support in this regard.

The British, led by Revington, wrote to their Surat Council, suggesting specific 'proposals' they should make to Shivaji. First, Shivaji 'should grant the prisoners their liberty, and restore what has been taken from them'.[26] If both things were not possible, he must restore 'at least our liberty', they emphasized. The British would back his campaign against Janjira, and he should pay for the English ships assisting the Marathas there. The Company should charge more for the ships than he'd be willing to pay, perhaps '10,000 pagodas for each of four ships', and demand all the money in advance. In short, a bait should be put out but difficult demands made so Shivaji himself would back off.

Plus, Shivaji must give the Company 'a convenient port town, with liberty to build a fort, he providing the labour and materials'. Shivaji's

'Braman at Rajapore' had promised the Company a 'handsome seat, called Meate Bunder, upon the coast'. *Meeth*, which the British wrote as 'Meate', is salt in Marathi; it suggests the offer was of a salt port. But Shivaji must also 'allow the English to receive half the customs revenue of that town, their own imports and exports being duty free'. And he must permit the British to establish a mint for silver coins and to buy saltpetre freely, apart from granting a warehouse in the port town he'd give.

There was every possibility that Shivaji wouldn't consent to any of this. 'Being a perfidious man himself', wrote the Englishmen, who had not too long ago praised him as 'noble', 'he may doubt whether the English will perform their promises, once he has released the prisoners. The answer should be that as the grant of a town (etcetra) is to be contingent on the English carrying out their contract, it would be more reasonable to expect security from him.'

And 'if he should be insolent', the imprisoned Englishmen observed, there were always threats that could be issued to him. They had already let it be known that if they weren't released, Surat officials would grant 'Oranzeebs [Aurangzeb's] desire in transporting an army into Decan'. So far they had desisted from doing so because they were friends with the Badi Sahiba of Bijapur, but now she too was deposed and gone. Another threat to be made was a British offer to help 'Shasta Ckaune' (Shaista Khan). The offer 'would be very acceptable to' the Khan 'and then Sevagi may be soon routed'.

One thing Revington and his co-prisoners were convinced about, and this they communicated to the Surat Council. The Janjira castle was 'the only aim' Shivaji had, and if he were persuaded to believe the word of the British, 'he would be real to us, therefore, whoever comes to him must make it his business to persuade him to believe us'.[27]

The Surat Council, in response to Revington's urging, wrote what it termed as 'many persuasive letters' to Shivaji for the release of the prisoners, 'yet they would not be taken notice of'.[28] Finally, the ill health of one official, following upon the death of another, changed things.

A month after the arrest of the eight British men, one of them, Richard Napier, had died. The Dutch *Batavia Dagh Register* recorded that he died of torture, but the British letters, which were not censored, make it evident that it was a natural death. Napier, according to British documents, 'came out of England a mellencholly [melancholy] person, and so continued'. He was 'dangerously ill, and not expected to live', and he passed away 'about a month since in Rajahpore', that is, before the English prisoners were moved out elsewhere.[29] Later that year, Revington himself fell gravely ill. From the start he appeared to have been uncomfortable at Songad and had begged to the Surat officials 'for some shirts, breeches, and cotton waistcoats', and also 'a small tooth comb, for among 170 prisoners he cannot himself so clean as he would do'.[30] (There were other prisoners lodged there too.) Around September or early October he came down with 'dropsey', which 'caused a feare of his death'.[31] He was let out by the Marathas along with his surgeon and returned to Surat, 'in a weake condition', on 17 October 1661; never recovering fully, he died in December that year.[32]

Shortly afterwards, the six British men who still remained imprisoned sent three desperate letters to the Surat officials, saying they should pay the Marathas whatever ransom they demanded and obtain their freedom. They did not get much sympathy.

In his reply of 10 March 1662, Andrews, president of the Surat Council, referred to the three letters and said the Council had its hands full with business and didn't want to spend time 'unnecessaryly in inditing and sending costly letters to a rogue that takes no notice of them'. Besides, the arrested officials seemed to have rubbed Surat the wrong way with some intemperate language. The Council chief referred to this with serious disapproval and underscored the fact that the prisoners had themselves to blame for their current predicament:

> How you came in prison you knowe very well. 'Twas not for defending Companies goods; 'twas for going to the Seige of Pannella and tossing balls with a flagg that was knowne to bee the Englishes ... It [Shivaji's action] was but as any other would doe, having power to revenge himself of such affronts; for marchants are not to sell their goods, when if of that nature as granadoes, to goe and shoote them off against an enemy; for

marchants while trading in a strainge country one may live quietly; if not, medling, must looke for a requitall of their deserts. Wee must tell you plainly that none but what rehearsed is the cause of your imprisonment; Mr Revington himself having mentioned the commands of Sevagee not to sell any.[33]

Despite this reproach, the president of the Surat Council did dispatch one letter to Shivaji and another to the Adil Shah of Bijapur, warning the captives simultaneously that if the ransom demanded were too big, 'wee have it not to spare'.[34] If the letters didn't work, it was proposed to 'employ force, by blockading the coast towns and seizing any vessels coming from Mokha or Persia'. It was pointed out that the queen of Bijapur, who had gone to Mecca, was set to return, 'and if it bee our good fortune to light on hir, surely the King will not faile to procure your release for hir'.[35] Shivaji still didn't send any reply, so on 21 July 1662 a consultation took place at Surat, and two British East India Company ships, the *Royal Welcome* and *Hopewell*, were instructed to go to Goa or some adjacent port for the monsoon and seize junks returning from Mokha. One of the ships, *Hopewell*, was advised 'to cruise off Rajapur and Kharepatan, while the other watched Vengurla, Dabhol, and the neighbouring harbours'. They were ordered to seize any ships belonging 'to any Decan people, either to the Kinge of Decan, Sevagy, or any marchants of the country'. The blockade should continue until 20 September, the ships' commanders were told, when both ships were to proceed to Karwar to fetch the pepper accumulated there. And a particular watch was to be kept for the 'Queen of Decan', who, if captured, was to be brought to 'Swally' (Suvali), with care taken to 'use hir with all the respect requisite to bee showed soe eminent a person'.[36]

Meanwhile, the English prisoners were moved by Shivaji's men to the fort of Rairi or Raigad. Neither the Badi Sahiba nor any ships of the Deccan were intercepted and seized by the Company's vessels. Negotiations with the Marathas dragged on for months, and Raoji Somnath, asked to supervise the captives, was himself away carrying out other responsibilities in Shivaji's other regions. He returned to Rairi on

17 January 1663, took the prisoners to Rajapur, and released them. The Surat Council, and the prisoners themselves, wanted reparations, but Shivaji wouldn't give any. What he did issue was a message carrying his seal. Read out to them at the time of their release in Rajapur, it said, 'Let us forget the past. We had on hand a war with Bijapur for which funds were needed, and so Rajapur had to suffer. We shall not repeat the affair.'[37]

Shivaji was responding to the British in a specific context, and in that context, as is unmistakable from the records available, he didn't budge an inch. He was hostile to the extent that the British would later remark that he saw them as inveterate enemies. But the Marathas naturally also looked at the British as traders whose business could yield the emerging Shivaji-led power decent tax and customs revenue as their goods moved back and forth. That is why Shivaji momentarily spoke of forgetting the past. The British East India Company too did not – barring the blockade idea – take any provocative action against the Marathas during this episode at least, despite the urgings of the imprisoned officials.

Though the Englishmen later restarted their trade at Rajapur, one of the officials sent to Surat an estimate of the losses the Rajapur factory had suffered. 'Shivaji's raid on Rajapur cost it in plunder the amount of 24,000 *hons*, the death of two persons and the detention of the factors for two years,' the official stated.[38] For long after the end of this episode, the British pressed Shivaji for reparations for the damages caused by the Maratha raid at Rajapur. He refused to yield beyond a point until the last, convinced he had done the right thing.

Some Maratha historians have cited this encounter with the British as proof of Shivaji having recognized right from the beginning the threat posed by the East India Company to the country, and its sinister motives. In popular fictional accounts, such as the play *Jaanta Raja*, Shivaji is shown ordering the imprisonment of the Englishmen at Rajapur and saying outright that 'these Englishmen say they are mere traders, but we need to be wary of them, because their real aim is conquest of the land'.

That's a classic case of reading history backwards. It is no one's contention that certain dangers were not apparent. For example, it was known to the Marathas, and indeed to other powers in the land, that the

English would want to have fortifications of their own. That was why, when the incarcerated British men told a Maratha official – whom they described simply as 'the Braman at Rajahpore' – that they should be released so they could offer some genuine help with the desired occupation of Janjira, his retort was that 'if we [the Englishmen] were not in his hands, our men would enter the [Janjira] Castle first, and keep it for themselves'.[39] Yet such fortifications were being built by all, and certainly by the Portuguese and the Dutch, who were much more powerful in that period than the British. And as mentioned earlier, Shivaji was looking at the British in a certain context.

Shivaji knew he would encounter the British East India Company again in the future, and also the other foreign powers such as the Dutch and the Portuguese. But that was if he could first somehow get the better of Aurangzeb's maternal uncle. That was going to be a significant challenge. Shaista Khan appeared to have got a firm grip on much of the Sahyadri belt and on the situation: he was already comfortably ensconced in the very home in which Shivaji had spent so many of his formative years.

6

The Nocturnal Strike

Shaista Khan, the *amir-ul-umra* and *subahdar* of the Deccan, was living the aristocratic life in Lal Mahal, Shivaji's own dwelling of his teenage years. Despite the 'Mahal' in its name, the single-storey house in Pune, with its straight-backed stone walls, was a nondescript and no-frills one. Shaista Khan and his attendants had turned it into as much of a picture of Mughal wealth as they possibly could. With the serious limitations of its Deccani plainness, though, they couldn't go very far, considering the very high levels of Mughal opulence, where white marble pavilions and canopies of gold were common.

Shaista Khan had got an open door leading to the kitchen covered completely, so that the sometimes overpowering trail of smells and the noise of the cooks did not breach the quiet cosiness of the inner chambers. In those chambers, he had got a number of bolsters placed, so that he could lean against them comfortably while holding a conversation with his officials or women from his harem, and look out of the open balcony whenever he wished to survey the surrounding mountainside, in style. He had also built what the Mughals described as a series of tents within. They weren't actually tents but layer upon layer of curtains, piled high. There were seven such layers in all, leading up to Shaista Khan's private bedchamber, so that his privacy, when he was in the company of any of his women, was perfect and undisturbed. And right at the heart of his chamber he had constructed a water tank, a mini-fountain as it were, to make up for the dearth of Mughal magnificence in that place, so that he could bear the heat and dust of Lal Mahal with equanimity and keep away any flies that swirled around.

Luxury did not distract him, however, from his given task of piling on the pressure on Shivaji. Shaista Khan combined comfort and conscientious Mughal duty almost effortlessly. With him in charge, the people in Shivaji's domains were, in the words of Shivaji's chronicler, Parmanand, 'frightened'.[1] Shaista Khan had stopped trying to break into Shivaji's forts after the unexpected difficulties he'd faced at Chakan, but on the ground, entire villages – and men, women, their houses, belongings and their cattle – were game for the Mughals. In Pune itself, the Marathas had, as we have seen, adopted a scorched earth policy, but elsewhere, the inhabitants had nowhere to hide.

An incident cited in a Persian document from Aurangzeb's reign illustrates the nature of Shaista Khan's deadly swoops:

> News was received that the villages belonging to the wretched enemy [Shivaji] were situated at the foot of Lohgad and other forts situated about forty miles away from Poona. The subahdar [Shaista Khan] sent Naamdar Khan [a general who was the son of another Mughal general, Jaffar Khan] and other mansabdars on Thursday the Eleventh in the direction of these villages. Naamdar Khan reached these villages the same day. He set on fire about seventy or eighty roadside villages. He destroyed grain and other material. He then halted at the foot of the fort of Tikona. The inhabitants of the villages had taken their cattle and goods to the hills. Naamdar Khan halted at the place for the next day. He sent his colleagues in pursuit of the inhabitants. They went up the hills and captured about one thousand cattle and three hundred men and women. On the third day, Naamdar Khan left the place. He set fire to villages situated between the forts Tikona, Lohgad, Isapur and Tungi. He then returned.[2]

Shivaji was well aware of this attack on lives and livelihoods. He wrote to his local officials with specific instructions on what they should do to protect the local people and what the ordinary peasants themselves should do to secure their safety. His letter to Sarjerao Jedhe, one of his trusted *deshmukhs* from Rohid Khore in the Mavals, offers insight into his thinking:

Shaka 1584 Kartik Va. [Vadya] 7 [23 October 1662]

'Mahadev' Mu. [Mudra] Va. [Vadya] See. [Seema]

Ra. [Rajashree] Shivaji Raje to Sarjerao Jedhe Deshmukh, Ta [*Tarf* or *tapa*, for region] Rohid Khore

Jasood [*jasoos* in Hindi or spies] have brought in information that the Mughals are going to raid your *tapa* [taluka or subdistrict]. As soon as you get this letter, you must send out warnings to all the villages in your *tapa* and, gathering all of the residents, along with their *lekrey-baale* [children; the expression can be termed the Marathi equivalent of the Hindi *bal-bacche*], send the peasant people to a strong and secure spot beneath the ghats. The spot should be such that it's safe from the enemy's attacks. Don't be lax, and act immediately. If the Mughals take away any captives owing to slackness on your part, the whole fault will lie with you. So bear in mind that you will carry the sin. Go across all the villages, work day and night, and take everyone below the ghats. Don't delay things for even a moment, and be absolutely on your guard. Some people may stay back to look after their fields. They should be told to find very safe spots on the hills and mountains, and if they spot the enemy at a distance, to flee in the direction opposite to where the enemy's headed. For your part, you must be extremely vigilant.[3]

Shivaji tried to retaliate against the Mughals in his own way. But the results were mixed. He himself led a force to Pen to attack Naamdar Khan, who had been among the most ruthless of Shaista Khan's generals. 'The Raja went in person to Mira Hill and made a surprise attack on Naamdar Khan,' the Jedhe Chronology states.[4] One of Shivaji's lieutenants, Waghoji Tupe, and several other Marathas were wounded in this encounter, and many died. Among the dead was Krishnaji Babaji, who'd been appointed governor of Jaawali by Shivaji after he'd taken it from the Mores.[5] Shivaji also deployed Netaji Palkar to cut off supplies, take away provisions and cause as much damage in the Mughal camp as possible; but far from doing any damage, he barely escaped with his own life.

Not all Maratha attempts were futile. When a Mughal general, Bulakhi, besieged the fort of Deiri in the Konkan, Kavji Kondhalkar, who had splendidly repulsed the challenge of Fatah Khan in Shivaji's first major battle near Pune in 1648, 'went there, killed 400 men and broke the siege'.[6]

All these moves were, in the end, going to be temporary. The skirmishes, whenever they did take place, were small, their effect was not widespread and often favourable to the Mughals, and the Maratha retaliatory raids were at best minor, patchwork measures. They weren't going to make Shaista Khan go away.

There was also no way Shivaji's army could fight pitched battles against Shaista Khan's men. The numbers were grossly disproportionate and, if the need arose, the Mughal general could summon plenty more men and arms from Gujarat, Rajasthan and elsewhere. Shaista Khan eventually did just that by calling in Maharaja Jaswant Singh of Jodhpur and his contingent in the middle of his Deccan campaign; this was something the Marathas simply didn't have the wherewithal to do. Also, Shaista Khan had reached a point where he had more or less occupied all of the territory Shivaji had won over the past decade and a half, leaving just a little bit at the southern end of the Sahyadris for him; to this Shivaji had now added the Bijapur part of the southern Konkan, which was almost all of the southern coastal belt up to the Goa border.

In order to focus on the looming threat from Shaista Khan, meanwhile, Shivaji had also given up Panhala. He had first thought he could end the siege of the fort, but soon realized it was futile to try. Furious at Shivaji's escape in the dead of night, the Adil Shah had taken control of the siege himself. He believed Siddi Jauhar had taken money from the Marathas and deliberately allowed Shivaji an opening. (Jauhar, poisoned to death on his return to Karnool, had to pay with his life for this mistrust.) Recognizing that the encirclement of Panhala was too strong to be breached, Shivaji told his men to give up the fort and focus elsewhere. It wasn't wise to fight on two fronts, against Bijapur as well as against the Mughals, he said in his message to Trimbak Bhaskar – whom he had appointed in-charge of the fort – advising the surrender of Panhala.[7]

With this retreat, Shivaji was also hoping for a thaw in the chill that had set in between Bijapur and him, since he didn't want to keep looking constantly over his shoulder while responding to Shaista Khan. Once Panhala was given up, there was indeed a modest thaw, which was more a setting of basic rules of engagement for the moment so that the threat of the Mughal empire – which loomed over all of Deccan and especially so for Bijapur, which was hit by tremendous durbari disorder – could be dealt with.[8]

But Shaista Khan had proven too difficult to handle for any such adjustment with Bijapur to have any real effect. Shivaji was faced with the most daunting challenge of his career so far, a challenge far more weighty, grim and problematic than the ones posed by Fatah Khan, the Mores of Jaawali, Afzal Khan and Siddi Jauhar. And he had another worry to contend with: Shaista Khan was winning over some officials of the fledgling Maratha order. To a couple of his officials, a palpably concerned Shivaji wrote on 3 April 1663:

> News has arrived from Sinhagad that there has been some *fitva* [betrayal] there, so for the moment we are not proceeding to the Konkan against Naamdar Khan as originally planned. You should leave for the fort of Sinhagad as soon as you get this letter, with your military troops and your infantry. And on the fort itself, be very alert and vigilant. Find out who all have committed treachery and write to me. Take along Tanhaji Naik and Kondaji Naik … and Kamloji Naik and Darekar and Rumaji Ahira and Gondaji Pandhra, and each one of you practise the greatest vigilance on Fort Sinhagad. Set apart the men involved in the treachery from the ones you're taking along.[9]

How was Shivaji going to get through this most difficult of trials that presented itself in the form of Shaista Khan and his army?

In the Maharashtrian historical imagination, and in the ever-burgeoning literature on Shivaji in Marathi, what happened next was near inevitable. According to this teleological approach, Shivaji was the sole driver of events, and he took them to predestined conclusions. The truth, on the contrary, was that Shivaji had suffered setback after grave setback for almost three straight years and was staring at a crisis which, if not surmounted, would spell the end of his ambitious enterprise to carve out a kingdom in the Deccan. He'd been driven out of almost all the areas he had made his own. His men, who had occasionally caused disturbances in the enemy camp, had been chased away, some were succumbing to Shaista Khan's offers, and without any major military battle to speak of, the Marathas appeared to have been considerably weighed down by the sheer unrelenting pressure of Mughal might. With his possession of vast tracts of land and his reserves of patience, Shaista Khan was on top of the situation and was truly establishing himself – as his title *amir-ul-umra* suggested – as the 'premier prince' of the Mughals, over and above his rank of *subahdar* of the Deccan.

Shivaji gave the matter a lot of thought and came up with the ingenious and extraordinary idea of personally mounting an attack on Shaista Khan. That, too, not in any field of battle, nor from any safe battlement of his own in the hills, but inside Lal Mahal. He made up his mind to hunt down the well-defended and cloistered general inside the very house in which he was holed up.

This plan was very different from the one he had hatched to defeat Afzal Khan. Afzal was lured, cleverly, into the hills, and Shivaji had arranged a meeting with him at a vantage point. Shaista Khan, on the other hand, had expelled Marathas from their territory. In Lal Mahal, the Khan had ring-fenced himself three times over. How was Shivaji even going to reach him? Shaista Khan's outermost layer of security covered Pune on all sides, the troops at least 10,000-strong. The second layer was inside the *kasba* of Pune. The entire town was effectively Shaista Khan's camp and now his military and administrative headquarters. Gaining entry would be very tough, and getting closer to Lal Mahal, where he was staying, even tougher. And even if Shivaji and his Marathas somehow reached the doorstep, how were they going to breach the security cover there? What, moreover, would happen if Shivaji, leading the charge himself, was caught? It would surely mean the end of him, an ignominious end. The jeopardy was too great, and the gamble almost not worth it. Except in Shivaji's mind. He was mentally mapping out the possibilities and determining the details. Many might have dismissed it as an act of insanity or a dive into disaster, but Shivaji, while very alert to the danger involved, was contemplating means by which the blood of Shaista Khan, just like that of Afzal Khan, could be somehow spurted out on to the Deccan soil. That was the only way he could win, the Marathas could win. To that end, he was firing himself up – and firing up his men too.

According to the Mughal historian Khafi Khan, whose father served in Shaista Khan's army, the *amir-ul-umra* had, after having lodged himself in the house 'built by that hell-dog Sivaji', issued orders that 'no person, especially no Mahratta [Maratha] should be allowed to enter the city [of Pune] or the lines of the army without a pass, whether armed or unarmed, excepting persons in the imperial service'.[10] To be safer, 'No Mahratta horseman was taken into service.' Whether such a strict enforcement of rules was possible or not is debatable given the not insignificant number of Maratha soldiers in the Mughal army and the continuous recruitment of many more. What is clearer is that the Mughals were confident that 'Sivaji, beaten and dispirited, had retired into mountains difficult of access, and was continually changing his position'.[11]

Shivaji prepared meticulously. He first obtained information through his spies about Shaista Khan's armed detachments on the route to Pune and how entry into Pune could be gained. Despite his precarious position, Shivaji had a couple of undoubted advantages: his profound knowledge of the region around Pune and its pathways, visible and invisible, and of Lal Mahal, which he knew inside out. He picked a squad of 400 trusted men, left Rajgad early in April 1663, and wound his way, mostly through the forests along the route, to get to Sinhagad, which was close to Pune. Along the route from Sinhagad to Pune, a distance of nearly 40 kilometres, he left behind small detachments at different spots for reconnoitring and to provide security in case of a skirmish on the journey back. Two groups, one led by Netaji Palkar and the other by Moropant Pingle, were directed to take positions a mile away from the Pune camp's borders. In the evening of 5 April 1663, Shivaji and some carefully chosen soldiers got off their horses and left the animals in a detachment placed under the leadership of Sarjerao Jedhe on the banks of the Mula river, just on the other side of Pune.[12] From there Shivaji and his select band walked on foot.

So far, so good. At the gates of Pune, however, the Marathas were stopped in the night and inquiries made of them, about their identities and their purpose of entry. At this point they were an approximately 100-strong force. Shivaji had with him two lieutenants, Babaji Bapuji and Chimnaji Bapuji, of Khed. At this tensest of moments, Shivaji and his men somehow succeeded in entering the encampment. There are two theories of how they slipped in undetected.

One is by Sabhasad. According to him, Babaji and Bapuji, whom he describes as being among Shivaji's 'favourites', walked at the head of the team, and 'behind them all the men and the Raje'. Shivaji himself was carrying, according to this chronicler, 'a shield and a sword in his hands'. Sabhasad writes that 'the Mahomedan army was vast', and 'at various places in the camp they questioned the Raje, "Whose men are you? Who are you? Where had you gone?" Babaji Bapuji and Chimnaji Bapuji replied, as they went on, "We belong to the army and had gone on sentry duty."'[13] What they meant was they were 'Deccani soldiers of the imperial army going to take up their appointed positions'.[14]

The second theory is Khafi Khan's. He speaks of twin acts by Shivaji's men. One group of Marathas formed a wedding procession in which the bridegroom rode ahead, with 'his head hung with chaplets of champak-blossom which concealed his features',[15] and the second, following closely, came in posing as a bunch of imperial captors and their captives. According to him:

> One day a party of Mahrattas, who were serving as foot-soldiers, went to the *kotwal* [the local police head], and applied for a pass to admit 200 Mahrattas, who were accompanying a marriage party. A boy dressed up as a bridegroom, and escorted by a party of Mahrattas with drums and music, entered the town ... On the same day another party was allowed

The Nocturnal Strike   113

to enter the town on the report that a number of the enemy had been made prisoners at one of the outposts, and that another party was bringing them in pinioned and bare-headed, holding them by ropes and abusing and reviling them as they went along.[16]

Once inside, Shivaji and his aides were in familiar territory and found a secluded corner, somewhere close to Lal Mahal, to 'put on arms'.[17] At midnight, Shivaji led some of his men – ten according to the Jedhe Chronicle[18] – inside Lal Mahal, while the rest waited outside. Shivaji, who knew every inch of the place, guided his men throughout. They first entered the kitchen taking a path known to Shivaji. It was the sixth day of the month of Ramzan, and many of the cooks had already woken up to prepare the meal that's usually taken before dawn. Shivaji and his men killed the cooks soundlessly, before making their way to Shaista Khan's harem. There was a wall separating the two areas of the house, but there had been a door there, as Shivaji well knew, which had recently been blocked with bricks and mud. As the Marathas began trying to bring it down, the noise of their pickaxes woke up some servants inside the harem. They rushed to Shaista Khan's chamber, separated from the harem by 'tents within tents, a maze like that of seven concentric houses'.[19] When the servants told him about the noise, Shaista Khan angrily rebuked them for having disturbed his sleep for no reason. The sleepy Khan 'scolded' them, writes Khafi Khan, 'and said it was only the cooks who had got up to do their work'. In the meantime Shivaji and his Marathas had breached the wall and were hacking away at the 'tents', which were large curtains elaborately placed one after the other, in a long row, as noted earlier, to afford privacy to Shaista Khan while he was with the women of his harem. Soon the seven layers of curtains were ripped apart and the frightened cries of women in the harem reached Shaista Khan, causing him to panic.

Before he could pick up his weapons, Shivaji was upon him, with Chimnaji Bapuji right behind. With a single stroke of his sword, Shivaji cut off three of the Khan's fingers on the right hand, according to Sabhasad.[20] Khafi Khan has it that it was Shaista Khan's thumb that was cut off, and the *Maasir-i-Alamgiri*, the official Mughal account of

Aurangzeb's reign, states it was the forefinger that was severed.[21] While this debate continues, it seems clear Shaista Khan was too startled by the suddenness of the attack to be able to respond coherently. He was provided cover by some of his 'slave girls' and assistants and somehow dragged to safety. In the commotion, some of the women put out all the lamps and flickering candles, which made things even more chaotic, the Marathas attacking wildly and two of them falling into a cistern they couldn't see. The water reservoir, as mentioned earlier, had been built recently for Shaista Khan and for the harem's women, and the Marathas who otherwise knew the place well, were taken unawares.[22] Two of Shaista Khan's women were also attacked, in the confusion. According to Maratha records, the darkness made it impossible for the attackers to see their adversaries. Khafi Khan describes the attack on the women, which he does not say was inadvertent, in gory detail. According to him, one of the two women 'was so cut about that her remains were collected in a basket, which served for her coffin'. The other woman, he says, 'recovered, although she had received thirty or forty wounds'.[23]

The Marathas now had the run of the house they knew so well. Some killed guards, derisively saying, 'This is how they keep guard!' Some stepped inside the *nagarkhana*, where all the kettledrums were kept, and ordered their players to beat the drums 'in the name of the Amiru-l Umra'. In the din, all the cries for help went unheard. Shaista Khan's son Abul Fath Khan fought the Marathas bravely, and killed two, but was soon wounded himself and succumbed to his injuries. 'A man of importance who had a house behind the palace of the Amiru-l Umra' heard the outcry, writes Khafi Khan, and 'finding the doors shut, endeavoured to escape by a rope-ladder from a window, but he was old and feeble, and somewhat resembled Shayista Khan. The Mahrattas mistook him for the Amiru-l Umra, killed him and cut off his head.' The assailants, Khafi Khan says, 'gave no thought to plundering, but made their way out of the house and went off'.[24] This raid presumably lasted not more than fifteen or twenty minutes; it was frenzied, feverish and chaotic.

Shivaji had no desire to linger. According to the Jedhe family's records and Sabhasad's narrative, he took the 'direct route' out of town and went across the river, which wasn't far from Lal Mahal.[25] The other men too slipped out unnoticed with him, and the Mughal soldiers looked for them inside the Pune camp in vain.

A story that has gained ground about Shivaji's escape from Lal Mahal is narrated in the Chitnis Chronicle, a latter-day, and not too reliable, document. According to this, Shivaji's men blew their horns while leaving Pune, as a signal to a Maratha unit hiding in the nearby Katraj pass to light torches tied to trees and to heads of bulls. The blazing torches gave the chasers the impression that the Marathas had gone that way, and a Mughal unit rode rapidly towards the lights while Shivaji, with his associates, went off in the opposite direction, towards Sinhagad. The popularity of this tale can be gauged from the fact that in Marathi, 'to lead someone up the Katraj pass' means to trick them with a red herring. It is one of the Shivaji era's more famous linguistic legacies, though the story itself is fictitious and has been junked by every bona fide historian.

At daybreak, the Mughals counted their losses. Apart from Abul Fath, Shaista Khan's son, six concubines and forty of Shaista Khan's soldiers had lost their lives. Two other sons of the Khan and a few women had been wounded. Shivaji's side, on the other hand, had lost six soldiers, and forty Marathas had been injured.[26]

The man who bore the brunt of Shaista Khan's anger in the morning was Jaswant Singh, the Jodhpur royal and governor of Gujarat. Neither he nor any of his men, numbering a few thousand, had stirred out in the night to help find Shivaji and his Marathas despite being in and around the town. On seeing him, Shaista Khan said sarcastically, 'I thought the Maharaja was in His Majesty's service when such an evil befell me.'[27] (He meant that Jaswant Singh ought to have come to Shaista Khan's rescue since he was on duty – hence 'in the Majesty's Service'.) Jaswant Singh had no reply to offer. He stood shamefaced in front of Shaista Khan, who had himself completely lost face.

The *amir-ul umra* did not remain in Pune for long. He shifted soon to Aurangabad, leaving Pune under the charge of Jaswant Singh. Early the following year, and still carrying the stain of humiliation, Shaista Khan was shunted out to Bengal as *subahdar* by a sorely displeased Aurangzeb. Shaista Khan was keen to see the emperor before he moved there, but his stock was so low that Aurangzeb didn't even grant him an audience. Shaista Khan pleaded with Aurangzeb in writing that he be allowed to stay put so he could wreak vengeance upon Shivaji. He wrote to his friends asking them to save him from removal and even offered to pay from his own pocket the expenses of the Deccan campaign. Nothing worked. 'Aurangzeb was immovable in his determination, and replied with severity that a man in a passion could never act with prudence, that the stay of Shaistah Khan in the Dakhin as leader against Shiva Ji could result in nothing but the loss of his army.'[28] Thus a final order was issued: Shaista Khan must, 'without further discussion',[29] leave for Bengal, a place seen as 'a penal province' at the time and described by Aurangzeb as 'a hell well stocked with bread'.[30] Aurangzeb was leaving no room for doubt that he was giving his maternal uncle a punishment posting.

Understandably, in the *Maasir-i-Alamgiri*, the reference to this episode is extraordinarily short and terse, as if it is too embarrassing to mention in any detail. It states that Aurangzeb was on his way to Kashmir when he heard, in the first week of May 1663, of what had happened:

On Friday, the 1st May/3rd Shawwal the Emperor resumed his journey [to Kashmir]. One of the occurrences in this period was the night attack of the infernal Shiva on the camp of the Amir-ul-umara, the cutting off of his forefinger during the encounter, and the slaughter of his son Abul Fath Khan. As this incident was due to the negligence of this premier noble, the Emperor punished him by transferring him from the viceroyalty of the Deccan [which was given to prince Muhammad Mu'azzam] to that of Bengal. On Tuesday, the 14th [of] May/14th Shawwal, the Emperor reached Bhimbar, which is the gateway to Kashmir.[31]

Word of Shivaji's astonishing audacity nevertheless spread far and wide, and extremely quickly. A letter sent by the Rajapur-based British official Phillip Gyffard to his Surat factory bosses is of considerable value because Gyffard got his information from Shivaji's chief official in

Rajapur, Raoji Pandit, and made it a point to write it all down without any delay. In his letter written on 12 April 1663, exactly a week after Shivaji sprang his surprise on Shaista Khan, Gyffard states that Shivaji himself had communicated to Raoji the details he was writing about:

> Rougy Pundit is returned ... Yesterday arrived a letter from the Rajah, written himself to Rougy, giving him an account [of] how he himself with 400 choice men went to Shasta Ckaun's camp. There, upon some pretence (which he did not incert in his letter) he got into his tent to Salam, and presently slew all the watch, killed Shasta Ckaun's eldest sonne, his sonne in law, 12 of his cheife women, 40 great persons attending him, their Generall, wounded Shasta Ckaun with his owne hand (and he thought to death, but since heares he lives), wounded 6 more of his wifes, 2 more of his sons, and after all this returnes, loosing but 6 men and 40 wounded, 10000 horse under Raja Jeswantzin standing still and never offered to persue him, so it's generally believed it was done with his consent, though Sevagy tells his men his permisera [*Parameshwara* or God] bid him doe it.[32]

Shivaji may have attributed the failure of Shaista Khan's mission against him to a divine favour, but his own personal prestige as a rebel military leader rose immeasurably in the wake of the nocturnal strike. His name resounded throughout the Mughal empire and in parts of the subcontinent where the empire did not hold sway. Several European travellers to India in the seventeenth century, writing of their experiences on the subcontinent, made note of it in as much detail as they could summon, given their limits of language and interpretation.

One of these Europeans was the Frenchman Francois Bernier. Born in 1620, Bernier, a protégé of the famous philosopher Petri Gassendi, had obtained a degree as doctor of medicine. Caught by the travel bug, he left to explore the East in 1656. After spending some time in Egypt, he sailed to Surat in 1658–59. On his way from Surat to Agra, he met Dara Shukoh, and reluctantly became his physician. After Dara was compelled to flee to Sindh in his battle with Aurangzeb, Bernier extricated himself from his household and reached Ahmedabad, where he lived under the protection of a Mughal noble. He travelled all the way up to Kashmir and was on his way to the north in 1663 when he heard of certain events in the Deccan. He recorded these goings-on as part of what he termed as 'Remarkable occurrences' in the first five years of Aurangzeb's rule:

> A revolt had taken place, headed by a *gentile* of *Visapour*, who made himself master of several important fortresses and one or two seaports belonging to the King of that country. The name of this bold adventurer is *Seva-gi*, or Lord Seva [Shiva]. He is vigilant, enterprising, and wholly regardless of personal safety. *Chah-estkan*, when in the *Decan*, found in him an enemy more formidable than the King of *Visapour* at the head of his whole army and joined by those Rajas who usually unite with that prince for their common defence. Some idea may be formed of *Seva-gi*'s intrepidity by his attempt to seize *Chah-estkan*'s person, together with all his treasures, in the midst of his troops, and surrounded by the walls of *Aureng-Abad*. Attended by a few soldiers he one night penetrated into *Chah-estkan*'s apartment, and would have succeeded in his object had he remained undetected a short time longer. *Chah-est* was severely wounded, and his son was killed in the act of drawing his sword.[33]

Another traveller, the Italian Niccolao Manucci had run away from Venice in 1653 at the age of eighteen. He boarded a vessel for the Turkish port Smyrna and, under the protection of an English noble whom he met on board, came to India, where he too, like Bernier, served under Dara Shukoh as an artilleryman. After Dara's defeat he didn't want to work directly with Aurangzeb and instead found employment with the Mughal noble Mirza Raja Jai Singh. He left that job later to head to Bassein or Vasai, 'where he narrowly escaped the Inquisition, and thence to Goa',[34] finally landing in Agra and Delhi. During his days with Jai Singh, he would meet Shivaji and later even be employed by the Portuguese in Goa to hold negotiations with Shivaji's son Sambhaji. But before that he had heard, while very much in Mughal service, of Shaista Khan's fiasco.

Manucci described the attack and added:

I leave it to the reader to imagine the confusion existing in the [Khan's] camp that night, everyone imagining that Shiva Ji was in their midst and slaying all men without intermission. In this confusion Shaistah Khan's sufferings from his wound were increased from not being able to call in any surgeon for fear that, in place of a surgeon, some traitor might gain admittance.[35]

If we set aside Parmanand's *Shivabharat*, the first systematic biography of Shivaji to have been written was in the Portuguese language. Its author, as mentioned earlier, was a Portuguese national, Cosme da Guarda, a Marmugao (Goa) resident in the seventeenth century. As the scholar Surendra Nath Sen has noted, da Guarda completed his work, *Life of the Celebrated Sevagy*, in 1695, a year before Sabhasad finished his account of Shivaji's life.[36] His observations on the Shaista Khan incident are interesting because, as a contemporary of Shivaji, he obtained his information from a number of people while he was in the Deccan.

Da Guarda was convinced that there was a secret pact between Jaswant Singh and Shivaji, which Shivaji had brought about with his wiles. 'Jassomptissingha [Jaswant Singh] was a Gentio [Hindu],' da Guarda stated, noting that:

> Sevagy took advantage of this [fact] for he was a [Hindu] and sent him one night a rich present of precious stones, a large quantity of gold and silver with many rich and precious jewels. With these marvellous cannons, Sevagy fought and reduced that fortress. The message was as follows: 'Though Your Highness has the greatness of a Sovereign King and [now] also that of the General of so powerful an Emperor, if you recollect that I am a Gentio like you, and if you take account of what I have done, you will find that all I have done was due to the zeal for the honour and worship of your gods whose temples have been destroyed by the Mouros [Moors]. If the cause of religion have precedence over all the goods of the world and even over life itself, I have for the same cause risked mine so many times.'[37]

Referring to the gifts he was sending across, Shivaji, wrote da Guarda, went on to say that he was offering Singh 'these trifles ... in the name of the gods themselves'.[38] And while he understood that Singh had 'to defend those whose salt and water you eat and drink' and could not, on account of holding a *jagir* of the Mughals, 'take the side of another', there were still ways in which he could offer assistance. Da Guarda quotes Shivaji as saying:

> You may so behave that you may not fail in the loyalty professed ... or in the respect due to your gods that I may mix with the people of Sextaghan [Shaista Khan], to be able to do as I like, and to do to him, without the knowledge of the Mouros, what I can.[39]

'Jassomptissingha was less devout and more ambitious' and 'was much obliged for the presents', da Guarda pointed out.[40]

We have no way of knowing whether Shivaji truly wrote such a letter to Jaswant Singh, but the contents of the purported letter indicate da Guarda had heard of Shivaji fighting in the name of the gods. It is a clue to the kind of conversations and discussions then going on in the Deccan. The theory of Shivaji attempting a Hindu revival was evidently in currency in his lifetime; apart from Cosme da Guarda, the two contemporary chroniclers closest to Shivaji, Parmanand and Sabhasad, have referred to it.

However, Shivaji's sense of Hinduness appeared to hold various faiths within its wide embrace. After Shaista Khan had occupied Pune and its surrounding regions, Shivaji had, through an order issued on 18 December 1660, ordered that grants given to Hindus and Muslims alike in those parts be continued as before. 'There are *inams* [grants] given to Hindus and Muslims in Poona, Indapur, Chakan, Supa and Baramati,' he wrote. 'Before Afzal Khan I had the *mokasa* [land rights] of these places, and *inam*-holders used to receive their grants. They will continue to receive them as before. Arrangements to this effect have been made.'[41]

Shivaji's new-found confidence after the defeat he inflicted on Shaista Khan is best exemplified by a letter he wrote to the Mughals soon after the Khan's humiliating withdrawal. In that taunting letter, an attitudinal tailpiece of sorts to stories that were circulating of his repeated triumphs, he accused senior Mughal generals and officials of sending totally fabricated reports of their activities in the Deccan to Aurangzeb:

Maharajah Shivaji to the Officers and Counsellors of the Emperor Alamgir

Letter drafted by Nila Prabhu Munshi

Farsighted and thoughtful men know that, for the last three years, famous generals and experienced officials [of the emperor] have come to these parts. The emperor had ordered them to capture my forts and territory. In their despatches to the emperor they write that the territory and the forts would be captured soon. They do not know that even the steed of unimaginable exertion is too weak to gallop over this hard country, and that its conquest is difficult. It is a matter of great wonder that they do not at all expect the fruit of shame from such writings filled with fictitious statements, but ... are not ashamed of sending false reports to the Emperor. My home, unlike the forts of Kaliani and Bidar, is not situated on a spacious plain, which may enable trenches to be run or assault to be made. It has lofty hill-ranges, 200 leagues in length and 40 leagues in breadth; everywhere there are *nalas* hard to cross; sixty forts of extreme strength have been built in this region, and some [of them are] on the sea coast. Afzal Khan, an officer of Adil Shah, came to Jaawali with a large army, but he was rendered helpless and perished. Why do you not report to the emperor what has happened [here], so that the same fate may not overcome you?

After Afzal Khan's death, the Amir-ul-umara [Shaista Khan], marched into these sky-kissing hills and abysmal passes, laboured hard for three years and wrote to the emperor that I was going to be defeated and my land conquered in a short time. The end of such a false attitude was only to be expected. He was disgraced and had to go away. This much is as clear as daylight.

It is my duty to guard my homeland. To maintain your prestige and save your reputation, you send false reports to the emperor. But I am blessed with Divine favour. An invader of the beloved country of this man, whoever he may be, has never succeeded.

[Lines in verse]
The wise should beware of this river of blood
From which no man (ever) carried away his boat (in safety).[42]

7

The Sack of Surat

The afternoon of 5 January 1664 began like any other for the *Loyall Merchant*, a ship of the British East India Company stationed in the waters of Swally (Suvali) on India's western coast. These shores of Swally formed the entry and exit for the port of Surat, and therein lay their significance. Surat was, in certain ways, more important to Mughal India than Agra or Delhi. If Agra and Delhi were its political centres, Surat was the empire's trading heart. Here it was that all kinds of 'Persian, Arabian, Egyptian, African, Chinese and European'[1] goods and commodities landed, to be distributed across the land; and it was from this economic hub that products from Gujarat, Lahore, Kashmir, Agra, Patna, Golconda, Bijapur, the Malabar coast and the wider Karnataka and Tamil parts found their way out to other, far-off shores. No other place in the Mughal empire could compete with it in terms of wealth, traffic and sheer grandeur. As if to complete the picture, there was also the element of religion: it was from Surat and its port that ships left for Mecca, taking several thousand pilgrims to Islam's holiest site and bringing them back every year. The numerous gardens in the city reflected its abundant prosperity: they had trees that were 'full of various fruits continuing all the year round'.[2]

On this particular afternoon, business in the port was brisk as always, with hundreds of ships and vessels loading and unloading their cargoes and the customs house occupied with its everyday, apparently countless clearances. For the English officers and sailors on the *Loyall Merchant*, things were likely to have been even ebullient: the ship was getting ready to leave for England on one of its trips. That mood was disrupted by a visit from one of the top messengers of the Company's Surat factory. At 3 p.m., the messenger arrived and gave the ship's captain, a certain 'Mr James,' a 'hot alarme' that Shivaji was 'within 10 or 12 miles of Surat'.[3]

All of Surat was taken completely by surprise. There had been no sign of Shivaji moving from his base towards the direction of Gujarat, and certainly not towards Surat. But clearly, he had left from his base in the Deccan several days earlier, and had rested with his men in the mornings and journeyed on horse mostly through the night. He had been spotted near Bassein and then near Nasik, no doubt, but then that was familiar ground for him – where he might venture every now and then to test either the Portuguese or the Mughals. But Surat? It had been deemed almost entirely out of the question because of the distance of over 400 kilometres involved.

According to Sabhasad, it was Shivaji's spy-in-chief, Bahirji Naik, who had shown the Maratha leader the quietest and most discreet route to the gates of the flourishing town. Bahirji's surname was Jadhav, and he was chosen by Shivaji as *naik* (from where he'd got his suffix or almost a new surname) or head of the *jasoods* or intelligence gatherers, because he was considered 'a very shrewd man'. Shivaji had sent him to Surat well in advance to collect information on the town's riches and defences, and Bahirji had reported on his return that 'if Surat is plundered, wealth beyond count would be found'. He also offered to act as principal guide on the route, saying to Shivaji, 'I shall conduct the army to a safe place, avoiding any meeting with the Mughals. Your Majesty should not be anxious.'[4]

The British factory's officials wanted the captain to immediately send forty armed men to the city to guard the Company's stocks. Surat was of extraordinary importance to the Company as well; Bombay, obtained barely three years ago by the British from the Portuguese as a dowry gift, was at the time little more than a mosquito-infested swamp. Soon, many more armed men were sent, so that in all, 200 of them – 150 Englishmen and 50 'peones'[5] – were in place to defend the factory.

Shivaji set up camp, with 8,000 of his soldiers accompanying him, at Gandevi, which was about 45 kilometres or a little over an hour's horse ride to the south of the city. The immensely wealthy merchants of Surat, described by the foreign traders as 'grave, judicious, neat, tall, goodly' and 'cloathed in long white callico or silk robes', panicked at once and started looking for ways to escape. The safest spots they could go to with as many of their riches as they could hurriedly gather, they felt, were the Surat fort, which was distinct from the city, and the factory of the British East India Company; the poor, on the other hand, tried to flee across the river nearby in boats with their families and whatever little they had got. Surprisingly, for a city so filled with money and incredibly precious items, whose total customs collection came to 12 lakh rupees a year,[6] it had no walls and barely any security cover. Perhaps its very prosperity had resulted in a sense of security bordering on complacency. Not that there was no official machinery in place. The city had a governor, Inayat Khan, who was also the fort commander and was supposed to keep a well-equipped defence force, but everyone, rich or poor, knew he was simply in the business of siphoning off funds. While he took funds from the Mughal treasury to maintain a force of 500 or more, he hired only a small number of soldiers, if any at all, and misappropriated the money meant for the rest. The local population knew all this, so naturally, the sense of alarm grew as evening fell.

Many traders wanted to get inside the British factory as early as possible for the protection of their lives and riches. They knew the Company's officials had, apart from calling in 200 personnel from Swally, made further preparations for the defence of the property. Swiftly, the president of the Company's Surat Council, George Oxenden, had procured four brass guns: two from the Company's own ships nearby, and two from a local merchant. The factory, which the British referred to in their written records as simply 'the house', was sought to be filled with 'victuals, water and powder', some of the men were 'set to melt lead and make bullets', and portholes were made in what Company officials called their 'great gate' so that any fire could be directed outside from there. Three of the guns were taken to the top of the factory to scour the two main streets outside, and one was positioned in such a way that it looked down from atop the next-door residence of Haji Said Baig, one of Surat's most affluent merchants. Baig's house was of the same height as the British factory, and the British thought if it were possessed by the enemy, their factory could be in genuine danger of being successfully attacked.[7] Officials at the Dutch factory in another part of the town were similarly alert and had made adequate preparations as well.

The rest of the city, though, stood mightily exposed, and the majority of the houses too were not such that they would take well the brunt of a powerful assault. Surat's total population was two lakh. Its overall shape was 'ill-contrived into narrow lanes' which were mostly 'without any forme'. The few homes of the ultra-rich were made of bricks, but these were scarcely two or three in number. Most of the local residents' houses were either made entirely of wood or a combination of brick and wood, 'the main postes' of which were simply timber, with the rest of the structure built of bamboos or cane; many dwellings had nothing but mud walls and floors.

> The whole towne is unforteified either by art or nature and its situation is upon a large plaine of many miles' extent ... They have only made against the cheefe avenues of the towne some weake and ill-built gates, and for the rest in some parts a dry ditch, easily passable by a footman, wanting a wall or other defence on the inner side; the rest is left so open that scarcely any signe of a ditch is perceiveable.[8]

Sometime in the evening, Shivaji sent two of his envoys to Surat's governor, Inayat Khan, with a letter asking the governor and the three most eminent and 'money'd men in the towne' – Haji Said Baig, Virji Vora and Haji Kasim – 'to come to him in person immediately'[9] and settle the terms of ransom for the entire city. According to the account left behind by Volquard Iversen, an eyewitness present at the Dutch factory there, Shivaji communicated to both the British and the Dutch 'that he was now in need of money to maintain his army and that a considerable sum must be advanced to him', failing which 'he would set fire to the whole town'.[10] He was determined to avenge the ruin of his land by the Mughals over the past three years. British records state that Shivaji sent a note to the president of the British Company's Surat Council, George Oxenden, stating that:

> he was not come to doe any personall hurt to the English or other merchants, but only to revenge himself on Orom Zeb (the Great Mogol) because he had invaded his country [and] had killd some of his relations, and that he would only have the English and Duch give him some treasure and he would not meddle with there houses; ells he would doe them all mischeefe possible.[11]

Oxenden himself remarked in a letter he sent to England that Shivaji's 'designe was not altogether riches but revenge upon this King [Aurangzeb]'.[12] Shaista Khan had destroyed the treasury of Shivaji's provinces, caused arbitrary injury to the local population, and the damage done to fields and marketplaces had punctured his sources of revenue. The governor refused to concede Shivaji's demand, but out of sheer fright, he himself sought refuge inside the Surat fort. The message to all of Surat's residents was transparent: their official commander, in charge of the city's defence, had gone into hiding.

At about eleven the next morning, 6 January 1664, Shivaji reached Surat and, while he was occupied with pitching his tent near a 'great garden ... a quarter of a mile'[13] beyond the city's eastern gate, his soldiers, on his explicit instructions, rode into the town and began sacking it and setting houses on fire. These were 'shock and awe' tactics aimed at securing a hefty ransom. With the forces lodged inside the castle, the Marathas had decided to engage in a very light way, not aiming to combat them, but to merely prevent them from blocking the sack. From within the fort, firing was at times regular and at other times intermittent, and from the British and Dutch accounts, it is evident it caused 'more damage to the houses than harm to the enemy'.[14]

Starting Wednesday, 6 January, the day the Marathas entered Surat, the city burnt for four straight days. Shivaji's men had a more or less free run, plundering and firing at will and setting all kinds of houses ablaze. The only resistance offered was by the British and the Dutch, who prevented them from getting into their factories by firing back from within. Shivaji had no desire to engage in battle; nor did he want to waste ammunition and the lives of his Marathas. He was in Surat only to gain ransom and to send a chill down the mighty Mughal empire's spine. So where resistance was offered – and it was only in these two places – he got his men to back away. But neighbourhoods even in the immediate vicinity of these factories were set aflame.

Of the three most moneyed merchants, Haji Kasim had his residence dug up and its contents plundered, after which his property was promptly set on fire. According to the British version of events, Shivaji's men also broke open and plundered Haji Said Baig's house and warehouse, situated right next to their factory, for one full night. Sensing imminent danger to its own property if Baig's home was either strengthened as a temporary station by the Marathas or set afire, the Company, wrote its Surat Council chief, 'caused a party of foote to sally forth and fight them, in which scuffle wee had three men slightly wounded, our men slew a horse and man, some say two or three'.[15] The Surat British factory having thus soon 'cleared its quarters', its officials 'shut up the doors and barricaded them and made a passage from our into his [Baig's] house, and kept a garrison in a balcony that cleared all the street'.[16]

Unlike Baig's property, Virji Vora's couldn't escape the conflagration. If Baig was a Muslim, Vora, reputed to be 'the richest merchant in the world' at the time with assets of 80 lakh rupees,[17] was a Gujarati Hindu, though the historian Jadunath Sarkar has mistaken him for a Muslim and incorrectly written his name as Baharji Borah.[18] From the 'magnificent house' of this 'Banyan [*bania*] merchant, Virji Vora', wrote a Dutch witness, 'gold, money, pearls, gems and other precious wares' were taken before it was reduced to ashes.[19]

On Thursday, 7 January, the second day of the Maratha offensive, an attempt was made on Shivaji's life. It enraged his followers so much that it might have resulted in a full-scale massacre if not for a timely alert that the assassination bid had not been successful. That morning, an emissary had come from the Surat governor to meet Shivaji and offered 'some conditions', which were presumably terms for settlement of the ransom amount. The proffered deal, the British noted, 'pleased Sevagee not at all', and he asked the emissary indignantly whether his master, the governor, 'cooped up in his chamber, thought him a woman to accept such conditions'.[20] The emissary angrily responded, 'We are not women', and adding, 'I have somewhat [something] more to say to you', he suddenly drew his dagger and ran 'full at Sevagee's breast'. Before he could get to Shivaji, a Maratha soldier reached him and with his sword struck off his hand. The would-be assassin, however, had 'made his thrust at Sevagee with all his might' and 'did not stop' but 'ran his bloody stump against Sevagee's breast and with force', with the result that 'both Sevagee and he fell together'. Shivaji's tunic was stained with blood, and many of his followers, thinking 'he was killed', sent out a cry of 'kill the prisoners', at which point some prisoners the Marathas had taken from the town, one of the Britishers wrote, 'were miserably hacked'.[21]

The soldier who'd hacked off the would-be assassin's hand had just 'cloven off' his 'skull' when Shivaji quickly got up from the ground and asked his men to stop the killings. Instead, he ordered them to 'bring the prisoners before him'.[22] There were more than a hundred of them, of various faiths, creeds and nationalities, as Surat boasted of people from faraway lands like the 'English, Dutch, Portuguese, Turks, Arabs, Armenians, Persians, Jews', apart from the 'Indians of several sorts (principally Banians) or else Moores, the conquerors of the country, Hindues or the ancient inhabitants or Parsees, who are people fled out of Persia ages ago and here, and some miles up the country, settled in great numbers'.[23]

Once the prisoners were lined up, an infuriated Shivaji ordered the heads of a few of them severed and the hands of many others to be cut off. In all, the British recorded, 'four heads and 24 hands' were cut off.[24] A British East India Company employee, Anthony Smith, was among those produced before Shivaji. The moment Shivaji commanded that his right hand be chopped, Smith 'cryed out in Indostan [Hindustani] to Sevagee rather to cut off his head'. To do that, Smith's hat too was taken off, 'but Sevagee stopped [the] execution', and his life was saved.[25] Shivaji demanded 3 lakh rupees as ransom for Smith's release but later heard he was only a 'common man' and eventually let him go for a ransom of 300 rupees, though not without 'a message full of threats and menaces' to the British factors.[26]

The historian Jadunath Sarkar came to the erroneous conclusion in his biography of Shivaji that once Smith's hat was taken off, Shivaji realized he was an Englishman and therefore spared his life.[27] The truth is, Shivaji had known all along that Smith was an Englishman and a Company employee. Smith needn't have taken off his hat for his face, identity and colour to be obvious. Shivaji had in fact asked him more than once over the previous two days to convey his demand for ransom to the English factors, as well as his demand that they not impede the Marathas when they sacked Vora's house, which was, like Baig's, near the English factory. Smith had landed at the Dutch port on Wednesday and was on his way to the English factory when he was taken into custody by Shivaji's soldiers and dragged to their camp. It was to Smith, according to the British version of events, that Shivaji first made it clear he intended no personal harm to the British; the same evening, he asked him to go to his employers' factory with a message from the Marathas. Smith agreed but insisted that he be accompanied by a guard, in case he was harassed or caught in a crossfire. Perhaps smelling a rat, Shivaji then called off the plan and packed him off to the part of the camp where all the other prisoners, including the ambassador of the king of Ethiopia, had been kept. Not a single document, not even the English ones which extensively cite Smith's case and his movements – noting that on the day after his life was spared, he did indeed go to the English factory with a fresh Maratha demand for '3 lakh rupees'[28] – states that he was identified as an Englishman at the moment of his hat being taken off in front of Shivaji. That bit is a work of imagination from Sarkar that mars his otherwise excellent writing on Shivaji. The Maratha leader had wanted Smith to carry his message to the British camp, and Smith had agreed to do that, more than once. That was evidently the reason his life was spared.

The fires that raged across Surat were the most terrible on Thursday (7 January) and Friday night, according to the account left behind by the local English chaplain, Reverend John L'Escaliot. On the night of Friday, 8 January 1664, the blaze, L'Escaliot said, was 'so great' that it 'turned the night into day, [just] as before the smoke in the day tyme had almost turned day into night, rising so thicke ... it darkened the sun like a great cloud'.[29]

In the midst of recording their details of the sack and the violence, three European travellers to India of that period, Bernier, Thevenot and Jean-Baptiste Tavernier, wrote of Shivaji's act of magnanimity as well. On the day of Shivaji's arrival in the city, Father Ambrose, who was chief of the local French Capuchin Mission, went up to him and earnestly appealed to him not to do any violence to the poor Christians living in Surat. Shivaji not only 'took him [the Reverend Father Ambrose] into his protection'[30] but issued instructions to his soldiers that 'the *Frankysh* Padrys are good men, and shall not be molested'.[31]

Shivaji, besides, spared the house and property of a local Hindu *dalal* of the Dutch Company, because he was informed that the man had been 'very charitable while alive'.[32] This '*shroff* or money-changer' was identified by Tavernier as 'Mondas Parek' (Mohandas Parekh), and he had died exactly three years before, in January 1661.[33] But his karma was such that he was much praised by all: he had 'bestowed much alms during his life on the Christians as well as on the idolators [Hindus]', and 'the Reverend Capuchin Fathers' had lived 'for a part of the year on the rice, butter and vegetables which he sent them'.[34]

Sometime on Saturday, Shivaji got wind that a Mughal army was on its way from the north to provide relief to Surat. By then the sack had been pretty thorough, and he was preparing to leave with his soldiers. The Dutch factory that morning sent out an Indian informant on twin assignments. The first was to pass on a message to the English factory that if Shivaji threatened them again, he should be told that the Dutch and the English would fight him together. The second was to find out what Shivaji was now up to. Having delivered the communique to the English factory, the spy left to take a look at the rest of the town, where he found 'the houses of the principal merchants ... laid in ashes', and from there headed for Shivaji's camp. He returned in the evening, the Dutch wrote.[35] At the Maratha camp situated just outside the city, 'he [the spy] saw Shivaji sitting on the ground and his men bringing him the plunder'. There were no tents at all to be seen anywhere, so it was assumed, correctly, that they had been already dismantled by the Marathas, and that 'their stay would only be short'.[36]

Shivaji and his men left for home, with the booty gathered, on Sunday morning, camping one night over 20 kilometres away before proceeding home via the Konkan coastline. The Portuguese, who ruled much of upper Konkan, suspected Shivaji chose this route deliberately with the aim of implicating them in the sack.

The day Shivaji departed Surat was 10 January 1664. For a full week after that, most of the traders and their families did not return to their houses or properties, afraid that the Marathas might come back any moment as rumours of their imminent return continued to circulate. It was only when the Mughal army entered the city on 17 January 1664 that the merchants came out of hiding. So did, at the same time, the Surat governor, Inayat Khan. When he finally walked out of the castle, secure in the knowledge that the Mughal army would provide him security, the townspeople who had returned 'derided him and flung dirt at him' for his extraordinary cowardice. Incensed, Inayat Khan's son vented his anger over this public humiliation of his father by shooting a 'poor Bannian' who had just come in from across the water, with his pack on his back. The helpless, unsuspecting *bania* got an arrow in his mouth and was killed on the spot, an act which the *Loyall Merchant*'s British officials described as one that showed 'the insulting pride and baseness of' the rulers of Surat. They had not had the courage to stand up to the enemy 'to save their estates, yet killed a poore Bannian that had not done them any injury', the ship's officials wrote acerbically.[37] The ship's departure from Swally's shores, of course, was delayed by Shivaji's advance; it ultimately left only at the end of January 1664.

What was the monetary worth of what the Marathas had carried away from the Mughal empire's Gujarati commercial centre for their otherwise depleted exchequer? Though estimates vary quite a bit, the historical consensus on the closest-to-accurate figure is between 1 crore and 1.5 crore rupees, cited by three different British sources.[38] The Mughal historian Khafi Khan wrote, 'Shivaji took from Surat an immense booty, in gold and silver, coined and uncoined. Millions in money and goods came into the hands of that evil infidel.'[39]

The Surat operation mounted by Shivaji and his Marathas is a good example of the ruthless medieval to early modern era tactic of stripping an attacking adversary of much of his prime economic power to make up for the losses suffered on one's own lands, of showing oneself to be as severe as possible, and wreaking enough destruction to build up one's own image as an equal foe, capable of inflicting intimidation and pain and leaving a permanent mark. Shivaji had already declared in his letter to Mughal officials after Shaista Khan's humiliation that he would defend his homeland until the last; in Surat, he provided a demonstration of the terrible ramifications that any destructive incursions into his lands would have for the aggressor. A convulsion of huge proportions, the Surat raid became part of the gathering storm of incidents and clashes all tending in the direction of a major Shivaji versus Aurangzeb conflict.

Almost immediately after the Maratha raid, Aurangzeb was inundated with requests from all the resident merchants of Surat, and from the British and Dutch companies, for exemptions in view of the massive losses they had suffered on the Mughal civil and defence administration's watch, which had turned out to be no watch at all. George Oxenden, the president of the Surat Council, had begun to press this demand on the very day the Mughal army reached Surat. He had put down his pistol in front of the military general in charge, saying it was now for the Mughal forces to protect the city. The general offered Oxenden 'a horse, a sword and a vest' to acknowledge the opposition the English had put up against the Marathas, but Oxenden told him those were 'things becoming a soldier, but they were merchants and expected the Emperor's favour in their trade'.[40] Aurangzeb agreed, allowing the local merchants, the British and the Dutch not to pay any customs duties for a year. After that, for the courage they had shown against the Marathas, the English and Dutch were also given a 0.5 per cent reduction in customs payments, but it would apply only to imports; for exports, they would continue to pay the regular 3 per cent.[41]

The other prompt fallout, as expected, was the ouster of the derelict city governor Inayat Khan and his replacement by one Ghiyasuddin Khan.[42] A worried Aurangzeb also instructed his officials to get a stone wall built around Surat for its protection. The more lasting impact was the scare Shivaji had created in the minds of the Mughals, their generals and officials, and the merchants in their territories. What the Surat Council of the British wrote to its counterparts in Karwar in the south barely months after the sensational sack shows how Shivaji had begun to evoke strange and phantasmagoric visions:

> Sevagy is so famously infamous for his notorious thefts that report hath made him an airy body, and added wings or else it were impossible he could bee at so many places as he is said to bee at, all at one time.
>
> Sometimes he is certainly believed to bee in one, and in a day or two in another place, and so in halfe a dozen remote one from another, and there burnes and plunders all without controule, so that they ascribe to him to performe more than a Hirculian labour that he is become the talke of all conditions of people.[43]

Shortly after Shivaji returned to his capital, Rajgad, his father Shahaji Raje Bhosle died in Karnataka. Shahaji fell off his horse in a hunting accident in Hodigere (now in Karnataka's Davangere district), and succumbed to his injuries on 23 January 1664.[44] The Adil Shah gave the rights to Shahaji's *jagir* in the Bangalore–Mysore and Thanjavur regions to his younger son Ekoji or Vyankoji. The Dutch recorded in a letter from their Vengurle factory that 'the old preying bird Shahaji, father of the great rebel Shivaji', had passed away.⁴⁵

Early in the twentieth century, the outstanding Maratha historian V.K. Rajwade discovered a document by one Jayram Pindye which credibly established Shahaji's fluency in the Sanskrit language and his patronage of Sanskrit scholars in his court, thus revealing a dimension of his personality other than his record as a military general and *jagir* holder. From the description the document offers, Shahaji in his later years 'appears to have kept a splendid court in Bangalore'.⁴⁶

Jayram Pindye was a poet who lived close to the town of Nasik. In his work,⁴⁷ which combines prose and verse, he stated that 'having heard of the fame of Shahaji and of the patronage he extended to learning', he thought of travelling from his home near Nasik to Bangalore. On reaching there, he was introduced to Shahaji 'through a man called Shivaraya Goswamin'. He straightaway placed twelve coconuts in front of Shahaji. Asked why he'd done that, he said it was to indicate he could compose poems in twelve languages. He was told to produce an example of his work, and he recited his Sanskrit poem, titled *Radha Madhav Vilas Champu*, a depiction of the love of Radha and Krishna.

Shahaji was happy but insisted that a poet's 'real test' was 'in the completing of a Samasya'. A 'Samasya', in Indian and particularly Sanskrit linguistic tradition, is part literary play and part challenge, where a poet or composer is given a portion of a stanza and asked to complete it and make it appear coherent and whole. 'Let us all give him Samasyas to fill,' Shahaji told all his officials in court, and began by setting a Samasya for the poet himself. He was followed by Malhari Bhatt, Naropant Hanmante and thirteen others at the court, with Hanmante in particular 'looking up, yawning, and shaking his body' in a deliberate display of languid cerebral style while providing his own literary puzzle; and then more officials – thirty-five in all are named – 'came forward to set Samasyas in different vernaculars'. The poet apparently 'acquitted himself satisfactorily, was given presents and was entertained by Shahaji at his court'.⁴⁸ Finally, when Rajwade found Pindye's *Radha Madhav Vilas Champu*, it had three parts: the first part the original which was recited in Shahaji's court, the second, also in Sanskrit, containing details of the poet's visit to Shahaji's court and his stay at the court, and the third an appendix of sorts 'which gives the poems in the vernacular composed by Jayram and other poets of Shahaji's court', set out 'separately in the end as it was not considered proper to include them in the body of the Sanskrit work'.[49] Going to Shahaji's court evidently resulted in an expansion of Pindye's body of work.

Shahaji's death came soon after his elder son Sambhaji's passing in a military campaign, a second major blow for Jijabai. Desolate, Jijabai decided, according to Sabhasad's version,[50] to become a sati by committing the traditional sacrifice carried out by a woman on her husband's funeral pyre. But Shivaji dissuaded her from doing any such thing. Such a practice was by no means unheard of in the Deccan, but it was hardly common among the Marathas, even if we were to take Sabhasad's version at face value.

Shivaji, writes Sabhasad, was 'very sad' and 'lamented much' the death of his father, remarking, 'I have no elder left after him now.' When his mother expressed her wish to immolate herself, 'the Raje sat on her lap', put his hands around her shoulders and 'made her take an oath that she would live and refrain from self-immolation'. 'There is none to witness my heroic deeds, you must not go,' Sabhasad quotes Shivaji as saying. 'With such exhortations,' he writes, 'the Raje, as well as all other great men, after great exertion made her desist.'[51]

8

A Naval Enterprise

With loot pouring in from Surat, Shivaji was now able to feed his fascination for the glistening waters of the Arabian Sea. He was on the lookout for a strong base in southern Konkan, substantial parts of which he was ruling now, to enhance his naval might against the Mughals, the Portuguese and even the Siddis, who still held on to Janjira, the one place Shivaji coveted. In the late 1650s, as we saw earlier, he had captured the ports of Kalyan, Bhiwandi and Prabalgad near Panvel in upper Konkan, but those places had slipped out of his hands later, with either the Mughals or the Portuguese having resumed their domination. The Malvan coastline just north of Goa was well suited to be precisely that kind of coastal headquarters in southern Konkan that Shivaji wanted: it had a reef-lined harbour and quite a few rocky isles.

On a visit there after the sacking of Surat in the early part of 1664, Shivaji noticed an island about 1.5 kilometres off the coast that appeared bigger to him than most of the others in those waters. He asked about it and was informed by two local officials accompanying him, Krishna Sawant Desai and Bhanji Prabhu Desai, that the island was locally known as 'kurte',[1] with a hard 't'. Shivaji was keen to take a close look and was carried there by boat. He noticed how cautiously the path had to be navigated to reach the spot: there were too many small rocks to go around, and that, from a military captain's point of view, was a very good thing. On setting foot on the island, he ordered the building of a robust fort there. Work was to start immediately, and the fort – an island fort, surrounded by water on all sides, as distinct from a coastal fort, which would have land on at least one side of it – would be named Sindhudurg.

With a perimeter of about 3 kilometres, the fort would be spread across 48 acres and have fifty-two bastions, with forty-five well-built steps leading to the top of each. Nearly 500 stonecutters, 200 ironmongers, 100 Portuguese workers and 3,000 other labourers got down to building it.[2] Construction was completed in three years, by 1667, and a letter issued the following year by Shivaji shows that the Maratha official Rajaji Bhosle was appointed *hawaldar* or commander of the fort.[3] A post-Shivaji era document estimates that the expenditure incurred towards construction was one crore *hons*, which is evidently an exaggeration because one *hon* was worth about 3.75 rupees, and the cost in that case would come to 3.75 crore rupees, at least 2.75 crore more than what Shivaji had got from Surat.[4] Even so, there's no doubt Shivaji spent a significant amount of money obtained from the sack on this fort.

Owing in part to its somewhat ragged shape, Sindhudurg remains a thing of rugged handsomeness in the Konkan, with two intriguing features: a couple of prints – one of a right hand and the other of a left foot – which a legend old enough to have found a mention in the *Bombay Gazetteer* of 1880 has claimed are those of Shivaji, and a temple dedicated to Shivaji, built after his passing. The temple is unique because it has perhaps the only representation of Shivaji we have without a beard. The idol of Shivaji installed there, purportedly built during the time of his younger son Rajaram, shows him sporting a moustache and, remarkably enough, according to the Maratha historian G.H. Khare, 'a topee that resembles that of a Koli (fisherman or boatman)'.[5] The Kolis and Bhandaris are the two original inhabitants of the Marathi-speaking part of India's western coast, including Mumbai, and it's a measure of the kind of identification the fisherfolk began to have with Shivaji that his image acquired the headgear of a Koli. For them, Shivaji was the one indigenous ruler of the seventeenth century who cared for the two communities, and who respected the sea and its power and potential. The 'outsiders' had always done so and had ruled unchallenged over the coast: Shivaji recruited the Kolis and the Bhandaris, mingled with them as one of their own, and won them over, as he won over the people of the hills. And he claimed the seas for the indigenous people and for their own raj, which was the raj or state he was establishing. For the Bhandaris too, just as with the Kolis, the identification with him was close: Shivaji came to have a Bhandari as one of his seniormost naval officials.

A little to the north of Sindhudurg, Shivaji discovered, at the time he was scouting the coast, a fortress locally called 'Gheria' on top of a mountain against which the sea waves crashed. It was surrounded by the sea on three sides. He instructed that it be restructured and rebuilt, and named it Vijaydurg. With three layers of fort walls, it provided strong security cover; after Shivaji's death, it was used by the famous Maratha admiral Kanhoji Angre to stock ammunition. A second existing sea fort, further to the north, was identified and reconstructed and its defences fortified; Shivaji gave it the name Suvarnadurg. The names themselves indicate he was attaching a great deal of importance to these citadels: one was named for the river Sindhu or Indus that distinguished Hindu civilization for the rest of the world, the second one for 'Vijay' or victory, and the third for 'Suvarna' or gold. Soon after these three forts were ready, he made a handsome annual allowance of 10,000 *hons* for the upkeep of each.[6]

Shivaji's focus at this point was also on the designing of frigates – which he had started acquiring, albeit in small numbers, in the second half of the previous decade – and on developing his overall naval fleet. English and Dutch records offer ample indication of his efforts in this regard. In June 1664, the British East India Company's officials in Surat wrote to their colleagues in Karwar about how they were 'alarmed' enough 'to expect him [Shivaji]' 'by sea' this time around. They had received reports that he was 'fitting up and building' sixty frigates. What was his reason for doing that? They offered two theories: one, that he intended to 'waylay' ships belonging to Surat on their return from 'Bussorah [Basra] and Persia', and two, that he had 'designs to run up the river of Cainbaya [Cambay]' and land his army there so it could 'march up to Ahmadavad' from there and sack that city.⁷ The following month, the Portuguese captain in Chaul near Alibaug wrote to his Goa headquarters that Shivaji was building fifty ships for combat, of which seven were ready in upper Chaul and would be out to sea soon. Should he obstruct these Maratha ships when they ventured out, the captain asked the Goa officials. If yes, he'd need reinforcements, he wrote; he didn't have enough men with him in Chaul. In its reply, Goa's Portuguese advisory council advised him not to lock horns with Shivaji and not to block his ships for the moment, but it decided to send fifty military men from Bassein (Vasai) to Chaul nonetheless, should the need for its defence arise.⁸

Aurangzeb, a sharp military general himself, was sufficiently concerned by these naval developments. He could see that Shivaji had started, from the late 1650s onwards, focusing on the seashore and was intently building his naval strength. The Dutch in Surat wrote in mid-1664 that the new Mughal governor of the city, Ghiyasuddin Khan, had approached them as well as the Britishers with a message from the Mughal emperor:

> [The Mughal] 'king had ordered him [Khan] by *firman* to request the English and us [the Dutch] to lend a ship each to His Majesty about 15th or 20th September, in order to meet, near St. John, His Majesty's ships, which are expected to arrive from Mocha and to protect them against all hostilities of the robber Siwasi who, as people said, was going to fit out a fleet against the Mogol.⁹

'St. John' here is an unsaintly mutilation of Sanjan, a port in Gujarat. Aurangzeb promised that any charges the European powers would incur 'would be refunded either in cash or by granting more freedom in ... business and exemption from toll'.¹⁰ The British agreed to send a convoy, and the Dutch too consented to deploy their vessel *Vlielant* to assist the Mughals, but not without some reluctance.¹¹ (The Dutch later wrote that 'the [Mughal] king's ships safely came back from Mocha with the English and the Dutch vessels.'¹²)

The Dutch reluctance was mainly owing to the fact that Shivaji was an emerging power in the region, and they didn't want to incur his displeasure by 'helping the Moors', especially when he, during his attack on Surat, 'did not attack our lodge there, although he certainly would have been able to capture it, or at least set fire to it' and when 'that rebel and his subaltern governors have not yet shown us any hostile feeling but have openly tried to keep up friendly relations'.[13] It's not that the Dutch officials trusted the Marathas. They in fact believed Shivaji was inclined to be cordial because 'he knows the Company's maritime power, which might inflict great losses on him'.[14] He wouldn't want losses at a time he'd sensed a chance to become a maritime power himself in both defence and trade, they reckoned, writing that 'he intends to open up an intensive traffic in many quarters, and tries to obtain a busy navigation in the parts he has taken under him'.[15] 'Commerce' was something 'he is taking up pretty busily by stimulating the merchants to traffic', they noted a second time, in another report.[16]

Shivaji indeed wanted a piece of the marine trading ecosystem. In fact, the very same year, at a port in southern Konkan controlled by the Marathas, one of Shivaji's officials, Raoji Somnath Pandit, 'received 2 small ships back from Mocha'; this 'brought him such a nice profit that he has at once made 8 or 9 ships ready to sail to Mocha, Congo, Persia, Mascata, Atsji, etc.'[17] The Dutch, momentarily anxious to keep the peace, had mixed feelings about this: they decided they would 'not give passes for those' ships.[18] They also noted with considerable concern that Shivaji 'has got 50 frigates on the stocks along the straits' and that his 'subedar Rauji Pandito and Bikasi Pandito have written several flattering letters to our people in Wingurla [the port of Vengurla then under Dutch domination] whereby they offered every friendship and service'.[19]

Apart from the talk that the Marathas' share in sea-based trade was slowly inching upwards, what worried the existing powers the most was a possible threat to their security. The Dutch made the point in their internal communication to their bosses that:

Siwasi has struck a great terror amongst the Moors. They think that they will be attacked by him from the sea also, although, as far as is known, he never before sailed on the sea. If he did, the awe he has inspired would enable him to inflict still greater losses on the Moghul with robbing and plundering. He is a man, as it is said, of great conceptions and designs which he knows how to contrive and execute with ingenuity. This might raise him to such a high latitude of power among the terrified Moors, especially now that he has come to perceive the timidity of these people in making his raid on the town of Suratte, of which exploit he will no doubt be very proud and boastful.[20]

Given these perceptions, it wasn't surprising that Aurangzeb asked Bijapur to help the Mughals in ousting the Marathas from southern Konkan at once. If Bijapur cooperated, Aurangzeb would redeem its yearly tribute; if not, he would lead an army himself and invade the Deccani Sultanate. The Adil Shah promptly deputed his forces, and they captured the coastal town of Kudal from the Marathas in mid-1664. The Bijapur army was told to press forward further, and Khawas Khan, an Abyssinian general, was sent at the head of a force of 10,000 cavalry. Accompanying him was a contingent led by Lakham Sawant of Konkan who, as we see in a previous chapter, kept changing sides. Interestingly, Bijapur's army included Shivaji's stepbrother Ekoji Bhosle who had inherited their father's Karnataka *jagir*. A Maratha general, Baji Ghorpade, was also heading there from his home town of Mudhol (further inland from Kudal along the coast) to provide further support with his own 1,500-strong infantry. Ghorpade, described by Dutch officials as 'one of the most excellent commanders', was crucially 'in charge of the [Bijapur] King's cash for paying Chaveschan's [Khawas Khan's] army'.[21]

In a sense, all three of these Marathas were Shivaji's kin, because Ekoji apart, the Sawant-Desais of Kudal and the Ghorpades of Mudhol had close family ties with the Bhosles. 'Ghorpade' was even known as an alternate surname of sorts for 'Bhosle'. But while the Sawant-Desais had played both sides, Baji Ghorpade had stood out as a confirmed enemy of Shivaji's family in particular. On a July morning in 1648, it was Baji Ghorpade who, along with two other Bijapur officials, had entered Shahaji Raje Bhosle's chamber in Jinji, put chains around him, and taken him to Mustafa Khan's camp, where he was imprisoned before being taken to the Adil Shahi capital by Afzal Khan. Mustafa Khan had died long ago, and Shivaji had killed Afzal Khan in 1659. Ghorpade was still around and still assisting Bijapur against the Bhosles – and the death of Shahaji, which had happened barely months ago, was fresh in Shivaji's mind.

Shivaji picked out Ghorpade and mounted so ferocious an assault on him and his men in Mudhol that the Bijapur general was seriously wounded and soon died of his injuries, leaving his men demoralized. Shivaji had unmistakably targeted his father's tormentor in the devastating attack. Next, Shivaji marched against Lakham Sawant and killed several of his men. The twin blows scared Khawas Khan into going back to Bijapur and Lakham Sawant into fleeing to Bardez in the Portuguese colony of Goa.[22] The Adil Shah later wrote to his officials 100 kilometres south of Kolhapur asking them to provide refuge to Sawant. 'As Shivaji caused him much harassment and he could do nothing against it, Lakham Sawant had to desert from his *watan*,' the Bijapur ruler said by way of explanation.[23] The Vengurla coast was barely 20 kilometres away from Kudal, and Vengurla's frightened local governor similarly ran away at the prospect of Shivaji and his men arriving there; so did the local Dutch official there, carrying away with him to Goa 'spices and other goods to save them from Shivaji'.[24] The Dutch reported that 'Sivasy's army consisted of 10 thousand foot-soldiers, 5 or 6 thousand horsemen, and 90 frigates, and this army was followed by 7 or 8 thousand "biggerys" [*begaris* or labourers] and 4 to 5,000 pack animals carrying provisions and diverse other necessaries for the army'.[25]

Pushing on with the success at Vengurla, Shivaji, from October to December 1664, 'seized at sea several Moorish frigates arriving at this roadstead from Persia and Mosquetta (Muscat)', wrote the Dutch officials, adding 'some of these belonged to his own lord [Bijapur, as they saw it] and others to the inhabitants'.[26]

The Dutch have left behind an account of how some ships were taken. On 3 November, they stated, Shivaji's fleet captured 'two little ships'.[27] 'One of them, belonging to Cannara, was taken by surprise, while it was riding at anchor … and was carried away without a shot being fired.' The second vessel had not yet cast anchor, and 'his [Shivaji's] men', the

Dutch pointed out, 'thought they could attack' it 'in a similar way'. The vessel belonged to 'the old queen', the Badi Sahiba of Bijapur, and the Marathas faced so much resistance that 'they could not have captured it if its powder had not been damp'. (Having got wet it could not be used effectively.) Shivaji got the vessel, but not before losing about sixty men, 'while no more than four men were wounded on the frigate'.[28] The moment they climbed on board, Shivaji's men found the frigate's captain 'had stabbed himself out of despondency, saying he would rather die than fall into Siwasi's hands'.[29]

The next morning the Marathas took the vessel to Kharepatan, 'unloading the stolen goods and storing them in the fortress of Giria [Gheria]'. When they were busy doing that, 'one third of their rowers ran away', which the Dutch felt wasn't a surprise, 'for many of them were peasants who had never plied an oar before, nor had even been at sea'.[30] Shivaji was truly building his naval fleet from scratch, and it's perfectly possible he had roped in farmers with no previous experience of being on the seas. Many of them could scarcely be blamed if they didn't comprehend that he was actually building a Maratha state, and many others might have been sceptical at that time about the success of the Maratha forces as they were genuine novices in the waters. Shivaji was breaking new ground and wading through waters totally unfamiliar to his flock; it was a measure of his ambition, his enterprise and his willingness to ride the storm.

On the evening of 8 November, 'two Musquet (Muscat) frigates appeared'.[31] The first, as soon as it heard 'news about Sivasi', didn't approach the shores but 'directed her course homeward to Cannara'. The second ship was from Yemen. Its master, a Christian named Manuel D'Andrade, anchored it in Vengurla, 'inquired about Sivasi's whereabouts' and asked the local Dutch officials to advise him on whether he should stay there. The Dutch told him Shivaji had promised 'safe conduct to the merchants and the frigates that came safely to anchor', and 'moreover, he [D'Andrade] had brave Arabs on board on whom he must rely more than on Sivasi's security'. He answered, 'I may trust him, but I trust my arms most. Very well, I will wait here for three days.'[32] Meanwhile, thirty of Shivaji's frigates came ashore. One of the Maratha captains, whom the Dutch records identify only as 'Mocquerly', approached the Dutch officials and told them he'd initially thought the ship belonged to their Company but had now found out it didn't. He'd proceed to take possession of the ship, 'Mocquerly' said.[33] The Dutch officials advised him not to do so as Shivaji had promised safe conduct to frigates in the seaports and 'handed him two letters of security granted by Sivasi to the Dutch, the English and the Portuguese'.[34] Further, they told him not to harm the ship before he had orders from Shivaji and said he and the Dutch both 'ought first to write about this matter to Sivasi' and 'obey' whatever reply he gave. In a huff, the Maratha official walked off to his armada, set on the course of action he had decided on, but was finally dissuaded by the Dutch not to go ahead.[35]

Another Maratha official, 'Daria Sarangh', wouldn't stay back, however. He pursued the Yemen ship with all of his own vessels, and though D'Andrade sailed safely past in the morning, the Maratha ships 'came up to him at about four o' clock in the afternoon'. They 'fired four shots' and got 'grape-shot' in return, the Dutch wrote, and 'Sivasi's fleet got some men killed and wounded, after which they returned in a great hurry without thinking of pursuing the vessel any farther'.[36]

But on another 'little ship to Surat', there were hardly any brave soldiers. This ship had a '200 tons burden' and 'was manned by more than 100 men', among them two Englishmen serving as gunners; it carried fourteen guns, besides. Yet, rather inexplicably as the Dutch perceived it, the ship's captains surrendered to Shivaji's fleet 'without resistance, to the surprise of all the inhabitants who … were firmly convinced that it could not be captured by Sivasi'.[37] When the Marathas boarded and captured the ship, the Dutch wrote, they 'divided her crew among their frigates' in order to prevent any kind of mobilization before towing her away.[38]

At sunrise on 7 December, a ship belonging to the Dutch Company's merchants 'Cassiba' (Kashiba) and 'Santubasinay' (Santuba Shenavi) had just about anchored itself when it was seized by the Marathas. The Dutch considered its capture ignominious because the Maratha naval official, 'Daria Sarangh', had himself offered the captain of the ship a lifeline: he had, said the Dutch, 'advised' the captain 'to cut the cable and sail away'.[39]

A few weeks later, at noon on 26 December, Dutch officials noticed, from the top of a mountain, a little ship being vigorously pursued by Shivaji's fleet. The Marathas chased it 'till late in the evening, nearly as far as Wingurla', but when they found out it was a Dutch ship called the 'Cadt', they sailed away.[40] The worried ship's master told the Company's officials early next morning when he came ashore that he'd been pursued by Shivaji's armada for twenty-four hours.[41]

Based on what they were seeing around them, the Dutch themselves got their own factory fortified against Shivaji by calling in nine men from their vessels and 2,000 pounds of gunpowder. They 'also enlisted 10 peons, especially to serve us at the guns'. 'With all these, together with some Arab merchants who had fled into the lodge, some Christians, and a few native inhabitants, we considered ourselves sufficiently strong to bear an attack from the admitted rebel, as his soldiers had already shown courtesy in many respects,' the Dutch officials wrote.[42]

The Dutch estimated the booty gained by the Marathas from the ships seized and from Baji Ghorpade's base during this short period to be '8,00,000 gold rups' – rupees, meaning *hons*; *hons* were called gold rupees by foreigners – and 'the spoils taken by land' to be '20,00,000 gold rupees'.[43]

To this, Shivaji added fresh gains from a sudden inland raid into Hubli, which was to the south of both Kolhapur and Belgaum in the Kannada-speaking parts of the Deccan. The British factors in Karwar recorded that Shivaji 'sent about 300 horse' to Hubli, 'robbed the town, and carried away some prisoners, so that Hubely is little better than spoiled'.[44] Luckily, when Shivaji arrived there, the British officials said, they had nothing except '1185 pagodas in ready money'.[45]

By the end of 1664, Shivaji not only had almost all of the southern or 'Tal' Konkan in his grip but had attacked parts of Bijapur territory in the uplands as well. The Britishers in Surat wrote that 'Sevagy ... is the sole talk of court and country' and 'raines [reigns] victoriously and uncontrolled [so] that he is a terror to all the kings and princes round about, dayly encreasing in strength'.[46] They'd already reported he had got sixty-five frigates, though they considered these vessels 'pitiful things' and weak enough for 'a hundred of them' to be destroyed by 'one good ship'; now, they said he had 'fitted up more vessels'.⁴⁷ And another British official from further south, Henry Gary, reported that Shivaji 'is destroying by fire and sword all that he can of the King of Vigapore's country'.⁴⁸ It was credibly reported, Gary stated, that 'he hath an army of 8,000 horse and 10,000 foote, all small shott [short] men'.⁴⁹ Surat's mandarins wrote that Shivaji was, along with his scouts, 'who range all over the country, making havoc', and added that he 'continues in great power and force, and much feared by all'.⁵⁰ After the Surat raid, they wrote, he had taken possession of 'eight or nine' of the 'most considerable ports belonging to the Deccan', and from each of these ports 'he setts out two or three or more trading vessels yearly to Persia, Bussora [Basra], Mocha' and other places.⁵¹

Thus Shivaji's naval power was, in the midst of all the clashes, also acquiring a degree of stability.

The question on everyone's mind was: would Shivaji attack Goa next? The British thought it highly unlikely, even as they hedged in an advisory to officials at their Karwar factory, asking them 'not to sleepe too secure but to be watchfull and procure what intelligence you can of him [so] that you may make a timely escape where you think you may be most safe'. They also felt a place like Karwar was so down south, being even beyond Goa, that he wouldn't 'fall down so low as where you are' as it would be 'bad travelling in the raines for either horse or foot; besides, he will have his hands full if ... the King of Vitchapoore setts out an army against him'.⁵²

The Dutch had a different take. According to them, Shivaji was looking at a pact with them so that they could fight Goa's rulers together. The Dutch claimed that in the middle of January 1665, 'Siwasi's grand governor, Raogi Pandito, asked our chief [of the Vengurle factory] Lenertsz' to send across 'a reliable person' with whom he could discuss 'important matters'. When the Dutch sent an official over, Raoji Pandit told him he'd got 'letters from his spies in Goa' saying there had been 'some estrangement between the Dutch and the Portuguese'. If that were true, 'his master Siwasi would be willing to enter into a contract with the Dutch for the town of Goa'. But if not true, Lenertsz should not talk about it [the Maratha offer]', and there the matter would end.⁵³

And what were the Portuguese thinking? They were apparently getting mixed signals. In the first place, Shivaji's frigates had taken, in October 1664, 'eight boats ... laden with elephants' teeth' which had left for Chaul from Goa, prompting the viceroy of the Portuguese colony to summon the 'northern armada' and pay and post soldiers 'on the frontier against him [Shivaji]'.[54] Then, early in January 1665, the Portuguese viceroy wrote to his king in Portugal that both Shivaji and the Adil Shah wanted to have a tie-up with Goa.[55] These conflicting signals were far from helpful to them in making up their minds.

But unlike the Britishers, the Portuguese weren't inclined to dismiss the Maratha ships as 'pitiful things' that could easily be taken care of. Shivaji's fleet was mostly made of *galleywats* (or *gallivats* or *galvetas*) or what in Marathi were termed *galbats*. These were chiefly rowing boats, but large in size for boats of that kind; they generally had two masts, of 40 to 70 tons; and they carried four to eight guns.[56] Small meant speedy, so these *galbats* could well have an advantage over the slow-moving, big Portuguese ships.[57] Thus, unwilling to take any chances in view of Shivaji's growing power, the Portuguese decided to keep 'a continuously strong watch on all the frontier places and points round Goa' and had all these spots 'continually provided with victuals and ammunition'.[58] The viceroy ordered the islands of Salsette, Bardez and Goa 'to be inspected and had a list made of all soldiers capable of bearing arms'. On Salsette were stationed 64,000 such soldiers, on Bardez 24,000 and in Goa, 12,000. From among them, 'the most capable black men' were selected – 8,000 from the first place, 5,000 from the second and 3,000 from the third. With 'shooting arms of their own', they'd all have to take their 'rounds each in their own cities giving notice to the others to be ready if need be, so that this rebel [Shivaji] is keeping all Goa in constant alarm'.[59]

Adding to the sense of alarm, the chief of the Portuguese naval fleet wrote to Goa's viceroy that the people of Mirjan, Ankola, Shiveshwar and Karwar were scared by rumours that Shivaji would soon be there, and the British officials in Surat too slightly revised their opinion, pointing to Bhatkal in the south as a likely target.[60]

While all this talk was on and these preparations were being made,

Shivaji neatly bypassed Goa and sailed well past Karwar and Bhatkal before suddenly curving in and hitting land in Basrur. Hardly anybody had thought he'd foray so deep into the Kannada-speaking regions; at the most, it was surmised, he'd go up to Karwar, which was the southernmost tip of the Marathi-speaking coastal belt. This was the first – and as it turned out, only – naval campaign undertaken by Shivaji in his life, where he rode the seas with the wind in his hair and his trusted men by his side in the newly minted Maratha *galbats*.

Early in February 1665, Shivaji 'himself in person set forth' from Malvan, the British factory officials in Karwar wrote to Surat.[61] He had with him 'a fleet of 85 frigots (frigates)' and '3 great ships'. He freely 'plundered' Basrur, which at the time was being ruled by a local chieftain, Somashekhara. Basrur's previous ruler was Somashekhara's father, the well-regarded Shivappa, the local king of Ikkeri. Shivappa had evicted the Portuguese from the place, but the son had, after the father's death in 1660, been ceding ground and had more or less been prepared to give the Portuguese a walkover. Shivaji had sensed an opportunity before the Portuguese stepped in and taken it. He didn't want to be enmeshed in a conflict in one place, not when he knew he'd soon have to reckon with serious Mughal retaliation for what he'd done to Shaista Khan. He had thus avoided the strongly fortified Goa and other well-defended spots and gone further south.

From Basrur Shivaji headed to Gokarna, where the Hindus had one of their famous places of pilgrimage: the temple of Mahabaleshwar dedicated to Lord Shiva, built along the seafront circa fourth century CE. There, Shivaji, a devout Hindu, 'washed his body, according to the ceremony of that place' and moved in the direction of Ankola, wrote the British. Before leaving Gokarna, he asked all his ships to go back and kept only 4,000 foot soldiers and horsemen with him, along with twelve frigates which would help him and his cohort cross the rivers on their way back home via the land route. On 22 February Shivaji reached Karwar, prompting the British to hurriedly 'clap all the Company's money and portable commodities aboard a ship' that belonged to the Imam of Muscat. Its captain promised the British he'd secure their goods and if needed sail out and take the Company's officials to whichever port they wanted to reach. Shivaji's major vessels, except the twelve he'd kept back, had gone past Karwar just the day before; that brought some relief to the British, though they were pretty sure Shivaji would still try to target them.

The very evening on which the British officials boarded the ship stationed in the port, there arrived Sher Khan, a lieutenant of the powerful Bijapur noble Bahlol Khan whose writ ran in the region. Sher Khan was there to make preparations for Bahlol Khan's mother's journey to Mecca; a ship belonging to one Rustom Jemmah was to take her to the holy site. Sher Khan sent one of his men to Shivaji with a message, saying he had heard the Maratha leader intended to pass through the town. He told him he desired him not to take that route, because 'if he did, he must use whatever means he could to stop his passage'. 'A great many goods of his masters were on the Bunder,' Sher Khan said, and for their security, 'he could not admit of so potent an enemy so near his quarters'. According to the British, several messages passed between the two, and Shivaji, 'knowing his [Khan's] power with his master and strength of Bullol Caune [Bahlol Khan] in this kingdom', finally 'condescended to go a little out of his way'. Instead of going through the town, he encamped with his army at the mouth of the river nearby.

But that wasn't the end of it. Shivaji sent his ambassador to Sher Khan, saying that he'd arrived and that he'd heard that aboard the Muscat ship were the English, plus there was another ship in the port belonging to the African kingdom of Kongo. Both, Shivaji said, were ready to resist him, so Sher Khan had better 'deliver up' the English ship or move away himself, permitting Shivaji to take revenge on the British, 'whom he stiled [styled] his inveterate enemies'. Sher Khan conveyed the message to the British and was told by them that they 'had nothing on board but powder and bullets, which if he [Shivaji] thought would serve him instead of gold he might come and fetch'. Shivaji was so exasperated and angered by this reply that 'he said he would have us [the English] before he parted'. Panicking, the Karwar governor persuaded the merchants in the town 'to agree to send him [Shivaji] a present, lest he should recall his fleet'. The Britishers too concluded, after having initially sworn defiance, that the best way out was to promise their own share of 112 pounds 'than runne the hazard of the Company's estate in Carwar, being about 8,000 pagodas', being invaded. With the booty thus gathered, Shivaji finally departed on 23 February but 'very unwillingly', 'saying that Sher Khan had spoiled his hunting at his Holi, which is a time he generally attempts some such design'.

The Marathas led by Shivaji became a coastal and specifically naval power to reckon with in a short period of time, despite their poor knowledge of the technology of shipbuilding, their limited ammunition and the fact that all the foreign powers in India at the time were way ahead of them in entering the maritime race. Shivaji's act of systematically building a navy makes him genuinely unique among all the military leaders of early modern India. Among them, he was the first mover. At a time when the Portuguese, Dutch, the British and the French had virtually exclusive rights over the seawaters, he figured out that in peninsular India, the coastline was far too important in terms of both defence and trade to be left in the hands of these powers. His vision was clear-cut, and so were his planning and execution. But who were the people who helped him build and keep his navy? Very, very little information has come down to us about these men, except that it's not a surprise that the majority of them were from the local communities that lived along the coast such as Kolis, Bhandaris and indigenous Muslims. We know for sure the identities of only three of his naval commanders: Darya Sarang, Daulat Khan and Mainak Bhandari.

Two of these three were Muslim, Daulat Khan and Darya Sarang, according to Sabhasad.[62] Sabhasad also gave some idea of the nature of the vessels Shivaji had: apart from *galbats*, he mentioned, Shivaji had such things as '*tarande*', which are big sailing vessels, '*gurab*', mainly two-mast ships of 150-tonnes burden 'built to draw very little water, being very broad in proportion to their length, narrowing however from the middle to the end', '*taru*', simply meaning a sailing vessel, '*sibad*', 'large, square-sterned and flat-bottomed vessel with two masts but no deck' and known to be chiefly used for trade, and '*pagar*', which was just a well-smoothed canoe.[63]

The British wrote that Darya Sarang's real name was 'Ventjee Sarungee',[64] which sounds like a Hindu name. But Sabhasad may be a more reliable source, and, as the Maratha historian G.B. Mehendale has pointed out, the surname Sarangee was indeed used among local Muslims – as against Arab, Persian or African Muslims – in the Marathi-speaking coastal corners.[65] Darya Sarang was thus most likely neither a name nor a post but a title Ventjee had been given, and the word '*darya*', which means the ocean, is indicative of that. Sarangee seems to have later fallen out of favour with Shivaji, for in the late 1670s, the British reported that Shivaji had ordered 'both Deria Saranga and his son' to be 'taken prisoner' and 'all [that] they have seized'.[66] What went wrong between Shivaji and his commander? The historical record is completely silent on that.

Mainak Bhandari was, as his surname makes evident, from the coast-dwelling Bhandari community. One post-Shivaji-era document has suggested his surname was Bhatkar.[67]

Sabhasad mentions one Ibrahim Khan along with Darya Sarang and Mainak Bhandari as a commander. Here, alas, it looks like he got things mixed up. Though quite a few historians have counted Daulat Khan and Ibrahim Khan as two separate people, the most plausible theory about Ibrahim Khan's name is that Sabhasad was referring to Daulat Khan and wrote it wrongly, as there's no mention of any Ibrahim Khan anywhere else, whereas the name Daulat Khan is corroborated by several sources. The veteran Communist Party of India leader Govind Pansare, who was tragically killed in 2015, wrote a small booklet, '*Shivaji Kon Hota?*', which portrayed Shivaji as a champion of the 'masses'. Looking through his communist ideological prism, Pansare got quite a few things wrong, and among those was his mention of Daulat Khan as 'Darya Sarang Daulat Khan'.[68] Darya Sarang and Daulat Khan, as Jadunath Sarkar has rightly pointed out, were two different people;[69] as noted earlier, Darya Sarang was emphatically not a position, and it was not a moniker ever applied to Daulat Khan, who was a commander in his own right.

9

Setback and Retreat

After Shivaji hammered Shaista Khan's confidence and made him look ridiculous, Aurangzeb became more determined than ever to sound the drumbeat of doom for the Maratha who had refused to row back his rebellion and, seemingly out of nowhere, was presenting a stiffer challenge to the Mughal empire than any of the other Deccan powers like Bijapur and Golconda. Asking Bijapur to block Shivaji's progress on the coast was just a sideshow; Aurangzeb's main act, as he surveyed a Deccan vastly changed in just a little over a decade, was to draft in a highly experienced Hindu general to do the job of wrecking Shivaji's emerging ship of state.

That Hindu was Mirza Raja Jai Singh. A member of the royal house of Jaipur, Jai Singh had entered Mughal service as an orphan at the age of eight and gone on to distinguish himself in campaigns across the empire, from Balkh and Kandahar in Afghanistan to Bijapur in the south and Mungir in the east.[1] Greatly skilled at military manoeuvres, he was also noted for his command of the art of diplomacy, and he had a penchant for taking things to their logical conclusion for his master – unlike Shaista Khan who, despite his frothy title of *amir-ul-umra*, had allowed complacency to set in during a largely successful campaign, with disastrous results. What made this Rajput prince of Amber, now a wise fifty-six years old, even more valuable to Aurangzeb was his absolute and unquestionable loyalty, strengthened no doubt by blood ties. They were bound by blood, three times over. One of Jai Singh's forebears had arranged his daughter's marriage to Emperor Akbar; his great-grandfather's sister was married to Prince Salim who later became Emperor Jahangir; and Jahangir had later also taken another girl from Jai Singh's family as his wife.[2]

Jai Singh had exceedingly competent generals like the Afghan Diler Khan accompanying him on his campaign against Shivaji. Altogether, 14,000 troops led by various captains, including Jai Singh's own son Kirat Singh, left for the Deccan along with him.[3] Those who'd been with Shaista Khan were still very much stationed in Maratha country; if their numbers were added, the total Mughal count behind Jai Singh stood at 70,000.[4] Statistically, Shivaji's Marathas appeared almost pitiful in comparison.

However, Jai Singh was keenly aware of problems created by size and the attendant Mughal bureaucracy. The first thing he told Aurangzeb was that he wanted full freedom in decision-making at all levels. Often local appointments, payments and various other civil and military matters were handled by regional straps, resulting in bottlenecks. Aurangzeb's son Prince Muazzam, appointed viceroy of the Deccan in place of the disgraced Shaista Khan, was especially indolent and hadn't done much in the few months he'd been there, and that may well have been one reason for Jai Singh making such demands. Aurangzeb acceded to this, perhaps cognizant of the prince's not-so-consequential presence there.

Once he had got all the powers he wanted, Jai Singh hit the ground running. He wasn't content with the existing numerical superiority; he wanted a crushing superiority, and to get that he would use persuasion, force, bribery, threats – whatever was necessary. As he marched across the Narmada in January 1665 and then – after genuflecting, at least physically, before Prince Muazzam in Aurangabad in February – reached Pune early in March, he wrote to the successors of the Mores of Jaawali. Hadn't Shivaji taken their lands from them? What better way to get them back than to join the Mughals to destroy Shivaji, he asked them.[5] He asked the Siddis of Janjira to help him stamp out the Maratha menace, for didn't Shivaji covet their sea fort like nothing else? Afzal Khan's son Fazl volunteered himself, and Jai Singh offered him a 5,000-horse post as a matter of honour.[6] Wasn't Fazl, too, hungry for revenge? The zamindar of Jawhar, a plateau situated to the north of Bombay, sent an envoy expressing his desire to join. Jai Singh wrote to Aurangzeb saying he was convinced the zamindar could be 'immensely useful'.[7]

With the Portuguese, Jai Singh used both persuasion and warning. He dispatched two Portuguese men working with him to Goa, asking the authorities there to cooperate in the Mughal bid to get rid of Shivaji. He wrote that he wasn't happy, though, that some Portuguese men had been actively involved with Shivaji, forcing the Goa viceroy to clarify that Shivaji might have employed some Portuguese for his naval activities, but that didn't mean they had the Portuguese state's approval. There were many delinquent Portuguese all across the Mughal regions and even in Bijapur, Golconda and other places, over whom Goa had no control, the viceroy wrote.[8] And, of course, he offered all assistance to Jai Singh, though the Goans, much like Bijapur, had increasingly come to see Shivaji's Maratha force as constituting some sort of buffer zone between them and the Mughal giant that could simply swallow them up.

Worried that the already cornered Bijapur might get together with Shivaji to fight the Mughals, Jai Singh set about 'trying to sow dissension',[9] bribing several Adil Shahi fort commanders and making generous offers of office and cavalry to Bijapur generals. Somashekhara, the son of Ikkeri's late ruler Shivappa Naik whose region Shivaji had partly plundered only recently, and the zamindar of Basavapatan were sent 'letters and robes of honour'.[10] And the *deshmukhs* and *deshpandes*, key officials in Shivaji's hill regions, were threatened with dire consequences if they covertly aligned with Shivaji.[11]

After cannily getting together a robust set of allies, Jai Singh was adroit about his camp selection as well. He picked Saswad to the east over the much more obvious choice of Pune. There, he would in a sense be between Shivaji's state and Bijapur: he would not only be able to keep an eye on both sides and move either way easily, but also preclude the possibility of the two rivals coming together. Unlike Shaista Khan, who had stopped touching Shivaji's forts after the difficult siege of Chakan and had contented himself with seizing territory, Jai Singh demonstrated a strong awareness that the hill forts formed the heart of Shivaji's political enterprise. If he struck at them, he would strike at the core of the state Shivaji was attempting to build. All the Deccan territory was of course needed, but 'we have primarily to attack the hill forts', Jai Singh wrote to Aurangzeb, asking him to send across, for that purpose, 'big guns' already lying with the Mughals and 'cannons which have been recently cast'.[12]

And in Saswad itself was one of Shivaji's most powerful citadels: Purandar. It was time to go all out against Purandar, one of the sources of Shivaji's pride, he decided. After Purandar to the south-west, there were also Sinhagad and Rajgad to the west of Saswad. Checkmate Purandar, and the checkmating of Sinhagad and Rajgad could logically follow, Jai Singh believed.[13]

While the Afghan Diler Khan was to lead the thrust against Purandar, on the ground level, a number of large military teams were to plonk themselves at strategic points across Maratha territory so that the local officials and populace would submit easily. For example, 4,000 troopers were stationed under Ihtisham Khan in Pune and 7,000 horsemen under Qutubuddin Khan in Junnar, with directions to the latter that 3,000 of them should position themselves in front of one fort, Lohgad, and 4,000 before another, called Nardurg.[14] Jai Singh also issued instructions that several surrounding places were to be ransacked to forestall any daring strikes. Well before the assault on Purandar started, Jai Singh had tried, but failed, to entice 'Almaji and Kahar Koli and two of his brothers',[15] all tasked by Shivaji to look after the Maratha artillery at the foot of the fort, by offering them honourable positions. Now his directions were that if any peasants or military men surrendered, they were to be welcomed into the Mughal camp and offered incentives to break the back of Shivaji's forces.[16] Jai Singh's plan, in short, was to make his offensive relentless and launch it from all sides.

Not surprisingly, the team led by Diler Khan approached Purandar with much enthusiasm. But its initial ardour was somewhat dampened by a bunch of Marathas who slithered down the hillsides and began raining muskets. The Mughals recovered quickly and chased the Marathas up the hill, all the way to the *machi* or the lower posts near the base of the fort, and even burnt all the houses that stood there. Despite the Marathas firing from the top, Diler Khan soon had the post under control and called for reinforcements, which Jai Singh sent promptly and generously. Among them was a force of 3,000 led by his son Kirat Singh and teams led by Qubaid Khan, Badal Bakhtiyar, Indraman Bundela and others, all well stocked with guns and other arms.

The Mughals covered Purandar from all sides, digging trenches, and on Jai Singh's orders first targeted its sentinel Rudramal, whose crest gave cover to the lower fortress of Purandar. Jai Singh told Aurangzeb in a letter, correctly, that Rudramal held 'the key to Purandar'.[17] If the Mughals wanted to get to Purandar's *bale-killa* or top fort, they first had to get to the lower fortress, and if they had to win the lower fortress, they had to go past Rudramal. Not an easy thing, for Purandar rose 4,500 feet above sea level and its base itself was at over 2,500 feet. It was rather laborious to carry the guns within striking distance of Rudramal's important points. The 10,000-strong Maratha garrison atop Purandar and its sentinel made the task even more difficult for over 20,000 of Jai Singh's men – Mughals, Rajputs as well as Europeans in the artillery department – by showering arrows, stones and other projectiles. Yet the determined Mughals got there in a matter of a few days in April 1665 and unleashed a volley of cannon fire. A breach was created by the fire, and Jai Singh's sappers exploded a mine placed along the walls of Rudramal to create another gaping hole, throwing Purandar open to a full-fledged assault. Though his army had lost eighty people and over a hundred men had been injured in breaching Rudramal, Jai Singh strategically offered free passage to the garrison that surrendered there, hoping it would give reason enough for the main garrison at Purandar to capitulate without any further fighting.

Jai Singh was evidently satisfied with what he had achieved so far. He wrote to Aurangzeb, stressing that until then it had been believed cannons could be used only against forts which stood close to the ground:

> But our campaign has established one thing. It is indeed possible to carry the big guns half-way up the hill forts, to the very place the people of these regions called the *machi*. From that spot, a highly effective assault

can be launched on the fort. That's precisely what we did in the case of Rudramal.[18]

There was no doubt, he stated, that Diler Khan and his associates had done an excellent job. 'But in truth, all of this happened because of the Badshah's great good fortune, his manifest destiny,' he added in supplicating fashion. 'The enemy [Shivaji] had never before experienced such a disaster. God willing, his situation will be even more disastrous in the future. Shivaji has been taught a real big lesson.'[19]

His men's aggressive boundary-pushing feat, which left only the main hurdle of Purandar to be surmounted, made Jai Singh think that he must move ahead elsewhere to try and undermine Shivaji's resolve. The breakthrough at Rudramal offered him a fine perch to launch attacks across the countryside, and that was what he directed his various units to do. In their formidable numbers, they set about razing the fertile ground in which Maratha ambitions were thriving. They showed up in the villages and districts along the hills, atop the hills and beneath the hills, unleashing a barrage of strikes and raids.

How he directed all the action is clear from Jai Singh's missives to Aurangzeb. First, he explained his reasoning to the emperor. He wanted to demonstrate to Shivaji that just because the Mughals were busy carrying out the siege of a major fort like Purandar, they would not remain confined to that action. No way. There were a great many of them, so even as the siege progressed, they could very well push their way into the rest of the Maratha country without a break. Second, he was convinced that the moment was right to make a hit and encircle the enemy from all sides, just when the attention of Shivaji's men was focused on what was for them, without doubt, the looming crisis of Purandar.[20]

Further, Jai Singh spoke of the exact nature of the attacks that were being organized and carried out. To the west of Purandar lay Shivaji's most important hill fort, Rajgad, where the Maratha had set up his residence at the time, and Kondhana (also known as Sinhagad); to Purandar's south stood Rohida. All three forts were in the heart of Shivaji's mountainous territory. Jai Singh sent out more than 6,000 troops, 'led by Daud Khan,

Raja Raisingh Rathod and others' with orders to 'depopulate and reduce to ashes' the whole region in which these forts lay.[21] Reaching the vicinity of Rohida on 27 April 1665, these generals and their forces 'set ablaze around 50 villages', Jai Singh reported to his emperor. Nestling securely in the hills there were also 'four populous and prosperous villages where no Mughal army had ventured before'. This time, the Mughal units reached there and requested the leadership for reinforcements, which were immediately sent. The result, Jai Singh wrote, was that 'the enemy ran away from the villages, and our armies set fire to all four villages and laid them waste. Many people and animals were caught and taken prisoner.'[22]

The approach to Rajgad was more ruthlessly violent: all the villages along the route were torched and all the lands and cultivation mercilessly destroyed. By 30 April the Mughal troops had reached the base of Rajgad and their leading unit 'even reached up to the fort's gates', Jai Singh stated, 'but those inside didn't have the courage to come out, so our forces, instead of just staying there, went out and completely burnt all the villages nearby'.[23] As that part was quite hilly, the Mughals, instead of setting up camp there, chose a less inconvenient flatland about 7 kilometres away to put up their tents for the moment, and from there they moved in the direction of Kondhana, causing large-scale devastation in its neighbourhood on 2 May.[24]

Meanwhile, Jai Singh received information that Shivaji was consolidating his forces near Lohgad, which was to the north-west of Purandar and almost at the western tip of the Sahyadris, overlooking the coastal parts. He rushed his already charged-up men there, with more than adequate arms and ammunition. In the fierce fighting that took place, a Mughal unit led by Qutubuddin Khan 'killed several Marathas and injured many, while those that remained withdrew in the direction of Lohgad'. Continuing their pursuit, the Mughals 'set up camp on the ground that stands between Lohgad and three other forts around it [Visapur, Tung and Tikona]'. Such was the grip that the Mughals had achieved in a short time, wrote Jai Singh, that they had 'defeated the enemy on the Balaghat [hilltops] as well as the Painghat [bottom of the hills] and totally destroyed enemy territory'.[25]

As for the siege of Purandar, it was going especially well, and though monsoon was approaching, the Mughals would have the fort sooner rather than later, Jai Singh told the emperor. 'Day and night I am occupied with the business of the siege,' he said, adding, 'thanks to your [Aurangzeb's] blessings, things which would have been impossible to do in a month are being accomplished in a day.'[26]

It was really a matter of time before Purandar fell to the battery of assaults. The leader of the Maratha garrison there, Murar Baji Deshpande, had put up a stiff fight with his men, but it was evident he couldn't hold out for long. Murar Baji had earlier worked with the Mores of Jaawali, Shivaji's bitter opponents, but after Shivaji took over Jaawali, he had joined him and had been steadfastly loyal. Seeing 5,000 Mughals led by Diler Khan trying to ascend the hill towards the *bale-killa* and sensing the inevitable, Murar Baji decided to make a dash into the enemy formation. With 700 chosen Marathas he stormed in, taking Diler Khan's men momentarily by surprise because they hadn't expected such a small group of fighters to make a sudden and apparently suicidal descent. Murar Baji was bent on making a final, desperate move. He and his Marathas killed 500 Mughals, Murar Baji himself cutting his way through into Diler Khan's own camp with a band of sixty soldiers.[27] Falling slightly back, Diler Khan asked his artillery, archers, lancers and 1,000 light-armed men to deal with Murar Baji's smallish squad. Of these attackers, sixty fell to Maratha blows, and Murar Baji went all the way up to Diler Khan. Face to face with the Afghal general, the Maratha commander, according to Sabhasad's account of the episode, asked himself how he could possibly 'show face' to Shivaji after 'men cherished by the favour of the Maharaja [Shivaji]' were 'dead' and decided that he must 'rush on straight'.[28] According to Sabhasad, a snappy exchange followed between the two rival captains:

Diler Khan: You take a *kaul*, an assurance of safety, from me. You are an extremely intrepid soldier. I will promote you.

Murar Baji: What is your *kaul*? Do I, a soldier of Shivaji Raje, take *your kaul*?[29]

Holding his sword aloft, Murar Baji stepped ahead, but the alert Diler Khan positioned his bow and arrow for the kill. He struck before Murar Baji could, snuffing the life out of the brave Maratha commander of Purandar. Around 300 Marathas died in the desperate fight, while the 400 who survived went back to the fort. Diler Khan, however, was rattled by the surprise attack and took off his turban, vowing he would put it back on only after he had captured Purandar. He proceeded to form 'a rampart of shields ... below the portals of the fort' and moved forward. But the garrison kept up its spirited resistance, saying, 'What if one Murar Baji is dead? We are as brave as he was, and we shall fight with the same courage!'[30]

Jai Singh himself was exultant at his domination of the war theatre. The siege of Purandar, he noted, 'was effectively conducted, five towers and one battlement were captured by us, his [Shivaji's] country was plundered by our cavalry'. He gloated that:

> his troops collected in such a long time were seduced by us – because I had by this time by giving passports and promises of safety summoned to myself many of his cavalry and induced them to enter the imperial service with proper *mansabs* [military ranks] and stipends of 10 or 15 [rupees], and by giving them 10 or 20 rupees above the promised rate in cash from the treasury.[31]

Worried again about Shivaji and Bijapur joining hands, the wily Jai Singh had also scared off the Adil Shahi state by issuing a series of threats and positioning the Mughal armies in strategic places, ensuring that it would not, for the sake of its own security and survival, want to assist the rebel Maratha in any way.

With Murar Baji Deshpande and hundreds of other Maratha soldiers gone, almost all of the territory Shivaji had taken (except for southern Konkan) more or less overrun, Purandar on the verge of being conquered by Diler Khan, and other Sahyadri forts similarly threatened by Mughal armies parked perilously close, Shivaji believed that the best option for him was to stop fighting and seek acceptable terms. He recognized that if Afzal Khan was a hard one to tackle and Shaista Khan twice as hard, then this was several times harder.

Shivaji would not have to take merely one or two but many steps back for Jai Singh to agree to a peace treaty with him. He had been driven into a corner. He had the other choice, of course, the choice many a warrior-leader had made on countless occasions before him, and would make during and after Shivaji's times. He could commit hara-kiri; he could self-destruct; he could go out, as it were, in a blaze of glory, to be remembered – like many battlefield giants – as a great martyr to his cause, who did not blink at the supreme sacrifice. But Shivaji thought twice, thrice, a number of times, and he made up his mind. He *was* going to swallow the excruciatingly bitter pill. This would count as one of the hardest and most wrenching decisions of his career. He had the far-sightedness to realize that even if it appeared, in May–June 1665, that Maratha forts would only be somewhat reduced in number if Purandar and some others like it were taken by the Mughals, those were extremely critical to his emerging raj. Once they fell, their loss would translate into pressure on other citadels and on whatever little territory was still left in his hands. Whichever way he looked at it, he could only perceive defeat, and if he didn't concede it now, it would lead to the extinguishing of his long-held dreams of independent statehood. Shivaji was going to do everything he could to prevent the blowing out of that flame. He was going to go through the wringer – not to be crushed, but to emerge beaten but still alive on the other side.

Much before the Purandar siege reached its tipping point, Shivaji had begun to make overtures to Jai Singh – just as he had previously, to Bijapur as well as to the Mughals, whenever he was in a spot of bother. Shivaji's first offer was of assistance to the Mughals in their drive against Bijapur, which was 'more likely to succeed', he said, 'than a war in his hilly and intricate country'; in exchange for that, he must be permitted to keep his forts, his territory and his part of the coastal belt.[32] That hadn't worked. When the tipping point came at Purandar, Shivaji made a fresh offer. This one carried a warning. He sent his envoy Raghunath Ballal Atre to meet the Rajput leader of the Mughal troops and promised tribute and some forts. If these terms were rejected, Shivaji said, he would 'restore a part of the Bijapuri Tal Konkan to the Sultan of Bijapur, join the Sultan and oppose the Mughals'.[33]

Jai Singh wouldn't accept the proposal. He insisted that Shivaji meet him in person and submit to the Mughal empire unconditionally; only then might the empire bestow its mercy on him. Atre soon returned to Jai Singh with a message from Shivaji: he was willing to send his son Sambhaji across to make the submission. That, too, Jai Singh dismissed out of hand. Jai Singh had already communicated to Atre that the Mughal emperor had given him neither the freedom nor the authority to negotiate with Shivaji, which meant he could hardly hold any conference with him openly. Shivaji wrote to him that if this was the case, 'if you cannot publicly grant me [any] promise and safe conduct, make the same promise in private', so that he could come and see him. Jai Singh replied to Shivaji's envoy on 9 June 1665, saying that if, after having arrived in his camp, Shivaji 'consents to obey the Emperor's orders, he would be pardoned and granted favours, otherwise he would be allowed to return in safety to his home'.[34] Jai Singh didn't want to stretch his advantage to breaking point. He warned Aurangzeb that his spies had brought him news that the sultan of Bijapur, who had wrested a few *mahals* from the Tal Konkan from Shivaji as proof of his loyalty to the Mughal empire, had 'secretly promised [Shivaji] every possible help' to keep the Mughals at bay ... To render Shivaji hopeless would only drive him into an alliance with Bijapur.'[35]

Jai Singh had set up camp close to the foot of Purandar. He was holding his durbar there on the morning of 11 June 1665 when, at 11 a.m., Atre walked in to say Shivaji had arrived, accompanied by six Brahmins and the bearers of his palanquin. Jai Singh immediately asked two of his officials, Udairaj Munshi and Ugrasen Kachhwah, to meet Shivaji on the way 'and tell him that if he agreed to surrender all his forts he might come, otherwise he should turn back'. Shivaji answered without hesitation, as if he were anticipating such an ultimatum, 'I have entered into [imperial] service. Many of my forts will be added to the imperial dominions.'[36] Satisfied, the two men led him in, and at the door of Jai Singh's tent he was escorted inside by Jai Singh's aide Jani Beg Bakshi. Jai Singh came forward, embraced Shivaji and asked him to sit by his side, while two of Jai Singh's armed men stood around, keeping guard.

Jai Singh had made preparations for a neat little scene for Shivaji's eyes, a scene almost guaranteed to break down any barriers that the Maratha might still want to keep intact. He had asked Diler Khan and his own son Kirat Singh, who were in the forward positions at Purandar, to be ready to launch a decisive attack. The moment Shivaji walked in, Jai Singh sent out word to Diler and Kirat; on cue, a part of the tent's curtain was pulled away. It was a distressing sight for Shivaji to behold: the assault on his stronghold had been renewed, and dust, smoke and the noise of artillery filled the air. The defenders hit back, but the attackers evidently had the upper hand, and more of the garrison lay dead and wounded as fighting intensified. Shivaji implored Jai Sigh to stop the killing and offered to give up the fort. Jai Singh replied, to drive the point home, that the Mughals were on the verge of vanquishing their enemy there. 'In an hour, in a minute', the garrison would be 'put to the sword', he said. If Shivaji had an offer to make to the emperor, it had better be of several other forts, he declared confidently.[37]

Shivaji did his best to keep his calm and appealed once again, saying he wanted the lives of his men defending the fort to be spared. Relenting, Jai Singh sent one of his own officials with a representative of Shivaji to Diler Khan and Kirat Singh, and the Mughals took possession of Purandar, allowing its garrison and other inmates to leave.[38]

The negotiations thus began for Jai Singh on just the right note, and they went on for hours, with the Rajput prince and two of his fellow interlocutors, Udairaj Munshi and Surat Singh Kachhwah, being of one voice and one mind: they wanted Shivaji to surrender all his forts. Shivaji, of course, was trying to keep as many of them as possible. The high-stakes talks went on till midnight, and Shivaji, believing Jai Singh's promise that he would be unharmed, ended up spending two nights in Jai Singh's camp until the final draft of the agreement was hashed out.

It was during his stay in the camp that Niccolao Manucci, the Italian who had been appointed commander of the Mughal artillery by Jai Singh on this campaign for a pay of ten rupees a day, met Shivaji.[39] Manucci's memoirs indicate that Shivaji had created grave apprehensions in the mind of Aurangzeb and across his empire. He wrote that when Aurangzeb had called Jai Singh to his court to discuss the Deccan campaign, the emperor had said 'he could no longer endure the insults of Shivaji' and 'had come to the resolve that he would go in person against this rebel'.[40] The situation was such that 'either he should go' or 'Rajah Jai Singh should undertake to suppress Shivaji', Aurangzeb had said, to which Jai Singh's reply was that he would take it upon himself to defeat Shivaji and 'repress his assaults'.[41] The pressure exerted on Shivaji seemed to have not eased these fears entirely yet. When Shivaji arrived at Jai Singh's camp, Manucci stated, 'much anxiety was caused in our camp, everybody assuming that he must be coming to attack our army'.[42] They felt relieved 'when it was known that he had very few people with him', and when Shivaji stayed at Jai Singh's camp for the negotiations, 'a tent was put up for him alongside the rajah's, and he had liberty to enter and leave as he pleased; he was always treated with great honour and respect'.[43]

Manucci was in the habit of going 'at night to converse and play cards with' Jai Singh. One night the Italian, Jai Singh and a Brahmin in Jai Singh's camp were having a game 'when in came Shivaji':

We all rose up, and Shivaji, seeing me, a youth well favoured of body, whom he had not beheld on other occasions, asked Rajah Jai Singh of what country I was the rajah. Jai Singh replied that I was a Farangi rajah. He [Shivaji] wondered at such an answer, and said that he also had in his service many Farangis, but they were not of his style. Rajah Jai Singh wanted to do me honour, and responded that as a rule Nature made a distinction between the great and the humble, and I being a rajah, she had given me a body and a mind very different from those of others. I rose to my feet as a mark of recognition for the compliment, and made the appropriate obeisance.[44]

This opening, Manucci further wrote:

> afforded me occasion many times to converse with Shivaji, since I possessed, like anyone else in the camp, the Persian and Hindustan languages. I gave him information about the greatness of European kings, he being of opinion that there was not in Europe any other king than the King of Portugal. I also talked to him about our (Christian) religion.[45]

Was Shivaji really safe in Jai Singh's camp? According to Manucci, not quite: 'Diler Khan, being habituated to treachery, wished several times to kill Shivaji, and to this intent solicited Rajah Jai Singh to take his life, or at least to give him [Diler Khan] leave to do so. He would assume all responsibility, and see that the rajah was held blameless.'[46] As a matter of fact, Diler Khan was convinced that 'the king [Aurangzeb] would rejoice at such a result. For Shivaji's valour and intrepidity would never give any rest to the Mogul.' But Jai Singh, 'who had pledged his word and oath not to allow of a murder ... never listened to the words of Diler Khan'.[47]

Two days into Shivaji's stay, the final agreement, known as the Treaty of Purandar, which put the Marathas completely on the back foot, was ready. Shivaji had thirty-five forts with him at the time. Of these, he agreed to surrender twenty-three or two-thirds,[48] of which the annual revenue, put together, was four lakh *hons*. He would get to hold the other twelve forts, with an annual revenue of one lakh *hons*, 'on condition of service and loyalty to the Mughal Empire'.[49] Apart from Purandar and Rudramal, among the forts to be given up were the vertical dynamo Kondhana, Lohgad, Rohida, Nardurg, Tung, Tikona, Mahuli and others. They were spread across the Sahyadris as well as the lower part of the Konkan. Among the ones Shivaji would retain were Rajgad and Rairi, which later became famous as Raigad.[50]

One of the terms of the treaty specified that whenever Shivaji was called upon by the Mughal governor of the Deccan to perform a duty, he had to render it 'without delay'.[51] To avoid the tag of being a Mughal noble, Shivaji had asked that he be exempted from *mansab* (military rank) or regular service, and the request was granted, chiefly because he did not openly specify the reason he didn't want a *mansab* for himself and said his son would hold it instead. So Sambhaji, it was agreed, would get the rank of a commander of 5,000 horses and an equal number of troopers. Because Sambhaji was still a child, he would be 'accompanied by Netaji [Palkar], who is surnamed the Second Shivaji', when he attended on the *subahdar* of the Deccan.[52] Shivaji had asked that he be permitted to take all the lands in the lower Konkan which were under Bijapur's control and also Bijapur's possessions in the Balaghat or uplands, which both he and Jai Singh intended to capture. In return he would pay the emperor 40 lakh *hons* in annual instalments of three lakh.[53]

Deprived of a triumphant march into Purandar by the deal between Jai Singh and Shivaji, Diler Khan was annoyed. So was Daud Khan, who had destroyed so many villages and torched so many settlements and lands. Diler Khan in particular had sent Shivaji a nasty letter in reply to his missive stating that he was willing to give up Purandar. Just over a year ago, Shivaji had, after having shocked Shaista Khan, sent a letter to senior Mughal officials across the Deccan, saying that his country was full of hill ranges and hard and harsh, and had underlined that no invader of his lands had tasted success. Diler Khan was now taking potshots at Shivaji for the defiant words he had used not too long ago. He stated in his response, almost from the very gates of Purandar:

> May Good Providence be your helper! My wish to see you is so strong that it is hard to measure it ... Your letter, with some palace guards [*mahaldars*], has been received. It calls for peace. Be it not concealed from your heart that the words most appropriate for saying on this occasion are 'First fight and then peace'. If a man craves peace without fighting it sounds as an unbecoming proposal to the imperial generals, who have come at the bidding of their master from the garden of Hindustan in order to travel and hunt in your hilly country. They have come solely for this that you would show yourself in battle. They are guests arrived in this hilly tract

with an intense desire for it but you have not appeared before them! In spite of your many 'strong forts, sky-kissing hills, abysmal ravines, and brave soldiers lying in ambush', you have not once shown any sign of yourself anywhere. And now you propose peace![54]

To assuage the egos of both his affronted generals, Jai Singh, before sending Shivaji away to his own dominions, 'mounted him on an elephant' and asked him to go with his son Kirat Singh to meet Diler Khan at the *machi* of the fort and then Daud Khan in his camp for a farewell interview.[55] Details of those interviews aren't available, but Shivaji had to swallow his pride all over again and have an audience with these generals. What is evident is that he did not respond to Diler Khan's provocative verbal challenge. Shivaji was not in the habit of obliging his opponents whenever and wherever they sought an open and pitched battle against him. He preferred to strike at a time and place of his own choosing. On this occasion, too, he kept his counsel, anxious not to engage in a confrontation when the enemy was in a far, far superior position. He was quietly settling into his new, albeit temporarily assumed, identity – of a man affirming his loyalty, and that of his would-be *mansabdar* son, to the 'Alamgir' or Emperor Aurangzeb. And if there was anything to salve the wound of his losses at the moment, he had his own sense of discretion.

Shivaji was to go back home to Rajgad on 14 June. That day, Jai Singh 'presented him with an elephant and two horses' and again sent Kirat Singh with him. Why? Jai Singh was eager that the prized fort of Kondhana be handed over by the Marathas as soon as possible, and he wanted Shivaji himself to head there and submit Kondhana's 'keys' to Kirat Singh. At noon, Shivaji reached Kondhana and delivered the fort to Jai Singh's son. From there he set off for home, taking with him another of Jai Singh's men, Ugrasen Kachhwah, 'who was to bring Shivaji's son away with him' to the Rajput general's camp for grant of commander status.[56] Soon the other forts too were taken, and a proud Jai Singh sent their 'keys' to Aurangzeb.[57] He added a personal touch: he would compensate the imperial treasury for what it had spent on the conquest of Purandar.

'The conquest of this fort is the first victory of the Deccan expedition, and my life and service are at the service of the Emperor,' he wrote to Aurangzeb.[58]

Jai Singh had every reason to feel magnanimous in his moment of victory. He had taken barely three months to get Shivaji to agree to terms humiliating to the Marathas. He had also got Shivaji to stamp with his own seal two letters in Persian to Aurangzeb drafted on his behalf by Jai Singh's secretary Jairaj Munshi. One of the letters, written in florid, courtly language, stated that 'this offender and sinner was deserving of all kinds of punishment', yet the 'gracious and favour-showering imperial court' had granted him 'mercy and grace'.[59] Hereafter 'he [Shivaji] will remain firmly engaged in performing the Emperor's work, as a reparation for his past life and an amendment of his uselessly spent days; he will never deviate from his position of rendering service, risking his life and carrying out the imperial mandates'. He expressed the hope that 'out of the storehouse of Your Majesty's grace, pardon of offences and cherishing of offenders, life to this slave may be granted, and an imperial *firman* may be issued pardoning his offences, granting security to his house and family, and bestowing life on him'.[60]

The second letter, sent after Aurangzeb issued him a *farman*, said:

> this sinner and evil-doer did not deserve that his offences should be forgiven or his faults covered up. But the grace and favour of the Emperor have conferred on him a new life and unimaginable honour ... He is confident that, through the grace of God and the lofty fortune of the Emperor, some valuable service may be rendered by this slave, as amends for his past failings, whereby he may earn the pleasure of the Emperor and discharge a small part of the heavy debt of gratitude which he owes for these favours.[61]

Aurangzeb in his reply severely chastised Shivaji and informed him of the duties he needed to carry out without any delay. Not for the first time, he wrote to Shivaji that his crimes were simply too many:

Although the offences committed by you up to now through your thoughtlessness about the consequences of your acts are beyond count, yet as this devoted Rajah [Jai Singh] has prayed for your pardon, I, out of my characteristic noble habit of shutting my eyes to faults and granting the pardon of lives, do forgive your past deeds and sins and grant all your prayers.[62]

He steered the subject immediately to the planned Mughal strike against Bijapur. 'Whenever Jai Singh would invade Bijapur, you would, at the head of a proper contingent of your own troops, co-operate most heartily with him and give him satisfaction by the excellence of your service,' he stated. Further, Aurangzeb directed Shivaji to 'always remain firm in fidelity, devotion and obedience and pay the tribute you have agreed to'. Only if cooperation and service were rendered in these respects, and only if that part of the Bijapuri Balaghats (uplands) still held by the Adil Shahi's forces was captured by Shivaji and brought under Mughal control would all those *mahals* be confirmed in his name, Aurangzeb clarified. In a telling comment on his approach to Shivaji, he ended the letter with:

> out of my practice of cherishing slaves, I confer the rank of 5,000 *zat* on your son, and I am sending you this royal edict, stamped with the impression of my royal palm and accompanied by a splendid robe of honour, in order to exalt your head. You ought to recognize the value of our royal favour and render thanks ... Always remain true and constant in loyalty and serviceableness.[63]

It was the norm for a 'slave' to travel several kilometres to receive a letter or robe of honour sent to him by the Mughal emperor, and Shivaji would soon be forced to undergo the additional humiliation of adhering to that custom. However grudgingly, Shivaji did that too.

Very soon, Shivaji was summoned by Jai Singh to join his new campaign. Jai Singh wanted to complete his triumph of the Deccan by annexing Bijapur; confidently, he began his march in its direction on 25 November 1665 with Diler Khan on one side and Shivaji, with his

9,000-strong force including the senior general Netaji Palkar, on the other.[64] Shivaji's forces, forging ahead on Jai Singh's orders, captured four places across the Nira river in less than a fortnight. First, they took Phaltan, where Shivaji had some of his kin, and then Tathavdagad, Khatav and Mangalvedha in the south-eastern parts of Maharashtra as defined by the Marathi-speaking regions.[65] Happy with the reports Jai Singh sent him, Aurangzeb wrote to Shivaji on 25 December, 'I have learnt from the despatches that ... you are, at the head of a good force, firmly engaged in my service and have exerted yourself greatly in the conquest of forts Phaltan and Thathvada ... and in punishing the Bijapuri army in the Tal Konkan.' In acknowledgement, Aurangzeb also sent him 'a robe of honour and a jewelled dagger' along with the *farman*.[66]

Pushing further south, a Mughal contingent led by Diler Khan and Shivaji took on a Bijapur force of 12,000 which was led mostly by Maratha generals. One of these generals was Vyankoji Bhosle, Shivaji's stepbrother.[67] Brother was fighting brother. This time the going wasn't smooth as the Bijapuris hit back strongly, but Jai Singh's forces finally pushed them back. Seated on the back of the same elephant, Shivaji and Jai Singh's son Kirat Singh took the battle to the enemy.[68]

Shivaji was in the enormously difficult and entirely indigestible situation of having to fight shoulder to shoulder with his arch enemies like Diler Khan and Kirat Singh. Diler Khan had brutally and relentlessly bombarded Purandar and killed many Marathas, including Shivaji's incredibly brave loyalist Murar Baji Deshpande. Diler had also written a letter full of malicious bile to Shivaji when the Marathas had found themselves encircled and had been forced to surrender that fort. Jai Singh, on the other hand, might have been outwardly civil and polite to Shivaji, but he was in truth the hostile Rajput general who had ultimately placed Shivaji in an extremely difficult position, so fighting alongside Jai Singh's son Kirat was equally tough for a man who was so hell-bent on pressing for his own autonomy and identity. The worst crisis of Shivaji's political career had plunged him into this dire extremity: the unwanted company of the openly hate-spewing Diler and the unsympathetic Kirat.

It is striking how, as the likes of Diler Khan rejoiced as Maratha power tottered, Shivaji put up with the humiliation, the tragic circumstances forced upon him, going through the ordeal with silent resentment. Shivaji's act of fighting on the same side as his sworn rivals is an exquisite and exceptional snapshot of his determination to endure. We find here a truly remarkable survivor. He was trying to preserve whatever he could of his political project so that he could emerge some day from this period of desperate uncertainty, hopefully more or less intact and without any lasting consequences from his present state of helplessness.

It is perfectly possible that many of his followers, even his close lieutenants, might not have been able to fully comprehend his actions. Did they really understand what he was doing, how he was prizing keeping his head above water over everything else so that he and his comrades could live to fight the Mughal empire another day? Did any of them see in their beloved leader's conduct authentic echoes of Lord Shiva swallowing the infernal poison to keep things going, or did they find the whole thing – Shivaji's decision to give up the majority of his hard-earned forts and to fight as part of the Mughal army – quite inexplicable and a deathly blow to all their efforts? Did they see the possibilities, however slim they appeared at that moment, of the paradoxical outcome (involving undeniable defeat but continued existence) that Shivaji had accepted as against a possibly irreversibly disastrous one? Or were they convinced that only unmitigated disaster lay ahead after such capitulation?

There are no records of the discussions that took place in Shivaji's inner circle at such an enervating moment, almost nothing that could allow us to excavate the views of his top lieutenants and close aides. But it seems safe to assume that acceptance of the difficult decisions might not have been universal, and that some of the acquiescence would have been reluctant, if not proffered after protest. Many would have endorsed, or been easily drawn into endorsing, an all-or-nothing approach, a fight to the finish at that precise moment. They might have seen the move to surrender forts as deeply alarming in its apparent promise to the Mughals of complete eventual takeover and triumph.

Shivaji was seeing things the other way. It was not as if a wipeout was certain if he decided to still contest Mughal claims over his lands and forts. The outcome of such a struggle was unknown; and later, in fact, Jai Singh failed in his attempt to wipe out Bijapur in similar fashion. But the handover of his forts, Shivaji reasoned, was going to give him precious breathing time to gather his wits, build up his resources further, instil even more fighting spirit in his Mavale, and then come back to fight the very fight his followers wanted to fight – one to the finish. His policy of four steps forward and two steps back had all along allowed him to enlarge his dominions, slowly but surely, and he wanted to eliminate the possibility of total annihilation by accepting a retreat in time. The difference, if any, with his colleagues, was over the timing of the big fight.

Whatever the differences and whatever the reverberations of his tough decisions, what we know for sure is that they did not open up any chasm amid the crisis. The loyalty of all of Shivaji's lieutenants and followers who remained with him – those who had not fallen prey to Jai Singh's offers, and there were plenty of them – remained natural and unaffected. The exception was Netaji Palkar, whose desertion was soon thereafter caused by his dismissal and not by differences over military strategy. In sum, Shivaji's men stood united behind him, continuing to see him as a revolutionary leader ultimately committed to the goal of independent statehood. The absence of any serious jolt to their convictions about Shivaji and his leadership in this great crisis showed both the firm and solidly dependable nature of that leadership and the steadfast nature of the followers' loyalties.

Meanwhile, buoyed by the fresh success against the Adil Shahi forces, Jai Singh chose to make the final thrust into Bijapur and was taken by surprise by the readiness the opponent demonstrated in defence. Having arrived within 16 kilometres of the Adil Shahi capital, the Mughals were compelled to beat a retreat in the first week of January 1666. This was largely because Jai Singh had, underestimating his rivals, neglected to carry big artillery and other equipment for a siege, whilst Bijapur had increased the strength of its garrison and laid waste territory up to about 10 kilometres, making the supply of basics and even of water difficult for the invaders.[69]

When the Mughal army retreated to a place about 25 kilometres from Parenda in mid-January 1666, Shivaji offered to go to Panhala near Kolhapur and seize it. As he told Jai Singh in a conversation the Rajput later mentioned in his report to Aurangzeb, he knew 'all the ins and outs' of Panhala,[70] where he had been besieged for months until he had escaped from under the watchful eye of Siddi Jauhar's Bijapur army. Thereafter, the Marathas had surrendered the fort to the Adil Shahi. Shivaji promised Jai Singh, 'I shall raise so much disturbance in that district that the enemy will be compelled to divert a large force from their army to oppose me.'[71]

Jai Singh wrote that he accepted the idea because Shivaji's 'words bore promise of action'.[72] There was nevertheless another reason for him to give the nod without a moment's hesitation. The latest Mughal retreat had resulted in a blame game of sorts in the Mughal camp, and the faction led by the powerful Diler Khan was pointing fingers at Shivaji, indicating that the Maratha either didn't have his heart in the campaign against Bijapur or was actively in collusion with the emperor's enemies. Entirely mindful of Diler's vehemence against Shivaji from the time the Afghan had offered to eliminate him and take responsibility for the killing and when he had written a disdainful letter to the Maratha over the surrender of Purandar, Jai Singh felt it might be a good idea for Shivaji to be elsewhere for a while.[73]

Rather perplexingly for Shivaji, his assault was quickly repulsed by Bijapur's defenders atop the fort of Panhala, and he had to make a retreat to Vishalgad. Just a little over five years ago, he had undertaken a similar journey from Panhala to Vishalgad, getting away from Siddi Jauhar's grip. While that was a triumphal escape, this time the getaway was extremely disconcerting. Why did it happen, he wondered, and discovered that his top general Netaji Palkar and his unit had not arrived in time to support him. Shivaji was very, very upset, and Netaji Palkar was peremptorily dismissed as commander-in-chief of the Maratha forces. In his place, Kudtoji Gujar, another highly competent general who was then heading the forces at Rajgad, was appointed the *sarnobat* or chief of the military, and given the title of 'Prataprao' – broadly, 'the man of brave exploits'.[74] 'Why didn't you turn up when you were asked to?' Shivaji asked Netaji Palkar, making no attempt to hide his anger and disappointment.[75]

Distressed over his removal and upset with the scolding he had received, Netaji Palkar went and promptly joined the Adil Shahi state.

Jai Singh was puzzled and worried. Just what was going on? Was this a genuine rift, or was it Shivaji himself who had planted Netaji there? Netaji Palkar had a robust enough reputation of his own. Jai Singh had referred to him as 'the Second Shivaji' in his letters to Aurangzeb. What if Shivaji himself defected and went back to his old ways soon? The momentary stalling of his Bijapur campaign was one thing, but Jai Singh did not want his grand success against Shivaji to be squandered and was anxious to do everything in his power to prevent a joining of hands between Shivaji and Bijapur. To add to his worries, the Qutub Shah of Golconda had, without warning, decided to extend his assistance to Bijapur in its defence against the Mughals. Two well-established Deccan kingdoms had come together. They were gradually weakening powers and could be handled, though it was going to be a tough task. Shivaji represented a new power, on the other hand – and new powers and the people associated with them often have a sense of purpose, a sense of resolve, and a sense of mission. When almost everything had been lost for Shivaji and his men, Murar Baji Deshpande, the commander of Purandar, had exemplified that sense of mission. It was absolutely urgent for Jai Singh to ensure that Shivaji's rebellion did not get a fresh lease of life.

With that end in mind, he had already started selling to Shivaji, even before his own reverses against Bijapur and Shivaji's reverses at Panhala, the idea of going north for an audience with the emperor. Such an audience, he believed, could solidify the connection between the emperor and his 'slave'. Once Shivaji saw the splendour, grace, power and glory of the famous jewel-studded Peacock Throne of the Mughals, he would not rethink his position or entertain thoughts of rebellion again but would be eager and happy to wield power as one of the Mughal empire's leading generals in the Deccan. The turn of events early in 1666 made Jai Singh intensify his pitch, to Shivaji as well as to Aurangzeb, in his dispatches to the north. Jai Singh wrote to the emperor, 'Now that Adil Shah and Qutb Shah have united in mischief, it is necessary to win Shiva's heart by all means and to send him to Northern India to have audience of Your

Majesty.'[76] And when Aurangzeb agreed, Shivaji, no matter how unwilling, was left with little choice.

He didn't want to go. One of the conditions he had stipulated – and got Jai Singh to concede during negotiations – was that he would neither hold military rank himself in Mughal service nor be obliged to attend the emperor's court. Yet Jai Singh held out all kinds of promises to him and, to use his own words, 'used a thousand devices' to convince him.[77]

Shivaji had absolutely no trust in Aurangzeb. If the likes of Diler Khan bore him ill will, then Aurangzeb, who had neutralized and murdered three of his own brothers to get hold of the Mughal crown, was all the more likely to do so. Diler Khan had been itching to kill Shivaji in Jai Singh's camp close to Purandar. What would the infinitely more powerful Aurangzeb do to him in the Mughal capital? He knew that in Aurangzeb's eyes he was an upstart who had simply too much gall for someone who had inherited neither a state nor a kingdom. How had he dared even conceive of cocking a snook at the Mughals in the Deccan, plundering their territories, including the precious town of Surat, attacking their much-feared military, and worst of all, chopping off the fingers of a leading Mughal general who also happened to be Aurangzeb's own maternal uncle? Shivaji was well aware these were the resentments that the Mughal emperor harboured as far as he was concerned.

Some Maratha chronicles indicate Jai Singh told Shivaji that the emperor could grant him viceroyalty of the Deccan and that Shivaji was open to that possibility.[78] None of the Persian documents breathes a word about any such offer, though most historians have kept an open mind on the subject and feel the viceroyalty might just have been a bait that was dangled, along with the handover of Janjira, the fort of the Siddis, and one of Shivaji's near-obsessions; almost right from the start of his political and military career, Shivaji had tried to conquer Janjira, but despite a number of attempts, it had somehow remained beyond his grasp and was at that time directly under Mughal control.[79] The other theory, put out by Sabhasad,[80] is that Shivaji had offered to capture the Adil Shahi and Qutub Shahi kingdoms for the Mughals during his talks with Jai Singh, and an audience with Aurangzeb, he thought, could help him to gain quick sanction for such an enterprise. While he would first seize the two Deccan kingdoms with the weight of the Mughal forces, he could afterwards cast off his shackles and use the gains thus accrued to strike out on his own again, efface the enormous losses he had suffered, and take on the Mughals afresh, with renewed vigour. Whether this was true or not, such an approach was far from inconsistent with the strategies Shivaji had employed earlier, of playing an eager-to-serve supplicant for a while in order to be able to later assert his freedom and sovereignty. One British historian of the Mughal empire writing in the early twentieth century felt that it would in fact be in accordance 'with the whole bent of his peculiar genius'.[81]

Still, what of the most important question – of personal safety? Here again, Jai Singh made all kinds of promises, including religious ones as a fellow Hindu,[82] vowing that no one would even touch Shivaji, so he needn't have any apprehensions on that count. Moreover, one of Jai Singh's sons, Ram Singh, would be present at Aurangzeb's court, and Jai Singh was going to direct him to escort Shivaji and look after him while he was there.

Initially, Shivaji was meant to visit Delhi, where Aurangzeb had been based – and from where he had ruled – for quite some time. Early in 1666 the venue shifted to Agra. On 22 January 1666, Shah Jahan, who had been imprisoned by his son Aurangzeb inside Agra fort from 1658 and was being looked after by his three daughters, died at the age of seventy-six. Following Shah Jahan's passing, Aurangzeb shifted his court from Delhi to Agra. Aurangzeb was feeling far more assured of his position now than he had ever done before: even the ailing father was finally out of the way. Shivaji, on the other hand, was going through the worst phase of his career. He had suffered his greatest defeat and, to put it in Aurangzeb's own words, was having to make a visit to Agra 'for the purpose of saluting the threshold of my Court'.[83]

Could things get any worse for Shivaji?

Perhaps they could. So, before he left for Agra, Shivaji devised proper plans for what would happen in his absence in his own dominions. His mother Jijabai would hold charge as the regent, and she would be assisted in the running of affairs by the prime minister, Moropant Peshwa, Nilo

Pant Mujumdar, the chief accountant who would take care of the finances and the coffers, and the new *sarnobat*, Prataprao Gujar.[84] To ensure that things went smoothly in his lands regardless of what fate had in store for him in Agra, Shivaji made a visit to many of the forts he still held, reiterating the rules he had previously laid down for their commanders and asking them to be extremely alert; similarly, he ordered the civil administration to follow the procedures and practices he had instituted.[85] Jai Singh wrote to Aurangzeb later that Shivaji's preparations were such that his state would function smoothly in his absence.[86]

On 5 March 1666, Shivaji proceeded from his premier fort Rajgad for Agra. He was accompanied by his son Sambhaji, who was just nine years old. The top officials and associates he had picked to accompany him were Niraji Rauji Sahana or Kotwal, Trimbak Sondev, son of Shivaji's official Sonaji Pant Sondev, Manko Hari Sabnis, Dattaji Trimbak, Hiroji Farzand, Raghoji Mitra and Davlji Gadge. There were 1,000 Mavale besides, and 3,000 of his military.[87] Aurangzeb had sanctioned one lakh rupees as costs for Shivaji's journey from the Deccan exchequer, and an officer from Jai Singh's army, Ghazi Beg, was to be Shivaji's guide along the way.[88]

10

Showdown and Escape

When Shivaji reached the gates of Khadki, one of his first stops on the over 1,200-kilometre-long journey to Agra, he discovered that his reputation had preceded him. In an age when there were no newspapers to signal his impending arrival, crowds had lined the streets to watch his entry into the Deccan town that Aurangzeb had renamed Aurangabad, after himself.[1] The Mughal emperor had apparently sent word to his officials that when Shivaji passed through their territory on his way to Agra, he should be received with honour. However, it turned out that the town's Mughal governor Saf Shikan Khan had sent his nephew to welcome Shivaji, while he himself remained holed up in his durbar, waiting for the Maratha leader to come calling. When the nephew relayed these expectations to Shivaji, the latter retorted, 'Who is Saf Shikan Khan? What does he do here? And why isn't he here before me?'[2] When Saf Shikan Khan discovered that the visitor had taken umbrage at his absence, he developed cold feet and immediately went to Shivaji's quarters, taking along all his important officials.[3] While welcoming him, Shivaji did not come all the way to the door, to show his displeasure.[4] The next day, however, when he paid the governor a return visit, he appeared to have forgotten the previous evening's incident, treating the Khan with the civility and decency befitting his position.[5] It was an early taste for

Shivaji of the intricate games he would have to play to keep his honour intact while dealing with the Mughals.

Shivaji had been asked to be present in Aurangzeb's court on 12 May 1666. The day was of great significance to the Mughal court: it would mark the sixth Mughal emperor's fiftieth birthday according to the lunar calendar. A show of extraordinary pomp had been planned. The Mughal empire, known for its ostentatious ways, had ordered a mammoth 1,400 carts to be brought all the way from Delhi loaded with all the glitzy paraphernalia possible, to light up Aurangzeb's new imperial durbar in the city of the Taj Mahal, where his father now lay buried next to his wife Mumtaz Mahal, in the tomb he had built for her.[6]

Shivaji made sure he too arrived in style. Accompanying Shivaji, according to an eyewitness account of his arrival in Agra, were 250 men mounted on horses, 100 with horses of their own and the rest of them *bargirs* or those with horses given to them by the state they represented. When Shivaji rode out in a palanquin, several tall, well-built men wearing Turkish caps walked ahead of him, while a hundred *banjaras* or porters walked at the other end of the entourage. Before Shivaji's *palki* also was an advance guard of troopers, their horses marked by gold and silver trappings, and a team of his loyal Deccani Mavale, and right in front of the palanquin strode a large elephant carrying his flag. Shivaji's silk flag was orange and vermilion with gold decorations. His senior officials rode in their own palanquins, though Shivaji's stood out for the silver plates across its body and golden ones at its poles. Behind him were two female elephants, each with her own *haud* or howdah. The contingent was small, by Mughal standards of strength, but it was 'very splendidly equipped'.[7]

The official in Jai Singh's employ who penned this account was particularly struck by Shivaji's personal appearance. 'Lean and short,' 'very handsome and wonderfully fair in complexion' was how he described him; he further remarked:

> Even without finding out who he is, one does feel instinctively that he is a ruler of men. The mere sight of him is enough to tell that he is a very

brave, high-souled man. He keeps a beard. His son is nine years old and is very marvellously handsome in appearance and fair in complexion.[8]

However, the Maratha leader's impressive bearing and elaborate entourage did not ensure him a warm reception. Aurangzeb had instructed Jai Singh's son Ram Singh, who was to be Shivaji's chaperon, aide and minder throughout his stay at the Mughal court, to 'advance one day's march from Agra and welcome Shivaji on the way and conduct him to the capital'. But when Shivaji arrived on schedule on 11 May at the serai of Maluk Chand some kilometres outside of Agra, after three months of almost non-stop travel in the sweltering summer heat, he discovered Ram Singh had sent one of his clerks, Munshi Giridhar Lal, to meet him. It was a blatant snub: Ram Singh, who was not a particularly exalted official (he had to his credit a modest rank of 2,500 horses, which meant those many horses and a proportionate number of horsemen were under him; sometimes, one horse would have more than one horseman), hadn't made himself available despite the emperor's orders.

Far from making amends the next day, Ram Singh – busy with the task entrusted to him, of placing patrols in the area around Aurangzeb's palace – once again sent off his clerk to escort Shivaji to Agra. He then belatedly rode out to welcome him, but by a route different from the one Shivaji was meant to take.[9] The two men eventually came face to face at the Nurganj garden. One of Jai Singh's officials later wrote that 'Shivaji wished it in his heart that the Kumar should make the first move by advancing and receiving him', so he stayed where he was. 'Then the Kumar himself moved forward and embraced Shivaji, who was still seated on his horse's back.'[10] The point to be noted here is that Ram Singh hadn't got off his horse to welcome Shivaji.[11]

The delays caused by these shambolic arrangements meant that there was no time for the entourage, already discontented by its reception, to rest. It got worse. Thanks to Ram Singh's tardiness, they missed the Diwan-e-Aam, where both high officials and the hoi polloi were granted an audience. It was at the Diwan-e-Khaas, for a select audience, chiefly senior officials, that Shivaji finally laid eyes on Aurangzeb.

Seated on his throne, Aurangzeb was the master of all he surveyed: a lavishly decorated, canopied marble hall with big pillars; a long line-up of nobles and other officials who stood in the best of robes, their hands in front and mouths shut in dutiful silence; courtiers in their green tunics and black turbans, with lances in their hands, who moved back and forth, ushering in and leading back guests and others who were brought in humbly before the throne; and expensive goods that were always being offered – and especially on the occasion of the emperor's fiftieth lunar birthday – for weighing him in gold and silver. All the gifts gathered would then be distributed among the emperor's favourites as a sign of his imperial beneficence. When Aurangzeb was informed that Shivaji had arrived, he asked the *bakshi* or paymaster Asad Khan to bring him forward so that he might grant him an audience.[12]

Led up to the emperor, Shivaji bowed thrice in front of him and presented him with 1,000 *mohars* (pieces of gold) and 2,000 rupees as *nazar* (presents) and 5,000 rupees as *nisar* (propitiatory offerings). Shivaji's son Sambhaji's offerings – 500 *mohars* and 1,000 rupees as *nazar* and 2,000 rupees as *nisar* – were similarly placed in front of the throne.[13] Aurangzeb didn't utter a word of acknowledgement or greeting, or offer a gesture of even mild recognition.[14] Instead, Shivaji was escorted back from the throne by court officials and made to stand in a line on the right meant for *paanch hazari* officials or those with a rank of 5,000 horse, which was the third row of ranking officials.[15] The proceedings of the court continued, as if nothing had happened. It was as if no one had noticed that Shivaji had greeted the emperor – or if they had, had promptly forgotten.

Shivaji's mind was in a state of intense turmoil. What was going on? First the botch-up when he was just about to enter Agra, followed by this grating display of imperial indifference. And Jai Singh, adept at handing out assurances, had forgotten about his promise of a *mansabdari* or authority to Shivaji to stamp out both the Adil Shahi and Qutub Shahi in the Deccan. When Shivaji, with rows of officials blocking his view of the emperor, questioned Ram Singh, and learnt from him that he was standing among the *paanch hazaris*,[16] he flew into a rage.

What? My son is nine years old, and he was made a *paanch hazari* without even having to turn up before the Emperor in court. Netaji Palkar, who works for me, is a *paanch hazari*. After all the services I have rendered, and after having come all the way to the court, is this low rank what I'm going to get?'[17]

Shivaji then demanded to know the identity of the official standing right in front of him. Ram Singh answered that it was Maharaja Jaswant Singh of Navkot in Marwar, and Shivaji turned apoplectic. 'An *umrao* like Jaswant Singh? My soldiers have seen the back of him! Why should I stand behind him?'[18] Barely a couple of years ago Shivaji's soldiers had foiled Jaswant Singh's assault on Sinhagad without much difficulty, forcing him to turn around.

Meanwhile, the ceremonies for the emperor's birthday were under way. Betel leaves were distributed, and Shivaji received one too. The *khilats* or robes of honour were given out next, and Aurangzeb's *wazir* Jafar Khan got one, as did Jaswant Singh, who stood in front of Shivaji – but not Shivaji himself.[19] At this, he 'became sad and fretful', and 'his eyes became wet with anger', recorded one of Ram Singh's officials.[20] Aurangzeb noticed the hubbub and told Ram Singh, 'Ask Shivaji what ails him.' Shivaji replied to Ram Singh, 'You have seen, your father has seen, your *padshah* has seen what a man I am, and yet you have deliberately made me stand so long. I cast off your *mansab*. If you wanted me to stand, you should have done it the right way.'[21] In an instant he turned his back to the throne and began walking away. Ram Singh caught hold of his hand, but Shivaji shook it off, went to one corner or recess of the durbar and sat there. Ram Singh followed him and tried to calm him down, but he was too disturbed to respond. He exclaimed, 'The day of my death has arrived. Either you kill me or I will take my own life. Cut off my head if you like, but I am not going to stand in front of the Emperor again.'[22]

Kumar Singh went to the emperor and, trying to attribute the fracas to Shivaji's long journey and the exhaustion it had caused, said: 'The tiger is a wild animal of the forests. He feels hot. Something has happened.'[23] May in Agra was undoubtedly ferociously hot, but that, of course, was not the reason for Shivaji's displeasure. Aurangzeb then ordered three of his nobles, 'Multafat Khan, Aqil Khan and Mukhlis Khan', to 'console Shivaji, invest him with a *khilat* and lead him back to the (imperial) presence'.[24] But Shivaji did not agree.

> I won't accept the robes. The Emperor has deliberately made me stand behind Jaswant Singh. He knows what kind of a man I am, yet he has willfully kept me standing. I decline the Emperor's *mansab*. I will not be his servant. Kill me, imprison me, if you like, but I won't wear the *khilat*.[25]

Aurangzeb, watching from the throne, then asked Ram Singh to take Shivaji back with him to his quarters, to speak to him, and to calm him down. They could both return to court the following morning, he said. But Shivaji was in no mood to be pacified. The only thing he reluctantly agreed to, after an hour of persuasion, was to send his son Sambhaji to court. The next day, Sambhaji appeared before Aurangzeb with Ram Singh and was given a full robe.[26] When Aurangzeb asked Ram Singh where Shivaji was, he answered, 'He had fever and therefore will not come today.'[27]

Aurangzeb had acted to a plan. Shivaji was the most trenchant, the most stubborn of rebels. He had had the temerity, in Aurangzeb's opinion, to attack Mughal lands, loot entire prosperous cities, and carry out a stealthy night attack that had sent a fancied Mughal governor and close relation of the emperor scurrying for cover. He was pronouncing himself a free man in the Deccan, in the face of the full might of the Mughal empire. And wasn't he the one who had warned all the Mughal generals that they would drown in a river of blood if they tried to conquer his lands? Aurangzeb's idea was to deliver a deliberate snub to Shivaji, and he had done it in such a way that every one of the generals, rajas and maharajas present in court could see it. He had barely acknowledged Shivaji's presence and, after giving him little or no time and absolutely zero attention, had made him stand in a row of junior officials. A chastened rebel was, for Aurangzeb, better than a dead one who might become, in the eyes of his people, a martyr and inspire them to rebellious deeds.

A chastened rebel, especially a man of such pride and of those famous tiger claws as Shivaji, also served as an example for others who might be getting ideas into their heads. If the bold and fearless Shivaji could be subdued thus, the rest of you are easy pickings, the emperor was telling all the officials in the court of private audience where the man from the Deccan had stood with his son.

And what explained Shivaji's angry outburst in court? Most historians have referred to his act of speaking out against his humiliation as the proud pronouncement of a rebel who just wouldn't take things lying down. Of course, the deep voice that rose inside the marble pavilion was that of a confirmed and adamant rebel. But it was more than that. Shivaji was giving expression to the realization that his worst apprehensions had come true. He had never wanted to travel all the way, over a thousand-odd kilometres, to be present in front of Aurangzeb in his royal durbar. He had zero desire to be part of Aurangzeb's circle of patronage. He saw the emperor's officials who bent before the 'Alamgir' and raised their right hands thrice to their foreheads – to indicate that the soil beneath his feet was holy enough for them to place on their deflated domes – as despicable. He knew what was in store for him: as a defeated rebel, he would be humbled more and possibly demeaned more in the presence of the emperor, whom he had already accepted as his overlord when he had agreed to give up the majority of his forts. He did not require any more humbling.

But Jai Singh had cajoled him, and Shivaji had allowed the Rajput general to persuade him, however reluctantly, to proceed to faraway Agra. Aurangzeb had himself said that Shivaji should be received well and treated with respect. And Jai Singh – possibly, though we don't know for sure – had held out the possibility of the emperor granting Shivaji viceroyalty of the Deccan, which the Maratha could use to his advantage before eventually discarding the garb of loyalty. Shivaji's natural instincts and his native intelligence had militated against taking any of these assurances or promises at face value, and indeed he had not done so. Yet, placed firmly on the back foot by Jai Singh and the serious reverses he had suffered in the Deccan, he had finally agreed to go when he could very well still have refused. He had already lost a great deal, and there wasn't much else he was going to lose if he didn't see his chief rival Aurangzeb face to face. And yet …

It was this that had gnawed away at Shivaji's proud heart and his sense of self as the inevitable happened inside the court. And at the act of humbling in the durbar itself, he had left the inhibition of the defeated rebel behind, as if he were liberated by the proof, so stark and visible, of his deep conviction that the pursuit of freedom was just the right purpose he had chosen for his life, and that Aurangzeb was a man too vile and crude to treat him as anything better than a low-life slave. Whatever Shivaji's achievements, his bravery, his acumen, his acuity and his actions, Aurangzeb would always view him in this light – the very way Shivaji hated being looked at. It was also the way he had always hated the people of the Deccan to be viewed by the Mughal empire and by the many sultanates that had flourished for so long. Wasn't his fight precisely against that kind of treatment? Against the unjust trampling of children of the Deccani earth, the real children of the land?

After the commotion in court, those who were looking for an opportunity to instigate an already displeased emperor to act against Shivaji, got down to business at once. What better moment could there be? There were two groups of instigators: a Rajput group hostile to Jai Singh and those who had been adversely affected in the past by Shivaji's actions. Their refrain was:

> Who is this Shivaji that in your royal presence he behaved with such insolence and yet Your Majesty permitted his conduct? If this goes on, many petty landholders will come here and act like him with impunity. How will the government run then? News will travel that a Hindu displayed such audacious rudeness, and everyone else will begin to be rude.[28]

Jaswant Singh, whom Shivaji had spoken of scornfully while standing behind him, said to Aurangzeb, 'Shivaji is a mere *bhumia* [small landholder], and he displayed such discourtesy and violence! It is up to

Your Majesty if you want to overlook it. But he ought to be punished.' Shah Jahan's eldest daughter, and Aurangzeb's sister, Jahanara, who had been receiving, on her father's orders, all of Surat's customs revenue, which amounted to lakhs of rupees every year, told Aurangzeb: 'He (Shivaji) has plundered Surat, he has carried away Shaista Khan's daughter, and acted with such rudeness ... And you ignore it! Is this advisable?'[29] (The story about him carrying away Shaista Khan's daughter was a false one that had been making the rounds.) Shaista Khan's sister, who was Aurangzeb's grand *wazir* Jafar Khan's wife, urged her husband to tell the emperor that the attack on her brother ought to be avenged. Shaista Khan himself sent a message to his brother-in-law, saying, 'Shivaji is intensely perfidious. He is learned in the black arts. When he came into my camp, he jumped over 40 yards and entered the house. The Badshah should not call such a man for an interview. If he is called, he will make a treacherous attack.'[30] Pushed by his wife as well as her brother, Jafar Khan promptly passed on their messages to Aurangzeb.

By now it had come 'into the Emperor's heart, or the policy was agreed upon in the Secret Council', wrote one of Jai Singh's officials, 'either to kill Shivaji or confine him in a fortress or throw him in prison'.[31] Shivaji had suspected something like this would happen soon and had called his officials for a discussion on how they could get out of Agra before Aurangzeb had them surrounded. 'The Badshah will not give us leave unless we undertake to render some service to him,' Shivaji told his men, and asked his official Raghunath Pant Korde to carry a petition to Aurangzeb.[32] In it Shivaji offered to conquer for the empire the two southern sultanates of Bijapur and Golconda; he also noted that if he were given a private interview with the emperor, he would 'meet and communicate something important' to Aurangzeb.[33] This proposal was an attempt by Shivaji to get out of the emperor's grasp. Aurangzeb didn't take the bait and simply wrote in reply, 'Wait a little, and I will do what you have asked for,'[34] which Shivaji took to be a non-committal response indicating there was 'suspicion in his [Aurangzeb's] mind'. Soon after, Shivaji heard that the *wazir* Jafar Khan had 'slandered him before the Badshah'; he sent Raghunath Pant to him with a request for a meeting.

It was granted, and Jafar Khan heard him out and even said he would petition the emperor to grant Shivaji a *mansab*, but Shivaji came away with the impression that Jafar Khan hadn't liked the drift of the conversation, and had 'not spoken frankly'.[35]

Barely twenty-four hours later, Aurangzeb issued instructions to the police chief of Agra, Siddi Fulad, to put Shivaji in the house of Radandaz Khan, which suggested punitive action was imminent. Radandaz Khan had been appointed commander of the Agra fort on account of his ruthlessness and lack of scruples, and prisoners were sent to his 'house' to be subjected to inhuman treatment. As well known for his bigotry, which had increasingly begun to appeal to Aurangzeb, as his cruelty, Radandaz Khan would, in just a few years' time, help the Mughal emperor crush the Satnami sect of the Hindus in Alwar, for which he would also get a promotion and the title of Shujat Khan. What Aurangzeb was signalling by asking for Shivaji to be sent to the Khan's 'house' was that he immediately wanted harsh punishment for Shivaji and was not in favour of a graduated approach that escalated penalty over time.

Greatly hurt by this decision – because it was now his father's 'word of honour' at stake – Ram Singh, who had himself treated Shivaji so casually and shabbily at the time of his entry into Agra, went to Aurangzeb's chief paymaster Muhammad Amin Khan and said, 'His Majesty has decided to kill Shivaji. But he has come here under my father's guarantee of safety. So it is proper that the Emperor should first kill me and only then put Shivaji to death or do anything else with him as he pleases.'[36] To this, Aurangzeb asked if Ram Singh would sign a security bond for Shivaji's conduct to prevent any escape bid and pre-empt any mischief. Ram Singh duly signed the bond, prompting Aurangzeb to keep the bond and remark, 'Go to Kabul with Shivaji. I'm posting him there under you.'[37]

The plan was for Ram Singh to deploy Shivaji in the fight there against the recalcitrant Yusufzais and Afridis, but that was not the crux of the matter. It was that Radandaz Khan had been appointed to command Ram Singh's vanguard on the march to Kabul. According to Aurangzeb's design, Shivaji was to be murdered there in cold blood, with the murder subsequently dressed up as an attack by hostile forces or a pure mishap or even suicide. 'The plan of killing was decided upon,' wrote Jai Singh's official.[38] This was deemed by Aurangzeb to be a safer method of elimination in that he could disown responsibility and prevent any possible uprising of the Marathas on hearing of their leader's death.

But Aurangzeb also didn't want to alienate his considerably efficient Hindu *mansab* holder Jai Singh, who had after all delivered Shivaji to him. He wrote to Jai Singh at the same time asking him about the precise assurances he had given to Shivaji as the Maratha was complaining of a breach of promises.[39]

The journey to Kabul would be deferred until Jai Singh replied from the Deccan, where he was still reigning. Shivaji used this window to bribe the *wazir* Jafar Khan and some other officials, with the result that the *wazir* presented Shivaji's petition to the emperor and said he ought to be pardoned for his offences.[40] Acceding to his prime minister's request, Aurangzeb cancelled the 'go to Kabul' order but in a parallel move, ordered guards to be posted around Shivaji's camp, making him effectively, if still not literally, a prisoner.

In the last week of May 1666, Shivaji sent a fresh plea to Aurangzeb, through the *bakshi* Muhammad Amin Khan, offering to pay the emperor two crore rupees if all the forts he had recently ceded to the Mughal empire were restored to him and he was permitted to go back home.[41] It provoked a furious response, with Aurangzeb saying, 'He [Shivaji] has gone off his head because of my mildness towards him. How can he be allowed to go? Warn him that he must not visit anyone, not even go to Ram Singh's camp.'[42] He couldn't step out any more and would remain confined in his quarters, which consisted of a cramped room surrounded by a very small courtyard. Now Shivaji was officially a prisoner.

Moreover, Aurangzeb had begun demanding of Shivaji that he should give up *all* his forts to the empire. Since he knew the Deccan so well, Aurangzeb realized that among the twelve forts Shivaji still clung on to were at least three important ones: Rajgad, Raigad and Torna. They could keep him, his ideas and his ambitions afloat and prevent his total annihilation. What Aurangzeb eagerly desired, however, was his complete ruin, and saw as now being easily possible with a single powerful blow.

When Ram Singh asked him to surrender the remaining forts, Shivaji said to him sardonically, 'Your father gave the Emperor 23 of my forts and got Tonk pargana [in Rajasthan] as his reward. You are now trying to get my other forts for the Emperor. What pargana are you thinking of gaining by doing that? Is it Toda?'[43]

Shivaji then sent out another petition to the emperor, once again through the *bakshi* Muhammad Amir Khan whom he had bribed. 'I am willing to cede all my forts to His Majesty as my tribute,' he wrote. For that, 'Let him permit me to go to my own country. My mere sending orders from here will not do, as my officers will not obey them. If I go there, I shall fight them and hand the forts over to the imperial agents.' Aurangzeb remained unimpressed and declined, asking, 'Why does he need to go there in order to hand over the forts to me? Will not his men yield them if he writes to them?'[44]

At once, the survelliance of Shivaji's camp was also intensified, and just a few days later, in early June 1666, a substantial force equipped with artillery was stationed outside Shivaji's quarters, with the police chief Siddi Fulad himself pitching his tent there.[45] There seemed to be no way out.

Jai Singh's reply had in the meantime reached the emperor. He had stated that as nothing was promised to Shivaji beyond what was stated in the Treaty of Purandar, 'nothing could be gained by imprisoning or killing Shivaji as the Maratha chief's wise arrangements [at the time of leaving for Agra] had made his government independent of his personality', and 'imperial interests would be best promoted by turning Shivaji into a friend'. Such an approach 'would also convince the public of the sacredness of the imperial officers' words', he wrote.[46] Yet Jai Singh, who had in the early part of Shivaji's visit to Agra said the emperor should send the Maratha leader back, was now decidedly against Shivaji's return to the Deccan! Jai Singh had come to the conclusion that the campaign against Bijapur was his own priority, and Bijapur could best be handled if Shivaji was away in Agra and not in a position to suddenly change sides and join hands with that Sultanate. 'Under the present circumstances it is not at all politic to permit Shivaji to come to this region,' he wrote to his emperor.[47] He told Ram Singh:

Also tell the Emperor that Shivaji should be detained there in a worthy manner [that is, not as a prisoner], so that his officers here may not despair of his return and thus be induced to join Adil Shah and create disturbances against us. This policy will avoid the necessity of His Majesty sending a fresh army to this side.[48]

Aurangzeb, of course, was sure he had got his man and didn't want to follow Jai Singh's advice of not keeping Shivaji as a prisoner; Sabhasad wrote that Shivaji at this stage himself 'began to feel distressed' and 'lamented much, holding Sambhaji Raje to his breast'.[49]

Over the next few days Shivaji reflected deeply on his predicament, which was actually a life-and-death situation. He came to the conclusion there was no point further petitioning the Mughal emperor or sending messages to him through his officials by either winning them over or offering them inducements.

In a series of well-thought-out moves, he first asked Ram Singh to withdraw the bond he had signed for his security and conduct, which the latter would not do. Instead, Ram Singh tried to 'reason with Shivaji and console him'.[50] Shivaji then directed his officials and the rest of his entourage to go back home. Aurangzeb and his officials were only too happy to grant them travel permits to return to the Deccan. If Shivaji, already in confinement, was letting go of the Mavale, the 2,500-strong band of soldiers he had brought along, most of his top officials and aides, who'd be left behind? He would have hardly any allies to rely on if he were planning anything deceitful or treacherous. He would only have with him the nine-year-old Sambhaji and a handful of aides to attend to essential matters. When most of his men had left Agra, Shivaji wrote to the emperor – a final petition of sorts was how he intended it to sound – to say that he wished to renounce the world and go to Varanasi or Benares to lead the life of a Hindu mendicant who had given up the worldly pulls of *sansar*. Aurangzeb replied, cleverly, 'Let him turn a *fakir* and live in Allahabad fort. My *subahdar* there will take good care of him.'[51] In the fort of Allahabad were state prisoners who had been cast away.

Weeks passed in this fashion, and Shivaji, now in the final stages of planning yet another daring escape, pretended to have fallen very ill. He bought various kinds of sweetmeats and ordered them distributed in wicker baskets to some Mughal officials and some holy men of the Hindu and Muslim faiths.[52] These were big baskets, each of them hanging from a wooden pole that needed two porters to shoulder it. Guards initially asked where the baskets were being sent and what they contained, and they had the bearers open some of the baskets to check that they were, indeed, carrying sweets. The watch was kept up diligently for a few days, after which it started slackening, with the guards no longer keen on checking baskets and only occasionally asking for one or two to be opened.[53]

During the afternoon of 17 August 1666, Shivaji informed his guards that he was extremely unwell and should not be disturbed. Hiroji Farzand, Shivaji's half-brother (Shahaji's son by another woman) and aide, who resembled him, lay flat on the wooden bed that Shivaji normally occupied. A quilt covered his body. The only part of his body that was visible was his right arm, which was stretched out. On the wrist was Shivaji's golden bracelet. A young servant sat by his side on the ground massaging his feet.

Shivaji and his son Sambhaji squeezed themselves, as noiselessly as possible, into two separate baskets. Like the other baskets, filled with sweets as usual, the two baskets, with their lids shut, were carried out of the camp by bearers, past the rows of guards, a little after sundown.[54] At an isolated, desolate spot outside the city, the baskets were placed by the bearers in front of some of Shivaji's *karkuns* or clerks whom he had sent out earlier from the camp after having fixed a meeting point. When the lids of the baskets were thrown open, Shivaji and Sambhaji clambered out of them. They then travelled almost 10 kilometres further to a village, where one of Shivaji's trusted officials, the *kotwal* Niraji Raoji, was waiting for him with horses. Shivaji, his son and some of those accompanying them smeared themselves with ash and dressed like renunciates, in the orange robes of sanyasis. They then proceeded in the direction of the holy city of Mathura; some others took a different route home.[55]

Back in Agra, Hiroji Farzand slept in Shivaji's bed for the night. In the morning, some guards peeped in and noticed his outstretched arm with the golden bracelet. At around 8 a.m., Hiroji walked out of the

Showdown and Escape

house with Shivaji's servant, telling the guards posted outside the gates to the quarters that they should not make too much noise as Shivaji was ill, and was undergoing treatment; he himself was stepping out to get some medicine for the master with the servant in tow, and no one must be allowed in.[56] When neither Hiroji nor the servant returned, the suspicions of some of the sentries were aroused, and at around 10 a.m., they went inside the house to check. The room was empty.

The British, who recorded the story of the great escape in a letter sent from Surat to England,[57] should have used the colloquialism 'gobsmacked' to describe the reaction of the guards who found that Shivaji and his son had disappeared. If ever the word was fit to be used, it was in this instance. The guards ran to the police chief Siddi Fulad, and he in turn ran to Aurangzeb. The British had already described Shivaji as being of an 'airy body', and the Mughals had begun to echo this description after the Shaista Khan episode. Siddi Fulad claimed there had been witchcraft to try and absolve himself. He told Aurangzeb:

> The Raja was in his own room. We visited the room repeatedly to inspect, but he disappeared all of a sudden. Whether he has fled, or entered into the earth, or gone up in the sky – we don't know. We have been very close to him. He vanished in our view. We don't know what magical trick he has played.[58]

Aurangzeb was far too rational to believe such tales, and he ordered a massive search across Agra and all along the route to the Deccan.

But Shivaji was more than twelve hours ahead of his pursuers. And he didn't head directly to the south or south-west in order to get to the Deccan. Against all expectations, he went in the opposite direction – to the north and north-west, making a brief halt in Mathura and from there drawing an arc through Bundelkhand, Gondwana and Golconda to get to his section of the Deccan and his home at Rajgad.[59] Little Sambhaji found it hard to keep up, so he was left behind in Mathura with three Deccani Brahmins – Krishnaji Pant, Kashi Rao and Visaji – who were brothers-in-law of Shivaji's *peshwa* Moropant Pingle.[60] Shivaji told them he would send them a message once he reached Rajgad, after which they could bring his son to the Deccan. Aware that he was in the vicinity of some of Hinduism's holiest spots, but had no time to visit them, he told the Brahmins, 'Get religious rites at Gaya and Prayag performed for me through men you know.'[61]

Shivaji then shaved off his moustache and beard, and once again donned the garb of a sanyasi, smearing himself with ash. He carried a sanyasi's staff, with gold coins and money concealed within it to pay for his expenses on the long journey back. Money was also apparently sewn into the clothes worn by his men.[62]

Shivaji returned to Rajgad on or about 12 September 1666, around twenty-six days after he had escaped from under Aurangzeb's nose.[63] The journey he made from Mathura was more than a 1,000 kilometres long, and he had obviously travelled at tremendous speed.[64] As soon as he returned, he circulated the rumour that his son Sambhaji had died along the way.[65] When this became well known, he let the three Brahmins in Mathura know that they could leave for the Deccan with his son, and they too set off dressed as mendicants.[66]

Shivaji had managed an almost miraculous escape from the Mughals, but not without cost to himself. He fell quite ill, evidently as the result of the sheer exhaustion of the frantic journey, but eventually made a full recovery.[67]

Escaping in a wicker basket, Shivaji had made the entire, giant Mughal empire a laughing stock. In Agra, a furious Aurangzeb instituted an inquiry into the grand fiasco. He asked the *wazir* Jafar Khan to give him the names of all the *mansab* holders, cavalrymen and guards who had been entrusted with the responsibility of keeping a watch on Shivaji. He asked the police chief Siddi Fulad to give him a sketch of all the checkposts set up around Shivaji's quarters.[68] Mughal horsemen set off at full gallop from Agra and went all the way to Rajasthan, Gujarat and Khandesh, the usual route to the Deccan which Shivaji had avoided. They came back empty-handed, of course.

Not surprisingly, Ram Singh's name came under a cloud, and rivals like Jaswant Singh did their bit to incite Aurangzeb against him.[69] According to various reports, some Maratha associates of Shivaji were arrested in Agra, from the house of the son-in-law of the chief Mughal spy, Pratit Rai.[70] Those arrested were Raghunath Pant Korde, Trimbak Pant and three others, according to one version; other versions say Trimbak Pant was among those who accompanied Shivaji during his escape.[71] There is not enough information available to reconcile these conflicting accounts, so we will never really know for sure who these men were. The captured Marathas, reportedly tortured, apparently admitted that Ram Singh had asked Shivaji to escape, if not actively connived in the escape.[72] The Marathas were kept behind bars before being released the following year. Four guards who had stood outside Shivaji's quarters were imprisoned, 'threatened with lashes and the thrusting of salt into their nostrils' and forced to 'confess' that Ram Singh had let Shivaji escape; they later retracted their statements, saying they had made them fearing torture.[73]

Ram Singh paid heavily for such allegations. He was soon dropped from the court on Aurangzeb's orders and deprived of his position and pay. Almost a year later, after his father had died, he was brought back into service and given the rank of 4,000 horse. Sent to Assam as part of the Mughal force tasked with winning back the fort of Guwahati from the local Assamese, Ram Singh spent a few months there before being sent to the north-west frontier, where he died of an illness in 1668.[74]

Raja Jai Singh's career started nosediving the moment news emerged that Shivaji had escaped. Apart from his son being accused of collusion, there was also the fact that Shivaji's soldiers in the Deccan were beginning to flex their muscles again. The Mughal commander of Rohida fort, among the twenty-three forts Jai Singh had obtained from Shivaji, was complaining bitterly of a lack of supplies and warning of an accumulation of war materials by Shivaji's men in the fort's vicinity.[75] The war against Bijapur too had gone nowhere after a promising start. To make the disgrace worse, Shivaji returned safely to Rajgad in September. It was not easy now to replicate Jai Singh's previous successes against Shivaji. There was a loss of morale, and a sense of annoyance, exhaustion and massive embarrassment over Shivaji's escape.

Jai Singh, who had advised Aurangzeb to treat Shivaji well, albeit for strategic reasons, and been civil with the Maratha leader during his fraught encounters with him, was now thirsting for his blood. He outlined in a letter to the Mughal *wazir* Jafar Khan a plan to murder Shivaji by deceiving him with an offer of marriage between one of Jai Singh's sons and one of Shivaji's daughters. Jai Singh said he would invite Shivaji to his camp to discuss it, though he added, spewing venom, that Shivaji's 'pedigree and caste' were 'notoriously low' and 'men like me do not eat food touched by his hand, and in case this wretch's daughter is captured I shall not condescend to keep her in my harem'.[76] Once things were 'arranged in such a way that the wicked wretch Shivaji will come to see me once', Jai Singh emphasized, 'in the course of his journey or return our clever men may get a favourable opportunity of disposing of that luckless man in his unguarded moment at some place'.[77]

Nothing came of the plan as it remained unapproved in the wake of the fresh debacle, and Jai Singh, dispirited and discredited, was relieved of his charge as governor of the Deccan and replaced by Prince Muazzam in May 1667.[78] That was the final blow: the same Muazzam, deemed indolent and inefficient, whom Jai Singh had not wanted to take orders from as governor of the Deccan and had therefore pleaded with Aurangzeb for autonomy in decision-making, was replacing him barely two years later. How the tide had turned. A disconsolate Jai Singh started on his journey back to Rajasthan but never reached. He died on the way, at Burhanpur, on 28 July 1667.

The question that still hung in the air and is still often debated is: was Ram Singh truly involved? Did he assist Shivaji in his escape?

Two British historians of the Marathas, Grand Duff and Scott Waring, feel that Ram Singh did help Shivaji whereas the eminent historian Jadunath Sarkar, whose discovery of Rajasthani letters (written by Jai Singh's officials) in the Jaipur state archives threw much light on the whole drama, stayed firmly non-committal, as have others. The one exception among recent historians has been A.R. Kulkarni, who has given Ram Singh a clean chit.[79]

My own conclusion is that Ram Singh had no role to play in Shivaji's escape. Shivaji had bribed the Mughal *wazir* Jafar Khan, the *bakshi* Muhammad Amir Khan, and some others, but there is no evidence that Ram Singh had been dealt with similarly. He passed on Shivaji's messages to the emperor diligently, and sometimes spoke up for him, but in the end, he always did Aurangzeb's bidding, urging Shivaji to cooperate with the court and to even hand over the remaining forts in the Deccan to Aurangzeb. The fact that both men belonged to the same faith doesn't appear to have come into play, because Jai Singh's family was thoroughly committed to the Mughal rulers. Ram Singh did indeed console Shivaji in moments of despair, but that could be attributed to pure civility.

The allegations against Ram Singh by certain Mughal officials, and the insinuations made against Jai Singh, were part of the power play at Aurangzeb's court. Those who were going to be censured themselves for Shivaji's inexplicable vanishing act needed to hold someone else guilty. And they did.

Shivaji, meanwhile, had emerged an even bigger hero in the eyes of his people, and the story of his incredible escape became something of a folk legend even during his lifetime.

11

A Push for Reforms

Shivaji himself had no time to savour his breathtaking escape from Agra. He was a hero, no doubt, but one who had lost time, men, materials, resources and the majority of his forts. His closest aides, like Raghunath Pant Korde and Trimbak Pant Dabir, were languishing in a dungeon in Agra following his own escape from the Mughal capital. It would be several months before they were released. Fortuitously for Shivaji, Aurangzeb's attention was taken up, soon after his audacious exit from the imperial court, by a threat of invasion by the Shah of Persia and a rebellion by the Afghan tribes along the Mughal empire's north-west frontiers. Eventually the Persian king, Shah Abbas II, an upholder of Shia Islam (as distinct from Aurangzeb's championing of the Sunni branch), didn't carry out his threat, but he handed over instead an acerbic letter for the emperor to Aurangzeb's envoy at his court, Tarbiyat Khan, in which Shivaji figured prominently.

'I learn that most of the zamindars of India are in rebellion because their ruler is weak, incompetent and without resources. The chief of them is the impious *kafir* Shiva,' he wrote.[1] Shivaji, noted the ruler of Persia,

> had long lived in such obscurity that no one knew his very name; but now, taking advantage of your lack of means and the retreat of your troops, he has made himself visible like the peak of a mountain, seized many forts,

slain or captured many of your soldiers, occupied much of that country, plundered and wasted many of your ports, cities and villages, and finally wants to come to grips with you. You style yourself a world conqueror [Alamgir] while you have only conquered your father and have gained composure of mind by the murder of your brothers. It is beyond your power to repress lawless men.[2]

The bearer of the taunting letter bore the brunt of Aurangzeb's anger: he was accused of being irresponsible and robbed of his rank.[3]

Shivaji, meanwhile, decided to buy time by making a new offer of peace, and Aurangzeb's reciprocal time-buying tactic was to accept the offer with alacrity. Shivaji wrote that he had fled from Agra not out of insubordination but in fear of his life, and that he was worried the emperor had already sent an army against him, 'which no one in the world ... could fight'. He sought pardon, saying that in the emperor's service lay his own welfare. His son Sambhaji would render that service with a contingent of 400 troopers. If the Emperor chose to give Sambhaji, who was only nine years old at the time, a *mansab*, good; if he didn't, Sambhaji would still serve. He had already given up his forts, Shivaji wrote, and added that the strongholds that remained, and his life itself, now belonged to His Majesty.[4]

Aurangzeb knew Shivaji far too well by now not to be taken in by his renewed affirmation of loyalty; Shivaji was once again, as earlier, adroitly avoiding the role of a *mansabdar* himself so that he did not hold any position within the very empire he was fighting against. But the statement of loyalty nonetheless suited Aurangzeb for the moment, because he wanted to focus on the instability in the north, and not on the Deccan. He wrote back to say that Shivaji's offences stood 'pardoned' and that his son Sambhaji 'had been enrolled as an imperial officer'.[5] Shivaji could seize parts of Bijapur and add them to Mughal territory or stay firm in his own territory, Aurangzeb said. Shivaji had complained in his letter that imperial collectors were impeding his effort to collect rent in his own fiefdom, despite the emperor having given him *deshmukhi* rights in the areas around the surrendered forts.[6] Aurangzeb got these rights restored.[7]

He went a step further, granting Shivaji the title of 'rajah', something he had rejected outright when Jai Singh had recommended it for the Maratha after the Treaty of Purandar.[8] 'Rajah' didn't mean much more than titular pretension; Jai Singh was a 'rajah' in Aurangzeb's service, and so were many others like Jaswant Singh.

Aurangzeb's real opinion of Shivaji had been expressed more frankly in the wake of his escape. When Shivaji was under house arrest in Agra, he had asked some Mughal couriers to carry his pearls, *hons* and gold *mohars* home. Midway to the Deccan the couriers heard of his escape and, returning to Agra, handed over everything to the emperor's officials, fearing they would be implicated in the escape. Aurangzeb's wrathful pronouncement was that it was all '*haram* [illegal] property'. He asked for the goods to be sold and the proceeds 'distributed among *fakirs*'.[9] Aurangzeb was even harsher with Netaji Palkar, the former chief of Shivaji's army. Netaji had, after his estrangement with Shivaji, first joined Bijapur but had soon afterwards gone over to the Mughals. Though now a Mughal 'commander of 5,000 horse' and stationed in Agra and other parts of the north, Netaji was imprisoned at once, 'lest he too should run away'. When he offered to turn Muslim if his life was spared, he was, according to the *Alamgir-nama*, converted, circumcised, given a new name, Muhammad Kuli Khan, and 'posted to the army of Kabul'.[10]

Shivaji, momentarily left alone by the Mughals, was able to establish a degree of quiet. As he saw it, if Aurangzeb believed that he feared reprisal after his escape and had slunk away to safety, it would be an advantage. It would give him the breathing space he needed to rebuild, and to prepare for a fresh round of resistance to the Mughals in the future. While his battle-hardened army got a much-deserved rest, Shivaji himself wasn't planning on resting. He wanted to use this time to carry out urgent administrative and legislative reforms. He had come to the conclusion that the lands that were still his were reeling under constant warfare and the administrative inefficiency and corruption brought on by the overlordship of several sultanates. He felt governing structures needed to be changed and improved, and measures taken to curtail the unlimited and unrestrained jurisdiction of certain privileged fief holders.

Thus began a new phase in Shivaji's life. For three years on the trot, he made no moves that would invite Mughal retaliation. Instead, he focused his energies on his lands, working tirelessly and not allowing disappointment over loss of territory to stand in the way of his mission. He also carried out far-reaching reforms in the functioning of his military forces. His thinking was that once his reforms gathered pace and took root, and members of his military state and its citizens saw for themselves the changes he had achieved, he could move from there, in a new surge of activity and battlefield oomph, towards regaining all his lost realms.

So it was that soon after his return from Agra, Shivaji asked one of his senior officials, Annaji Datto (who later became his minister for land revenue), to carry out the measurement of his lands so that new rules could be set for revenue collection. The *watandari* system was the root of most ordinary people's troubles in that period, and Shivaji carried out a major revision in the way it was run. The system was not altogether without merit: the roles performed by *deshmukhs* and *deshkulkarnis* – in other words zamindars who collected revenue from cultivators and passed on a share to the state – and by *mirasdars* and others, provided a measure of stability to village administration even in the midst of conflict. But land and revenue collection rights had become hereditary over centuries, spawning fratricidal conflicts and blood feuds. Also, the system squeezed the peasantry, who were forced to pay exorbitant sums to these rights holders, of which only a small part was sent to the state exchequer. Such an arrangement also meant that no matter who was ruling a region, *watandars* were non-accountable and unmoved by any change in authority; they simply transferred their allegiance to the new rulers. And the common people had no one to turn to for redressal if the local *watandar* didn't provide a just administration.

Shivaji fixed revenue dues in cash and grains 'according to the yield of a village'.[11] Officials could no longer extract rents arbitrarily, but only according to centrally fixed rates. Wealthy *watandars* had taken to building castles (*wadas*) and bastions in the villages. Shivaji demolished these edifices and barred these officials from building any 'bastioned castles'. They could only build houses, he told them, like the rest of the population.[12] Another rule he introduced was that 'every government servant, civil or military, officer or ordinary soldier', would be 'paid directly by the government – either in cash or by orders of payment on the treasury'.[13] This was meant to end random collection and misappropriation. If officials could not pay themselves, casual decentralization could be checked, felt Shivaji.

For agriculture, Shivaji adopted the *batai* system where farmers paid a share of their actual produce to the state. He chose this over the *bighawani* system that was just as widespread, under which tax was levied at flat rates determined by quality of land. Annaji Datto wrote to *watandars* that they should, roping in responsible individuals in their villages, do their own land surveys; he himself would select one village in each district for a sample survey and compare the results of the two surveys, theirs and his, to arrive at the right revenue settlement figure.[14] Shivaji decided that an estimate of crop per *bigha* would then be made, and 'after dividing the grains into five shares', 'three' would be 'given to the cultivators and two ... taken for the government'.[15] Later, the share of government was raised to 50 per cent.[16]

For the state to demand such a high share of crop revenue was significant. But with Shivaji, 40 per cent or 50 per cent meant *just that*. Earlier, whatever the written rules stated, collections were random, unsystematic, indiscriminate and without any proper count or assessment made by anyone, and the people and peasants found themselves harried and hassled. Shivaji had in fact started implementing a similar set of rules in the twelve Mavals near Pune soon after he had shifted to Pune in his teenage years. Gradually, as his territories grew, so did the scope and scale of implementation, and a semblance of order began to spread across the land. After the Agra drama, he focused far more stringently on establishing this order properly.

That's why none of his enemies could cite a single instance of the local population in any of Shivaji's administered regions protesting or rebelling against the rules he was putting in place. So many of Shivaji's territories had been destroyed, repeatedly so, for more than a decade. Whether it was Afzal Khan or Shaista Khan or later Jai Singh, entire villages were laid waste by each one of them, people were displaced, houses burnt and properties destroyed. Why did the local populace (as distinct from some *watandars*), whose members comprised Shivaji's army, then still stick with Shivaji when they could have easily taken shelter under the umbrella of the bigger, far more established and older powers? Why were they backing this newbie champion of the Deccan? It was because someone whose house had been left in a smouldering ruin by a powerful army could expect from Shivaji's rule a degree of justice, of fairness and of method in the midst of all the early modern age warfare.

Apart from Shivaji's charismatic personality, and his personal bond with his men, this was another reason why someone like Baji Prabhu Deshpande, who had served other powers as well in the Mavals before Shivaji's advent, had laid down his life for the intrepid rebel. It also helped explain why a man like Murar Baji Deshpande, who could have easily taken up the prominent post offered to him by the Mughal general Diler Khan, instead chose to die in the act of protecting Purandar. Baji Prabhu and Murar Baji at least gained immortality; the Marathas who died alongside them – a few hundred in each incident – are nameless, their identities obscure and forgotten. Bravery cannot fully explain their sacrifice: they clearly saw themselves as being part of a cause, and they perceived the cause to be worthy enough for them to stake their all on it. They were convinced that Shivaji was the man who needed to be in charge if they, their families and their children were to have a better future. Shivaji's genius lay in creating this sense of belief, and self-belief, in the ordinary, faceless and nameless people of the Deccan.

Shivaji also fostered confidence among the people by tackling one of the most daunting challenges confronting both ruler and populace in that era: the problem of too many wastelands and how to make them useful and bring livelihood to the local people and revenue to the state.

In order to encourage cultivation, Shivaji instructed that 'new farmers who come to settle should be given cattle ... and grain and money ... for providing themselves with seeds'. These were not intended as gifts: he said 'the sum should be realized in two or four years according to the means of the *rayats* (peasants)'.[17] In a letter to an official in the 1670s,

Shivaji said if a farmer had the ability and workforce to till his land but no oxen, he should be given cash to buy oxen and the advance later 'realized gradually and according to his [the peasant's] ability without charging any interest'.[18] Funds were set aside for such assistance so that wastelands could be brought under cultivation. Similarly, land was granted rent-free for establishing a market town, and though customs duties were retained as earlier, in an important reform measure, the many taxes and cesses routinely imposed were all abolished by Shivaji once the *batai* system was introduced.[19]

There were invariably those who resisted change. For instance, a temple complex at Chinchwad near Pune had for long been given the privilege of buying goods from neighbouring districts at concessional rates, and the loss thus suffered by the exchequer was recovered by imposing taxes on local residents. Shivaji had put an end to all taxes by bringing in the crop-sharing arrangement, yet the temple authorities continued to buy from farmers at cheap rates and locals continued to be taxed as well by the district authorities. Learning about these twin blows, Shivaji wrote to the district *subhedar* asking him not only to at once stop imposing taxes because cultivators were already paying half their produce to the state but to forbid the temple establishment from purchasing goods at low rates from farmers. He ordered the *subhedar* to send the temple complex provisions from government stocks at subsidized rates.[20] Though a devout Hindu, Shivaji did not see respect for faith as a grant of licence for religious establishments to cause trouble or harm to the local population. He may not have put it this way, but this was, in a small yet important way, a separation of church and state.

In the Deccan, the *mansab* holder was also the *jagir* holder with the right to collect taxes. Shivaji stopped appointing *jagir* holders altogether in his territories, eliminating a line of authority that had become notorious; taxes were collected by the administrative in-charge already in place, the one holding a clerical and purely administrative position – not the *watandar* with hereditary rights but a state-appointed official specifically for that task.

Shivaji's other, equally momentous achievement during this phase was to underline that the civilian system of administration was as significant as military preparedness, efficiency and valour. Sure, the conquest of new lands was a perennial pursuit with him, just as it was for the other powers. But his peacetime measures showed how much more there was to him, and how keen he was to establish a stable and just new order.

As we have seen, every state in the Deccan in the seventeenth century was a military state, and almost every civilian official was at the same time a military official. Naturally, there were times officials saw greater glory in military duties. In 1670 Nilopant Sondev, whom Shivaji had appointed chief of finance, requested him to appoint someone else while he himself went off to capture some forts. Shivaji in his reply firmly emphasized that 'to stay in the country for administrative work was also an important task' and directed him to focus on the region's affairs. Nilopant, in turn, reading and interpreting Shivaji's message accurately, acknowledged that if Shivaji Raje 'considers both these duties as equal, I shall stay in the country'.[21]

Shivaji's military was entirely his own creation. All his life he focused on building forts and fortifying existing ones, knowing his greatest strength lay in their unassailable character. He focused equally on the bravery of his men, the Mavale, and appealed to their Maratha pride to fuse them into a unit and drive them to greater feats. But discipline was key, and he emphasized that 'every pass' be 'commanded by forts', that 'regular fortifications' bar 'all open approaches', and 'every steep and overhanging rock' be 'occupied as a station to roll down great masses of stone'.[22]

Shivaji mandated, in keeping with the established rules of the age, that three officials of equal status and responsibility assume charge of every fort. These were the *havaldar* (commander), the *sabnis* (officer in charge of accounts), and the *sarnobat* (who held charge of personnel at the ramparts). A hands-on *karkhanis* doing commissariat work would assist these three, affixing his seal to orders before the three signed, overseeing stores of grains and war materials, verifying roll calls and details of cash and treasury department arrangements, requisitioning goods and commodities, and overseeing construction work. The *karkhanis* reported directly to the *sabnis*, who was ultimately responsible for all accounts. The *sabnis*, besides, carried out correspondence with government or other officials.[23] This was not very different from what the other powers were doing; as the following example illustrates, it was the actual implementation that was different, heralding the start of an era.

In one respect the *havaldar* of Shivaji's forts had unfettered authority: the keys of a fort would always be with him, and he was to shut and lock the fort gates every evening. In the morning, he'd go out again to open the main gates.[24] According to an incident cited in a Maratha chronicle, Shivaji went up to Panhala one night, and guards at the gates told the *havaldar* the Maharaj was seeking entry. The commander, after checking, disallowed him, saying the king's own orders prohibited him from opening the gates. When Shivaji told him 'the regulations are mine and the order involving their breach is also mine', he still refused. In the morning the *havaldar* opened the gates and, with folded hands, asked the king for punishment, but the king instead voiced his appreciation for the man's sense of duty.[25]

Conscious of caste rivalries and intrigues, Shivaji specified how appointments at forts were to be made. While the Ramoshis and Parwaris 'kept watch' at the gates,[26] Sabhasad writes that Shivaji had instructed

> the garrison in the fort, the *havaldar*, and the *sarnobat* should be Marathas of good families. They should be appointed after someone of the royal personal staff had agreed to stand surety [for them]. A Brahman known to the king's personal staff should be appointed *sabnis* and a Prabhu, *karkhanis*. In this manner each officer retained should be dissimilar [in caste] to the others. The fort was not to be left in the hands of the *havaldar* alone. No single officer could surrender the fort to any rebel or miscreant.'[27]

Dividing up work among people of different castes was presumably to prevent people of one caste getting together to carry out subversive activities or join hands with the enemy and hand over a fort. The idea of putting three officials in charge was, similarly, to preclude treachery and betrayal. It didn't always work. On occasions officials faced charges of misappropriation of funds,[28] and in a previous chapter we saw how Shivaji had written a letter to his officials in 1663 about the fort of Sinhagad having been compromised by its officials, making it necessary for loyalist forces to march there and take possession.

For Shivaji, light infantry and light cavalry were hugely critical in view of the hilly nature of his terrain which necessitated swift movement, and he laid down the chain of command for both. In the cavalry, the *bargirs* or those 'equipped with horse and arms by the state' would form the heart of a unit, while *shiledars* – those who brought their own horse and sometimes a body of troops equipped at their own expense – would be 'under the jurisdiction of the *paga* [unit]' and would therefore not be at liberty to turn into self-styled dons.[29] *Shiledars* were known to be unwieldy and for their penchant to dictate terms, and their body of troopers often did the exact opposite of what the ruler commanded. Shivaji did not want the rules he was laying down breached and prima donna *shiledars* calling the shots. And while both infantry and cavalry heads were important, as was the naval in-charge, the cavalry chief was overall head of the military forces, reporting to Shivaji.

Shivaji recruited Muslims in his army along with Hindus, just as he had two senior Muslim officials, Daulat Khan and Darya Sarang, in his navy. His first infantry chief in fact was Noor Beg, a Muslim, about whom no other information is available except his name and the fact that after the conquest of Jaawali, he was succeeded by a Maratha, Yesaji Kank.[30] According to one Maratha document, a group of 700 Pathans who offered to join Shivaji's army were recruited by him in the face of opposition from most of his officials, with the notable exception of his veteran colleague Gomaji Naik Pansambal, who backed the decision on merit.[31]

Shivaji had, according to Sabhasad, put together a code of conduct for his army. Since the army spent eight months out on expeditions, it was permitted to levy contributions from outside territories for subsistence and maintenance; in that era, armies of states depended almost entirely on the resources of the place they camped in. Shivaji's code stated explicitly that 'in enemy territories, women and children should not be captured', 'cows not taken' and 'Brahmans not molested';[32] the cow was a holy animal for Hindus, and Brahmins had a place of privilege in the deeply entrenched caste order. Further, Shivaji said 'there should be no women, female slaves or dancing girls in the army', 'he who would keep them should be beheaded', and 'no one should commit adultery'.[33] One of Shivaji's harshest critics was the official Mughal chronicler Khafi Khan; he once described the Maratha as a 'hell-dog'.[34] Khafi Khan wrote that 'fortune so favoured' the 'treacherous, worthless' Shivaji that 'his forces increased, and he grew more powerful every day'. He had to concede this, however:

> But he [Shivaji] made it a rule that wherever his followers went plundering, they should do no harm to the mosques, the Book of God, or the women of anyone. Whenever a copy of the sacred Koran came into his hands, he treated it with respect, and gave it to some of his Musulman followers. Whenever the women of any Hindu or Muhammadan were taken prisoners by his men, he watched over them until their relations came with a suitable ransom to buy their liberty ... Shivaji had always striven to maintain the honour of the people in his territories. He persevered in a course of rebellion, in plundering caravans, and troubling mankind, but he entirely abstained from other disgraceful acts, and was careful to maintain the honour of women and children of Muhammadans when they fell into his hands. His injunctions upon this point were very strict, and anyone who disobeyed them received punishment.[35]

If Shivaji's army wanted anything, he directed it was to be 'obtained by peaceful purchase'. Armies of the period were known to enter villages at will and take grain or whatever else they laid their eyes on the strength of their sword. While this was deemed an acceptable tactical move in that age and carried out by just about everyone in enemy territory, if it happened inside a state's home territory, there was nothing the affected peasants or villagers could do, no one they could appeal to, and no one they could turn to for help. Shivaji made serious efforts to change this pattern of behaviour.

During his journey through Golconda in the 1670s, Shivaji warned his soldiers not to create trouble for ordinary people and made an example of a few offenders.[36] In 1673, he wrote a noteworthy letter to his regiment stationed at Chiplun in his own territory, warning it not to harass people in the neighbourhood or forcibly take provisions from them.[37] Shivaji knew his troops had exhausted most of their supplies, and though provisions had been sent from elsewhere, including for the horses, he thought it likely they would 'feed recklessly' and there would be nothing left at 'the height of the rainy season'. 'You will have to starve, and the horses will begin to die. That will mean you will have killed the horses,' he wrote. Then, Shivaji noted:

> you will begin to trouble the country ... Some will take the grain of the cultivators, some bread, some grass, some vegetables and things. When you begin to behave like that, the poor peasants ... holding on to their homes and somehow making a living will begin to run away. Many of them will begin starving to death. They will think you are worse than the Mughals who overrun the countryside! So much agony there will be, and all the curses of the peasants and horses will descend on you.[38]

He was, therefore, laying out his expectations of his soldiers:

> Whether you are a *Sipahi* or a *pavkhalak* [foot soldier], keep your conduct right. Some of you may be staying along the *paga* [military unit] or in different villages in the *muluk* [land]. Don't give the *rayats* [peasants] the slightest trouble – you have no business straying out of your camping places. Money has been given to you from the government treasury. Whatever any soldier may want, grain or vegetable or fodder for animals, duly buy it if it comes around to be sold or go to the bazaar and buy it duly there. Don't force anybody. Don't tyrannize anybody. Provisions assigned to government stables must last through the rainy season. The *karkuns* [clerks] will give rations of grains with this in mind: take only what is needed, so you don't have to go without food; there will be something to eat every day, and the horses will gradually gain strength. Don't lose your temper with the *karkun* for no reason or say 'give me this' and 'give me that', and don't violently enter the store-room and seize things from it.[39]

He highlighted how small things could lead to big disasters.

> The men attached to the stables are probably already living and will live in single stacks. Some of them will make fires, some will make their *chulhas* and cook in all sorts of unsuitable places; some will take live coals to light their pipes with, without thinking of whether there is any grass lying about, or whether there is a breeze. And suddenly there will be an accident. When one haystack catches fire, all the others will catch it and get burnt down. If some spark falls from somewhere on a few blades of grass, all the grass will be ablaze. The horses would die of hunger and the cavalry would be ruined. Then even if the heads of some peasants are cut off or punishment dealt to the *karkuns*, hay could not be procured and not a single haystack built ... So be careful and let the officers go around always and see that there is no cooking or lighting of fires [at unsuitable places] or that a lamp is not kept burning at night, so that a mouse can come and take a burning wick with it. Let there be no accident from fire. See that the grass, the rooms, are safe. Then the horses will survive the rainy season. If disaster strikes, it will not be necessary to tie the horses or feed them; the establishment itself would have been extinguished! And you won't have any worries left! That is why I have written to you in so much detail. All the officers – *jumledars*, *havaldars* and *karkuns* – should hear this letter in all its details and be alert. I will keep myself informed regularly, every day, and those who commit wrongs will be punished.[40]

The Bijapur army had become infamous during Shivaji's times for its lack of discipline, and the march of Mughal armies was often marred by indolence, indulgence and excesses. In such a situation Shivaji was seeking to create order and discipline in his military, something which was almost always a work in progress. In September 1671, he received information that one of his soldiers had attacked the *sabnis* of his regiment with a sword; the following year, Shivaji pulled up one of his top officials because the troops had given trouble to pilgrims of the fair at Chaphal, where lived the saint Ramdas, revered by Shivaji and by people across the state for his devotion to Lord Ram.[41] It was particularly embarrassing for the

Maratha state that such things were happening in the land of a towering religious authority and figure like Ramdas.

Yet John Fryer, a surgeon with the British East India Company who travelled across the Deccan and who saw the Marathas as nothing but a source of trouble for him and his masters, made an interesting comparison between Shivaji's army and that of Bijapur. He recorded that:

> the hilly people are of a rougher temper, more hardy and less addicted to the soft vanities of musick, cloathing, pomp or stateliness ... Seva Gi's men [are] thereby fitter for any martial exploit, having been accustomed to fare hard, journey fast, and take little pleasure. But the other will miss of a booty rather than a dinner; must mount in state and have their arms carried before them, and their women not far behind them, with the masters of mirth and jollity; will rather expect than pursue a foe; but then they stand it out better; for Seva Gi's men care not much for a pitched field, though they are good at surprising and ransacking; yet ... they are both of stirring spirits.[42]

Shivaji had undoubtedly wanted the phase from 1667 to 1669 to be a very quiet one, where he could regain his strength and carry out reforms. Yet, it was bang in the middle of this decidedly quiescent period that he launched his first – and, as it turned out, only – attack on the soil of Goa against the Portuguese. Why did he target Goan territory when he disturbed neither the Adil Shahi nor the Mughals at this time? Was there any provocation?

There had actually been a build-up of tensions between Shivaji and the Portuguese. Though the decline of Portugal as a global power was well under way with its repeated conflicts with the Dutch in the seventeenth century, the Portuguese were still the predominant power on India's west coast. They ruled not only Goa but Daman, Diu, Bassein (Vasai, near Bombay) and Chaul (near Alibaug); and Bombay too had belonged to them, until they gave it away to the British in 1662. It was precisely on this stretch that Shivaji had started building his navy from the late 1650s. His first sea forays were in Kalyan, Bhiwandi and Panvel, and part of his fleet was being built in upper Chaul – that part of the northern Konkan, just a little north and a little south of Bombay, where the Portuguese called the shots, and where they did not want a rival to come up. Initially they did not respond to Shivaji in a hostile manner: they had always professed to be neutral in their dealings with all the powers on the land, be it the Adil Shahi or the Mughals, and they watched Shivaji's early activities silently but intently.

Soon, they realized that Shivaji wanted Janjira, a fort more than 70 kilometres south of Bombay that was held by the Siddis. The fort was of strategic significance: anyone who wanted to control the coastal corridor needed to have it in order to move their fleet easily between north and south Konkan. The hold of the Siddis in the areas adjoining Janjira too was strong, so naturally, Shivaji wished to neutralize them.

From the beginning of Shivaji's attempted assaults on Janjira in the late 1650s, the Portuguese tacitly assisted the Siddis. They were convinced that the Siddis had no desire to go beyond their small sphere of control; Shivaji, on the other hand, was eyeing far bigger things and could emerge as a direct competitor. As attack after Maratha attack on Janjira was resisted by the Siddis, Shivaji realized that the Siddis were doubtlessly doughty fighters, but the only reason they could withstand repeated onslaughts was the active assistance offered to them by the Portuguese in terms of vessels, arms and ammunition.

Subsequently, Shivaji took, one by one, various towns to the north of Goa held by local satraps who were vassals of Bijapur. The geographical boundaries of Goa were then very different from the present ones: areas such as Ponda, Perne, Bhatagram (Bicholim) and Sattari (Sanquelim) were not inside Goa then, but to its north. And the local *desais* were the rulers there. By the end of 1664 Shivaji had captured most of these areas, forcing the *desais* to flee. Just before he left for Agra in 1666, Shivaji had also besieged the Ponda fort, but the Adil Shahi general Rustam-i-Zaman had come down the ghats, lifted the siege and also brought the areas previously occupied by Shivaji under the Adil Shahi banner.[43] (Shivaji believed that the Bijapur territory of southern Konkan was his by agreement with Bijapur, but Bijapur had now reneged on this by repossessing these areas.) Shivaji knew that Ponda had been able to hold out until Rustam-i-Zaman's arrival only because the Portuguese had secretly supplied ammunition to it. On his return from Agra, Shivaji regained all of the south Konkan territory of the Adil Shah, except Ponda and a few other smaller spots (though the Portuguese received information that he had probably captured some villages around Ponda fort).[44]

The Portuguese did not want Shivaji too close to the borders of Goa, but there he was. The viceroy of Goa worriedly reported to the king of Portugal on 20 September 1667 that Shivaji 'is now our neighbour at Ponda'. But while highlighting the peril Goa faced, the viceroy also paid Shivaji a huge compliment in the same letter to the Portuguese king. 'His [Shivaji's] alacrity, valour, alertness and military foresight are of the order of Caesar and Alexander. He is omnipresent,' he wrote.[45]

The immediate provocation for Shivaji to enter Goa now was that the Portuguese had provided shelter to all the *desais* and their *dalvis* or high officials evicted by him from the areas north of their state. The Portuguese were also helping these *desais* to make incursions into their former territories and create trouble for Shivaji there.

Almost all the *desais* and *dalvis* had taken refuge in Bardez inside Goa. From there, they went back to their old *watans*, and harassed and attacked the local population, with Portuguese assistance. Bardez itself was in the grip of serious religious frenzy. The viceroy, Conde de San Vincente, had baptized 7,000 Hindus in this part of north Goa and efforts were under way to convert the remaining 3,000; a Christian priest recorded optimistically that they would soon 'adopt the faith'. In September that year, the viceroy also issued a notification asking all Hindus to leave Bardez within two months as 'their presence affected the loyalty of the Christians to their religion'. The same month, Narba Sawant, nephew of Lakham Sawant, who had been the *desai* of Kudal, entered Vengurla with the help of the Portuguese, perpetrated violence and caused trouble to the Dutch who had their factory there.

On 22 November 1667, Shivaji began his offensive inside the Portuguese-ruled territory: he invaded Bardez with 1,000 cavalry and 5,000 infantry. The Portuguese, having received information that he was on his way, successfully sheltered the *desais* whom Shivaji wanted to target. But villages weren't spared: a number of them were attacked and hundreds of people were captured, including women and children, who were usually left alone by Shivaji's soldiers; these were clear violations of Shivaji's code of conduct. A report by local Franciscan padres stated that Shivaji headed straight to Colvale, where one of the *desais*, Keshav Naik, was supposed to be hiding. The rector of Colvale who emerged from the church to inquire about the noise outside was 'cut down', and so was another padre, who suffered eighteen wounds. Some other Christians too were killed.[46]

The viceroy ordered troops and ships from outside Bardez for support, and the villages of the local Ranes along the borders were used by the Portuguese as bases against the Marathas. The fighting went on for two days, but negotiations for peace began on the third day itself, with both sides saying they desired peace. Negotiations were speedy as Shivaji was close by, at Bicholim, and a treaty of friendship was concluded on 5 December 1667. The viceroy informed his bosses in Portugal that 'Shivaji duly returned all the plunder and women and children that his troops had seized',[47] and Shivaji, in return, extracted from the Portuguese the promise that they would not provide refuge to the *desais* inside their territory. All the *desais* were expelled from Goa the following year.

Did Shivaji's invasion have anything to do with the driving away of Hindus by Goa's viceroy? No. Shivaji was clear he was upset with the Portuguese for having harboured the *desais*. Not just the final treaty, but even the 'note of instructions' the Portuguese envoy carried from the viceroy to Shivaji during negotiations, which spoke of the points to be discussed with the Maratha leader, made no mention of the issue of religious persecution.[48] That means it never figured in the talks. A pragmatic man, Shivaji even allowed the Portuguese to open a factory at Dabhol in 1668.[49] And the treaty signed by him with the Portuguese stated that Goa's rulers would not provide shelter to the *desais* working against Shivaji. (Another treaty was signed between the two in 1670 to facilitate trade between Shivaji's territories and Goa, though tensions between them remained unresolved until Shivaji's death, with the

Marathas accusing the Portuguese of continuing to clandestinely help their enemies whenever they could.)

However, a theory emerged and gained currency that there was a religious angle to Shivaji's actions in Goa, thanks to an Englishman's letter of 30 November 1667 that cited the padres' apparent refusal to convert to Hinduism as the reason for their killings. That was simply not true. All the records – of the Portuguese, the Marathas and the Dutch – are clear about this. P.S. Pissurlencar, who dug up the records, concluded correctly that the Marathas' attack on the padres wasn't premeditated, and that they were killed as they were found out of doors and seen as hostile elements who might mount an attack. Apart from the fact that Shivaji didn't attack people of faith whatever their religion or denomination, it's important to note, as Pissurlencar stated, that 'padres often participated in battles as armed soldiers and therefore met with resistance from the enemy. That they were not non-violent preachers must not be lost sight of.'[50] The Portuguese also recorded that the Marathas thought of Portuguese priests as 'excellent soldiers'.[51]

Having said that, Shivaji was far from indifferent to the prejudicial policies of the Portuguese with regard to Hindus. He demonstrated an interest in the matter by restoring and repairing the temple of Saptakoteshwara in Narve, Bicholim, which had been demolished first by the Bahmani rulers and then by the Portuguese. The Kadamba dynasty that ruled Goa worshipped Lord Shiva as Saptakoteshwara, their family deity. In the twelfth century the Kadambas built a massive stone temple for the deity in Narve on the island of Diwadi. Destroyed by Muslim rulers in the fourteenth century, the temple was reconstructed by Madhava, a minister of the Vijayanagara state. A Portuguese priest, Minguel Vaz, ordered it to be razed again in 1540; within eight years, the Hindus reconstructed it in a small way but a little away, beyond Diwadi. Shivaji carried out repairs to the Saptakoteshwara temple and rebuilt it in November 1668 at the same spot beyond Diwadi.[52]

This was, significantly, during a period when Aurangzeb was targeting Hindu shrines. He had demolished the famed Somnath temple in

Gujarat and the temple of Lord Vishwanath at Kashi,[53] perhaps the most prestigious of the twelve *jyotirlingas*, and replaced it with a mosque known today as the Gyanvapi mosque. Mathura, considered the birthplace of Lord Krishna, was a particularly sore spot in Aurangzeb's eyes. In January 1670, he directed that the Krishna temple there be razed, and his chronicler recorded that 'in a short time ... the destruction of this strong foundation of infidelity was accomplished, and on its site a lofty mosque was built'.[54] Places of worship in Ujjain, where another of the *jyotirlingas* stood, were similarly targeted, as were Hindu religious sites in Bihar, Bengal and Orissa.[55]

Shivaji had been careful not to create a rupture with the Mughals as he went about restabilizing his provinces, refurbishing forts, setting up the patterns of his administration and, in the case of the Saptakoteshwara temple, reconsecrating a Hindu place of worship. He had also sent a military unit led by Prataprao Gujar and Niraji Raoji to Aurangabad to report to Prince Muazzam and had taken up the *jagir* offered in his son Sambhaji's name in Warhad in northern Maharashtra.[56] The Maratha force of 5,000 spent most of its time split into two, half of it encamped in Aurangabad with Muazzam's men and the other half guarding Sambhaji's *jagir*.[57] Shivaji's relations with Muazzam too were reported to be relatively peaceful and sound, and there was hardly a word about discord between them.

But the truce was far too unnatural to last very long.

12

Shivaji Strikes Back

Shivaji's truce with Aurangzeb and the Mughals had always been a shaky one. It had been a trial, as severe as many of the other trials he had faced. But towards the end of 1669, Shivaji was confident he had seen the ordeal through; with three full years of rebuilding starting from 1667 behind him, he was ready to abandon all pretences and fling himself into the business of confronting Aurangzeb all over again.

As it happened, Aurangzeb himself provided reason for Shivaji to throw off the garb of loyalty. Aurangzeb distrusted his son Muazzam's motives in the Deccan and had certainly not forgiven Shivaji for what he had done in Agra. He heard that his son's relations with Shivaji were good and were in fact improving by the day, and suspicion quickly rose in his mind that Muazzam might be preparing himself for a succession war in alliance with the Marathas.

Unable to hold himself back any longer, Aurangzeb directed the confiscation of portions of the *jagir* granted to Sambhaji ostensibly for recovery of the one lakh rupees he had advanced to Shivaji for his travel to Agra. At the same time, according to Sabhasad, the Mughal emperor hatched a plan to arrest Shivaji's senior officials at Aurangabad who, like Shivaji himself, were getting on rather too well with Muazzam.[1]

Along with these two aggravations, there was a third one: Aurangzeb wanted Shivaji to back off from the boundaries of Janjira. Shivaji's very first offensive in 1669, after having regained much of his strength, was aimed at the long-desired capture of Janjira, the sea fort that had eluded him for so long, and this time he came extremely close to winning it. Despite the '572 pieces of ordnance'[2] the Siddis had with them, Shivaji took their fort, Danda-Rajpuri, opposite Janjira and drove the chief official, Siddi Fateh Khan, to first seek the help of the Portuguese and the British, which they secretly offered, and then of the Mughals. Even so, the Marathas looked well placed to take Janjira, and Fateh Khan was on the verge of surrendering when three of his generals rose in revolt and, motivated by Siddi pride, deposed him and kept up the resistance. Bijapur, which nominally ruled over the Siddis, could not help, so the three Siddi generals approached the Mughals, as Fateh Khan too had earlier, and a Mughal *farman* was issued ordering Shivaji to instantly withdraw.

Shivaji was thoroughly annoyed: his argument was that, on the one hand, the Mughal–Maratha treaty signed by Aurangzeb had directed him to capture as much Bijapur territory as he could, and on the other, the emperor was directly and blatantly blocking his moves.

Was Shivaji also repelled by Aurangzeb's growing religious fanaticism, apart from his other provocations? There is no direct statement from him at this precarious moment, yet two contemporary documents specifically refer to this. One is a letter by a British official Henry Gary, who reported to Surat from Bombay that 'the arch rebel Sevagee is again engaged in arms against Orangsha [Aurang-shah or Aurangzeb] who, out of a blind zeale for reformation, hath demolished many of the Gentue [Hindu] temples and forceth many to turne Musslemins'.[3] The other is the Jedhe family chronicle, which states that 'from 17 August to September 1669 Aurangzeb harassed Benaras and destroyed temples. In the month between 14 December [1669] and 11 January 1670, the peace between the Mughals and Shivaji came to an end. Prataprao and Anandrao, who with their contingents were with the Prince [Muazzam] at Aurangabad, returned to Rajgad.'[4]

Evidently, for a variety of reasons, Shivaji decided he had had enough.

The first place he chose to target was the one that stared him in the face. From the top of Rajgad, where he and his mother were then staying,

Shivaji could see in the distance the impressive fort of Kondhana or Sinhagad. It was among the earliest forts he had taken, but he had had to give it up in the wake of his father's arrest in 1648. In subsequent years it had come back to him and had been a part of his dominions for over a decade until it was given away again in 1666, as part of the Treaty of Purandar. In places the fort was so steep the climb was almost vertical, and while all its heights were hard to ascend, those at the western end were considered impassable.

One of Shivaji's Mavale aides, Tanaji Malusare, offered to lead the onslaught. Tanaji hailed from the village of Umratha to the south-east of Mahad in the Konkan and was in charge of a Maratha infantry force of 1,000.[5] We don't know his exact age at the time of the battle of Kondhana, but he had struck up a close friendship with Shivaji right from their childhood and was of the same generation. Shivaji was thirty-nine in 1669, so Tanaji would be around the same age, give and take perhaps a couple of years. Known to be extremely tough, spirited and uncompromising as a soldier, Tanaji had figured prominently in various military campaigns, most notably against Afzal Khan's army and during Shivaji's foray into southern Konkan. And he always had his younger brother Suryaji by his side, helping him in all his endeavours.

The rival Tanaji was set to face was of a similarly solid martial reputation. Udaibhan Rathod, a thirty-eight-year-old Rajput from Jodhpur, was the highly competent leader of the Mughal garrison at Kondhana.[6] Most of his men there were fellow Rajputs. There were 1,200 of them versus Tanaji's 500 Marathas.[7] But the Maratha method was reliant not on numbers or on prolonged sieges, but on surprise and skill. Surprise included attacking in the dead of night, and that was Tanaji's plan too.

At around midnight on 4 February 1670, Tanaji reached the bottom of the fort with his men and asked two 'good and fearless' Mavale to begin their climb.[8] With consummate skill they went up the precipice and reached the ramparts, where they fixed a rope ladder for Tanaji and the others to ascend. Around 300 Mavale thus crept up slowly and stealthily, the wind gently whistling in their ears and the noises made by bats and other creatures breaking the dead silence of a dark night. The Rajputs were soon alerted to the presence of the enemy. Jadunath Sarkar has written that the Rajputs atop the fort were 'stupefied with opium',[9] a dubious claim that undoubtedly helped a Bollywood filmmaker (who made an otherwise very watchable film on Tanaji) come up with a scene of delirious revelry showing the garrison as negligent and foolish. Udaibhan Rathod and his men were, in truth, agile and alert, and as soon as they realized that the Marathas had already climbed up quietly, the 'gunners, archers and expert swordsmen' picked up their weapons, lit their torches and *chandrajyotis* (candles filled with powders), and rushed to repel the attackers. But the surprise had indeed worked, and as blade clashed against blade, and archers and lancers took aim, a massive confrontation broke out, the Marathas demonstrating a fierce spirit and filling the air with cries of '*Har Har Mahadev*'.

Sometime in the midst of the fight the rival commanders came face to face, raining blows on each other and also defending themselves valiantly with their shields. At one point the shield that Tanaji held in his hand broke, and a second shield didn't arrive in time. Without a break he fought on, 'making a shield of his left hand' and pluckily and dauntlessly taking Udaibhan's blows on it. Soon the two, 'fired with anger' and fighting furiously, struck each other fatal blows with their swords and fell to the ground. Tanaji's brother Suryaji immediately stepped up and rallied all the Marathas, ensuring their assault did not flag at that critical moment. All the 1,200 defenders ended up dead, many of them 'leaping down the cliff' in the heat of the unanticipated clash.

The Marathas took control of the fort, and in a signal to their supreme leader who had stayed up all night to track the attack, they set fire to the stacks in the stables. Shivaji, according to Sabhasad, saw the blazing flames and cried out, 'The fort has been captured! Victory has been achieved!' Early the next morning, an informer told Shivaji what had happened. Crushed to hear of Tanaji's death, Shivaji said, 'One fort has been taken, but another fort [Tanaji] is gone.' Shivaji praised Suryaji Malusare as well for his courage and conferred Tanaji's *suba* (province) on him; all the soldiers who participated in the epic clash were given 'gold bracelets' and 'gold-embroidered clothes'.

Buoyed by their triumph at Kondhana, the Marathas set out to recapture their other lost forts – they had given up twenty-three of thirty-five forts to the Mughals – and so swift and smooth was their success that within a matter of only four months, almost all of the twenty-three citadels they had given up were back in Shivaji's possession. Their restored chutzpah was exemplified by the conquest of the prestigious Purandar in March 1670, during which the Marathas took the Mughal *qiledar* (fort commander) Raziuddin captive. Their dominance was similarly overwhelming in Nanded, whose *faujdar* (military unit chief) Fateh Jung Khan fled in such fright that the irascible Aurangzeb felt compelled to dispossess him of the word 'Jung' in his title. Ludi Khan, the governor of Konkan, was routed twice and forced to leave the coastal areas, and the Mughal commander in Kalyan–Bhiwandi, Uzbek Khan, was attacked and killed by Shivaji. The *qiledar* of Mahuli near Thane, Manohardas Gaud, fought hard and well, but here too, the Marathas had the upper hand throughout, forcing a hapless Gaud to send in his resignation to Muazzam at Aurangabad because he knew he could not defend it any longer. The commander who replaced him, Allahvardi Khan, was killed by the Marathas and the fort taken.[10] The Mughal governor of Khandesh,[11] Daud Khan, was summoned by Aurangzeb to deal with the Marathas, as was Diler Khan, who was then in Gond country and who had given the Marathas a tough time at Purandar only four years earlier. Their arrival, however, failed to stem the tide. 'A number of Mughal officers arrived in Aurangabad in a very miserable condition,' wrote the historian Bhimsen Saxena who was then working with the Mughals in the Deccan.[12]

Apart from reclaiming forts, Maratha forces also plundered places near Ahmadnagar, Junnar and Parenda, and in particular carried out major raids in Warhad, where Sambhaji had earlier been granted a *jagir* by Aurangzeb and from which parts had been seized to purportedly recover the advance given for Shivaji's Agra visit. A Mughal newsletter stated 20,000 Marathas had arrived in the region and taken 20 lakh rupees.[13] The British at Bombay and Surat noted that Shivaji's 'motions have ever been so quick that his designs were rarely yet anticipated' and that Shivaji 'now marches not before as a thief but in gross with an army of 30,000 men, conquering as he goes, and is not disturbed though the [Mughal] Prince lies near him'.[14]

The recapture of twenty-three lost forts in just four months was an almost impossible feat. Mere familiarity with the terrain could not account for such astonishing success. How was it all done? Barring the case of Sinhagad, there are no surviving records which give any details of how the other forts were won, one after the other, in an avalanche of attacks. But if the glimpse provided by the charged atmosphere and inspired action at Sinhagad is any indication, Shivaji had chalked out an elaborate strategy and assigned specific tasks to specific teams after mapping out all the details of the near-simultaneous push and thrust to be made. All of it must have been backed up by vows, by a sense of opportunity, and by the inspiration provided by Tanaji and his spirited men for their fellow Marathas at the very beginning of the bold repossession initiative.

What is pretty certain is that most of the attacks on the forts were mounted by the Marathas in the night, incorporating their famous element of surprise. And we know thanks to British records – among the very few available records which throw some light on the regaining of forts, apart from Sabhasad's details about the Sinhagad mission – that the Maratha action did not cease even during the monsoon. This undoubtedly was a standout factor, for all armies, especially those in the mountains, hills and mountain passes and also those along the coastline corridors, were known to rest during the rains. Shivaji had intelligently made an exception. The British officials in Bombay wrote to Surat, 'Shivaji is not so slothful as the Mughal's forces, for he not only makes hay while the sun shines, but then when it is obscured by violent rains also.' Since the Mughal army had 'withdrawn forces up the hill [Sahyadris] for a quiet wintering, his have not been idle, but have recovered for him Lohgad, Kohoj ... and very lately made an assault again upon Mahuli'.[15]

While the Maratha forces had definitely benefited from a three-year break from conflict and by Shivaji's efforts to put his house in order, and been re-energized by his re-entry into planned aggression, the Mughal response was in part hamstrung by internal conflict. Prince Muazzam and his top general Diler Khan didn't see eye to eye. Diler Khan was deeply suspicious of Muazzam, and believed the prince was planning to throw him into prison and get him killed. He was also the chief purveyor of 'reports' to the emperor that Muazzam was hand in glove with Shivaji and was waiting for an opportunity to usurp Aurangzeb's throne. Muazzam, on the other hand, accused Diler Khan of not attending his court – Diler Khan had indeed stayed away from it for fear of being killed – and wrote to his father demanding action against the insubordinate general. Aurangzeb sent an official to the Deccan to probe charges made by both sides. Meanwhile, Diler Khan, finding his position increasingly untenable in the south-western parts, fled in the direction of Ujjain and was chased in September 1670 by Muazzam and Muazzam's aide Jaswant Singh before they were ordered by the emperor to return to Aurangabad. The Gujarat governor Bahadur Khan took this opportunity to avail of the services of the able Diler Khan and asked Aurangzeb if he would move him to Kathiawar, which the latter promptly did.[16]

If Aurangzeb had hoped that dust would settle on these internal disturbances, and the status quo would prevail, he was in for a rude surprise. On 3 October 1670, Shivaji entered Surat with a force of around 15,000 cavalry and infantry, and sacked the trading town once again, for two consecutive days. The British had anticipated such an offensive and had in the previous month itself moved all their goods to Swally, but little else had changed despite the walls finally having come up around the town after Shivaji's first sack six years earlier, in 1664. The local governor had with him a pitiful force of 300, and just as they had the first time, most Mughal officials and defenders fled the city the day before the Marathas arrived. The Hindu and Muslim traders ran away to the fort, as they had in 1664, and the Marathas had a run of the place except, as on the previous occasion as well, the factories of the English, Dutch and the French, where either resistance was offered or bribes paid. The British openly bad-mouthed the French factory officials, complaining that they had 'made a private peace for themselves, on what terms we cannot learn, and so never shot off a gunn, though at first, being strong in menn, they vapoured as if they would have fought the whole army themselves'.[17]

The others who put up a fight were those at the *serai* of the Persian and Turkish merchants and at the Tartar *serai* close to the French factory. Inside the Tartar *serai* was the former king of Kashghar, and the men there stood firm for most of the first day but could go on no more and escaped to the fort in the night. The English wrote that Shivaji got from the Tartar quarters 'a vast treasure in gould, silver, (a) rich plate, a gould bed, and other rich furniture'.[18]

At noon on 5 October, Shivaji left Surat almost as quickly as he had come 'to the wonder of all men', wrote the British, though 'no enemy was near, nor the noise of any army to oppose him'. But, they guessed, 'he had gott plunder enough'.[19] 'The great houses' had been ransacked 'at leisure' and 'nearly half the town' had been 'destroyed', and at the time of going away, the Company's officials recorded, Shivaji sent a letter to the officers and chief merchants saying that if they did not pay him a yearly tribute of 12 lakh rupees, he would come back the next year and burn down the remaining part of Surat.[20]

As he had done the previous time, Shivaji had in fact written a letter to the governor and to Surat's leading merchants before riding down to the city, demanding for 'the third' and 'last time' the *chauth* or quarter part of the annual revenue:

> As your Emperor has forced me to keep an army for the defence of my people and country, that army must be paid by his subjects. If you do not send me the money speedily, then make ready a large house for me, for I shall go and sit down there and receive the revenue and custom duties, as there is none now to stop my passage.[21]

The official Mughal newsletter estimated the total loot to be worth 66 lakh rupees.[22]

Shivaji's twin accomplishments of speedily winning back the surrendered forts and pulling off the second sack of Surat were followed by a string of incredibly efficacious raids across the north and north-east of the Marathi-speaking regions covering entire stretches of Baglana and Berar. The Marathas' belligerent military push which began at the end of 1670 and frenetic Mughal reactions to it kept armed hostilities continually raging in the Deccan for three years, up until 1674. There were many instances of individual exploits by Shivaji. Besieging one fort, Salher, with a 20,000-strong contingent, Shivaji with his muscled arms, superbly fit despite now being over forty years old, himself used rope ladders to climb up to the fort's ramparts. After the fort commander Fathullah Khan was killed, Salher's garrison surrendered to Shivaji. All of this resulted in Shivaji's name echoing across the land for the scope and scale of his ambitions and his relentless audacity in challenging an empire that, in the size of its army and expanse of territory, was at the height of its powers (under Aurangzeb).

An irate Aurangzeb had asked his general Daud Khan, the governor of Khandesh based in Burhanpur, to intercept Shivaji and his men on their return home from Surat in October 1670. The Khan moved quickly to catch the Marathas near Chandor, where the pathway from the northern parts to Nasik passed through the hills. A particularly violent battle ensued, with the Marathas on one side and the Bundelas as part of the Mughal army demonstrating great military skill and mobility. The pounding of the Mughal artillery forced the Marathas to eventually retreat, but not before the fighting had gone on until late in the night and the blows inflicted by them had made the Mughals set up a temporary camp at the spot for 'burying the dead and tending the wounded'.[23]

Dissatisfied with the fight his forces were putting up, Aurangzeb nominated a new commander for the Deccan, Mahabat Khan, formerly governor of Kabul.[24] Soon Aurangzeb was dissatisfied with his progress too, so Diler Khan and Bahadur Khan, who had moved up north, were sent back, Bahadur Khan as the new top Deccan general. He and Diler besieged Salher fort, which Shivaji had climbed to capture. Shivaji's men, known for their skill in defending forts in the hills, won this time by attacking the besiegers from outside. This battle, and another at Mulher at the end of 1671, carried Shivaji confidently into the new year and compensated for the loss of Pune to Diler Khan at around the same time.

In the middle of 1672, Shivaji captured Jawhar and Ramnagar, which gave him a boost by opening up the route to Surat. The Portuguese at

Daman used to pay one-fourth of their revenue to Som Shah, the Koli king of Ramnagar ousted by Shivaji. Now Shivaji demanded it from them, and the Portuguese agreed to pay *chauthai* (one-fourth of revenue) though they never really kept their word.[25]

More ambitious inroads into Warhad and Telangana in 1673 were blocked by the Mughals who gave chase to Shivaji's men, with much loss of life (400 men) and materials for the Marathas. That year was a much more mixed one for Shivaji, with the Mughal pushback finally acquiring some strength. But a further outlet for his revitalized military came in the form of disorder at the Bijapur court following the death of Ali Adil Shah II. Quick to seize an opportunity, Shivaji recaptured Panhala and Satara. Panhala's recovery brought him a great deal of satisfaction; he had had to surrender it after Siddi Jauhar's siege, and when he had tried to take it back in 1666, he had been forced to withdraw, resulting in his row with his general Netaji Palkar. Now Shivaji set up camp at Panhala for a month to 'direct operations against Bijapur' from there.[26]

The Adil Shahi had meanwhile got a new *wazir*, Khawas Khan; he was a firm opponent of Shivaji. He ordered the locally in-charge military general, Bahlol Khan, to regain Panhala. An Afghan, Bahlol Khan, with his largely Afghan force of 12,000, defeated the Marathas at Bankapur near Dharwad while Bijapur's new *wazir* simultaneously solicited assistance from the Mughals. Shivaji ordered Pratoprao Gujar to attack Bahlol Khan, saying he was 'stirring too much'.[27] A battle ensued at Umrani near Panhala, where Bahlol Khan's unit had camped. The rival sides fought all day, and when the Bijapuris flagged, Bahlol Khan went up to Shivaji's *sarnobat* and begged for mercy. And Pratoprao Gujar, showing magnanimity, promptly left. The shrewder Shivaji, finding this turn of events inexplicable, asked his commander, 'Why have you concluded peace?'[28] It turned out that he had been right to be sceptical. In January and February 1674, Bahlol Khan was again near Panhala to get it back. Wanting him out, Shivaji wrote a message to Pratoprao Gujar, stating peremptorily, 'Bahlol Khan is on his way. Go with the army and rout him. Otherwise don't show me your face again.'[29]

Stung by the rebuke, Prataprao, discovering that Bahlol was at Nesri to Panhala's south, rushed recklessly to the spot on 24 February 1674, hoping to catch him on a pass in the hills. Prataprao, according to some accounts,[30] led a party of six men and was killed, as were all the other six. From this account emerged the legend that only seven brave men had charged against Bahlol Khan's 10,000-strong force. What documents attest to is that he rushed to attack Bahlol Khan with six men in the middle of a larger battle and was 'killed by a sword cut'.[31] Sabhasad states categorically that 'a great battle was fought' and 'many fell' in it, and 'a river of blood flowed'.[32] The legend, regardless, has assumed a life of its own as an example of Maratha military valour. The Jnanpith award-winning Marathi poet V.V. Shirwadkar wrote stirring verses on it; set to music by composer Hridaynath Mangeshkar in the 1970s, it was immortalized in song by Lata Mangeshkar. The song, *'Vedaat Marathe veer daudley saat'*, is still played across Maharashtra at almost all social, cultural and political festivals.

Shivaji was 'greatly distressed' at the loss of his number one commander and said, 'I have lost a limb. I had written to Prataprao not to show me his face without securing a victory. He has won great merit and applause by making the ultimate sacrifice.'[33]

Still, Maratha raids into Bijapuri lands continued despite the Mughal general Diler Khan joining hands with Bahlol Khan to ward them off. The Mughals had foiled a Maratha bid to seize Pune. Their new Deccan governor Bahadur Khan had defiantly set up camp at Pedgaon on the banks of the river Bhima near Pune and renamed it after himself as Bahadurgad. Yet the imperialists were mostly playing catch-up, chasing the Marathas in Aurangabad, in the Panhala region and, as Shivaji's men went about sacking Ramgir, in the Andhras; the Mughals tried and failed to win all but one or two of the forts captured by the Marathas in Baglana.[34] The Englishmen at Surat wrote in February 1674 that Diler Khan 'had lately received a rout by Sevajee and lost 1,000 of his Pattans [Pathans], and Sevajee about 4 or 500 of his men'.[35] Shivaji blocked Mughal passage into southern Konkan as well. The Mughals stirred the

Siddis, who had won back the fort of Danda-Rajpuri from the Marathas a couple of years before, asking them to attack Shivaji's naval fleet, but this did not come to much.

Hobbled by worsening disturbances on the north-west frontiers, the Mughals were in no position to intensify their efforts against Shivaji. The revolt of the Afghans had assumed serious proportions. And just as in the Deccan, Aurangzeb was having to shuffle his top officials there. After two generals were shunted out in quick succession, Radandaz Khan, known for ill-treating prisoners in Agra fort, was sent to Peshawar; he was ambushed and killed by the rebels there in February 1674, just when Diler Khan was experiencing defeat at Shivaji's hands in the Deccan. The disasters compelled Aurangzeb to move himself to Hasan Abdal in the Punjab in April 1674 to direct operations; a month on, he also called Diler Khan to the northern frontiers.

Shivaji had begun the post-Agra phase of his career by avoiding direct military conflict with the Mughals. He had instead bolstered his defences and repositioned his forces, so that he could strike back at the right moment to recover possessions. Once the counterstrike began, Shivaji's campaign had gone almost perfectly according to plan, save for the truly irrecoverable loss of close associates like Tanaji and Prataprao, who, he acknowledged, had made it all possible. Shivaji's men had dealt significant blows to the Mughals, getting back everything that had been lost with astonishing rapidity and thwarting Mughal progress in the Deccan. Aurangzeb and his generals like Jai Singh had believed that their put-down of Shivaji would help write him off forever. But after Shivaji had seen himself through a deliberately quiet phase, he had seen to it that the Mughals lost their grip on events, and he was now the one defining and shaping the Mughal–Maratha conflict and most of its outcomes. Alongside the war he was waging with Aurangzeb, he was reconstructing the political order in the Deccan the way he wanted; he was making the era of revolt also one of serious reform, attempting to improve everyday life, resetting various aspects of administrative and military life. Above all, through patience, planning and decisive action, he had run rings around

Aurangzeb; the reconquering of forts from Aurangzeb's troops had been a masterpiece of fleet-footedness.

It was no longer Shivaji but the Mughal empire that was on the back foot in the Deccan. Shivaji's domains were now stable enough in both shape and character for him to declare his independence and sovereignty, and wear the crown.

13

The Crown

One day Shivaji had an unexpected visitor from the enemy camp. He was busy planning new offensives against the Mughals and Bijapur in the early 1670s from a spot near Satara when his guards informed him that a young man named Chhatrasal Bundela wanted an audience with him. Intrigued, Shivaji asked them to show him in.

Chhatrasal, all of twenty years old, was a soldier in the Mughal general Diler Khan's camp. He belonged to a clan that had fought hard, as Mughal soldiers, against Shivaji. Their own homeland, Bundelkhand (now divided between modern-day Uttar Pradesh and Madhya Pradesh), lay close to Delhi, and they had at first battled the Mughals. Aurangzeb, after ascending the throne, had come down hard against them, forcing a famous Bundela warrior, Champat Rai, to end his life along with that of his wife Rani Lal Kunwar in 1661. Two of Champat Rai's orphaned sons sought employment with the Mughals in 1664 and joined Jai Singh's forces: one was Angad, and the other, barely fifteen years old then, was Chhatrasal.

The teenaged Chhatrasal had joined Jai Singh on his Deccan mission against Shivaji, and he and his brother had distinguished themselves at the siege of Purandar.[1] After Jai Singh's death in 1667, Chhatrasal became a part of Diler Khan's contingent, but felt he was undervalued. Stories of Aurangzeb's growing bigotry against Hindus, which were by then being widely circulated, also made him uncomfortable; alongside, Shivaji's dazzling brilliance against the Mughals fuelled his desire to meet the Maratha leader.

Thus, one morning, on the pretext of going hunting, he waded through forests and crossed two rivers, the Bhima and Krishna, to meet Shivaji; that's how he had finally reached Shivaji's camp. Shivaji welcomed the young man and, when Chhatrasal had narrated his story, said to him, 'You are the crown prince of the Kshatriyas. *Jeet apni bhoomi ko, karo desh ko raj* (Go and win your homeland and rule over it).'[2]

According to Chhatrasal's court chronicler, Shivaji further told him to destroy the Mughals. Shivaji said, according to this account:

> I have Goddess Bhavani's blessings, that's why I am not scared of the Mughals. They have sent *umraos* against me, and I have unsheathed my sword against them. Eliminate them the way Keechaka was killed (by Bhima in the Mahabharata). Go to your country, mobilise your army, and use your swords to slay the Turkic forces.[3]

He dissuaded Chhatrasal from joining the Maratha army. 'If I keep you here,' Shivaji said, 'the credit for your feats will come to me, not to you. So proceed to your country and destroy the Mughals. Let the stories of your feats come to my ears.'[4] Shivaji gifted Chhatrasal a sword before he left. The young man, who would live until the age of eighty-one, was quick to put this advice into action. He built up a military and asserted his independence in Bundelkhand, though for a brief while he also made peace with the Mughals.

What the Chhatrasal episode tells us is that Shivaji now had star power beyond his realm. He had gained great recognition in his homelands of course, but, importantly, equally in the opposing camp.

Shivaji's handling of his crisis at the Mughal court in 1666 in particular had magnified his appeal. Within the city of Agra, voices had risen in praise of Shivaji immediately after the durbar drama, with one Rajput officer close to Jai Singh writing to another that though Shivaji's valour and courage had been noticed earlier, the people of the city had been especially impressed by him after his 'strong replies' at the emperor's court.[5] The officer regretted that no one had properly advised Shivaji against travelling to the imperial court, a comment that indicated how sympathy for him had grown among Rajputs, particularly during his imprisonment at Agra. And his subsequent escape and pushback against Aurangzeb had added immeasurably to his aura.

As Maratha tensions with the Mughals spiked, a deep appreciation for Shivaji's state-building capabilities and his constructive vision came from closer home, from the revered saint Ramdas, who had his enclave at Chaphal near Satara. Ramdas was a worshipper of Lord Ram and of Shakti. He described Shivaji's growing self-assertiveness against Aurangzeb as redolent of Maharashtra dharma, referring to a broad set of values and ethical principles, including spiritual and religious principles. Ramdas openly declared that Shivaji was singularly responsible for the survival of Maharashtra dharma.[6]

This social and cultural approval had a political dimension, given that politics at the time was always allied to faith. But there was also now, importantly, another kind of political recognition for Shivaji, which had more to do with power relations, the interface between states and their leaders, and diplomacy. Various powers were repositioning themselves vis-à-vis Shivaji.

We saw in the previous chapter that the Portuguese, earlier not so amenable to Shivaji's demands, had agreed to pay *chauthai* to the Marathas after Shivaji's capture of Ramnagar near Daman. Around the same time, the neighbouring Deccan kingdom of Golconda led by Abul Hasan Qutub Shah, of which Hyderabad was a part, consented to pay an annual tribute of one lakh *hons* to Shivaji because Golconda saw him as a buffer of sorts between the Mughals and Bijapur.[7]

The British too had come around from their earlier antagonism towards Shivaji. They were anxious to conclude a treaty with him as soon as possible. They had three reasons for doing so. The first was his growing power, which they could no longer deny (as mentioned, they had recently admitted he was no longer marching 'as a thief but in gross with an army of 30,000 men, conquering as he goes').[8] The second was they were still haggling over compensation from him for their losses at Rajapur during the Maratha raid of the 1660s. And the third was that a rival power, the Dutch, had recently offered to help Shivaji capture British-controlled Bombay, an offer he did not eventually take up but which caused alarm.

The issue of the Rajapur compensation had been complicated by two other matters: damage caused by Marathas to the British factory at Hubli during a raid, and the safe passage the British desired for their supplies through Shivaji's territories, with their men at Bombay dependent on inland areas for their requirements. Talks between the British and Shivaji went on through 1672 and 1673, with Shivaji offering 20,000 rupees as relief for Rajapur while the British asked for 'one hundred thousand'.[9] In his half-hour meeting with the British envoy Lieutenant Stephen Ustick in 1672, Shivaji firmly said he was willing to restore 'what was entered into his books', not more than that.[10] The British were not pleased, but they had to keep up relations with Shivaji because of Bombay's dependence on his territory for provisions, timber, firewood, etc.[11] Trade had been obstructed once already, in 1670, when Shivaji had refused to allow the British to cut and take wood from his lands after they had refused to sell him 'grenadoes, mortar pieces' and other ammunition he wanted against the Siddis.[12]

The British tried again by sending another envoy, Thomas Niccolls, in 1673. Shivaji treated Niccolls with great courtesy, offering him 'betel net and Pawne', taking him by the hand and asking him to sit on his left, 'near one of his side pillowes'.[13] But Niccolls achieved nothing, Shivaji telling him he would 'send on an answer' to the British demands ... by one of his own people named Beema [Bhima] Pundett [Pandit]'.[14] By the end of October 1673, however, the British traders were reporting with relief to their bosses that they were on the verge of concluding an agreement with Shivaji, which came at the end of the year, with the Marathas agreeing to pay just 10,000 rupees as damages for the Rajapur raid, the two sides agreeing to carry out trade, and the Britishers getting access to goods from Shivaji's lands.[15]

These talks and agreements with various powers were all evidence that a de facto state was being acknowledged by those around Shivaji. But when would the de facto state become a de jure state? The transformation was absolutely crucial for all the pacts and agreements to acquire legitimacy and legal sanctity, and for the people in Shivaji's lands to feel secure about the validity of his administration's orders and regulations if his adversaries came calling and raised questions. Shivaji was acutely aware that his opponents, while fearing his military prowess, were disinclined to give him his due as a statesman, arguing that he was the son of an Adil Shahi *sardar* and therefore a mere vassal of Bijapur. The stamp of sovereignty was a must, and Shivaji decided to confer it on himself at the place that had become his de facto capital: the fort of Raigad. He planned to get himself crowned king or, in his idiom, Chhatrapati – bearer of the *chhatra* or royal umbrella which bestowed kingship and sovereignty. It would be an event unprecedented in early modern India, since the sprawling Mughal empire did not allow lesser powers, like the sultanates, for example, to declare themselves independent in this fashion.

For some years Shivaji had treated Raigad, situated in Mahad, southwest of Pune, as both his capital and home, though Rajgad still held the status of official capital. In the 1660s, though, he began carefully fortifying and developing it as his chief fortress. Raigad stood at 2,800 feet above sea level, and its greatest attribute was that it provided easy access to the sea. Believed to have been built during the Satavahana era, Rairi, as the fort was originally called, had in the mid-fifteenth century been seized from a local Maratha chief by the Bahmani ruler and had towards the end of the century come under the control of the Nizam Shahi Sultanate. When the Mughals and the Adil Shahi divided that state between themselves post-1636, Rairi went to the Adil Shahi and was for the next couple of decades held by the Mores of Jaawali on their behalf.[16] Shivaji conquered it after defeating the Mores in 1656, gave it the more formal nomenclature of Raigad, and started constructing a large number of stone houses, offices and quarters there. There were two important waterbodies there; to these, Shivaji added a third reservoir.

And now, Raigad was getting all decked up for the moment of Shivaji's crowning glory. It must have been a surreal and supremely special moment for him and his proud Marathas. Shivaji had been dismissed and attacked for years as a bandit, a robber, a rover, by his enemies – most notably, as a 'mountain rat' by Aurangzeb.[17] But these pejorative terms had not proved, for Aurangzeb or for Shivaji's other adversaries, a helpful cudgel with which to go after him. Or to put him down. If anything, they had only stirred him. Spurred him on. Made him plot his moves ever more carefully and determinedly and bend his neck closer to the shimmering mane of his stallion to move it at a gallop. He had launched himself on to the big stage and more than stood his ground when Aurangzeb and his generals had bared their teeth and attempted a crackdown.

However rude and curt his words for Shivaji, Aurangzeb had wholly comprehended the powerful emergence of the Maratha rebel when he had declared to Jai Singh, after Shaista Khan's disgrace in 1663, that things were serious enough for him to need to proceed to the Deccan himself. Aurangzeb's march to the Deccan became a certainty after Shivaji's escape from Agra and especially after his second sack of Surat and recapture of all of his twenty-three forts surrendered to the Mughals. Shivaji had lost those forts in just three or four months in 1665, and once he had launched his moves to get them back early in 1670, he had recovered them in a major swoop in just as many months. Small had turned big. Rebel had turned rival. And the Mughal empire itself was now floundering against this Maratha of 'acute intelligence', 'quick in action, lively in carriage', 'with a clear and fair face' and 'dark big eyes so lively that they seemed to dart rays of fire'.[18] Aurangzeb's worry was that Shivaji could inspire other aspiring rebels too, and could even be a magnet for them.

But Aurangzeb couldn't head to the Deccan straightaway. There was too much trouble in the north, as we have noted, and things had to be quietened there before his southern campaign could even start. Shivaji knew this predicament and also the potential of his own rebellion to trigger a bigger rising which could, his 'Parmeshwara' willing, take down the whole empire. His act of announcing the advent of his own political raj was thus aimed as much at further checkmating his major rival Aurangzeb as it was at seeking his personal jurisdictional legality.

Significantly, given Aurangzeb's increasing championing of what he saw as the real tenets of Islam and growing reports of his discrimination against Hindus, who formed the majority of the Mughal empire's subjects, Shivaji chose to be consecrated as king according to the well-established Hindu rituals of kingship. He followed those rules closely and scrupulously for this special occasion. The prodigious use of ritual in the ceremonies was intended equally emphatically for Shivaji's very own people: it would go down very well with a massively tradition-bound Hindu society and help to firm up his state's lawful status in their eyes.

Shivaji called in Gaga Bhatt, a Brahmin priest, all the way from the holy city of Kashi or Benares to conduct the rites for the coronation ceremony and to preside over it. Gaga Bhatt's family was from Paithan in Maharashtra but had moved to Benares a few centuries earlier; his great-grandfather was the priest who had reconsecrated the Vishwanath or Vishweshwara temple after it was rebuilt in the wake of its first demolition. Gaga Bhatt's real name in fact was Vishweshwara. The priests of this family were given to writing religious texts and tracts, and when Gaga Bhatt came to the Deccan for Shivaji's coronation, he too wrote a tract on it called the *Shivrajyabhishek Prayog*, which provided details of the various rituals to be carried out.

The coronation ceremony itself was spread over a week starting 30 May 1674, and the *muhurat* for the enthronement determined by Gaga Bhatt was just a few minutes short of 5 a.m. on 6 June. When Henry Oxenden, an official dispatched by the East India Company's Bombay Council, reached Pachad, a town at the base of Raigad fort on 19 May, he learnt that Shivaji had left for Pratapgad. It was for him a special place: it was there he had built a shrine for Goddess Bhavani. He was now going to bow his head before her for her blessings and perform some ceremonies. For the goddess he had 'carried with him several presents', among them, Oxenden noted, 'a Sombrero of pure gold weighing about 1¼ maunds'.[19]

Shivaji belonged to the Kshatriya caste, one of the three 'twice-born castes', sandwiched between Brahmins and Vaishyas. Yet Shivaji's Kshatriya family, as the Brahmins saw it, had abandoned certain practices linked to the 'twice-born'. In particular, they hadn't bothered with the sacred thread ceremony, which in any case was largely confined to Brahmins at that time in the Deccan region. Nor, at the time of his various marriages, had Shivaji worn a sacred thread, so they could not be regarded as proper Vedic ceremonies, Gaga Bhatt and the other Brahmin priests felt.

Thus Shivaji had to not just go through a sacred thread ceremony, but had to be married all over again, before he could be anointed Chhatrapati.[20] Sabhasad wrote:

> an enquiry being held about the Raja's family, it was found the Raje was a Shuddha Kshatriya; a Sisodia family had come from the north to the Deccan, [and] that was the Raja's ancestral family. Having previously decided that the sacred thread ceremony should be performed as the Kshatriyas of the north assumed the sacred thread, the Bhat Gosavi [one of Gaga Bhatt's associates] conferred the sacred thread on the Raje.[21]

The day after Shivaji was invested with the sacred thread (29 May), he was married to his surviving wives again in keeping with Vedic customs. On that day, the priests performed the ritual puja for Lord Ganesha – as Ganesha is the Hindu deity ritually propitiated at the time of new beginnings.[22]

Over the next few days, a host of other rituals were carried out, and at the break of dawn on 6 June 1674, the climactic moment arrived. A splendid throne 'made of 32 maunds of gold' was ready to receive its occupant; water 'from the seven holy rivers' and from 'famous places of pilgrimage' had been brought in; and 'many gold lotuses inlaid with gems of nine varieties and various other golden flowers and clothes were distributed in advance'.[23] Shivaji first performed the *mangal-snan* or ablution; prayed to 'Sri Mahadev and Sri Bhavani, his family gods'; gave ornaments and clothes to the priests; and sat on a golden seat for the *abhishek*, where the eight officials he was appointing as his ministers or *pradhans*, along with the Brahmins, poured holy water over him from golden jars and vessels. 'According to the prescribed forms of charity', wrote Sabhasad, 'sixteen *maha-daans* (major acts of alms-giving)' were carried out. 'The eight pillars of the throne were studded with gems', and by each one stood one of the eight ministers. Similarly, all the officials and guests stood at their appointed spots, and the *chhatra* or 'golden umbrella inlaid with gems and having pearl fringes was held over the Raja's head'.[24] Shivaji was now Chhatrapati, Lord of the Umbrella.

Slowly the guests trooped in, among whom was the Briton, Oxenden. Raigad, he wrote later, recording his impressions of the rugged capital of the newly minted Maratha kingdom, was:

> fortified more by nature more than art, being of very difficult access, and [it has] but one advance to it, which is guarded by two narrow gates, and fortified with a strong high wall and bastions thereto. All the other part of the mountains is a direct precipice, so that it is impregnable except [if] the treachery of some in it betrayes it. On the mountains are many strong buildings as the Rajah's Court and houses for other Ministers of State, to the number of about 300. It is in length about 2½ miles and breadth 1 mile, but no pleasant trees not any sort of graine growes thereon.[25]

Shivaji was to hold his durbar immediately after being crowned. Oxenden, walking in at 'seven or eight' in the morning:

> found the Rajah seated in a magnificent throne and all the Nobles waiting on him [in] very rich attire, his Sonne Sombagy (Sambhaji) Rajaah, Peshua Moro Punditt and a Braminy of great eminence seated on an ascent under the Throne, the rest, as well officers of the army as others, standing with great respect.[26]

Oxenden continued:

> I made my obeysence at a distance and Naransinay [Narayan Shenvi, an envoy of the British] held up the diamond ringe which was to be presented him. He presently took notice of us and ordered our coming nearer, even to the foot of the Throne, where being vested, we were desired to retire, which we did, but not so soon but that I took notice on each side of the

throne there hung (according to the Moores manner) on heads of gilded lances many emblems of Government and dominion, as on the right hand were two great fishes, heads of gold with very large teeth; on the left hand several horses' tailes, a pair of gold scales on a very rich lance head poised equally, an emblem of justice, and as we returned at the Palace gate there was standing two small elephants on each side and two faire horses with gold bridles and rich furniture, which made us admire which way they brought them up the hill, the passage being so difficult and hazardous.[27]

Shivaji took four momentous decisions at the time of his coronation. Apart from appointing eight *pradhans*, he had given new Sanskrit names to their ministerial posts, doing away with the long-established Persian titles. This was a further assertion of his identity as a Hindu ruler and of his Hindu heritage, a statement of civilizational continuity that he wished to make, as Aurangzeb, in a puritanical turn, had banned music and imposed a series of discriminatory levies against the Hindu population in the Mughal empire (more on this later). Moropant Pingle, Shivaji's *peshwa* or prime minister, was to be called *mukhya pradhan*; Niro Nilkanth and Ramchandra Nilkanth the *mujumdars* were to be jointly termed *amatya*; the *waknis*, Dattaji Trimbak, was redesignated as *mantri*; Annaji Pant the *surnis* would now be *sachiv*; Ramchandrapant Sondev would be called not *dabir* but *sumant*; and Hambirrao Mohite would be the *senapati* or commander-in-chief and not *sarnobat*, which came from the Persian *sar-i-naubat*; Ravji was *pandit rao* or the royal priest, and Niraji Raoji would be the *nyayadhish* or chief justice. The council would be known as the Ashta (Eight) Pradhans. At the same time, the scholar Raghunath Pandit was asked to find replacements for numerous Persian terms commonly used in state correspondence, and Pandit soon prepared what came to be known as the 'Rajyavyavaharkosh' or dictionary of such terms. Shivaji also declared the opening of a new era, 'Rajya Shaka', from the date of the coronation,[28] and documents sent to him after his coronation referred to him as 'Kshatriya Kulawatans Shri Raja ShivaChhatrapati'. He got gold and copper coins minted with 'Raja ShivaChhatrapati' inscribed on them, indicating that was the official title he had taken for himself.[29]

After the coronation, Shivaji took a ride to a temple on an elephant,[30] and a few days later, having previously done his *tula* or weight in gold and having 'weighed 17,000 pagodas or about 160 pounds', made a 'great distribution of gold to the weight of his body ... and the same of silver, copper, spelter, tin and iron and of very fine linen, camphor, salt, nails, nuts and mace, with some of other native spices, butter, sugar', and 'of all fruits and all sorts of eatables, betel and arrack included'.[31]

Shivaji had already established his residence a while ago at his new capital. His mother, Jijabai, had set up her home at the base of Raigad fort, in the little town of Pachad. Her son had constructed for her what came to be known as the 'Pachad *wada*', which was actually a small fort with a moat around it. Here, barely eleven days after witnessing her son's glorious coronation, Jijabai breathed her last at over seventy years. She died in the knowledge that her son had done things entirely out of the ordinary. He had never assumed any formal position under any kingdom, even when he looked after his father's Bijapur *jagir*. Afzal Khan had accused him of having the gall to behave like an 'independent king', underscoring the fact that he was not one; Aurangzeb had offered him a *mansab* but he had not taken it, allowing his little son to be a *mansabdar* instead, even though this was a time of enormous difficulty for him; the only thing he had accepted was the title of 'Rajah', which the emperor had granted only after being pressed by Jai Singh. He'd always held his own as a free man and a leader of men and women, when in fact he had been surrounded by one of the biggest empires the world had ever seen, and when, all around him in the Deccan as well, there were older states which had for long been legal entities. He had stood up to everyone; he had survived – had more than survived. He had in fact become a sovereign, codifying his own rule of law and establishing his own order.

However, the loss of his mother, in the moment of his greatest triumph, was traumatic for Shivaji. Jijabai had been the real *chhatra* of the Chhatrapati, providing shelter, support and succour. She had also dabbled occasionally in administrative matters, issuing land grants or orders whenever someone approached her and she felt entitled to settle the matter, and declaring donations for religious places, among other things. During her son's absence in Agra, she had calmly handled the situation as his regent, when there was no certainty he would return alive. And at the time of her death, she had left for him a sum of over 25 lakh *hons*.

But there are always those who prey on people's griefs, and the time produced one such character, a tantric priest named Nischalpuri Gosavi. He had evidently felt sidelined as Vedic priests dominated Shivaji's coronation ceremony and had probably got fewer gifts than them. Nischalpuri found grievous faults with the various rituals that had been performed and attributed certain occurrences and tragedies, including that of the death of Shivaji's mother, to them. Nischalpuri's litany of complaints was severe and openly alarmist in character.[32] As was his prescription that Shivaji should undergo another coronation, this time according to tantric rites. Shivaji agreed. A product of his times in many ways, he must have been worried by the ramifications of the events around him, as spelt out by the tantric priest, who was of course being opportunistic. The second single-day coronation of Shivaji took place on 24 September 1674.

It was raining hard by then. The Deccan was cool and lush, but Shivaji wasn't resting on his laurels. His eyes were fixed on Pedgaon where the Mughal governor Bahadur Khan had entrenched himself. The Marathas, eventually led by Shivaji himself, cleaned up his camp, taking with them one crore rupees which basically paid for Shivaji's coronation.[33] Two months later, the Mughals again failed in averting a Maratha attack on towns near Aurangabad and into northern Maharashtra, where Shivaji's men also raided an English factory. And again a by-now familiar pattern played itself out: early in 1675, Shivaji proposed peace and offered his son's services as *mansabdar*, and Aurangzeb, perhaps clenching his teeth but hobbled in the north-west, accepted it at the moment, though not without warning Bahadur Khan not to be 'deceived by the words of that cunning person [Shivaji]'.[34] A little while after Aurangzeb's *mansab* for Sambhaji arrived from the north, in August 1675, a Mughal delegation led by the official Malik Barkhurdar went to Purandar to meet Shivaji. On the first day Shivaji played the gracious host, and the guests stayed back as he provided them excellent facilities. The next morning, he was totally dismissive: 'What brave deeds have you done that I should make peace with you? Get away from this place soon, else you will be disgraced.'[35]

Shivaji had started negotiations with the Mughals because he saw an opportunity in Bijapur, and he didn't want the Mughals interfering. Not for the first time, the Adil Shahi was in turmoil, with the feuding camps of the Pathans (led by Bahlol Khan) and the Deccanis and Abyssinians (led by Khawas Khan) at each other's throats. Before he dismissed the Mughal envoys at Purandar, Shivaji had taken several Bijapuri places from Kolhapur to Karwar, with a Muslim official Ibrahim Khan serving him excellently.

Meanwhile, both the Mughals and the British were helping the Siddis against Shivaji, who was still continuously striving, as ever in vain, to get the sea fort of Janjira. The renewed striving didn't help. Shivaji never got Janjira. Why? First, the Siddis deserve credit for this, for they invariably put up a tremendous fight, and second, they were almost always backed by one or the other opponent of Shivaji, sometimes by more than one opponent at a time.[36]

The far more alluring prospect for both the Mughals and the Marathas was away from the coast, in the south, where the internecine conflict in Bijapur had turned so ugly that the leader of one of the factions, Khawas Khan, was murdered by the other early in 1676. Shivaji's plans in this direction were temporarily stalled by a grave illness he suffered in January 1676, which laid him low for a month at least. (This has not been explained in the records, where mentions of this illness are without detail. His non-stop exertions must have begun taking a toll.) On his recovery, the Marathas got into action again, making some gains but suffering serious setbacks too. The Mughals also began energetically invading Bijapur territories, having got the Deccani faction over to their side. At this point, Shivaji reached out to Bahadur Khan for a pact that would ensure each side did not disturb the other as they made advances into different areas of the south: the Mughals deep in the south and Shivaji just as deep in the south-eastern parts. Shivaji was keen on going through Golconda to the eastern parts, all the way up to the coast if possible. Golconda had entered into an alliance with Bijapur against the

Mughals, but the Qutub Shah, Abul Hasan, was brought around easily by Shivaji, and the kingdom agreed to cooperate with the Marathas. Bahadur Khan too easily agreed as the arrangement suited the Mughals as much as it did the Marathas.

Meanwhile, just before he headed south, Shivaji, faced with an unexpected surprise in his backyard, became instrumental in remoulding a Hindu tradition. One day in mid-1676, his estranged confidant and erstwhile commander-in-chief, Netaji Palkar, arrived at Raigad. After his conversion and renaming as Muhammad Kuli Khan, Netaji had been sent by Aurangzeb to the north-west, and he had lived there for nine long years. He had been sent back by the emperor, possibly along with Diler Khan, for the campaign against Bijapur. Somehow, Netaji slipped out of the Mughal camp and arrived at Shivaji's capital.

The point was: how was he going to be received? Hadn't Shivaji had a bitter falling-out with him after Netaji had arrived at Panhala too late for a planned strike? Shivaji had fired him on the spot, and he too had gone away, straight into Aurangzeb's arms and into the faith Aurangzeb was increasingly claiming to uphold. Netaji was now repentant and wanted to be taken back into the Maratha fold, but how was that going to be possible? Shivaji didn't easily forgive such breaches of trust as Netaji had committed. Just months before Netaji's return, he had sternly warned his chief official at Prabhavali, whom he suspected of having deliberately slowed supplies to the Maratha fleet against the Siddis, saying that his behaviour was unacceptable and that he would not be spared even though he was a Brahmin if his misconduct were established.[37] Moreover, the Hindu religion did not have any practice of reconversion once someone had embraced another faith. The religion, at that time, even had formidably strong walls built between the various castes. What hope then could someone who had already stepped outside the Hindu fold have of being accepted back?

Shivaji's reaction turned out to be unexpected. He did not have any searing words for Netaji, only those of reconciliation. And breaking all the rules for him, he allowed him to reconvert, with rites possibly made up as they went along. The Jedhe Chronicle matter-of-factly noted that

'Netaji Palkar took *prayaschitta* [vows of repentance] and was purified'.[38] The welcoming of his long-lost comrade by Shivaji in this fashion was revolutionary at many levels. Netaji was given a reasonably high post, according to historical sources, though the top posts had been taken up since his leaving by others, and Shivaji took care not to replace or disturb them. When Shivaji got ready for his south-eastern campaign, Netaji was among the many generals accompanying him. So intensely focused on ritualism at the time of his coronation, Shivaji was now turning the well-established Hindu convention of prohibited reconversion upside down. It was a politic move, and also political. Hadn't his chief rival, the Mughal emperor, in a way converted Netaji to spite Shivaji himself?

Either on the day of Dassera in 1676 or shortly thereafter, Shivaji left Raigad for perhaps the most ambitious military enterprise of his career: his planned conquest of the south from the Tungabhadra to Vellore, and from Vellore to Jinji and Thanjavur. Up all the way from the Karnataka regions to the Tamil coast! Parts of the erstwhile Vijayanagara state had mostly been divided between Bijapur and Golconda, with Bijapur holding 'northern and eastern Mysore and the Madras plain',[39] and Golconda possessing the long strip along the eastern coast from Chicacole (Srikakulam) in the Andhras to Sadras on the Tamil lands. The Bijapur stretch had two separate governors: Nasir Muhammad Khan at Jinji, and the Afghan Sher Khan Lodi who was based lower south in Walgondapuram. Still further south were two Hindu states, Madura and Thanjavur, the latter ruled by Shivaji's brother Ekoji or Vyankoji as a vassal of Bijapur.[40]

Interestingly, Vyankoji's own hold on some of these parts had become loose. Having taken charge of his father's *jagir* after Shahaji's death, Vyankoji had been sent by Bijapur to Thanjavur in 1674 to put the previous ruling dynasty there back in power and evict the invading Madura *nayak*. Instead, Vyankoji had captured Thanjavur early in 1676 and, perhaps with the example of his half-brother very much on his mind, crowned himself in March that year.[41] His capital thus had moved from Bangalore to Thanjavur.[42]

Golconda was eager to exploit Bijapur's weakness and seize its south-eastern parts, and Shivaji offered a partnership, agreeing to share the spoils. Once Shivaji reached the capital of Golconda, Hyderabad, the exact terms were thrashed out. Golconda had earlier agreed to pay one lakh *hons* a year to Shivaji as tribute and to permit him to keep his envoy, Prahlad Niraji, at its court. For the southern campaign, Abul Hasan Qutub Shah promised the Marathas 3,000 *hons* a day, plus a military unit under the Golconda general Mirza Amin.[43] Shivaji said he'd hand over to Golconda regions not held earlier by his father Shahaji. And Shahaji had had a lot of them: the *parganas* listed in 1663 were 'Trincomalee, Jungmohan, Vetavalam, Velpur, Vriddhachal, Balangdas, Alwananur, Junnar, Koprapur, Tiru-kolur, Kolar and Bangalore'.[44]

Shivaji's visit as a royal guest of the Qutub Shah was an important moment in terms of his wider acceptability and the projected, albeit limited, Deccan solidarity. Leading an army of 50,000, Shivaji in February 1677 entered what Sabhasad called 'the Bhaganagar (Hyderabad) territory'[45] with fanfare, winning the hearts of the Qutub Shah as well as his people with his gestures. Shivaji gave orders to his army not to cause 'the slightest trouble to *rayats*'[46] in those parts. Some miscreants whose misdemeanours reached his ears 'were beheaded', and wherever Shivaji made a halt, items were purchased from the local bazaars; nothing was taken by force. The Qutub Shah was pleased and decided to advance a few miles ahead to welcome Shivaji. But Shivaji sent him a message, saying, 'You should not come forward to meet me. You are my elder brother.' So the *wazir* Madanna, a Hindu, and his brother Akanna came forward to welcome Shivaji and lead him into the city.

The intrepid Shivaji had generated an extraordinary amount of curiosity among the people, and when his army marched in, adorned with rich gold ornaments, 'citizens stood by the streets in millions to have a glimpse of the king'. The Qutub Shah had done his guest genuine honour by adorning his capital city. 'Streets and lanes were all around coloured with a thin layer of *kumkum* powder and saffron. Festive poles and triumphal arches were erected and flags and standards hoisted all over.' The women welcomed Shivaji by 'waving innumerable lamps around him, flowers were showered on him'. For his part he distributed wealth and countless clothes among the people on his way to Dad Mahal, the sultan's palace. At the gates of the palace, too, he sent a message to the Qutub Shah, asking him not to proceed downstairs. 'I will come to you, upstairs,' he said. After he had ascended the flight of stairs with five of his officials, Abul Hasan Qutub Shah came forward and gave Shivaji 'a friendly embrace'. The two sat on the same seat, and a long conversation – stretching over three hours – ensued. On his way back to his accommodation, Shivaji again 'distributed coins to the townspeople'. The next day Shivaji had food cooked by Madanna's mother at their place, after which he met the Qutub Shah, where details of the agreement were discussed and finalized.

Shivaji stayed for a month in Hyderabad before proceeding to Jinji. On the way there, he halted at Sri Shailya, the site of the Mallikarjuna *jyotirlinga* in the Andhras, a place of stunning beauty above the river Krishna; the temple compound, at the heart of which is the Mallikarjuna shrine, has sculptures, pillars and inscriptions which tell the stories of Hinduism's great epics.[47] Moved by the sheer other-worldliness of the place, Shivaji, after taking a bath in the Neel-Ganga there and praying at the temple, felt an irresistible desire, we are told, to give up his life as an offering to the god, but was dissuaded from doing so with reminders about all the duties that remained for him to perform.[48] Fascinatingly, the theme of Shiva is in a way a constant in Shivaji's life – from the time his grandfather repairs a shrine in the Deccan, his own naming, his worship of the deity, the war cry of *Har Har Mahadev* that he adopted, and Aurangzeb's razing of a number of famous temples dedicated to Shiva, to this visit to Sri Shailya, where Shivaji is moved enough to want to give up everything.

The victory in the south was a sweeping one. At the end of May 1677, the commander of Jinji, Nasir Muhammad Khan, surrendered the fort to Shivaji. In the first week of June, Vellore was encircled, and the Bijapur garrison there led by Abdullah Khan held it 'resolutely for fourteen months', but Shivaji kept hammering away, resulting in the gallant defence finally collapsing. The Jesuits of the region wrote that once Shivaji took over the district of Jinji, he 'applied all the energy of his mind, and all the resources of his dominions to the fortifications of all the principal places. He constructed new ramparts around Jinji, dug ditches, erected towers.'⁴⁹

The Bijapur governor of those parts, Sher Khan Lodi, and officials of the French East India Company, who had their factory at Pondicherry, began a dialogue on how to deal with Shivaji. Lodi and the French had often worked together, the Afghan taking the assistance of the *firangs* against intra-kingdom rivals. The French governor Francois Martin saw that 'the overthrow of Chircam [Sher Khan] was already in sight'⁵⁰ and prioritized his own factory's interests. He sent a Brahmin envoy to Shivaji requesting that the French territories be spared. Shivaji, wrote the French governor,

> assured our envoy that we might stay in complete security at Pondicherry without taking the side of either party; that if we offered the least insult to his people there would be no quarter for us or for those of our people who were in the [French] factory at Rajapour, that he would send an (h) avaldar in a few days to govern Pondicherry and that we might have to live with him in the same manner as we had done with the officers of Chircam.⁵¹

The French agreed not to step in. Before Shivaji's forces arrived, however, the French governor went and met his friend Sher Khan Lodi and asked him what he was going to do. Lodi was frank in the private conversation. He said:

> If Sivagy sent only four to five thousand horse against him he would hazard a battle, but if he came with all his forces he (Chircam) would have to retire under the guns of one of his fortresses, and that what caused him the greatest trouble was the lack of funds.⁵²

Martin told him sympathetically that 'we were touched to see him in so little state [ill-equipped] to resist Shivaji, whose army consisted of twelve thousand horse and many thousand infantry'.⁵³ As Lodi ran for the woods of Ariyalur in Tiruchirapalli, Shivaji chased him and caught up with him at the end of June. On 5 July, Lodi surrendered all his territories to Shivaji.

From there, Shivaji moved his camp at Tirumalawadi, 16 kilometres to the north of Thanjavur. Here, two agents of the French who witnessed the arrangements recorded that 'the camp of Sivagy was without pomp, without women, there were no baggages, only two tents but of simple cloth, coarse and very scanty, one for him and the other for his prime minister'.[54] It was at this camp, on the northern bank of the Kolerun river, that Shivaji invited his half-brother to meet him.

Initially there was a lot of warmth as the two brothers spent eight days together, exchanging gifts and presents. Then the reunion soured as Shivaji pressed his paternal claims. Sabhasad refers to Shivaji asking Vyankoji for their father's twelve *birandes*, an archaic, out-of-use word which has been commonly translated to mean titles, including robes of honour.[55] 'You should give me only the 12 *birandes* of my father you have, and I shall display them. Of course I can have new ones, but I am demanding these, as I should have what was earned by my father,' Shivaji said.[56] Was the father's southern *jagir* also discussed? Sabhasad is silent on this. But the French governor of Pondicherry, Francois Martin, noted that 'Ecugy [Ekoji or Vyankoji] had in his possession one-third of the lands of Gingy which their common parent Sagimagro [Shahaji Maharaj] held on his part. There were also his personal property and valuable effects. Sivagy demanded his share of these goods.'[57]

Vyankoji did not yield and, in the silence of the night, quietly fled from Shivaji's camp, taking a boat across the Kolerun river to his side of the territory. Shivaji was quite confounded to hear the next morning that his half-brother had escaped:

> Why has he fled? Was I going to imprison him? What should I do with the *birandes*? My own *birandes* have spread over the eight directions ... My fame has spread, what then should I do with those *birandes*? I had asked for them as one should have his patrimony. If he did not like to part with them, he was at liberty not to give them. Why did he flee for nothing? He is young, very young, and he has acted like a child.[58]

Before leaving for home, Shivaji appointed Raghunath Narayan Hanmante as *mujumdar* or auditor for the newly acquired parts and temporarily kept back his commander-in-chief Hambirrao Mohite for defence of the southern territories.[59] On his way back, the Mysore region up the ghats which Vyankoji had ruled was easy: Kolar, Koppal, Balapur, Belavdi and Sampagaon were captured, though in Mysore itself local ruler Chikkadevaraja beat back the Marathas, and Shivaji appointed Rango Narayan as his governor for his section of Mysore.[60] At the end of the year, after skirmishes between Vyankoji's army and Shivaji's, in one of which Shivaji's general Santaji Bhosle had to backtrack,[61] a truce was established: Shivaji got to keep the Mysore uplands and Jinji, and Vyankoji retained his lands south of the Kolerum river and a tiny part to the river's north.[62]

Shivaji's southern expedition had been a smashing success. He had seized territory which yielded 20 lakh *hons* a year, captured 100 forts, destroyed Bijapur's influence in those parts, and crossed over from the Marathi-speaking territories into the Kannada heartland and parts of Tamil country. The campaign was proof of the implications of Shivaji's coronation not merely for Maharashtra but for the shape of Indian history. Shivaji's state was no doubt deeply a Maratha state, but his conquests encompassing present-day Karnataka, Andhra and Tamil Nadu provided the clearest indication that he was setting himself up not just as a king of the Marathi-speaking parts but as Aurangzeb's principal rival across the length and breadth of peninsular Hindustan, as India was then known.

Golconda got absolutely nothing out of Shivaji's expedition despite having borne some of the costs and having sent a 5,000-strong military unit. Not a single fort. Shivaji also refused to hand over Jinji when the Qutub Shah demanded it. Aggrieved, the Qutub Shah walked out of his alliance with Shivaji and looked for an understanding with Siddi Masaud, who had taken over as the new regent at Bijapur. Unlike the Afghan Bahlol Khan who had fallen ill during Shivaji's absence from the Deccan and had died, Masaud was a Deccani, and the Qutub Shah was more comfortable dealing with him. Meanwhile, Diler Khan had taken over from Bahadur Khan as Mughal governor of the Deccan and had tried to attack Golconda but had been repulsed. He, however, got Bijapur's new regent to pledge allegiance to the Mughal empire and successfully signed him up for action against Shivaji.

Even better for him, Diler Khan managed to win over someone who was incredibly close to Shivaji. A piece of Shivaji's heart, as it were.

14

The Final Phase

Shivaji's son Sambhaji had been barely two years old when he had lost his mother Saibai in 1659. He had grown up under the shelter and watch of his father and, importantly, his grandmother, Jijabai. He had lived through an unforgettable experience in Agra with his father and had been part of his thrilling escape. Shivaji had appointed tutors to educate him, and the boy had developed, much like his paternal grandfather, a particular liking for the Sanskrit language, which he would go on to master. From the early 1670s, Shivaji had started getting him involved in important administrative work, and at the time of the coronation, Sambhaji, then seventeen years old, had been given the honour of sitting 'on an ascent', as the British envoy had remarked.[1]

Once Shivaji became king, Sambhaji naturally became the heir apparent. But there was trouble – of an all-too-familiar nature among royal families – brewing within the household.

Just as Sambhaji had been given due honour at his father's coronation, so had Soyrabai, as the seniormost among Shivaji's surviving wives. Soyrabai had given birth to a son on 24 February 1670. He was named Rajaram. The boy was just four at the time of Shivaji's crowning, but Soyrabai already seemed keen to make him, rather than the elder son, the heir apparent. Shivaji had only these two sons, though he had married eight times (most of which were political matrimonial alliances in view of his rising power).² During her lifetime Sambhaji's mother Saibai was his seniormost wife, and after her death, Soyrabai. He had six daughters as well, all of whom were married into various Maratha families, but they have been largely invisibilized by the historical record as they played no role in his entire political enterprise, subsequent to their marriages. Three of these daughters – Sakwarbai or Sakhubai, Ranubai and Ambikabai – were born to his first wife, Saibai; and three other wives bore him one daughter each: Soyrabai gave birth to Dipabai, Sakwarbai to Kamaljabai, and Sagunabai was the mother of Rajkuvarbai. Shivaji's other four wives – Kashibai, Putlabai, Laxmibai and Gunwantabai – did not have any children.³

When Shivaji had fallen severely ill for a month early in 1676, rumours started swirling in parts of the Deccan that he had died. It was around this time that news of serious differences within Shivaji's household spread all across the Deccan. Among them were reports of Sambhaji's allegedly unruly conduct. But Sabhasad – who later worked with Soyrabai's son Rajaram, whom she was setting up against Sambhaji – makes no mention of them, and the historian Kamal Gokhale, who wrote a scholarly biography in Marathi of Sambhaji, says stories of Shivaji's elder son's alleged misconduct began to originate only after the coronation of 1674 and were most likely spread by Soyrabai to discredit him.⁴

What was nevertheless true was that tensions had started rising in the family, and Sambhaji appeared to have been extremely dissatisfied about his place within it, and with how things were moving. In 1674, his grandmother, his major source of solace, had also died. So, on 13 December 1678, Sambhaji, at the age of twenty-one, took a step that left his father stupefied. He left Satara, where he was staying at the time, for Pedgaon and joined the Mughals under Diler Khan.⁵ The records don't make clear what the immediate trigger was for his defection.

For the Mughal empire, this was an extraordinary slice of luck, but it would not last long. Sambhaji was with Diler Khan when the Mughal governor attacked and seized the fort of Bhupalgad to the south-west of Pandharpur from the Marathas in April 1679. Diler Khan treated the garrison that was captured, and the local village population that had moved into the fort for shelter, with great cruelty. One hand of each member of the garrison was hacked off, and many villagers were reduced to becoming slaves.[6] Diler Khan also launched a campaign against the Adil Shahi, and Siddi Masaud wrote to Shivaji for help as the Mughals threatened the state capital of Bijapur. Shivaji immediately offered his assistance, sending a force of '10,000 horse and 10,000 oxen laden with grains' to protect Bijapur, and also personally carrying out raids in Mughal territories of the Deccan, including Jalna, which was both pillaged and captured.[7]

Diler Khan had to lift the siege he had mounted on Bijapur, partly because it was well defended, and partly because the top Mughal decision-makers could not agree on whether an attack should be launched on the Adil Shahi capital. On his way back, Diler Khan sacked the town of Tikota and, for no reason, imprisoned 3,000 of the town's ordinary inhabitants. From there, he moved to Athani, where again he perpetrated atrocities on the populace despite the complete absence of any provocation.[8]

Sambhaji, having grown up in the Shivaji ethos, where wanton harassment especially of ordinary civilians was not the norm, was immensely disturbed by Diler Khan's actions and decided that he did not really fit into the Mughal scheme of things.[9] He escaped from Diler Khan's camp on 20 November 1679, and father and son were reunited, after a rebellion that lasted less than a year but sent shock waves through the Maratha kingdom. The issue of succession nevertheless remained unresolved, though, according to Sabhasad, Shivaji planned to divide his territories between his two sons. Sabhasad's version states succinctly that there was 'much rejoicing' as father and son met each other after almost a year of serious separation.

Shivaji said to Sambhaji:

My boy, do not leave me. There is enmity between us and Aurangzeb. He intended to commit treachery against you. But the Sri [God] has kindly rescued you and brought you safely back. A great deed has been done. Now you, my eldest son, have grown big, and I have learnt that it is in your mind that you should have a separate kingdom. This is also in my interest. I shall give you a kingdom then. I have two sons. You, Sambhaji, are one; and Rajaram is the second. So I shall divide all my kingdom into two. The kingdom of Jinji – stretching from the Tungabhadra to the Kaveri – is one. The second is a kingdom on the other side of the Tungabhadra extending up to the river Godavari … You are my eldest son. I confer on you the kingdom of the Karnataka; the kingdom on this side I give to Rajaram. You two sons should rule over these two kingdoms. I shall henceforth meditate on the Sri and thus secure my welfare.[10]

To this, Sambhaji replied, 'My fortune lies at the feet of Your Majesty. I will live on milk and rice [at peace] and meditate at your feet.'[11]

The anguish of separation having been acute on both sides, the exhalation of relief at the reunion was similarly considerable. Shivaji had zealously laboured to build his own raj, and he fervently desired that his elder son Sambhaji should be on his side to secure its present and its future.

Thoughts of all of his family members were evidently occupying Shivaji's mind, for soon thereafter, he wrote a letter to his half-brother Ekoji or Vyankoji urging him to take proper care of his southern territories; as we have seen, the two brothers had partitioned their father's southern estate between them. Shivaji had heard that Ekoji had suddenly withdrawn into his shell, had turned indifferent to his own state machinery, was neglecting affairs of state, and was seriously contemplating becoming an ascetic. Shivaji reminded him of their father's renown as a military general, of his own ceaseless striving that had helped him establish his own kingdom; he urged Ekoji not to entertain thoughts of turning into a recluse but to take care of his own health and matters of state, and to expand his state and run it competently so that he could earn 'fortune and renown'. 'If you exert your best efforts and attain fortune and happiness in those parts, I will only be contented and full of pride that my younger brother has accomplished so much,' Shivaji wrote in his outreach to his half-brother.[12]

Around the same time, Shivaji dictated to his secretary, Neel Prabhu (who wrote his Persian letters), easily his most memorable letter, a letter that reflected the breadth of his thought, the depth of his belief in the oneness of humanity, and his distaste, as a Hindu ruler, for religious bigotry and intolerance. Shivaji had, while underlining the Hindu nature of his reign, practised a policy of religious tolerance in peace and in war, enjoining upon his soldiers and followers to treat Muslim women, Islamic saints and other people of the religion and the holy book of the religion itself, the Quran, with the greatest respect. He had continued in his territories the *inams* or grants to mosques, tombs and any other commemorative spots which had been given by previous rulers. In recruiting soldiers, too, he had never been hesitant about taking in those of the Islamic faith, and his two Muslim navy admirals and other officials were examples of the religious equality he practised conscientiously.

Shivaji's letter was addressed to Aurangzeb who, apart from targeting temples, had also taken to targeting the Hindu population within the Mughal empire. He had, in the mid-1660s, issued an ordinance stating that Hindus in the empire had to pay 5 per cent customs duty while Muslims could pay half of it; two years later, he had exempted Muslim traders from paying customs duty altogether and retained the 5 per cent imposed on Hindus. He had also started offering positions and handing out promises of settlement of property disputes and exemption from prison terms for 'unbelievers' who agreed to convert to Islam. Gradually, only Muslim collectors of rent were permitted and Hindu chief clerks and auditors were ordered to be sacked; he walked back on this step subsequently, after he realized the practical impossibility of doing such a thing. Some converts were also paraded on elephants, and some were paid very small allowances.[13] In April 1679, Aurangzeb's religious policy was on steroids: he imposed the *jaziya*, a tax for 'unbelievers' who lived in a theocratic Islamic state, on the Hindus. The Hindus of Delhi appealed to him to withdraw the inequitable law; when a big group stood in front of the Jama Masjid to make a plea in this regard, he sent elephants in their direction to crush all those who came in their path and disperse others.

Shivaji was angry and upset that Aurangzeb had taken a fanatical path. Asking Aurangzeb to desist from implementing such discriminatory policies, he stated in his letter:

To the Emperor Alamgir. This firm well-wisher Shivaji, deeply grateful for divine favour and your kindness as clear as daylight, begs to inform your Majesty:

I returned from your presence without seeking your permission. It is my misfortune. But I am ready to serve you in every possible way. May your kindness be felt by everybody. As a well-wisher I am placing some matters before you.

Recently it has come to my ears that owing to your war against me, your treasury has become empty. You have decided to meet the expenditure through the imposition of *jaziya* on the Hindus.

Your Majesty, Akbar, the founder of your empire, ruled for 52 years. He had adopted the excellent policy of treating with peace and equality Christians, Jews, Muslims, Dadupanthis, Stargazers, Malakis, Atheists, Brahmins, Jains, in fact all the communities. His aim was to ensure the welfare and protection of all. That is why he came to be known as the *jagadguru*. The result was that to whatever direction he turned, success and glory attended his arms. He brought most of the country under his sway.

After him, Nooruddin Jahangir ruled for 22 years. He led a life full of good deeds and became immortal. Shah Jahan ruled for 32 years. He too made his life fruitful through good deeds. That is why these rulers were successful in whatever direction they turned. During their rule a number of provinces and forts came under their sway. They have passed away, but their name endures … One measure of their greatness is that Alamgir has tried to imitate them but without success. He is at a loss to understand why this should be so.

The previous rulers, had they so desired, had certainly the power to impose *jaziya*. But they felt that all men [and women], big and small, were the children of God, and all religions but means to the worship of the Almighty. They never allowed the feeling of religious hatred even to touch them. The memory of their kindness and the good deeds they did is always fresh in the world. All men great and small praise and bless them. During their rule the people had peace, and … their glory increased.

But during your regime, many provinces and forts have gone out of your hands. The remaining provinces and forts too will be lost to you. I will not spare any effort to ruin your provinces. Your subjects are crushed. The income from your parganas and *mahals* is decreasing day by day. It is difficult to realize even 1,000 from places the income of which was one lakh previously. Poverty is striking kings and princes. The plight of nobles and *mansabdars* is apparent ... Your soldiers are discontented, the Muslims are in anguish, and the Hindus are scorched. Men are pining for bread ... They are in such deep distress, and yet you have imposed *jaziya* on them. How could you do this? This evil news will spread from east to west. People will say, 'The Emperor of Hindustan has taken a begging bowl and is out to realize *jaziya* from Brahmins, Jains, Sadhus, Jogis, Sanyasis, Bairagis, the poor and the starving. He takes pride in doing so. He is laying in dust the name of the Taimur dynasty.' Such will be the deep feeling of the people.

Your Majesty, in the Quran, God has been described as the Rabbul Alameen, the Lord of the entire universe, and not as Rabbul Mussalmin, the Lord of the Mussalmans. In fact, Islam and Hinduism are both beautiful manifestations of the Divine Spirit. The call for prayers is given in the mosques, bells ring to the Divine glory in temples. Anyone bearing fanaticism and religious hatred must be said to be acting against the commands of God. To presume to draw lines on these pictures is verily to lay blame on the Divine Artist [God]. To point out blemishes in any creation only means you are blaming the creator. Do not do so.

Jaziya cannot be justified on any grounds. It is an innovation in India. This is unjust. If you feel that on grounds of religion and justice the imposition of this tax is essential, you should first realize it from Raja Raj Singh. For, he is the leader of the Hindus. It will be then not be difficult to collect it from this well-wisher.[14]

The bluntness of the letter indicated Shivaji was now happy to burn all his boats with the emperor. As Chhatrapati, he now felt far more well positioned to admonish Aurangzeb directly and to point out the unreasonableness, blatant bias and criminality of his discriminatory faith-based policies and actions.

His reflections, in his writing, might have been profound, but events were still allowing Shivaji no rest.

While tense relations with the Mughals continued, Shivaji did conclude a peace treaty with the British early the next year, that is, 1680, over the contentious issue of the island of Khanderi, which had suddenly blown up a few months before. The Marathas had begun fortifying the small island, situated right opposite British-controlled Bombay, when a squad of alarmed English officials recklessly attempted to land there, drawing fire from the Marathas and losing a number of soldiers. The British naval fleet was considerably more advanced than that of the Marathas, and so were their guns; the Marathas took refuge in Naigaon but carried on with the fight and with their work on the island, refusing to vacate it. They also managed somehow to keep the island if not exactly awash in supplies, then sufficiently provided at all times, without exposing their fleet to British guns. At one point in the conflict, after the British had solicited the help of the Siddis, most of Khanderi's defenders wanted to give in, but according to the Company's officials, Shivaji's official Mainak Bhandari, his son and a Muslim soldier of Shivaji swore to keep fighting as Shivaji had apparently sent word that he didn't want them to quit.[15] As the historian Setumadhavrao Pagadi put it, in this case, the Marathas had in a way adapted guerrilla tactics to naval operations.[16]

The affair of Khanderi had ended honourably for the Marathas. But there was ferment on other fronts. Siddi Masaud of Bijapur had turned against the Marathas and joined hands with the Mughals; the Siddis were still holding on to Janjira (with Shivaji still bent on taking it); and the Portuguese were, just like the British and the Dutch, swaying towards whichever side suited them best.

Conflict was of course part and parcel of Shivaji's life, but now a serious personal health setback complicated the picture. In March that year, Shivaji celebrated the marriage of his younger son Rajaram to the daughter of his late lieutenant Prataprao Gujar at Raigad; Sambhaji was at Panhala then, Shivaji having kept him away, presumably to protect him from the intrigues of Soyrabai.[17] Days after Rajaram's wedding, in the middle of March, Shivaji took to his bed at Raigad with high fever. Twice earlier, after his escape from Agra, he had had serious illnesses lasting up to a month, once immediately after his return in 1666 and then exactly a decade later, in 1676. He had recovered from these. But the relentless pace of his life had clearly taken its toll; in the past few years, there had also been domestic strife, over the question of succession. Shivaji never recovered from this illness. Less than two months after he had turned fifty years old, close to noon on 3 April 1630, he had a strong feeling that death was close at hand. According to Sabhasad, he summoned all his counsellors and trusted aides, including his dear friend Tanaji Malusare's brother Suryaji and his half-brother Hiroji Farzand who had heroically taken Shivaji's place in Agra during his famed escape.[18]

'The term of my life has ended. I am going to Kailas to see my Sri [God],' Shivaji said as they all gathered around him. 'At these words from the king,' Sabhasad wrote, 'everyone's throat was choked, and tears began streaming from their eyes.'[19] Looking at them, Shivaji said, 'Do not grieve. This is a world where death is inevitable. All who were born in this world had to depart. Keep your mind free of sorrow and be of pure thought. You may now withdraw. I will now meditate on the Sri [the Divine].'

Having sent everyone out, 'Shivaji bathed in the waters of the Bhagirathi [Ganga], applied sacred ash on his body, put on the *rudraksha* or holy beads and through yoga, breathed his last.' The day Shivaji died, 3 April 1680, was a Saturday, and the time was around noon. For the cremation of their great king, the Marathas used sandalwood and *bel* wood.[20]

In the rival Mughal camp, Khafi Khan wrote, 'The infidel, the unbeliever, has gone to hell.'[21] And the Britishers, who had heard so much about his extraordinary exploits, were scarcely willing to believe word of his passing even eight months later, in December 1680. They wrote, 'Shivaji has died so often that some begin to think him immortal. It is certain little belief can be given to any report of his death till experience shows it.'[22]

Sabhasad wrote the following at the time of Shivaji's death:

[Shivaji's] authority was invoked from the banks of the Narmada to Rameshwar. He conquered these provinces and defeated armies and annexed the territories of the four Badshahis (on land), the Adil Shahi, the Kutub Shahi, the Nizam Shahi and the Mughlai, and the twenty-two Badshahs of the sea. A new kingdom was founded and the Maratha Badshah became a duly enthroned Chhatrapati or Lord of the Umbrella.[23]

Shivaji had survived challenge after demanding challenge, overcome difficulty after gargantuan difficulty, and braved crisis after burgeoning crisis to emerge as a super-survivor against forces that were usually vastly superior. And he had created, from scratch, an independent state that held its own against one of the most powerful empires the world had seen. Shivaji lit more than just a fuse under the foundations of the Mughal empire: he launched a blazing fire that eventually consumed Aurangzeb's empire and changed the face of all of Hindustan.

Hoping to wipe out the Marathas who refused to give up after Shivaji's death, Aurangzeb came down to the Deccan and spent close to twenty-five years there, struggling to accomplish his goal. His best officials, military and administrative, roamed the land of Shivaji, to stamp out his successes; his durbar was held there; the members of his household and top generals – Muslim and Hindu, including Rajputs – were desperately keen to go back home to the north after spending years attempting to subdue Shivaji's successors. But it was the Mughal empire that was corroded, slowly but surely, first due to the indomitable courage of Sambhaji and then the inexorable exertions, despite many damaging internal differences, of Rajaram, Rajaram's wife Tarabai and Sambhaji's son, Shahu.

Shivaji was succeeded by Sambhaji, and it was in 1681–82 that Aurangzeb embarked on his long-contemplated Deccan mission where he hoped to eliminate all the rival kingdoms. Aurangzeb soon destroyed the Bijapur and Golconda states, taking their rulers captive. Sambhaji, who kept up the Maratha fight as the new Chhatrapati, was taken a prisoner by the Mughals from Sangameshwar in Ratnagiri in 1689. He was taken to the Mughal camp at Bahadurgarh and paraded through the town on Aurangzeb's orders. The moment Aurangzeb saw Shivaji's son appearing before him as a prisoner, the Mughal emperor knelt to the ground to thank his god. Sambhaji was told to submit to him or face the worst possible consequences, but he refused to bow down and instead heaped abuse on Aurangzeb. That same night, Aurangzeb ordered Sambhaji's eyes to be gouged out. Even after the blinding, Sambhaji was tortured horrendously for a fortnight on Aurangzeb's instructions that Shivaji's son must be done to death because he had 'slain, captured and dishonoured Muslims and plundered the cities of Islam'. On 11 March 1689 Sambhaji's limbs were hacked off and he was executed, and after that, in a display of utmost bestiality, his severed head was taken around the main cities of the Deccan for all to see.[24]

Unapologetic, unchanged and undaunted, Shivaji's Marathas crowned his younger son Rajaram at Raigad. The Mughals pursued Rajaram relentlessly, forcing him to seek shelter at Jinji to keep up the confrontation from there; Sambhaji's wife Yesubai was imprisoned by the Mughals along with their son Shahu. Inside Jinji fort and encircled by the Mughals, Rajaram finally escaped with his wife Tarabai in 1697, and once back in the Deccan, the Marathas under him launched a counter-attack against Aurangzeb, for the first time going north of the Narmada river in 1699.[25] Rajaram died the following year, at the age of just thirty, but his wife Tarabai carried on the fight; while the succession struggle was still far from resolved, from then on, the Marathas as a whole went from strength to strength.

When Aurangzeb died in the Deccan, in Aurangabad, in February 1707, never having gone back to Agra or Delhi again in the second phase of his career in his determination to stamp out the Marathas, Shivaji's people were still a growing power and the decline of the Mughal empire had firmly set in. Towards the end of Aurangzeb's life, he was left a disappointed man, frustrated in his ambition to snuff the life out of Shivaji's Marathas. Soon the Marathas, under the leadership of the Peshwas, would go across all of the north and the east; in the east, they would reach Bengal, and in the north, they would go all the way up to Attock, in the Punjab province of modern-day Pakistan, before the decline of their own power began post 1760 along with the rise of the British. Shivaji had, entirely on his personal initiative and his brilliant leadership, lit the fire of their freedom, a fire that ultimately blazed through Aurangzeb's empire.

Notes

Introduction

1. Robert Orme (1782), quoted in Dennis Kincaid, *The Grand Rebel* (Rupa Publications, 2020 edition), 264.
2. Anil Samarth, *Shivaji and the Indian National Movement* (Somaiya Publications, 1975), 7–11. The information and quotations in this segment are from Samarth's book.
3. Ibid., 11.
4. Ibid., 59–61.
5. Ibid., 62–63.
6. Ibid., 68.
7. Ibid., 79.
8. Ibid., 84.
9. Ibid., 98.
10. Gajanan Bhaskar Mehendale, *Shivaji: His Life and Times* (Param Mitra Publications, 2011), 133–134.
11. Anil Samarth, *Shivaji and the Indian National Movement* (Somaiya Publications, 1975), 89.
12. Ibid.
13. Surendra Nath Sen, *Life of Siva Chhatrapati: Being a translation of the Sabhasad Bakhar*, Extracts and *Documents Relating to Maratha History*, Volume 1 (University of Calcutta, 1920), 32.
14. As for the argument that the term Hindu was practically non-existent before the twentieth century, Upinder Singh (the scholar-daughter of former Prime

Minister Manmohan Singh), has written about how the river Indus or Sindhu gave rise to the terms 'India', 'Hindu' and 'Hindustan', with ancient Chinese sources referring to the land of 'Shen-tu', Greek texts referencing 'India', and Persian inscriptions describing 'Hidu' as one of the subject countries of the Achaemenid ruler Darius. While Megasthenes, who came to Chandragupta Maurya's court in the fourth century CE, looked at the entire subcontinent as 'India', later Persian texts used 'Hindustan' for the land and 'Hindu' for its inhabitants. Thus the cultural identity is a rather old one. Upinder Singh, *A History of Ancient and Early Medieval India: From the Stone Age to the 12th Century* (Pearson, 2009), 3.

15. Hindawi started out in the thirteenth and fourteenth centuries as a language that 'moved away from Persian'. Gradually, the term began to indicate the indigenous people of India. Setumadhavrao Pagadi, *Shivaji*, (National Book Trust, 1983), 98; Pavan K. Varma, *The Great Hindu Civilisation: Achievement, Neglect, Bias and the Way Forward* (Westland, 2021), 194.

16. This account of Chhatrasal was penned by his court poet Gore Lal, better known as 'Lal Kavi'. The official account written in verse, 'Chhatra Prakash', covers events till 1707. Quoted in G.S. Sardesai, *Shivaji Souvenir* (Keshav Bhikaji Dhawale, 1927),154–160, published as part of *Chhatrapati Shivaji: Coronation Tercentenary Commemoration Volume*, ed. B.K. Apte (Bombay University, 1975), 141–144.

17. Diarmaid MacCulloch, *Thomas Cromwell* (Penguin Books, 2019), 4.

18. Aurobindo Ghose published what he called an imaginary dialogue between Shivaji and the Rajput general Jai Singh, whom Aurangzeb had sent to the Deccan to subdue Shivaji. In the conversation, Aurobindo quoted Jai Singh as saying to Shivaji, 'Where is the seal upon your work, the pledge of His (God's) authority?' To this, Shivaji replies, 'I undermined an Empire and it has not been rebuilt. I created a nation and it has not yet perished.' Aurobindo Ghose, *Karmayogin*, Vol. 3 (Sri Aurobindo Birth Centenary Library, [1910] 1972), 483–485, quoted in Samarth, *Shivaji and the Indian National Movement*, 148.

1. A Child of the Deccan

1. B.M. Purandare, better known as Babasaheb Purandare. No relation of this biographer. He has been easily the most well-known Shivaji eulogist in

Maharashtra since the 1960s and 1970s, and has done much to popularize the Shivaji legend. The name of the play referred to here is *Jaanta Raja*, which is almost always mistakenly written in English as *Janata Raja*. *Jaanta* means enlightened in Marathi, and the title of the play is translated as 'Enlightened King', while *Janata* means 'the people'.

2. Chitnis Bakhar (Chronicle), 23, quoted in G.B. Mehendale, *Shri Raja Shiv Chhatrapati*, Vol. 1 (Marathi) (Diamond Publications, 2008). Henceforth referred to as Mehendale (Marathi); all translations from it are mine.

3. *Shivabharat*, by Parmanand, translated into Marathi from the original Sanskrit by S.M. Divekar (Bharat Itihas Sanshodhak Mandal, Shalivahan Saka 1849 [1927]), 55. Henceforth referred to as *Shivabharat*; all translations from it are mine.

4. James Fergusson and James Burgess, *The Cave Temples of India* (Oriental Books, [1880] 1969), 248–252. Some of the details of the Shivneri caves are from Vidya Dehejia, 'Early Buddhist Caves at Junnar', *Artibus Asiae* 31 (1969), 147–166.

5. Stewart Gordon, *The Marathas: 1600–1818*, The New Cambridge History of India, Vol. 2, Part 4, (Cambridge University Press, 1993), 14–15.

6. 'Maharashtra' here is the word used for the Marathi-speaking regions of the Deccan and not the linguistic state with the boundaries that came into being in 1960.

7. Stewart Gordon, *The Marathas: 1600–1818*, The New Cambridge History of India, Vol. 2, Part 4, (Cambridge University Press, 1993), 12–13.

8. Ibid.

9. Hsuan Tsang quoted in A.R. Kulkarni, *Studies in Maratha History* (Diamond Publications, 2009), 1.

10. Afterword by Martha Ann Selby in Arvind Krishna Mehrotra, trans., *The Absent Traveller: Prakrit Love Poetry from the Gathasaptasati of Satavahana Hala* (Penguin Books, 2008), 72.

11. Ibid., 72–73.

12. Richard M. Eaton, *A Social History of the Deccan, 1300–1761: Eight Indian Lives* (Cambridge University Press, South Asia edition, 2020), 9–22.

13. Ibid., 91.

14. G.S. Sardesai, *New History of the Marathas*, Vol. 1 (Munshiram Manoharlal, 1986), 60.

15. Jadunath Sarkar, *House of Shivaji* (S.C. Sarkar & Sons, 1948), 33–41.
16. Ibid., 41–44.
17. Mehendale (Marathi), Vol. 2, 524.
18. Alexander Rogers and Henry Beveridge, trans., *Tuzuk-i-Jahangiri or Memoirs of Jahangir: From the First to the Twelfth Year of His Reign* (Royal Asiatic Society, 1909), 312–313.
19. Ibid.
20. William Foster, *The English Factories in India, 1618–1621* (Clarendon Press, 1906), 332.
21. Sarkar, *House of Shivaji*, 14, 20.
22. *Shivabharat*, by Parmanand, quoted in R.P. Patwardhan and H.G. Rawlinson, *Source Book of Maratha History* (K.P. Bagchi & Company, 1928), 3; *Shivabharat*, 19.
23. This Sambhaji was the son of Maloji's brother and Shahaji's uncle, Vithoji.
24. A.R. Kulkarni and G.H. Khare, *Marathyancha Itihas*, Vol. 1 (Marathi) (Continental Prakashan, [1984] 2021), 77.
25. Mehendale (Marathi), Vol. 1, 478–481; Sardesai, *New History of the Marathas*, Vol. 1, 63–65.
26. Ibid.
27. G.S. Sardesai, *Marathi Riyasat*, Khand [Vol.] 1 (Popular Prakashan, [1902] 2017), 55.
28. *Shivabharat*, by Parmanand, quoted in Patwardhan and Rawlinson, *Source Book of Maratha History*, 9.
29. *Badshah Nama* of Abdu-l Hamid Lahori, translated and quoted in H.M. Elliot and John Dowson, *The History of India, as Told by Its Own Historians*, Vol. 7 (Trubner and Co., 1887), 24.
30. *Shivabharat*, 58.
31. Ibid., 60–63.
32. The English chaplain L'Escaliot quoted in Jadunath Sarkar, *Shivaji and His Times* (Orient BlackSwan, [1920] 2010), XV.
33. B.G. Paranjape, ed., *English Records on Shivaji (1659–1682)* (Shiva Charitra Karyalaya, 1931), 73.
34. 'Life of the Celebrated Sevagy, Cosme da Guarda', in Surendra Nath Sen, ed., *Foreign Biographies of Shivaji* (Kegan Paul, Trench, Trubner & Co. Ltd; Calcutta: Girindranath Mitra, 1927), 2.

35. G.B. Mehendale, *Shivaji: His Life and Times* (Param Mitra Publications, 2011), 680.
36. Ibid.
37. Ibid.
38. *Shivabharat*, 82.
39. Ibid., 83–84, 90; *Sabhasad*, 3–4.
40. *Shivabharat*, 85.
41. Ibid., 88.
42. Patwardhan and Rawlinson, *Source Book of Maratha History*, 55.
43. Dennis Kincaid, *The Grand Rebel* (Rupa Publications, 2020 edition), 43.
44. Mehendale (Marathi), Vol. 2, 1125.
45. Ibid.
46. James Grant Duff, *History of the Mahrattas*, Vol. 1 (R. Cambray & Co., 1912), 113.

2. Notice to the Adil Shah

1. Mehendale (Marathi), Vol. 1, Map No. 8, 592–593 and 596–598.
2. Sardesai, *New History of the Marathas*, Vol. 1, 98–99.
3. Ibid., 98–99; Kincaid, *The Grand Rebel* (Rupa Publications, 2020 edition), 48–49.
4. Among them was an English chaplain, L'Escaliot, quoted in Sarkar, *Shivaji and His Times*, XV.
5. Both the stories are part of the Class 4 textbook in Maharashtra titled *Shiva Chhatrapati* (Maharashtra State Bureau of Textbook Production and Curriculum Research, Reprint, 2020), 21–23, 56.
6. The two letters appeared in the fifteenth volume of *Marathyanchya Itihasachi Sadhane* (268–269), a collection of Maratha documents gathered from across the Deccan by the historian V.K. Rajwade in the late nineteenth and early twentieth centuries. Among the top-ranking historians of the Marathas with a profound understanding of seventeenth-century Marathi who have called the letters fakes are G.H. Khare, Setumadhavrao Pagadi, D.V. Apte and K.V. Purandare. Recently the letters were described as forgeries by the historian Gajanan Bhaskar Mehendale. See Mehendale (Marathi), Vol. 2, 899–915.
7. Adil Shah's letter quoted in Mehendale (Marathi), Vol. 1, 624; Sarkar, *House of Shivaji*, 79; Setumadhavrao Pagadi, *Chhatrapati Shivaji* (Pune: Continental Prakashan, Reprint, 2017), 59.

8. Sarkar, *House of Shivaji*, 82; Sardesai, *New History of the Marathas*, Vol. 1, 104.
9. Kulkarni and Khare, *Marathyancha Itihas*, Vol. 1, 99.
10. Pagadi, *Chhatrapati Shivaji*, 59; Sarkar, *House of Shivaji*, 79.
11. Sarkar, *House of Shivaji*, 66.
12. Quoted from the Hindi translation of *Busatin-us-Salatin*, in Pagadi, *Chhatrapati Shivaji*, 59.
13. The original in Sanskrit is *Pratipacchandralekhev Vardishnurvishwavandita Saahasoonos Shivasyaisha Mudra Bhadraya Rajate*, quoted in Mehendale (Marathi), Vol. 1, 639 and Pagadi, *Chhatrapati Shivaji*, XIV.
14. Mehendale (Marathi), Vol. 1, 641–642.
15. A.R. Kulkarni, *Medieval Maratha Country* (Diamond Publications, 2008), 47.
16. Ibid.
17. Saqi Mustad Khan, *Maasir-i-Alamgiri: A History of the Emperor Aurangzib-Alamgir*, translated into English and annotated by Sir Jadunath Sarkar (Royal Asiatic Society of Bengal, 1947), 284.
18. Ibid.
19. Sardesai, *New History of the Marathas*, Vol. 1, 105.
20. Mehendale (English), 138.
21. Surendra Nath Sen, *Life of Siva Chhatrapati: Being a Transalation of the Sabhasad Bakhar*, Extracts and Documents Relating to Maratha History, Vol. 1 (University of Calcutta, 1920), 5.
22. Pagadi, *Chhatrapati Shivaji*, 61.
23. Sardesai, *New History of the Marathas*, Vol. 1, 109.
24. Sen, *Translation of the Sabhasad Bakhar*, 5; Sardesai, *New History of the Marathas*, Vol. 1, 109–110.
25. Mehendale (English), 135.
26. Ibid., 138–140.
27. Ibid., 138.
28. Ibid., 140.
29. Ibid., 140–141.
30. *Shivabharat*, 151.
31. Ibid., 145
32. Ibid., 144.
33. Ibid., 167–168.

34. Pagadi, *Chhatrapati Shivaji*, 63–64; an article by Lt Col M.G. Abhyankar, Director, Kunzru Centre of Defence Studies and Research, in the special issue on Chhatrapati Shivaji published by the Maharashtra government on his three hundredth death anniversary, with contributions by eminent historians, 1980, 45–51. M.G. Abhyankar, 'Chhatrapati Shivaji: A Heaven-Born General', *Chhatrapati Shivaji* (1980), 45–51 (published in the same aforementioned special commemorative issue).
35. *Shivabharat*, 161.
36. Pagadi, *Chhatrapati Shivaji*, 67, 73.
37. Ibid., 66–68, 72.
38. Ibid., 73.
39. Ibid., 72.
40. Ibid., 67.
41. Ibid., 60.
42. More Bakhar [family chronicle of the Mores], quoted in Sardesai, *New History of the Marathas*, Vol. 1, 119.
43. Ibid., 118–119.
44. Pagadi, *Chhatrapati Shivaji*, 70.
45. Sardesai, *New History of the Marathas*, Vol. 1, 119.

3. Notice to the Mughals

1. Jadunath Sarkar, *A Short History of Aurangzib* (Orient BlackSwan, [2009] 2019), 6, 9–11, 15–20.
2. Ibid., 21.
3. Ibid., 15–20.
4. Among the other places captured were Ghosale, Kangori, Tung and Tikona. Sardesai, *New History of the Marathas*, Vol. 1, 115–116.
5. Mehendale (Marathi), Vol. 1, 844.
6. Parmanand quoted in ibid., 855.
7. Mentioned in Sarkar, *Shivaji and His Times*, 43.
8. Sardesai (English), 116–117; Sardesai (Marathi), 174.
9. *The Times of India*, 13 November 1980; *Economic and Political Weekly* 15, No. 48 (29 November 1980); V.S. Bendrey, 'The Bhavani Sword of Shivaji the Great', *Journal of the Royal Society of Arts* 86, No. 4482 (14 October 1938).

10. Letter from *Adaab-e-Alamgiri*, a collection of letters dictated by Aurangzeb, quoted in Mehendale (Marathi), Vol. 1, 858.
11. Ibid., 817–818; Sarkar, *House of Shivaji*, 121.
12. Mehendale (Marathi), Vol. 1, 819.
13. Jadunath Sarkar, *History of Aurangzib*, Vol. 1 (M.C. Sarkar & Sons, 1912), 217–218.
14. Sarkar, *Shivaji and His Times*, 37–38.
15. Sarkar, *History of Aurangzib*, Vol. 1, 248–252.
16. Ibid., 281–282.
17. Sarkar, *Shivaji and His Times*, 38.
18. Ibid.
19. Mehendale (Marathi), Vol. 1, 825–826.
20. Aurangzeb's letters to Multafat Khan and Nasiri Khan, April–May 1657, quoted in Mehendale (Marathi), Vol. 1, 820–827.
21. Aurangzeb's letter to Nasiri Khan, circa early May 1657, quoted in ibid., 828.
22. Aurangzeb's letter to Nasiri Khan, circa 10 May 1657, quoted in ibid., 830.
23. Aurangzeb's letter to Nasiri Khan, circa 15 June 1657, quoted in ibid., 833–834.
24. Aurangzeb's letter to Nasiri Khan, circa May–June 1657, quoted in ibid., 835.
25. Aurangzeb's letter to Multafat Khan, circa May–June 1657, quoted in Mehendale (Marathi), Vol. 2, 1143–1144.
26. Quoted in Sarkar, *House of Shivaji*, 123.
27. Quoted in Mehendale (Marathi), Vol. 1, 866–868.
28. Quoted in Sarkar, *House of Shivaji*, 125–126.
29. Quoted in Sarkar, *Shivaji and His Times*, 41.
30. Ibid.
31. P.S. Pissurlencar, *Portuguese–Mahratta Relations*, translated by T.V. Parvate (Maharashtra State Board for Literature and Culture, 1983), 35–36.
32. Ibid.
33. Mehendale (English), 191.
34. Ibid., 191–192.
35. Pissurlencar, *Portuguese–Mahratta Relations*, 35.
36. Mehendale (English), 191.
37. Ibid.
38. Details of the appointments in Sarkar, *Shivaji and His Times*, 43–44; Pagadi, *Chhatrapati Shivaji*, 73–74, 89–90.

4. Daggers Drawn

1. Quoted in Sarkar, *Shivaji and His Times*, 48.
2. Ibid., 48–49.
3. Pissurlencar, *Portuguese–Mahratta Relations*, 68; Mehendale (English), 202.
4. Mehendale (Marathi), Vol. 1, 901.
5. Sabhasad, 8–9.
6. Ibid., 8.
7. Mehendale (Marathi), Vol. 2, 1126.
8. Sabhasad, 9; Sarkar, *Shivaji and His Times*, 45.
9. Aurangzeb's letter of 1656 to Shah Jahan, quoted in Mehendale (English), 200.
10. Sabhasad, 9; Mehendale (English), 199.
11. Sarkar, *Shivaji and His Times*, 56–57.
12. Adil Shah's *farman* to Kanhoji Jedhe, quoted in G.S. Sardesai, ed., *Shivaji Souvenir* (Keshav Bhikaji Dhawale, 1927), 142–143, published as part of *Chhatrapati Shivaji: Coronation Tercentenary Commemoration Volume*, ed. B.K. Apte (Bombay University, 1975), and in Patwardhan and Rawlinson, *Source Book of Maratha History*, 80.
13. Both of Afzal Khan's letters quoted in Patwardhan and Rawlinson, *Source Book of Maratha History*, 81–82.
14. *Shivabharat*, quoted in Mehendale (English), 199.
15. *Shivabharat*, 205–206.
16. Quoted in Patwardhan and Rawlinson, *Source Book of Maratha History*, 81.
17. Ibid.
18. A.R. Kulkarni, ed., *Jedhe Shakavali-Kareena* [both the original in Marathi and translation in English] (Diamond Publications, 2007), 197 (Marathi) and 301 (English).
19. Sarkar, *Shivaji and His Times*, 46.
20. Ibid., 46–47.
21. Mehendale (English), 203–204.
22. *Shivabharat*, quoted in Mehendale (English), 207.
23. Quoted in Sarkar, *Shivaji and His Times*, 47.
24. *Shivabharat*, 210–213.
25. Sabhasad, 10; Sarkar, *Shivaji and His Times*, 48.

26. *Shivabharat*, 214–215.
27. Sarkar, *Shivaji and His Times*, 50.
28. *Shivabharat*, 230; Sarkar, *Shivaji and His Times*, 49–50.
29. Ibid., 227.
30. *Shivabharat*, 225.
31. Ibid., 222–224; Sarkar, *Shivaji and His Times*, 49.
32. Mehendale (English), 212–213; Sarkar, *Shivaji and His Times*, 51.
33. For details of the Shivaji–Afzal Khan encounter, the days immediately before it, and its immediate aftermath, I have relied on *Shivabharat*, 230–245; Sabhasad, 18–24; Sarkar, *Shivaji and His Times*, 49–58; Mehendale (English), 211–215; Kincaid, *The Grand Rebel*, 110–116.
34. Sabhasad, 19.
35. Sarkar, *Shivaji and His Times*, 53.
36. Ibid.
37. Kulkarni, *Jedhe Shakavali-Kareena*, 304.
38. Among the clearest enunciations of this theory is by a Marathi scholar and writer, Narhar Kurundkar. Narhar Kurundkar, *Chhatrapati Shivaji Maharaj Jeevan Rahasya* (Marathi) (Deshmukh and Company, Reprint, 2019), 34–37.

5. Narrow Escapes and British Prisoners

1. Sardesai, *History of the Marathas*, Vol. 1, 131.
2. *Shivabharat*, 290–294.
3. English Factory Records quoted in Bal Krishna, *Shivaji the Great*, Vol. 2 (D.B. Taraporewala Sons & Co., 1932), 71.
4. *English Records on Shivaji*, 4.
5. Ibid.
6. Ibid.
7. Ibid., 20.
8. Ibid., 6.
9. Ibid., 9.
10. While the highly trustworthy Jedhe Chronicle and the Jedhe Chronology simply say Baji Prabhu laid down his life and his men did not allow Jauhar to ascend the pass, the post-Shivaji era 91 Kalmi Chronicle states that he took his last breath only after he heard the gunfire from the fort of Khelna. All three have been quoted in Mehendale (English), 236.

11. *Shivabharat*, 307–308.
12. Sarkar, *Shivaji and His Times*, 63.
13. Ibid., 63.
14. Mehendale (English), 242; B.M. Purandare, *Raja Shiva Chhatrapati*, Uttarardha [Part 2] (Purandare Prakashan, Pune, 2018 edition), 339–340.
15. *Shivabharat*, 324.
16. Patwardhan and Rawlinson, *Source Book of Maratha History*, 117.
17. Ibid., 325–326.
18. Ibid., 327.
19. B. M. Purandare, *Raja Shiv Chhatrapati*, Purvardha [Part 1] (Purandare Prakashan, Pune, 2018 edition), 430–431.
20. Quoted in Krishna, *Shivaji the Great*, Vol. 2, 132.
21. Ibid., 133.
22. Ibid., 132.
23. Ibid.
24. Quoted in William Dalrymple, *The Anarchy: The Relentless Rise of the East India Company* (Bloomsbury, 2019), 22.
25. Sardesai, *A New History of the Marathas*, Vol. 1, 141.
26. This and all the other suggestions mentioned in William Foster, *English Factories in India, 1661–1664* (Clarenden Press, 1923), 6–7.
27. *English Records on Shivaji*, 32.
28. Ibid., 34.
29. Foster, *English Factories in India*, 3; *English Records on Shivaji*, 27.
30. Foster, *English Factories in India*, 8–9.
31. *English Records on Shivaji*, 34.
32. Mehendale (English), 699.
33. *English Records on Shivaji*, 37; Foster, *English Factories in India*, 87; Sardesai, *A New History of the Marathas*, Vol. 1, 142.
34. Foster, *English Factories in India*, 87–88.
35. Ibid., 88.
36. *English Records on Shivaji*, 40; Foster, *English Factories in India*, 88.
37. Sardesai, *A New History of the Marathas*, Vol. 1, 142.
38. Ibid.
39. *English Records on Shivaji*, 23–30.

6. The Nocturnal Strike

1. *Shivabharat*, 289.
2. Quoted in Pagadi, *Chhatrapati Shivaji*, 122; Mehendale (English), 250–251. I have stuck here almost entirely to the translation from the Persian done by Pagadi, though in his footnotes he has by mistake mentioned the source as *English Records on Shivaji* when what he really meant – and Mehendale has correctly mentioned as the source – was *Selected Documents of Aurangzeb's Reign* (Persian), ed. Yusuf Husain Khan, Central Records Office, Government of Andhra Pradesh, 1958, 27.
3. The letter is part of N.C. Kelkar and D.V. Apte, eds., *Shivkalin Patra Saar Sangraha* (Marathi), Vol. 1 (Shiva Charitra Karyalaya, 1930), 217. Translation is mine.
4. Quoted in Mehendale (English), 251.
5. Pagadi, *Chhatrapati Shivaji*, 123.
6. Jedhe Chronology, quoted in Mehendale (English), 250.
7. *Shivabharat*, 309.
8. Two letters, one by Pilaji Nilkanth, Shivaji's chief official at Prabhavali in southern Konkan, and another by Shivaji to Pilaji, speak of Bijapur's recognition of Maratha claims on the Konkan. Pagadi, *Chhatrapati Shivaji*, 121.
9. Kelkar and Apte, *Shivkalin Patra Saar Sangraha*, 224. Translation is mine.
10. *Muntakhabu-l Lubab* of Muhammad Hashim, Khafi Khan, translated and quoted in Elliot and Dowson, *The History of India*, Vol. 7, 57–58.
11. Ibid.
12. Sabhasad, 42–43.
13. Ibid., 43.
14. Sarkar, *Shivaji and His Times*, 69.
15. Kincaid, *The Grand Rebel*, 139.
16. Khafi Khan, in Elliot and Dowson, *The History of India*, 58.
17. Ibid.
18. Quoted in Pagadi, *Chhatrapati Shivaji*, 126.
19. Sabhasad, 43.
20. Ibid., 44.
21. Khafi Khan, in Elliot and Dowson, *The History of India*, 59.

22. Cosme da Guarda in Sen, *Foreign Biographies of Shivaji*, 66–67, quoted in Mehendale (English), 792.
23. Khafi Khan, in Elliot and Dowson, *The History of India*, 59.
24. Ibid.
25. Quoted in Pagadi, *Chhatrapati Shivaji*, 126.
26. Mehendale (English), 255; Sarkar, *Shivaji and His Times*, 70.
27. Khafi Khan, in Elliot and Dowson, *The History of India*, 59.
28. William Irvine, trans., *A Pepys of Mogul India 1653–1708: Being an Abridged Edition of the 'Storia Do Mogor' of Niccolao Manucci* (E.P. Dutton and Company, 1913), V–VI.
29. Khafi Khan, in Elliot and Dowson, *The History of India*, 59.
30. Sarkar, *Shivaji and His Times*, 71.
31. Saqi Mustad Khan, *Maasir-i-Alamgiri*, 19.
32. *English Records on Shivaji*, 53–54.
33. Francois Bernier, *Travels in the Mogul Empire, A.D. 1656–1668*, A revised and improved edition based upon Irving Brock's translation by Archibald Constable (Archibald Constable and Company, 1891), 187–188. Accessed at the Columbia University website: http://www.columbia.edu/cu/lweb/digital/collections/cul/texts/ldpd_6093710_000.
34. Irvine, *A Pepys of Mogul India*, V–VI.
35. Ibid., 106.
36. Sen, *Foreign Biographies of Shivaji*, XV.
37. Ibid., 64–65.
38. Ibid., 65.
39. Ibid., 65–66.
40. Ibid., 66.
41. Pagadi, *Chhatrapati Shivaji*, 117.
42. The translation here is a combination of the translations made respectively by Sarkar in *House of Shivaji* (126–128) and Pagadi in *Chhatrapati Shivaji* (129–130). In my selection of their translated lines, I have depended as much on fluency, crispness and flavour as on accuracy and correctness.

7. The Sack of Surat

1. Krishna, *Shivaji the Great*, Vol. 2, 163.
2. Ibid.
3. Log of the *Loyall Merchant*, 5 January 1664 and Consultations at Surat, 6 January 1664, quoted in *English Records on Shivaji*, 60–62.
4. Sabhasad quoted in Krishna, *Shivaji the Great*, Vol. 2, 225.
5. Ibid., 60–61.
6. The traveller Monsieur de Thevenot quoted by Sarkar in *Shivaji and His Times*, 71.
7. All of these details of preparations made by the East India Company's officials to protect their property and lives were recorded by the chaplain in Surat, the Rev. John L'Escaliot, in a letter dispatched to Sir Thomas Browne in January 1664. The letter is quoted in *English Records on Shivaji*, 75.
8. Ibid., 72.
9. Letter from the president of the Surat Council, East India Company, to the Company, quoted in ibid., 66.
10. Iversen quoted in Krishna, *Shivaji the Great*, Vol. 2, 195.
11. *English Records on Shivaji*, 76.
12. George Oxenden's letter to Bantam, quoted in *English Records on Shivaji*, 86.
13. L'Escaliot's account in ibid., 75.
14. Iversen quoted in Krishna, *Shivaji the Great*, Vol. 2, 192.
15. *English Records on Shivaji*, 67.
16. Ibid.
17. Ibid., 78.
18. Sarkar, *Shivaji and His Times*, 74. Iversen's account from the Dutch factory correctly mentions the name as Virji Vora. Quoted in Krishna, *Shivaji the Great*, Vol. 2, 196. The chaplain of the British factory also named him correctly as 'Verge Vora', though he got the spelling wrong.
19. Iversen, quoted in ibid., 196.
20. *English Records on Shivaji*, 79.
21. Ibid.
22. Ibid.
23. Ibid., 72.

24. Ibid., 79.
25. Ibid.
26. Surat Council's letter quoted in Krishna, *Shivaji the Great*, Vol. 2, 181.
27. Sarkar, *Shivaji and His Times*, 76.
28. *English Records on Shivaji*, 75–78.
29. Ibid., 80.
30. Thevenot, in Sen, *Foreign Biographies of Shivaji*, 180.
31. Bernier, *Travels in the Mogul Empire*, Vol. 2, 188.
32. Ibid., 188–189.
33. Ibid.
34. Ibid.
35. Letter from the Governor General of the Dutch factory in India, in Sen, *Foreign Biographies of Shivaji*, 189.
36. Ibid., 189–190.
37. Log of the *Loyall Merchant* in *English Records on Shivaji*, 61–62.
38. The English chaplain L'Escaliot and Henry Gary, an employee of the East India Company, believed it was 1 crore rupees, while the log of the *Loyall Merchant* mentioned 1.5 crore rupees and above.
39. Quoted in Krishna, *Shivaji the Great*, Vol. 2, 175.
40. Mehendale (English), 271.
41. Ibid.
42. Ibid., 272.
43. Letter of 26 June 1664 from Surat Council to Karwar, *English Records on Shivaji*, 88.
44. The Marathi Sabhasad chronicle and the Dutch records cited by Mehendale (English), 278.
45. Dutch records cited in ibid., 278.
46. Rawlinson and Patwardhan, *Source Book of Maratha History*, 26.
47. Ibid.
48. Ibid.
49. Ibid.
50. Sabhasad, 90–91.
51. Ibid., 91.

8. A Naval Enterprise

1. Gajanan Bhaskar Mehendale and Santosh P. Shintre, *Shiv Chhatrapatinche Armaar* (Marathi) (Param Mitra Publications, 2010), 165.
2. Ibid., 165–167; *The Sahyadri Companion* (Sahyadri Prakashan, 1995), 231.
3. Letter No. 426 in Shankar Narayan Joshi and Ganesh Hari Khare, eds., *Shiv Charita Sahitya*, Vol. 3 (Bharat Itihas Sanshodak Mandal, 1930), 37.
4. Chitragupta Bakhar quoted in Mehendale and Shintre, *Shiv Chhatrapatinche Armaar*, 166.
5. Khare quoted in Mehendale and Shintre, *Shiv Chhatrapatinche Armaar*, 164.
6. Ibid., 43.
7. Letter from Surat to Karwar, 26 June 1664, in *English Records on Shivaji*, 88–89.
8. Portuguese letter of 25 August 1664 quoted in Mehendale and Shintre, *Shiv Chhatrapatinche Armaar*, 37; Mehendale (English), 278.
9. Krishna, *Shivaji the Great*, Vol. 1, Part 2, 234.
10. Ibid., 235.
11. Ibid., 234–235.
12. Ibid., 495.
13. Report of the Dutch official Pieter Van Antvliet to the Governor General and Council of the Dutch East Indies, ibid., 513.
14. Ibid., 514.
15. Ibid.
16. Ibid., 501.
17. Ibid., 114.
18. Ibid.
19. Ibid., 116.
20. Letter of 23 December 1664 from the Dutch Governor General and Councillors for India to the Lords Seventeen, ibid., 495.
21. Krishna, *Shivaji the Great*, Vol. 1, Part 2, 533.
22. The Dutch Dagh Register, two Adil Shahi *farmans*, and Sabhasad, quoted in Mehendale (English), 284–288.
23. Adil Shah's *farman*, ibid., 287.
24. Ibid., 288.
25. Krishna, *Shivaji the Great*, Vol. 1, Part 2, 527.

26. Ibid., 518.
27. Ibid., 529.
28. Ibid.
29. Ibid., 530.
30. Ibid.
31. Ibid.
32. Ibid.
33. Ibid., 531.
34. Ibid.
35. Ibid.
36. Ibid.
37. Ibid., 532.
38. Ibid.
39. Ibid.
40. Ibid., 536–537.
41. Ibid., 537.
42. Ibid., 536.
43. Ibid., 532–533.
44. *English Records on Shivaji*, 95.
45. Ibid.
46. Letter of 26 November 1664 written from Surat to the Company, ibid., 91–93.
47. Ibid., 92–93.
48. Henry Gary's letter of 1 December 1664 to Surat, ibid., 93.
49. Ibid.
50. Letter of 12 March 1665 from Surat to the Company, ibid., 97.
51. Ibid.
52. Letter of 26 June 1664 from Surat to Karwar, ibid., 89.
53. Krishna, *Shivaji the Great*, Vol. 1, Part 2, 518.
54. Ibid., 506.
55. Quoted in Mehendale (English), 293.
56. Pissurlencar, *Portuguese–Mahratta Relations*, 64.
57. Ibid., 37.
58. Dutch records on Portuguese preparations against Shivaji in late 1664 and early 1665, quoted in Krishna, *Shivaji the Great*, Vol. 1, Part 2, 519.

59. Ibid., 519.
60. Portuguese report quoted in Mehendale and Shintre, *Shiv Chhatrapatinche Armaar*, 42; Surat letter of 26 November 1664 quoted in *English Records on Shivaji*, 92.
61. The entire account of the Basrur campaign (including the foray into Karwar) is drawn from the 14 March 1665 letter sent by the British East India Company's Karwar factory officials to Surat, quoted in *English Records on Shivaji*, 97–99.
62. Sabhasad, 93–94.
63. Sabhasad, 89 (fn 120), 93–94.
64. Letter of 21 November 1970 from Bombay to Surat, quoted in *English Records on Shivaji*, 179.
65. Mehendale and Shintre, *Shiv Chhatrapatinche Armaar*, 173.
66. Letter of 6 November 1678 from Rajapore to Surat, quoted in *English Records on Shivaji*, Vol. 2, 187.
67. Kalmi Bakhar quoted in Mehendale and Shintre, *Shiv Chhatrapatinche Armaar*, 175.
68. Govind Pansare, 'Who was Shivaji?', translation of '*Shivaji Kon Hota?*' by Uday Narkar (Lokayat and Socialist Party [India], 1988), 26.
69. J.N. Sarkar, *The Modern Review* (December 1918), quoted in the translation of Sabhasad by Surendra Nath Sen, 94.

9. Setback and Retreat

1. Sarkar, *Shivaji and His Times*, 80–81.
2. Mehendale (English), 299.
3. Sarkar, *Shivaji and His Times*, 80; Sarkar, *House of Shivaji*, 131.
4. Mehendale (English), 298.
5. Jai Singh's letter to Aurangzeb which mentions details of all the rulers and people he was trying to recruit against Shivaji is part of *Haft Anjuman*, a collection of his missives to the emperor while he was on the Deccan campaign. Several of these letters, which are in Persian, have been translated by Jadunath Sarkar in English and are part of *House of Shivaji*. They have been translated more exhaustively in Marathi by the historian Setumadhavrao Pagadi and are part of *Samagra Setumadhavrao Pagadi*, Vol. 3, edited by D.P. Joshi and Usha Joshi (Marathi Sahitya Parishad, 2010).

6. Ibid., 65.
7. Ibid., 61.
8. Mehendale (English), 304–305.
9. Extract from *Haft Anjuman* quoted in Mehendale (English), 304.
10. Ibid.
11. Ibid., 301.
12. Pagadi, *Chhatrapati Shivaji*, 140.
13. Sarkar, *Shivaji and His Times*, 85.
14. Mehendale (English), 301.
15. Ibid., 302.
16. B.M. Purandare, *Raja Shiva Chhatrapati*, Uttarardha [Part 2].
17. *Haft Anjuman*, quoted in Pagadi, *Samagra Pagadi*, Vol. 3, 68.
18. Ibid.
19. Ibid., 69.
20. Ibid.
21. Ibid., 72.
22. Ibid.
23. Ibid., 73.
24. Ibid.
25. Ibid.
26. Ibid., 74.
27. Sabhasad, 53; Sarkar, *Shivaji and His Times*, 92–93.
28. Sabhasad, 53.
29. Ibid., 54.
30. Ibid.
31. *Haft Anjuman*, quoted in Sarkar, *Shivaji and His Times*.
32. Jai Singh's letter to Aurangzeb, quoted in Sarkar, *Shivaji and His Times*, 93; Sarkar, *House of Shivaji*, 134.
33. Sarkar, *House of Shivaji*, 134.
34. Ibid., 134–135.
35. Ibid., 134.
36. Ibid., 135.
37. Ibid., 136; Sarkar, *Shivaji and His Times*, 94; Kincaid, *The Grand Rebel*, 192.

38. Mehendale (English), 312.
39. Manucci, *A Pepys of Mogul India*, Vol. 2, 121.
40. Ibid., 120.
41. Ibid.
42. Ibid., 136.
43. Ibid.
44. Ibid., 136–137.
45. Ibid., 137.
46. Ibid.
47. Ibid.
48. The exact percentage is 65.7. I have rounded it off for clarity.
49. Ibid.
50. Ibid., 137–140.
51. Ibid., 137.
52. Ibid., 143–144.
53. Ibid., 144.
54. Diler Khan's letter to Shivaji, June 1665, translated by Jadunath Sarkar, *House of Shivaji*, 149–150. I have retained Sarkar's original text except in a couple of lines where the translated words sounded particularly archaic. Thus for the line 'My wish to see you is so strong that it baffles measuring', I have replaced 'baffles measuring' with 'is hard to measure it.' Similarly, for the line 'It treats of peace', I have written, 'It calls for peace.' The rest is the same.
55. Ibid., 138.
56. Ibid., 138–139.
57. Ibid., 139.
58. Ibid.
59. Shivaji's letter to Aurangzeb, June 1665, translated by Jadunath Sarkar, ibid., 148.
60. Ibid., 148–149.
61. Shivaji's letter to Aurangzeb, September 1665, ibid., 153–154.
62. Sarkar, *House of Shivaji*, 151.
63. Aurangzeb's letter to Shivaji of 5 September 1665, ibid., 150–152.
64. Sarkar, *Shivaji and His Times*, 98.

65. Ibid.
66. Aurangzeb's letter to Shivaji, 25 December 1665, quoted in Sarkar, *House of Shivaji*, 157.
67. Sarkar, *Shivaji and His Times*, 99.
68. Ibid.
69. Ibid., 99–100.
70. Ibid., 100.
71. Ibid.
72. Ibid.
73. Ibid.
74. Sabhasad, 78.
75. Ibid.
76. Ibid., 102.
77. Sarkar, *Shivaji and His Times*, 103.
78. Ibid., 103–104.
79. Ibid., 104.
80. Sabhasad, 59.
81. Sidney J. Owen, *The Fall of the Mogul Empire* (John Murray, 1912), 66.
82. Ibid.
83. Aurangzeb's letter to Shivaji, 5 April 1666, quoted in Sarkar, *House of Shivaji*, 157.
84. Sarkar, *Shivaji and His Times*, 104–105.
85. Ibid.; Mehendale (English), 322–323.
86. Mehendale (English), 323.
87. Sabhasad, 60–61.
88. Sarkar, *Shivaji and His Times*, 105.

10. Showdown and Escape

1. Sarkar, *Shivaji and His Times*, 105.
2. Bhimsen Saksena, *Tarikh-e-Dilkhusha* (Persian), translated by Setumadhavrao Pagadi in Marathi, *Samagra Pagadi*, Vol. 3, 218, English translation is mine; Mehendale (English), 323. Saksena was a chronicler who was a kin of a Mughal official posted in the Deccan at the time of Shivaji and Aurangzeb, and was present in Aurangabad when Shivaji reached there on his way to Agra.

Notes

3. Sarkar, *Shivaji and His Times*, 105.
4. Mehendale (English), 323.
5. Sarkar, *Shivaji and His Times*, 105.
6. Ibid.
7. All these details are in a letter of 29 May 1666 written by Jai Singh's officer Parkaldas, based in Agra, to Jai Singh's diwan Kalyandas, based in Amber. The letter has been reproduced in full by Sarkar in *Shivaji and His Times*, 105–106, and by Mehendale in *Shivaji: His Life and Times*, 324 – it is from these two sources that I have drawn the details.
8. Quoted in Mehendale (English), 324; Sarkar, *House of Shivaji*, 106.
9. Ibid.
10. Ibid.
11. Sarkar, *Shivaji and His Times*, 109.
12. Sarkar, *House of Shivaji*, 160.
13. Ibid.
14. Sarkar, *Shivaji and His Times*, 109; Mehendale (English), 326.
15. Sarkar, *Shivaji and His Times*, 109.
16. Ibid., 110.
17. Ibid.; Sarkar, *History of Aurangzib*, Vol. 4, 102.
18. Sabhasad, 63; Sarkar, *Shivaji and His Times*, 110; Sarkar, *History of Aurangzib*, Vol. 4, 103.
19. Sarkar, *Shivaji and His Times*, 110; Mehendale (English), 326; Sarkar, *House of Shivaji*, 160.
20. Sarkar, *House of Shivaji*, 160.
21. Ibid., 161; Sarkar, *Shivaji and His Times*, 110.
22. Ibid.
23. Sabhasad, 63.
24. Sarkar, *House of Shivaji*, 161.
25. Ibid.
26. Ibid., 162.
27. Ibid.
28. Ibid., 163; Sarkar, *Shivaji and His Times*, 112.
29. Ibid., 163–164.
30. Sabhasad, 65.

31. Sarkar, *House of Shivaji*, 164.
32. Sabhasad, 64.
33. Ibid., 64–65.
34. Ibid., 65; Sarkar, *History of Aurangzib*, Vol. 4, 104.
35. Ibid., 65–66.
36. Sarkar, *Shivaji and His Times*, 112; Sarkar, *House of Shivaji*, 164.
37. Sarkar, *House of Shivaji*, 165.
38. Ibid.
39. Sarkar, *Shivaji and His Times*, 112–113.
40. Mehendale (English), 329.
41. Ibid., 330; Sarkar, *House of Shivaji*, 170–171.
42. Ibid.
43. Ibid., 170–171.
44. Ibid.
45. Sarkar, *Shivaji and His Times*, 113; Sarkar, *House of Shivaji*, 168–169; Mehendale (English), 330; Sabhasad, 66.
46. Sarkar, *History of Aurangzib*, Vol. 4, 107.
47. Sarkar, *House of Shivaji*, 171.
48. Ibid.
49. Sabhasad, 66.
50. Sarkar, *House of Shivaji*, 170.
51. Sarkar, *Shivaji and His Times*, 113.
52. Sarkar, *Shivaji and His Times*, 115; Sabhasad, 67.
53. Sarkar, *Shivaji and His Times*, 115.
54. Ibid.
55. Ibid.
56. Sarkar, *Shivaji and His Times*, 116; Sabhasad, 68.
57. Their letter has been quoted in Krishna, *Shivaji the Great*, Vol. 1, Part 2, 261–262.
58. Sarkar, *Shivaji and His Times*, 116; Sabhasad, 69–70.
59. Sarkar, *Shivaji and His Times*, 117.
60. Ibid.; Sabhasad, 71.
61. Ibid.
62. Sarkar, *Shivaji and His Times*, 117.
63. Mehendale (English), 339.

64. Sarkar, *House of Shivaji*, 175.
65. Sarkar, *Shivaji and His Times*, 118; Mehendale (English), 338.
66. Sarkar, *Shivaji and His Times*, 118; Mehendale (English), 339.
67. Sarkar, *House of Shivaji*, 175.
68. Mehendale (English), 335.
69. Ibid., 334.
70. Ibid., 335.
71. Ibid., 335; Sabhasad, 68, 72.
72. Mehendale (English), 335.
73. Sarkar, *House of Shivaji*, 173–174.
74. Mehendale (English), 341–342; Sarkar, *Shivaji and His Times*, 116.
75. Sarkar, *Shivaji and His Times*, 119.
76. *Haft Anjuman*, quoted in Sarkar, *Shivaji and His Times*, 120.
77. Ibid.
78. Sarkar, *History of Aurangzib*, Vol. 4, 113.
79. Kulkarni, *Medieval Maratha Country*, 59–73.

11. A Push for Reforms

1. Quoted in Sarkar, *A Short History of Aurangzib*, 90–91.
2. Ibid.
3. Ibid.
4. Shivaji's letter to Aurangzeb of 22 April 1667 quoted in Sarkar, *Shivaji and His Times*, 126–127; Mehendale (English), 349.
5. Sarkar, *House of Shivaji*, 179.
6. The *deshmukhi* rights allowed him to collect revenue on behalf of the government.
7. Sarkar, *House of Shivaji*, 179–181; Mehendale (English), 349.
8. Mehendale (English), 351.
9. Sarkar, *House of Shivaji*, 174.
10. Ibid., 177–178.
11. Sabhasad, 38.
12. Ibid.
13. Mehendale (English), 367.
14. Ibid., 375–376.
15. Sabhasad, 37.

16. Mehendale (English), 367.
17. Sabhasad, 37.
18. Letter of 5 September 1676 to *subhedar* Ramaji Anant of Prabhavali district, quoted in Mehendale (English), 373–374.
19. Surendra Nath Sen, *Administrative System of the Marathas* (L.G. Publishers, [1925] 2021), 52.
20. Shivaji's letter to the *subhedar* of Junnar division, quoted in Mehendale (English), 376.
21. Correspondence between Shivaji and Nilopant Sondev, quoted in Mehendale (English), 362.
22. Sen, *Administrative System of the Marathas*, 77.
23. Sabhasad, 29; Sen, *Administrative System of the Marathas*, 78–82.
24. Sen, *Administrative System of the Marathas*, 79.
25. Ibid., 79–80.
26. Ibid., 85.
27. Sabhasad, 29–30.
28. When Shivaji had gone to Jai Singh's camp, there was no *havaldar* at Rajgad, and the charge of the fort was temporarily with Keso Narayan, the *sabnis*, who allegedly misappropriated a large sum from public funds. Case cited in Sen, *Administrative System of the Marathas*, 82.
29. Ibid., 85–86.
30. Mehendale (English), 386.
31. Chitnis Chronicle, quoted in Sen, *Administrative System of the Marathas*, 86–87.
32. Sabhasad, 82.
33. Ibid.
34. Khafi Khan, in Elliot and Dowson, *The History of India*, 58.
35. Ibid., 48–49, 93.
36. Sen, *Administrative System of the Marathas*, 90–91.
37. I have, in part, relied on the translations of R.P. Patwardhan, H.G. Rawlinson and Surendra Nath Sen for this letter, but have changed many of their archaic wordings and constructions, by looking very closely at the Marathi original, to make the language contemporary and, at the same time, absolutely accurate. The original letter is Document No. 28 in Vol. 8 of V.K. Rajwade's *Marathyanchya Itahasachi Sadhane* [Sources and Documents of Maratha History]. Rajwade's

works are available online on www.samagrarajwade.com, and the link to the letter from Vol. 8, should the reader want to check, is: https://samagrarajwade.com/index.php/marathyanchya-itihasachi-sadhane-khand-1/marathyanchya-itihasachi-sadhane-khand-8?start=81. Patwardhan and Rawlinson's translation of the letter is in their *Source Book of Maratha History*, 152–154, and Sen's translation is in *Administrative System of the Marathas*, 91–92.

38. Ibid.
39. Ibid.
40. Ibid.
41. Sen, *Administrative System of the Marathas*, 91.
42. Rawlinson and Patwardhan, *Source Book of Maratha History*, 302; Sen, *Administrative System of the Marathas*, 92.
43. The areas brought by Shivaji under his control, which were taken by the Adil Shah, were Kudal, Pernem, Bhatagram (Bicholim) and Sattari (Sanquelim).
44. P.S. Pissurlencar, *Portuguese–Mahratta Relations*, translated by T.V. Parvate (Maharashtra State Board for Literature and Culture, 1983).
45. Letter of Goa's viceroy, Vice-Rei Conde de San Vincente, to the king of Portugal, ibid., 45–46.
46. Ibid., 51–52.
47. Ibid., 54.
48. Ibid., 51.
49. Ibid., 55.
50. Ibid., 51–52.
51. Ibid.
52. V.T. Gune, ed., *Gazetteer of the Union Territory: Goa, Daman and Diu District Gazetteer*, Part I (Goa) (Panaji: Government Printing Press, 1979), 64; Pissurlencar, *Portuguese–Mahratta Relations*, 56.
53. Ibid., 55.
54. Saqi Mustad Khan, *Maasir-i-Alamgiri*, 60.
55. Sarkar, *History of Aurangzib*, Vol. 3, 301, 304.
56. Sarkar, *A Short History of Aurangzib*, 172–173.
57. B.M. Purandare, *Raja Shiva Chhatrapati*, Uttarardha [Part 2] (Marathi) (Purandare Prakashan, 2018 edition), 231–233.

12. Shivaji Strikes Back

1. Sarkar, *A Short History of Aurangzib*, 173; Pagadi, *Chhatrapati Shivaji*, 201.
2. Letter of 16 October 1669 from British officials at Bombay to Surat, quoted in Mehendale (English), 357.
3. Letter of 23 January 1670 in *English Records on Shivaji*, 140.
4. Quoted in Pagadi, *Chhatrapati Shivaji*, 202.
5. Sabhasad, 72; Purandare, *Raja Shiva Chhatrapati*, Part 2, 356–359.
6. Ibid.
7. Sabhasad, 72–73.
8. For this description of the battle of Kondhana I have relied on Sabhasad, 72–75.
9. Sarkar, *Shivaji and His Times*, 129.
10. Pagadi, *Chhatrapati Shivaji*, 204–206; Sarkar, *A Short History of Aurangzib*, 174.
11. Khandesh is the region comprising Jalgaon and its surrounding areas in northern Maharashtra.
12. Bhimsen Saxena's *Tarikhe Dilkusha* quoted in Pagadi, *Chhatrapati Shivaji*, 204.
13. Pagadi, *Chhatrapati Shivaji*, 204–205; Sabhasad, 72; Sarkar, *A Short History of Aurangzib*, 174.
14. Letter of 29 March 1670 from Bombay to Surat and letter of 30 March 1670 from Surat to the Company, *English Records on Shivaji*, 143–144.
15. Letter of 11 June 1670 from Mumbai to Surat, quoted in Mehendale (English), 418.
16. Sarkar, *A Short History of Aurangzib*, 174–175.
17. Letter of 20 November 1670 from Surat to the Company, *English Records on Shivaji*, 173–179.
18. Ibid.
19. Ibid.
20. Ibid.
21. Pagadi, *Chhatrapati Shivaji*, 208.
22. Sarkar, *Shivaji and His Times*, 136.
23. Ibid.
24. Pagadi, *Chhatrapati Shivaji*, 215.
25. Purandare, *Raja Shiva Chhatrapati*, Part 2, 307.
26. Pagadi, *Chhatrapati Shivaji*, 226.
27. Sabhasad, 107.

28. Ibid.
29. Ibid., 109
30. Purandare, *Raja Shiva Chhatrapati*, Part 2, 339–343.
31. Sabhasad, 109.
32. Ibid.
33. Ibid.
34. Pagadi, *Chhatrapati Shivaji*, 222–223, 225–227
35. Letter from Surat to Bombay, *English Records on Shivaji*, 321; Pagadi, *Chhatrapati Shivaji*, 230.

13. The Crown

1. Sarkar, *History of Aurangzib*, Vol. 5, 392.
2. This account of Chhatrasal was penned by his court poet Gore Lal, better known as 'Lal Kavi'. The official account written in verse, 'Chhatra Prakash', covers events till 1707. Quoted in G.S. Sardesai, *Shivaji Souvenir* (Keshav Bhikaji Dhawale, 1927),154–160, published as part of *Chhatrapati Shivaji: Coronation Tercentenary Commemoration Volume*, ed. B.K. Apte (Bombay University, 1975), 141–144.
3. Ibid.
4. If we leave aside Chhatrasal's official chronicler's hyperbole, the question arises: was Shivaji strategizing here? Possibly, because if unrest broke out in Bundelkhand, a new and independent front in the north would be created against the Mughals, and this might deplete the energies they could expend elsewhere.
5. Letter of 29 May 1666 from Rajput official Parkaldas to Kalyandas, quoted in Mehendale (English), 330.
6. Ramdas wrote his poem dedicated to Shivaji, 'Nischayacha Mahameru' circa 1670–1674.
7. Y.N. Deodhar, 'Shivaji and Golconda', *Chhatrapati Shivaji: Coronation Tercentenary Commemoration Volume*, ed. B.K. Apte (Bombay University, 1975), 132.
8. *English Records on Shivaji*, 143–144.
9. Sarkar, *Shivaji and His* Times, 266–271.
10. Ibid.
11. Ibid.
12. Ibid.

13. Account of Thomas Niccolls, 19 May to 17 June 1673, *English Records on Shivaji*, 251–257.
14. Ibid.
15. Sarkar, *Shivaji and His Times*, 271.
16. *The Imperial Gazetteer of India*, Vol. 21, 48–49; *The Sahyadri Companion*, 136–137.
17. Robert Orme (1782), quoted in Kincaid, *The Grand Rebel*, 264.
18. Cosme da Guarda, *Life of the Celebrated Sevagy*, quoted in *Foreign Biographies of Shivaji*, edited by Sen, 2.
19. Oxenden's account of the coronation, *English Records on Shivaji*, 371.
20. Gaga Bhatt's 'Shivrajyabhishek Prayog', Jedhe Shakavali and Sabhasad quoted in Mehendale (English), 484–485, and Pagadi, *Chhatrapati Shivaji*, 237–238.
21. Sabhasad, 114.
22. Gaga Bhatt's 'Shivrajyabhishek Prayog', Jedhe Shakavali and Sabhasad quoted in Mehendale (English), 484–485, and Pagadi, *Chhatrapati Shivaji*, 237–238.
23. Sabhasad, 115.
24. Ibid., 118–119.
25. Oxenden's letter of 13 July 1674, *English Records on Shivaji*, 372.
26. Ibid, 375.
27. Ibid, 375.
28. The era was to start from Jyestha Shuddha 13, 1596 (6 June 1674) according to the Hindu calendar. Mehendale (English), 488.
29. Sabhasad, 116; Sen, *Administrative System of the Marathas*, 23–25; Mehendale (English), 488.
30. Mehendale (English), 487.
31. Pagadi, *Chhatrapati Shivaji*, 239; Mehendale (English), 487.
32. Mehendale (English), 489–490; Pagadi, *Chhatrapati Shivaji*, 244–245.
33. Sarkar, *A Short History of Aurangzib*, 181; Purandare, *Raja Shiv Chhatrapati*, Part 2, 379–381. *The Imperial Gazetteer.*
34. Quoted in Pagadi, *Chhatrapati Shivaji*, 248.
35. Ibid.
36. Ibid., 245, 54.
37. Letter No. 1718 from Shivakalin Patrasar Sangraha, Vol. 2, quoted in ibid., 246, eds. N.C. Kelkar and D.V. Apte, Shiva Charitra Karyalaya, Pune, 1930.
38. Quoted in ibid., 261.

39. Sarkar, *A Short History of Aurangzib*, 182–183.
40. Ibid.; Pagadi, *Chhatrapati Shivaji*, 268.
41. Pagadi, *Chhatrapati Shivaji*, 269.
42. Ibid., 272–273.
43. Ibid.
44. Letter of 11 March 1663 of Ali Adil Shah II to all the *desais* and *nayakwars*, quoted in Sarkar, *House of Shivaji*, 89.
45. Sabhasad, 125.
46. This account is based on the work of Sabhasad, who was most probably an eyewitness to the events. I have relied on two translations: Sen, *Life of Siva Chhatrapati* (Sabhasad), 120–124, and Patwardhan and Rawlinson, *Source Book of Maratha History*, 164–166.
47. Diana L. Eck, *India: A Sacred Geography* (Three Rivers Press, Random House, 2012), 250.
48. Sabhasad, 124.
49. Quoted in Pagadi, *Chhatrapati Shivaji*, 283.
50. Francois Martin's account in Sen, *Foreign Biographies of Shivaji*, 281.
51. Ibid., 278.
52. Ibid., 284.
53. Ibid., 285.
54. Ibid., 305–306.
55. Sabhasad, 125.
56. Ibid., 125–126.
57. Sen, *Foreign Biographies of Shivaji*, 302–303.
58. Ibid.
59. Ibid., 129.
60. Ibid., 127–129; Pagadi, *Chhatrapati Shivaji*, 289–290.
61. Sarkar, *Shivaji and His Times*, 238.
62. Ibid., 239.

14. The Final Phase

1. Oxenden's letter, *English Records on Shivaji*, 375.
2. The names of Shivaji's eight wives, with their maiden surnames where available, are: Saibai Nimbalkar, Soyrabai Mohite, Sakwarbai Gaikwad, Kashibai Jadhav,

Putlabai Palkar, Sagunabai Shirke, Laxmibai and Gunwantabai. Mehendale (English), 680; Mehendale (Marathi), Vol. 2, 1130.
3. Mehendale (Marathi), Vol. 2, 1137–1138.
4. Kamal Gokhale, *Shivaputra Sambhaji* (Marathi) (Continental Prakashan, [1971], 2019), 45–72.
5. Pagadi, *Chhatrapati Shivaji*, 300–301.
6. Sarkar, *A Short History of Aurangzib*, 185.
7. Pagadi, *Chhatrapati Shivaji*, 309–311; Sarkar, *A Short History of Aurangzib*, 186.
8. Pagadi, *Chhatrapati Shivaji*, 315.
9. Ibid., 316.
10. Sabhasad, 131–132.
11. Ibid.
12. Letter from Thanjavurche Rajgharane, quoted in Mehendale (English), 615–616.
13. Sarkar, *A Short History of Aurangzib*, 126.
14. I have preferred Pagadi's translation of the letter to Sarkar's excessively flowery style, which provides a literal translation but muddles the text quite a bit. Pagadi, *Chhatrapati Shivaji*, 311–314; Sarkar's translation is in *History of Aurangzib*, Vol. 3, 325–329.
15. Details of the fight in Pagadi, *Chhatrapati Shivaji*, 319–325.
16. Ibid.
17. Gokhale, *Shivputra Sambhaji*, 71.
18. Sabhasad, 149.
19. Ibid., 151–152. There is much else that Sabhasad quotes him as saying, especially about how Maratha matters would pan out after him. But as Sabhasad was writing all this in 1694, that is, fourteen years after Shivaji's death, and as he was also writing for Shivaji's younger son Rajaram, it is best discarded as perhaps narrated 'to order' in view of the succession dispute that subsequently unfolded. About the overall situation at Raigad at the time of Shivaji's death and the broad conversation that happened, though, he is indeed credible.
20. Ibid., 153.
21. Quoted in Mehendale (English), 617.
22. Letter from Hugli to Bombay, 13 December 1680, in ibid., 618.
23. Ibid., 153–154.
24. Sarkar, *A Short History of Aurangzib*, 252–253.
25. Eaton, *A Social History of the Deccan*, 177–181.

Select Bibliography

Books

A History of Ancient and Early Medieval India: From the Stone Age to the 12th Century, Upinder Singh, Pearson, Delhi, 2009

A Pepys of Mogul India, 1653–1708: Being an Abridged Edition of The 'Storia Do Mogor' of Niccolao Manucci, translated by William Irvine, E.P. Dutton and Company, New York, 1913

A Short History of Aurangzib, Jadunath Sarkar, Orient BlackSwan, Hyderabad, 2019 edition

A Social History of the Deccan, 1300–1761: Eight Indian Lives, Richard M. Eaton, Cambridge University Press, South Asia edition, 2020

Administrative System of the Marathas, Surendra Nath Sen, first published in 1925, L.G. Publishers, Delhi, 2021

Chhatrapati Shivaji: Coronation Tercentenary Commemoration Volume, edited by B.K. Apte, Bombay University, 1975

Chhatrapati Shivaji Maharaj Jeevan Rahasya, Narhar Kurundkar, Deshmukh and Company, Pune, 2019

Chhatrapati Shivaji, Setumadhavrao Pagadi, Continental Prakashan, Pune, 2017

English Factories in India, 1661–1664, William Foster, Clarenden Press, Oxford, 1923

English Records on Shivaji (1659–1682), Volume 1, Shiva Charitra Karyalaya, Pune, 1931

Foreign Biographies of Shivaji, edited by Surendra Nath Sen, Kegan Paul, Trench, Trubner & Co. Ltd, London, published in India by Girindranath Mitra, 4/4A, College Square, Calcutta, 1927

Gazetteer of the Union Territory: Goa, Daman and Diu District, Part I (Goa), V.T. Gune, Government Printing Press, Panaji, Goa, 1979

History of Aurangzib, Jadunath Sarkar, Volumes 1 to 5, M.C. Sarkar & Sons, Calcutta, 1912

History of the Mahrattas, Volume 1, James Grant Duff, R. Cambray & Co., Calcutta, 1912

House of Shivaji, Jadunath Sarkar, S.C. Sarkar & Sons, Calcutta, 1948

India: A Sacred Geography, Diana L. Eck, Three Rivers Press, Random House, New York, 2012

Jedhe Shakavali-Kareena, edited by A.R. Kulkarni, Diamond Publications, Pune, 2007

Life of Siva Chhatrapati: Being a Translation of the Sabhasad Bakhar, Extracts and Documents Relating to Maratha History, Volume 1, Surendra Nath Sen, University of Calcutta, 1920

Maasir-i-Alamgiri, A History of the Emperor Aurangzib-Alamgir (Reign 1658–1707 AD), of Saqi Must'ad Khan, translated into English and annotated by Jadunath Sarkar, originally published by the Royal Asiatic Society of Bengal, Calcutta, 1947, reprint by B.R. Publishing Corporation, Delhi, 2019

Marathi Riyasat, G.S. Sardesai, Khand [Volume] 1, Popular Prakashan, Mumbai, first published in 1902, 2017 edition

Marathyancha Itihas, A.R. Kulkarni and G.H. Khare, Volume 1, Continental Prakashan, Pune, first published in 1984, 2021 edition

Marathyanchya Itihasachi Sadhane, V.K. Rajwade, 21 volumes; Volume 1 published in 1899 and then the subsequent volumes; the last, Volume 21, was published in 1918 (Accessed on www.samagrarajwade.com)

Medieval Maratha Country, A.R. Kulkarni, Diamond Publications, Pune, 2008

New History of the Marathas, G.S. Sardesai, Volumes 1 to 3, Munshiram Manoharlal Publishers Pvt Ltd, New Delhi, 1986

Portuguese-Mahratta Relations, a translation by T.V. Parvate of P.S. Pissurlencar's Portuguese-Marathe Sambandha, Maharashtra State Board for Literature and Culture, Bombay, 1983

Raja Shiva Chhatrapati, B.M. Purandare, Purvardha [Part 1] and Uttarardha [Part 2], Purandare Prakashan, Pune, 2018 edition

Samagra Setumadhavrao Pagadi, Volume 3, edited by Professor D.P. Joshi and Dr Usha Joshi, Marathi Sahitya Parishad, Hyderabad, 2010

Shiv Charita Sahitya, Volume 3, edited by Shankar Narayan Joshi and Ganesh Hari Khare, Bharat Itihas Sanshodak Mandal, Pune, 1930

Shiv Chhatrapatinche Armaar, Gajanan Bhaskar Mehendale and Santosh P. Shintre, Param Mitra Publications, Thane, 2010

Shivabharat by Parmanand. Translated into Marathi from the original Sanskrit by S.M. Divekar, Bharat Itihas Sanshodhak Mandal, Pune, 1927

Shivaji and His Times, Jadunath Sarkar, Orient BlackSwan, Hyderabad, 2010 edition

Shivaji and The Indian National Movement, Anil Samarth, Somaiya Publications, Bombay and New Delhi, 1975

Shivaji Kon Hota, [English translation 'Who was Shivaji?'], Govind Pansare, translated by Uday Narkar, published by Lokayat and Socialist Party (India), Pune, 1988

Shivaji Souvenir, edited by G. S. Sardesai, Keshav Bhikaji Dhawale, Bombay, 1927

Shivaji the Great, Volumes I and II, Bal Krishna, D.B. Taraporewala Sons & Co., Kitab Mahal, Hornby Road, Bombay, 1932

Shivaji, Setumadhavrao Pagadi, National Book Trust, 1983

Shivaji: His Life and Times, Gajanan Bhaskar Mehendale, Param Mitra Publications, Maharashtra, 2011

Shivaputra Sambhaji, Dr Kamal Gokhale, Continental Prakashan, Pune, first published 1971, 2019 edition

Shivkalin Patrasaar Sangraha (Marathi), Volumes 1 to 3, edited by N.C. Kelkar and D.V. Apte, Shiva Charitra Karyalaya, Pune, 1930

Shri Raja Shiv Chhatrapati, Gajanan Bhaskar Mehendale (Marathi), Volumes 1 and 2, Diamond Publications, Pune, 2008

Source Book of Maratha History, R.P. Patwardhan and H.G. Rawlinson, K.P. Bagchi & Company, Calcutta, 1928

Studies in Maratha History, A.R. Kulkarni, Diamond Publications, Pune, 2009

The Absent Traveller, Prakrit Love Poetry from the Gathasaptasati of Satavahana Hala, selected and translated by Arvind Krishna Mehrotra, Penguin Books, India, 2008

The Anarchy, William Dalrymple, Bloomsbury, London, 2019

The Cave Temples of India, James Fergusson and James Burgess, first published in 1880 by the British Raj in India, Oriental Books, Delhi, 1969

The English Factories in India (1618 to 1621), William Foster, Clarendon Press, Oxford, 1906

The Grand Rebel, Dennis Kincaid, Rupa Publications, 2020 edition

The Great Hindu Civilisation: Achievement, Neglect, Bias and The Way Forward, Pavan K. Varma, Westland, 2021

The History of India as Told By Its Own Historians, The Muhammadan Period, The Posthumous Papers of the Late Sir H.M. Elliot, edited by Professor John Dowson, Susil Gupta (India) Ltd, Calcutta, first published in 1877, second edition, 1952

The History of India, as Told By Its Own Historians, H.M. Elliot and John Dowson, Volume 7, Trubner & Co., London, 1887

The Imperial Gazetteer of India, Volume 21

The Marathas: 1600–1818, The New Cambridge History of India series, Stewart Gordon, Cambridge University Press, New York, 1993

The Sahyadri Companion, Sahyadri Prakashan, Mumbai, 1995

Thomas Cromwell, Diarmaid MacCulloch, Penguin Books, UK, 2019

Travels in the Mogul Empire (A.D. 1656–1668), Francois Bernier, a revised and updated edition based upon Irving Brock's translation, by Archibald Constable, Westminster, Archibald Constable and Company, 14 Parliamentary Street, 1891. (accessed on the Columbia University website: http://www.columbia.edu/cu/lweb/digital/collections/cul/texts/ldpd_6093710_000)

Tuzuk-i-Jahangiri or Memoirs of Jahangir: From the First to the Twelfth Year of his Reign, translated by Alexander Rogers and Henry Beveridge, Royal Asiatic Society, London, 1909

Periodicals

Artibus Asiae, a journal of the Museum Riettburg Zurich, Switzerland, Volume 31, 1969

Economic and Political Weekly, Volume 15, No. 48, 1980

Journal of the Royal Society of Arts, Volume 86, No. 4482, 1938

The Modern Review, December 1918

Acknowledgements

Thanks to Chiki Sarkar and Parth Mehrotra of Juggernaut Books for making this book possible.

Thanks to Anjali Puri who cast a sharp critical eye on the text – her interventions as editor were extremely valuable. Thanks to Rimli Borooah, my copy editor, for diligently working on the text. My thanks to Devangana Ojha, Arani Sinha and to the entire Juggernaut Books team for the way this book has turned out.

My heartfelt thanks to two eminent Sanskrit scholars: Dr. Amrita Narlikar, president of the German Institute for Global and Area Studies and professor of international relations at Hamburg University, and her mother Aruna Narlikar. They deciphered a key part of the poet Parmanand's Sanskrit text *Shivabharat* for me.

And thanks in particular to all the scholars of the brilliant historical movement in the Deccan towards the end of the nineteenth century and the beginning of the twentieth century, whose relentless efforts resulted in the unearthing of documents related to Chhatrapati Shivaji's life and times.

Without my family's firm support, there's no way I could have written this book while still holding a full-time job. So a big thank you, as ever, to my wife Swapna and son Vikrant, my parents Jagdish and Jyotsna Purandare, and my brother Kunal and sister-in-law Avani.

Index

Abaji Sondev, 56, 68
abhishek, 237
Abul Hasan, 242, 245, 246
Adil Shah, 25, 31, 38, 44, 54, 58, 65, 68, 70, 72, 73, 76, 79, 86–87, 108, 134, 142, 143, 148, 175, 213
    and Badi Sahiba, 50
    death, 50
    discriminatory regulations against Hindus, 40
    issuing *farman*/directive to Kanhoji Jedhe, 39
    paralytic attack, 50
    sending fighting unit to Bangalore base, 46
    Shahaji and, 45
Adil Shahi, 1–3, 9, 25–27, 29, 31, 34, 37–39, 44–46, 48, 50, 54–56, 69, 70, 74–75, 83–84, 93, 143, 155, 161, 173–176, 182, 211–212, 226, 234, 242, 253
Adil Shah I, 23
Adil Shah II, 56, 226
Afagis, 23
Afzal Khan, 46, 56, 69, 70–84, 86–89, 91–92, 98, 110–111, 143, 154, 202, 219, 240

Agra, 14, 29, 55, 117, 118, 123, 177–178, 179–183, 185, 187, 188, 190–195, 198–202, 212–213, 217, 221, 231–232, 235, 240, 251, 259, 261
Ali Adil Shah, 50, 70
Ali Adil Shah II, 226
Allahvardi Khan, 221
amatya, 239
Ambar, Malik, 24–25, 34, 55
Ambar Khan, 75, 83
Ambikabai, 252
amir-ul umra, 105, 110, 111, 115, 153
Ankush Khan, 75, 80
Annaji Datto, 201, 202
Annaji Pant, 239
Antonio de Melo de Castro, 67
Antulay, A.R., 57
Aqil Khan, 184
Arab-Turkish Muslims, 23
Ariyalur, 247
Asad Khan, 46, 182
Atre, Raghunath Ballal, 162
Attock, 4, 261
Aurangzeb, 1–4, 9, 11, 55, 57, 58–59, 60–62, 63–64, 65, 86, 88, 95, 96, 116, 118, 133, 134, 140, 153, 155, 157, 163,

165, 170, 176, 177, 179, 181–182, 184, 186, 188–191, 193, 194, 197, 199, 200, 215, 217, 218, 221, 223, 225, 228, 230, 235, 240, 255, 260, 260–261, 261
   against Golconda, 88
   and Bijapur forts, 59–60
   capturing the Bidar fort, 59
   conflict with Shivaji, 3, 133
   and Daud Khan, 225
   death of, 261
   and Deccan, 224, 236
   as governor of the Deccan, 55
   and Jafar Khan, 183, 187
   and Jai Singh, 155, 156, 157, 158, 163, 165, 168–169, 174, 176–177, 178, 189, 196, 200
   journey to northwards, 62–63
   letters wrote by Shivaji to, 58–59, 175
   and Mir Jumla, 65
   momentous clash of Shivaji with, 15
   Mughal chronicler of reign of, 43
   as Mughal emperor, 64–65
   Mughal–Maratha treaty signed by, 218
   Mughals under, 12, 55
   and Nasiri Khan, 63
   and Ram Singh, 177, 181, 184, 188
   real opinion of Shivaji, 200
   religious fanaticism, 218
   religious policy, 256
   'Remarkable occurrences' in the first five years of ruling of, 118
   Shah Jahan and, 53, 59
   and Shaista Khan, 88, 116
   trust of Shivaji in, 176
Aurobindo Ghose, 7, 16

Babaji, Krishnaji, 107
Badal Bakhtiyar, 157
Badi Sahiba, 50, 70, 71, 86, 100, 102, 144

Badshah Nama, 28
Bahadur Khan, 223, 225, 227, 241, 242, 249
Bahirji Naik, 124
Bahlol Khan, 150, 226–227
Bai, Sai, 31, 32, 47, 72
Baig, Haji Said, 126, 128
Bajaji Naik Jedhe, 47
Baji Ghorpade, 39–40, 46, 87, 142, 146
Baji Prabhu Deshpande, 3, 7, 50, 92, 203
Bakhsh, Murad, 64
bakshi, 182, 189, 190, 197
Bakshi, Jani Beg, 164
bale-killa, 43
bal-e-qila, 157, 160
Balkrishnapant, 30
Ballal, Haibatrao, 47
Ballal, Raghunath, 30, 162
balutedars, 38
Bandal, Krishnaji, 50
Banerjea, Surendra Nath, 7
Bapuji, Babaji, 112
Bapuji, Chimnaji, 112, 113
bargir-giri, 25
Bargis, 26
batai system, 202, 204
battle of Bhatvadi (1624), 25
Benaras, 218
Bernier, Francois, 15, 117
Bhagavad Gita, 22
bhakti movement, 22
Bhandari, Mainak, 151, 152, 258
Bhanji Prabhu Desai, 137
Bhaskar, Krishnaji, 69, 74, 77, 78, 82
Bhaskar, Trimbak, 109
Bhatari, Abdulla, 70
Bhatt, Malhari, 135
Bhavani (Durga), 57, 76, 81, 236
'Bhavani Mandir', 7

Bhimashankar, 19
Bhosle, Maratha Shivaji Raje, 1
Bhosle, Ekoji, 142
Bhosle, Rajaji, 138
Bhosle, Santaji, 249
Bhosle, Shahaji Raje, 2, 17, 31, 39, 71, 134
Bhupalgad, 252
Bijapur, 2–4, 14, 25, 30–31, 38–40, 43,
    45–53, 54–57, 59, 63, 68, 71–73, 75, 80,
    86–87, 91–94, 102–103, 108–109, 142–
    144, 153, 155, 162–163, 167, 170–171,
    173–175, 190, 195, 200, 211–212, 218,
    226, 230, 234, 240, 244, 253, 258
Bijapuri Tal Konkan, 163
bin Tughluq, Sultan Muhammad, 22
birth of Shivaji, 18
Bombay Gazetteer of 1880, 138
Brahmins, 6, 10, 40, 93, 163, 194, 236–237,
British East India Company, 5, 14, 98, 103,
    125, 129, 139, 211
British prisoners, narrow escapes and,
    86–104
Bundelkhand, 193, 230, 231
business in Surat, 123

Cadt, 146
'Cassiba' (Kashiba), 145
Chakan, 49, 78, 94, 106, 120, 155
Champat Rai, 230
Chandrajyotis, 220
Chandrarao, 51, 52
Chandraseniya Kayastha Prabhu, 93
Chaphal, 210, 232
Charles II, 99
chauthai, 226, 232
Chhatrapati (title), 1, 10
Chhatrasal Bundela, 230–231
Chimnaji Bapuji, 112, 113
Chitnis Chronicle, 19, 115

Cromwell, Thomas, 14
crown, 4, 64–65, 231, 234, 238, 244, 251,
    261

Dadaji Naras Prabhu, 37
Dad Mahal, 245
Dadoji Konddev, 29, 34, 38, 39, 43, 44
daggers drawn, 70
da Guarda, Cosme, 15, 29, 119–120
dalvis, 213
Danda-Rajpuri, 54, 56, 67, 77, 218, 228
D'Andrade, Manuel, 144–145
Dara Shukoh, 48, 55, 64–65, 117, 118
Daria Sarangh, 145
Darya Sarang, 151, 152, 207
Dattaji, 26
Daud Khan, 158, 167, 168, 221, 225
Daulat Khan, 9, 10, 151, 152, 207
Deccan, 1–4, 9, 22–28, 36, 37, 42, 51,
    55, 59–62, 65–66, 94, 105, 109–112,
    119–121, 136, 142, 153–154, 165–167,
    170, 175–180, 185–186, 189, 190,
    193–197, 203–205, 211, 225, 229, 235,
    241, 252, 260, 261
Deccani Muslims, 11, 23
setback and retreat, 153–178
Delhi, 22–23, 78, 118, 123, 177, 180, 230,
    255, 261
desais, 212, 213–214
Desh, 21
deshkulkarnis, 38, 41, 201
deshmukhs, 25, 36, 38, 47, 49–50, 62, 73, 74,
    75, 76, 201
deshpande, 38, 45
de Thevenot, Jean, 15
Diler Khan, 154, 156–158, 160, 161, 164,
    166, 167, 170, 171, 174, 176, 203, 221,
    223, 225, 227, 228, 230, 243, 249–250,
    252–253, 253

Dipabai, 252
Diwadi, 215
Diwan-e-Aam, 181
Diwan-e-Khaas, 181
Duff, Grand, 196
Duff, James Grant, 31
Dutch factory, 126, 131
Dutt, R.C., 7
Dynaneshwar, 11, 22

Ekoji, 29, 30, 134, 142, 244, 254
Elizabeth, Queen, 57
Ellora, 20, 24, 25, 33

Falgun Vadya Tritiya 1551, 17
farmans, 39, 41, 73, 169, 171, 218
Farzand, Hiroji, 178, 192, 259
Fatah Khan, 46, 47, 48, 108, 109
Fateh Jung Khan, 221
Fathullah Khan, 225
faujdar, 221
Fazl Khan, 83, 87, 92, 154
firangs, 4, 57, 66, 247
French East India Company, 247
Fryer, John, 211

Gadkari, Ram Ganesh, 7
Gaga Bhatt, 236–237
galbats, 148–149, 151
galloywats, 148
Gandevi, 125
Gary, Henry, 147, 218
Gathasaptasati, 21
Gaud, Manohardas, 221
Gaya, 194
Ghats, 21
Gheria, 139
Ghiyasuddin Khan, 134, 140
Ghorpade, Baji, 39–40, 46, 87, 142

Goa, 15, 23, 57, 58, 67–68, 97, 102, 108, 118, 137, 140, 143, 147–149, 155, 211, 212–215
Gokhale, Kamal, 252
Golconda, 2, 14, 60, 88, 187, 193, 208, 232, 242, 244–245, 249
Gomaji Naik Pansambal, 207
Gondwana, 193
Gopal Hari Deshmukh, 6
Goswamin, Shivaraya, 135
Gunwantabai, 252
Gyffard, Phillip, 90, 98, 116–117

Haibatrao, Vithoji, 74
Haji Kasim, 126, 128
Harchand Rai, 96
'Har Har Mahadev', 7, 11
Hasan Khan, 75, 80, 83
havaldar, 205–206
hawaldar, 138
Hindawi, 11
Hindawi Swaraj, 37
Hinduism, 10, 194, 215, 257
Hinduness, Shivaji's sense of, 120
Hindus, 8–10, 40–41, 120, 131, 149, 188, 207, 213–215, 230, 235, 255–257
Hiroji, 29, 178, 192, 193, 259
Hopewell, 102
Hridaynath Mangeshkar, 227
Hsuan Tsang, 21

Ibrahim Adil Shah I, 23
Ibrahim Khan, 152, 242
Ihtisham Khan, 156
Inayat Khan, 125, 126, 132, 134
Indraman Bundela, 157
Ingle, Shivaji, 47
Iraz Khan, 61
Iversen, Volquard, 126

Jaanta Raja, 103
Jaawali, 50, 51, 52, 53, 54, 55, 57, 63, 68, 70, 73, 74, 77, 78, 79, 82, 83, 84, 87, 97, 108, 109, 154, 160, 207, 234
Jadhavs, 20, 24, 25, 26, 27
Jado Ray, 25
Jadunath Sarkar, 13, 128, 130, 152, 196, 219
Jafar Khan, 183, 187, 188, 189, 194, 196, 197
Jagdev, Murar, 34
jagir, 24, 29, 30, 32, 34, 35, 37, 40, 43, 44, 45, 47, 49, 50, 61, 65, 68, 78, 86, 96, 120, 134, 135, 142, 204, 216, 217, 221, 240, 244, 248
jagirdar, 24, 35, 42, 86, 96
Jagtap, Godaji, 47
Jai Singh, 118, 153–171, 173–178, 180, 181, 182, 185, 186, 187, 189–190, 191, 195, 196, 197, 200, 202, 228, 230, 231, 235, 240
Jama Masjid, 255
Janjira, 54, 56, 67, 87, 99, 100, 104, 137, 154, 176, 212, 217–218, 242, 258
jasoods, 124
Jaswant Singh, 108, 115, 119–120, 183, 184, 186, 195, 200, 223
Jauhar, Siddi, 87, 89, 91, 94, 108, 109
Jayram Pindye, 135
jaziya, 9, 255–257
Jedhe Chronology, 17, 107
Jedhe Shakavali, 17, 18, 44
Jemmah, Rustom, 150
Jijabai, 1, 11, 17, 19, 24–28, 29, 30, 32, 33, 34, 40, 81, 87, 136, 177, 240, 251
Jinji, 45, 46, 71, 142, 244, 246, 249, 254, 261
Jumla, Mir, 60, 65
Jotirao Phule, 6, 11
jyotirlinga, 19, 216, 246

Kachhwah, Ugrasen, 163, 168
Kadamba dynasty, 215
Kalidasa, 22
Kamaljabai, 252
Kanhoji Angre, 139
Kanhoji Jedhe, 39, 50, 73, 74, 75, 84
Kank, Yesaji, 37, 68, 83, 207
karkhani, 205, 206
karkuns, 192, 209, 210
Kartalab Khan, 61, 95, 96
kasba, 34, 35, 43, 88, 110
Kashibai, 252
Kasim, Haji, 126, 128
Kavji Kondhalkar, 47, 108
Keshri Singh, 56–57
Khafi Khan, 9, 111, 112, 113, 114, 133, 208, 259
Khanderi, island of, 258
Khandoji Khopde, 39, 74, 84
Khan Muhammad, 71
Khare, G.H., 13, 14, 138
Khawas Khan, 142, 143, 226, 242
khilats, 183
Kincaid, Dennis, 14, 31
Kirat Singh, 154, 157, 164, 168, 171
Konddev, Dadoji, 29, 34, 38, 39, 43, 44
Kondhana, 13, 14, 39, 44, 58, 158, 159, 166, 168, 219, 221
Krishnaji Bhaskar Kulkarni, 64, 69, 74, 77, 78, 82
Krishna Sawant Desai, 137
Kshatriya, 231, 236, 237, 239
Kshatriya Kulawatans Shri Raja Shiva Chhatrapati, 239
Kudtoji Gujar, 174
Kulkarni, A.R., 196
kulkarnis, 38
Kumar Singh, 183
Kunbis, 11

Lakham Sawant, 142, 143, 213
Lala Lajpat Rai, 7
Lal Mahal, 34, 39, 105, 106, 110, 111, 113, 115
Lata Mangeshkar, 227
Laxmibai, 252
liberator, Shivaji as, 5
Life of the Celebrated Sevagy (1695), 119
Lodi, Sher Khan, 244, 247
Lokmanya, 6
Lord Ram, 11, 210, 232
Loyall Merchant, 123–124, 132
Ludi Khan, 221
Lukhji Jadhav, 26, 27
Lukhji Jadhavrao, 20, 25

Maasir-i-Alamgiri, 113, 116
Madhava, 215
Madura, 244
Mahabaleshwar, temple of, 149
Mahadev, Abaji, 69
Mahala, Jiva, 81, 83
Maharashtra dharma, 11, 232
Maharashtri, 21–22
Mallikarjuna shrine, 246
Maloji, 24–25
Maluk Chand, 181
Malusare, Tanaji, 13, 37, 68, 97, 259
Mambaji Bhosle, 74, 80, 83
Mangaji, Gangaji, 68
mansab, 59, 167, 183, 184, 188, 189, 194, 199, 204, 240, 241
mansabdar, 168, 199, 240, 241
mansabdari, 182
Marathas, 2–4, 7, 9, 12, 18, 20, 22–25, 47, 48, 56, 57, 67, 73, 88–90, 92–95, 97–99, 101–104, 108, 110–115, 211, 218, 220, 221, 233, 242, 260
Marathi Riyasat, 13

Martha Ann Selby, 22
Masaud, Siddi, 249, 253, 258
Mavals, 35, 36, 37, 43, 45, 50, 69, 107, 202–203
Meeth, 100
Mehendale, G.S., 152
Mian Rahim Muhammad, 44
mirasdars, 38, 201
Mission Shivaji, 73
Mocquerly, 145
Mohite, Hambirrao, 239, 249
Mohite, Sambhaji, 29, 49
Mohite, Tukabai, 29
mokadam of Ranjhe village, 41
mokasas, 29
More, Hanumantrao, 52
Moropant Peshwa, 177
Moropant Pingle, 111, 193, 239
Moro Trimbak Pingle, 68
Muazzam, Prince, 154, 196, 222, 223
Muazzam Khan, 59
Mughal empire, 1, 23, 24, 58, 59, 109, 117, 123, 153, 163, 172, 177, 180, 184, 186, 189, 194, 229, 234, 235, 239, 250, 252, 255, 260, 261
Mughal–Maratha conflict, 18, 228
Mughal rule, 5, 96
Mughals, 2, 5, 11, 12, 14, 24, 25, 27–29, 42, 48, 54–55, 57–63, 65–69, 79, 86, 88, 94, 95, 105, 107–111, 115, 120, 124, 134, 137, 140, 154, 156, 157–160, 162–164, 173, 175–177, 194, 200, 212, 217–218, 221, 225–228, 230–232, 241–243, 252, 253, 258, 260, 261
Muhammad Amir Khan, 197
Muhammad Kuli Khan, 200, 243
Muhammadnamah, 71
Muhammad Amir Khan, 190
mujumdar, 30, 239, 248

Mujumdar, Nilo Pant, 177–178
Mukhlis Khan, 184
Mukhopadhyay, Bhudev, 7
mukhya pradhan, 239
Mulla Ahmad, 56
Multafat Khan, 58–59, 61, 184
Munshi, Jairaj, 169
Munshi, Udairaj, 163–164
Murad Bakhsh, 48
Murar Baji, 160–161, 171, 175, 203
Murar Baji Deshpande, 160, 161, 171, 175, 203
Musa Khan, 47, 48
Muse Khan, 75, 78, 80, 83
Muslims, 9–11, 23, 24, 31, 40, 83, 120, 151–152, 207, 255–257, 261
Mustafa Khan, 39, 45, 46, 143

Naamdar Khan, 106, 107
nagarkhana, 114
naik, 124
Narba Sawant, 213
Nardurg, 156
Naropant Hanmante, 135
narrow escapes and British prisoners, 86–104
Nasiri Khan, 61, 62, 63, 65
Nasir Muhammad Khan, 244, 246
naval enterprise, 137–152
Nayaka, Kapaya, 9
Neel Prabhu, 254
Nehru, Jawaharlal, 10
Netaji Palkar, 68, 86, 87–88, 108, 111, 171, 173–175, 200, 226, 243–244
Niccolao Manucci, 15, 118, 165
Niccolls, Thomas, 233
Nila Prabhu Munshi, 121
Nilkanth, Niro, 45, 239
Nilkanth, Ramchandra, 239

Nilkanth, Shamrao, 30
Nilopant Sondev, 205
Nilo Sondev, 68
Nimbalkar, Bajaji Naik, 76
Nimbalkar, Mudhoji Naik, 31
Niraji Raoji, 192, 216, 239
Nischalpuri Gosavi, 241
Nizam Shahi, 1, 2, 14, 24, 25, 27–29, 34, 44, 55, 58, 64, 234
nocturnal strike, 105–122
non-violence, 8
nyayadhish, 239

Oxenden, George, 125, 127, 133, 134, 236, 238

paanch hazari, 182
Pachad *wada*, 240
pagar, 151
Pal, Bipin Chandra, 7
palki, 180
Pandharpur, 21, 76, 252
Pandito, Bikasi, 141
Pandito, Rauji, 141
pandit rao, 239
Panhala, 87–91, 93, 97, 108–109, 174–175, 206, 226–227, 243, 258
Pansare, Govind, 152
pargana, 25, 35, 36, 43, 49, 245
Parmanand, 14, 15, 17, 19, 47–48, 56, 87, 93, 96, 106, 119, 120
Pasalkar, Baji, 37, 48
patils, 38, 41, 42, 62
peshwa, 30, 193, 239
Peshwas, 12, 261
Pissurlencar, P.S., 15, 215
Ponda, 212–213
powada (ballad), 6
Prabhavali, 243

pradhans, 237, 239
Prakrit par excellence, 22
Pratapgad, 52, 74, 79, 80–81, 84, 236
Prataprao, 75, 83, 174, 218, 227, 228, 258
Prataprao Gujar, 178, 216, 226, 258
Pratit Rai, 195
Prayag, 194
prayaschitta, 243
Pune, 5, 13, 24, 27, 29–36, 39, 43–46,
    50, 52, 56, 68, 75, 87, 88–89, 94, 108,
    110–112, 115, 120, 154–155, 156, 202,
    204, 225, 227, 234
Purandar, 41, 45–48, 69, 78, 156–164,
    166–167, 168, 171, 174–176, 190, 200,
    203, 219, 221, 230, 241, 242
Putlabai, 252

Qubaid Khan, 157
Qutub Shah, 175, 176, 182, 232, 242,
    245–246, 249
Qutub Shahi, 2, 55, 60, 95, 176–177, 182
Qutubuddin Khan, 156, 159

Radandaz Khan, 188, 228
Radha Madhav Vilas Champu, 135
Raghunath Narayan Hanmante, 248
Raghunath Pant Korde, 187, 195, 198
Rai Bagan, 95, 96
Raigad, 7, 12, 52, 89, 102, 166, 189, 234,
    236, 238, 240, 243, 244, 258, 261
Raireshwar, temple of, 37
Raja Jai Singh, 118, 153, 195
Rajapore Merchant, 90
Rajapur, 83, 89, 90, 97, 98–99, 102, 103,
    116–117, 233
Rajaram, 138, 251, 252, 258, 260, 261
Raja Shiva Chhatrapati, 239
Rajgad, 43, 44, 50, 56, 75, 81, 87–89, 134,
    156, 158, 159, 168, 174, 178, 193–195,
    234
Rajkuvarbai, 252
Rajwade, V.K., 12, 135
Rajya Shaka, 239
Rajyavyavaharkosh, 239
Ram, Udaji, 96
Ramchandrapant Sondev, 239
Ramdas, saint, 11, 210, 232
Ram Singh, 177, 181–184, 188, 189, 190,
    191, 194, 195–197
Ranade, M.G., 7, 13
Ranadulla Khan (Junior), 75, 83
Ranadulla Khan, 29, 39, 40, 45, 70, 71, 75,
    83
Ranga, Kasturi, 71
Ranubai, 252
Raoji Pandit, 117, 147
Raoji Somnath, 99, 102, 141
Rathod, Raja Raisingh, 159
Rathod, Udaibhan, 219, 220
rayats (peasants), 6, 203, 245
reforms, push for, 198–216
Remarkable occurrences, 118
Revington, Henry, 89, 98
Rohid Khore, 37, 107
royal tigress, 95
Royal Welcome, 102
Rudra, Pratapa, 9
Rustam-i-Zaman, 97, 212, 213

Sabhasad, 14, 15, 44, 112–113, 119, 124,
    136, 151–152, 160, 176, 191, 206, 207,
    217, 220, 222, 227, 237, 245, 248, 252,
    253, 259
Sabhasad Bakhar, 14
sabnis, 30, 205, 210
Saf Shikan Khan, 179

Sakhubai, 252
Sakwarbai, 252
Salabat Khan, 95
Samasya, 135
Sambhaji, 19, 26, 27, 30, 46, 49, 71–72, 81, 83, 118, 136, 163, 167, 178. 182, 184, 191–194, 199, 216–217, 221, 241, 251–254, 260–261
Sambhaji Kate, 47
Sambhaji Kavji, 81, 83
Sambhaji Raje, 191
Samiti, Anushilan, 7
Sanskrit, 9
'Santubasinay' (Santuba Shenavi), 145
Saptakoteshwara, 215, 216
Sarang, Darya, 9, 151–152, 207
Sar-i-naubat, 239
Sarjerao Jedhe, 107, 112
Sarkar, Jadunath, 13, 128, 130, 152, 196, 219
sarnobat, 174, 178, 205, 206, 226
Savarkar, V.D., 7
Sawant, 57
Sen, Surendra Nath, 119
Shah Abbas II, 198
Shahaji, 25, 26, 29, 32
Shahaji Bhonsla, 39
Shahaji Raje Bhosle, 1, 2, 17, 31, 39, 71, 97, 134, 142
Shah Jahan, 26, 27, 28, 48, 53, 55, 59, 62, 63, 64, 177, 187, 256
Shaista Khan, 25, 61, 65, 88, 94, 97, 104–111, 113–121, 127, 133, 149, 153, 154, 167, 187, 193, 202, 235
Shakavali, Jedhe ,17, 18, 44
shamiana, 71, 81, 82
Shasta Ckaune, 100
Shayista Khan, 114
Sher Khan, 150, 151

Sher Khan Lodi, 244, 247
shiledars, 207
Shirwadkar, V.V., 227
Shivabharat, 30, 98, 119
Shivaji, Chhatrapati
   Agra visit, 14, 190, 221
   and Afzal Khan, 80, 82–83, 143
   and Annaji Datto, 201
   and Aurangzeb, 59, 60, 63, 170, 171, 180, 182, 199–200, 217, 218, 235, 255
   Babaji and Bapuji as favourites of, 112
   and Bahadur Khan, 242
   and Bahirji Naik, 124
   batai system, 202
   biography of, 7–8
   birth, 18, 19
   'Braman at Rajapore', 100
   Chhatrapati (title), 10
   childhood of, 3
   conflict with Aurangzeb, 3, 133
   death, 12, 259
   on the designing of frigates, 139
   and Diler Khan, 167, 170, 171
   and Ekoji Bhosle, 142
   English works on, 13–14
   escape from Lal Mahal, 115
   on farmers, 203–204
   and Fatah Khan, 108
   and Ghorpade, 143
   in Goa, 213, 215
   and Gokarna, 149
   and Golconda, 232
   Hindu identity, element of, 9
   illness of, 259
   Jaawali conquest, 75
   and Jai Singh, 162–165, 167, 168, 169, 170–171, 176, 185, 195, 196
   and Jaswant Singh, 186

Jawhar and Ramnagar capture, 225
and Jijabai, 29–30, 33, 34, 240
karkuns, 192
and Khafi Khan, 112
Kshatriya family, 236
leadership, 94
as liberator, 5
and Marathas, 110, 113, 133, 142, 195
Mission Shivaji, 73
and Mughals, 107, 194, 216, 217, 218, 242
Muslims recruitment in army, 9, 207
and Neel Prabhu, 254
and Netaji Palkar, 174–175
official imprint, 41
palki, 180
and people, 5
peshwa, 193
post-Agra phase, 228
as a protector of faith, 10
and Purandar, 45, 46, 48
and Qutub Shah, 245–246
and Ram Singh, 181, 188, 196–197
rebellious activities, 31
recapture of Panhala and Satara, 226
relationship with Muazzam, 216
relationship with stepbrother, 29, 142, 171
and Sabhasad, 136, 207
and Sambhaji, 192, 251, 260
sarnobat, 226
and Shahaji, 32
and Shaista Khan, 106
and Sher Khan, 150
Shivaji movement, 7
strikes back, 217–229
in Surat, 223
twin accomplishments, 224
and Vyankoji Bhosle, 171

on western coastline, 57
women, attitude towards, 56
Shivaji and His Times (Jadunath Sarkar), 13
Shivaji Jayanti, 18
Shivaji Jedhe, 74
Shivaji Kon Hota, 152
Shivabharat, 14
Shivneri, 17–20, 27–29
Shivrajyabhishek Prayog, 236
showdown and escape, 179–197
Shyamraj Nilkhanth, 68
Siddi Fulad, 188, 190, 193, 194
Siddi Hilal, 87
Siddi Jauhar, 87, 89, 91, 94, 109, 174, 226
Siddi Masaud, 249, 253, 258
Siddis of Janjira, 67, 87, 99, 154
Sindhudurg, 138, 139
Sindkhed, 25, 27, 33
Smith, Anthony, 129
Soyrabai, 251–252, 258
straight-bladed dagger, 82
subahdar, 48, 55, 62, 65, 105, 106, 110, 116, 167, 191
Surat, 26, 90, 98–103, 116, 117, 123–129, 131–135, 137–142, 147, 176, 224
Surat Council, 99–103, 128, 133, 134
Surat Singh Kachhwah, 164
suryadarshan, 28
Suryaji, 219, 220, 259
Swayambhu Shiva temple, 23

Tagore, Rabindranath, 7, 10
Tanaji, 13, 14, 37, 68, 97, 219, 220, 222
Tanaji Malusare, 13, 37, 68, 97, 219, 259
tarande, 151
Tarbiyat Khan, 198
Tavernier, Jean-Baptiste, 15
Thanjavur, 18, 29, 134, 244

The Modern Review (1911), 10
Tilak, Bal Gangadhar, 6, 7, 10, 18
Tiruchirapalli, 247
Tirumalawadi, 248
Treaty of Purandar, 166, 190, 200, 219
Trimbak, Dattaji, 178, 239
Trimbak Pant, 195
Trimbak Pant Dabir, 198
Tughluq dynasty, 22
Tungabhadra, 244
Tupe, Waghoji, 107

Udairaj Munshi, 163, 164
upri, 38
Ustick, Stephen, 233
Uzbek Khan, 221

Vellore, 244, 246
Ventjee, Darya Sarang, 9
Ventjee Sarungee, 151
Viegas, Fernao Leitao, 66
Viegas, Roe Leitao, 66
Vijayanagara dynasty, 60
Vijaydurg, 139

Vishalgad, 86, 174
Vishwasrao, Shriniwas, 27
Vora, Virji, 126, 128, 130
Vyankoji, 29, 244, 248

Wagh, Bhimaji, 47
wagh-nakh, 81, 82
waknis, 239
Ward, Robert, 98
Waring, Scott, 196
watan, 45, 76
watandar, 38, 201, 202, 203, 204
watandari system, 201
western coastline, 21, 57, 58
Westerners, 23
Western ideas of enlightenment, 6

Yakut Khan, 75
Yaqut Khan, 80, 83
Yashwantrao, 46, 52
Yesubai, 261
Yusuf, Mohammed, 58

Zunzarrao Ghatge, 83

A Note on the Author

Vaibhav Purandare is the author of the acclaimed *Savarkar: The True Story of the Father of Hindutva*, *Hitler and India: The Untold Story of His Hatred for the Country and Its People*, *Sachin Tendulkar: A Definitive Biography* and *Bal Thackeray & the Rise of the Shiv Sena*. He works as a senior editor with *The Times of India*.